D0916727

TERROR

TERROR

A Historical Novel

Hugo Wolfgang Holzmann

Copyright © 2008 by Hugo Wolfgang Holzmann.

Library of Congress Control Number:		2008900809
ISBN:	Hardcover	978-1-4363-1871-6
	Softcover	978-1-4363-1870-9

All rights reserved. No part of this book may be reproduced or transmitted
in any form or by any means, electronic or mechanical, including photocopying,
recording, or by any information storage and retrieval system,
without permission in writing from the copyright owner.

This book was printed in the United States of America.

To order additional copies of this book, contact:
Xlibris Corporation
1-888-795-4274
www.Xlibris.com
Orders@Xlibris.com
47071

CONTENTS

DEDICATION

This book is dedicated to a little girl by the name of Judis, who, in the arms of her mother, turned to the man and offered him a Little Green Twig, pleading "don't hurt my mommy and me" and was shot by the SS officer.

And to my classmates. In November 1941, we were only sixteen students left, fifteen of them were killed by the Nazis, shot in Fort IX on November 25, 1941. That these beautiful children, who were like family to me, are not forgotten; I enclose our class picture.

PICTURE TAKEN IN 1938 OF THE THIRD GRADE OF THE JEWISH PUBLIC
SCHOOL IN MUNICH, GERMANY

These children, and their teacher Kissinger, were shot by the SS on 25 November, 1941,
in Fort IX, Kovno, Lithuania.
** *My dear friend Bertel Sandbank died in the gas chamber of Chelmno.*
The other children in this picture had emigrated. Out of the sixteen children left in the
class by November 1941, only the author Hugo Holzmann survived.

ACKNOWLEDGMENTS

Without the enthusiastic support of my wife, Isabella, I would have never written this novel about terror.

To my grandson Daniel Ryaboy who helped with the editing.

To my dear friend and former classmate, Gerda Newman, who escaped the Nazis after the horror of the Crystal Night, and was with me in thoughts throughout writing the book.

To Dr. Andreas Heusler of the Munich Archives, whose book *verzogen, unbekannt, wohin,* detailed the fate of the thousand Jewish citizens from Munich deported to Fort IX.

To the librarians of the Solana Beach and Del Mar public libraries, who were so helpful in finding for me sources and material on the technical and historical aspects of my writing.

PREFACE

This novel is presented in three books. Each book is a different time period of the life of the protagonist, Anton Nagil, the son of a German war criminal. The first two books are historical. Many of the incidents desribed were actual happenings, such as the deportation of one thousand Jewish families from Munich, who upon their arrival in Kovno (Kaunas), Lithuania, were marched to Fort IX and machine-gunned.

The characters of SS Colonel Karl Jaeger, the gestapo chief in Lithuania, and SS Lieutenant Franz Hamann, commander of a roving killer squad are historical. In book 1, Anton Nagil becomes the accuser, judge, jury, and executer—the avenger.

In book 2, "Flight from Afghanistan," the description of the bombing of the American embassies in Kenya and Tanzania are factual as are the missile attacks on al-Qaeda camps in retaliation. The characters of Mohamed Atta, Osama bin Laden, and al-Zawahiri are historical, as well as Ahmed Shah Massoud, "the Lion of Panjshir" and warlord of the Northern Alliance.

Book 3, "Police Inspector Anton Nagil in Munich," is the sequel to the two historical books. It describes terrorist and criminal cases of an unusual nature which Inspector Nagil solved. Anton Nagil is the son of SS Colonel Otto Nagil, a war criminal.

PROLOGUE

November 25, 1941. It was a cold, dreary afternoon when the 994 resettlers from Munich were finally permitted to leave the train. It had been a long ride from Munich; in fact they had been underway for three days, traveling at night and stopping somewhere during the day, always away from towns and guarded by the Munich Police and SS.

It had been a miserable ride. The cars provided by the Reichsbahn railway were of the third class, ten compartments to a car. Each compartment had wooden benches meant for six persons to sit on with nets above for luggage. The day before the people entered the cars, their luggage, and for children their mattresses and beddings, had been brought in by details from the camp which filled not only the nets but also the seats. With ten persons assigned to each compartment, they had to rearrange everything to make room; and even then, only half of the men, women, and children could find a seat and the others had to stand. Though they would alternate between sitting and standing, this was not a comfortable way to travel, not even for a day; and for three days and nights, to travel in this fashion was dreadful. Along the compartments ran a corridor which led to the single toilet; an SS man was always present who would give permission to enter the corridor for the use of this facility. Already after the first day, most of the toilets were drained of flushing water which added to the discomfort of the travelers. The same, the faucet for each washbasin was soon emptied; and after a couple days, thirst became intolerable for the resettlers. How can you tell a child that there was no more water to quench its thirst? And there were 175 children with their families. The resettlers had been told that their trip to Riga in Latvia would last three days and to bring along provisions of food and liquids. Many had brought bottles with water, tea and coffee—it did not last for three days of travel and two days sitting on a siding in Kovno.

On the morning of the twenty-third of November, they had arrived at their destination which was not Riga but Kaunas (Kovno) in Lithuania. There the German policemen and SS company were relieved and returned back to Munich while a new company of SS guards surrounded the train. All entreatments for water were of no avail, and soon the resettlers realized that these SS men did not even understand German—they were Lithuanians.

Therefore, the resettlers were relieved when in the afternoon they were told to leave the train and get ready for the march to their destination. After they had formed in little groups before their compartments, an SS officer with a bullhorn addressed the multitude, introduced himself as SS Lieutenant Huber and told them that they are destined for the Kovno Ghetto; there was no need for them to carry their luggage and bedding as all would be brought in trucks to the ghetto. However, if they wished, they could carry things for the one night as they would be processed first at another facility where they would also get to drink and be fed.

This calmed the people, and most would carry a bag or suitcase with their most valuable things, never trusting the Nazis to keep their promise. The march soon got underway to the facility which was, as they had been told, two hours' distant.

However, it was a slow walk with the many children. Some small who had to be carried, and there were many old people. After two hours, they marched by the ghetto where people stood behind the barbed-wire fence and asked where they came from, "Munich." And where were they going? "To a place where we would spend the night and be processed into the ghetto."

The ghetto inhabitants knew of their destination, it was Fort IX. They also knew that anyone taken there would not return. They had already witnessed the march-by of a thousand deportees each from Frankfurt and Berlin in the morning, who thought that they would join the ghetto in the afternoon, but none had come.

From the ghetto, the road went uphill, and their walk became even slower and the column now spread out in a long line of tired people. During the march, the guards surrounding them had been noncommittal, only urging them on to walk faster, "Schnell, schneller, los lauf mal" (fast, faster, run); and some urged them to carry even their older children, though only few of them spoke German.

And then in the distance, loomed the high brick walls and towers of the fort, with their destination in sight, the march went faster as here they would receive water and food. The big gate was opened, and through it, the resettlers walked into the large courtyard and as the first ones entered the lights in the fort came on as it was dusk.

Here, they were received by more Lithuanian SS, and at once, it became a nightmare. These SS did not carry rifles as the guards had but instead whips, clubs, and those who spoke German yelled at the resettlers to deposit their luggage in one heap in the middle of the yard and immediately used their whips and clubs if one showed the slightest hesitation to comply. The brutality of the SS frightened the people and added to their apprehension of what was going to happen to them here, locked in by high walls on all sides. Adding to their fear was the appearance of these soldiers, many of whom had bottles they drank from and passed around; some appeared already drunk. And when some of the people asked the soldiers who spoke German when they get water, these soldiers laughed or grinned and answered, "No water, all boom-boom," and made gestures as if shooting. The resettlers had formed little groups of mostly family members, many of the children crying that they were thirsty, the older children as fearful as their elders. Some of those who had heard and seen these SS men make these gestures of shooting were even more frightened as they had a foreboding of their fate, and while many suspected what would happen to them, others refused to believe. "This could not happen! Even if they were hated by the Nazis—to be killed, shot—not even Nazis could commit such murder."

Fear spread among the families, and it could be seen in the faces of many as if realizing that something horrible was to happen to them. Mothers or fathers would shield their little children when they saw those clubbed or whipped viciously—they themselves already in a state of terror. Some were openly crying; men were reciting the Shema, a short prayer of devotion to the Oneness of God. More frightening were those who said the Kaddish, the recital of the death.

Then the gates clunked shut as the last of the resettlers had entered Fort IX. Again, it was the SS officer who had spoken to them at the train, who now stepped on a small platform before the people and, in a commanding voice, announced that all those with children will be processed first. "Families with children first, Form a single line to my right. There must be eighty persons in each line. Take off your coats, you won't be needing them. And you better make haste, or my men will use their clubs and whips. *Macht schnell, lauft ihr Judenschweine!* (Run you Jew pigs)" At once soldiers came among the people to expedite those with children and to take off their coats. Most just threw them on the ground, many already shivering from the icy wind that blew in from the north.

They used their clubs and whips freely, even hitting children to form them into a long line, and pointed to the place where the column was forming. At the beginning of the line stood a soldier and counted them. The last was a woman who had a small child in her arms and one clinging to her. The next one was a teenage boy with a small boy on his shoulders; the two were numbers 81 and 82. When the woman pleaded that they were family, the soldier smirked and let them join the woman, but cruelly hit the teenager and the little boy with his whip.

The command was given for the column to get going, "Schnell, immer laufen sonst bekommt ihr Hiebe, ihr Judenhunde!" (Fast, always run, or you get beaten you Jew dogs!) Those who remained behind saw the column of men, women, and children disappear behind some earthenworks. Soon they heard crying, wailing, and screaming—what sounded like single shots—and then the shooting of machine guns.

Those who remained knew of what fate awaited them. Each of them—man, woman, or child—would have to face death by machine gun, his or her own tragic end. Each would run around the earthen dam which extended the length of a long ditch along a narrow dirt path, lined with fearsome-looking SS men, who beat them as they ran by, then facing the ditch filled with the bodies of those who had been killed and so await the rapid fire of the machine guns placed above them on the earthen dam. For a last time, parents hugged their children, kissed them. All in a state of fear and shock. The terror unimaginable. The commander of Fort IX and in charge of the killings was SS Lieutenant Colonel Otto Nagil.

["Unpleasant scenes" SS Lieutenant Colonel Nagil wrote in his war diary. Meaning, when he witnessed families bade each other—Good bye.

Did he ever think about the indescribable terror the families faced during these last moments of their precious lives?

What can a mother say to her child as a last good bye? "The bullets won't hurt my love?"

"Mama I am so scared." Last frightening words a child should never have to utter.

"We are going to God in heaven, my love."

A trembling embrace . . . last kissing of the beloved face wet with tears . . . of sweet lips twisted in agony . . . eyes showing the horror felt.

"Daddy, can't you help me? I don't want to die!" A cry of despair.

The soul-wrenching helplessness of a father who cannot protect his family.

These are the unpleasant scenes SS man Nagil saw and apparently did not like.]

BOOK 1

A LITTLE GREEN TWIG

CONTENTS

PRINCIPAL
CHARACTERS

IN CAIRO:

The Nagil family:
    Otto Nagil. Born September 3, 1920, in Munich.
    Joined the Hitler Youth in 1934, the SS in 1938. Until July 1941, SS major in Dachau concentration camp. Transferred to Kovno and Jaeger's deputy in charge of Fort IX, Kovno, Lithuania, later chief of the gestapo in Lithuania. Missing after the war; then declared by his wife that he died in 1959. When Jaeger was arrested and gave a deposition that Nagil was his deputy, he was sought as a war criminal. He became an Egyptian citizen under Nasser with the name of Omar Nabil. Leader of ex-Nazis and war criminals in Cairo, member of the Teutonic Order. His actual death was in 1978.

Otto's wife, Rosemarie Nagil. Born September 30, 1923, in Planegg by Munich. Married Otto Nagil in 1941. Fled with Otto to Cairo after the war. A gentle woman who suffered greatly under her husband, especially when she visited her Jewish physician Dr. Zapruder. Returned permanently to Planegg near Munich in 1995 to the house she inherited from her parents.

Their son, Anton Nagil. Born in Munich March 27, 1965. After his birth, his mother returned with him to Cairo. He was made an Egyptian citizen with the name of Achmed Nabil. Traveled to most Middle Eastern countries as an Egyptian, to Afghanistan in 1998. Moved permanently to Planegg-Munich in December 2004 and joined the Munich Police Department.

Ali Muhammad Nasr, Egyptian. Ali was the same age as Anton, and they became the best of friends, attended the same schools. Ali was a devout Muslim. His father belonged to the Moslem Brotherhood, Ali became a member when of age.
    Ali became an imam at the famous Al-Azhar Mosque in Cairo.

When Ali went to Afghanistan in August 1998, Anton went with him as his "protector."

Zahi Abu Nasr, Ali's father. A government official and active Brotherhood member.

Gerhard Lutz. Otto Nagil's deputy in Fort IX. Fled with his wife Elke to Cairo after the war and was a close friend of Otto. Sought as war criminal in Germany.

The Jewish Zapruder family:

Dr. Avraham Zapruder was the personal physician of Rosemarie Nagil.

His wife Amal was born a Moslem but converted to Judaism.

Their daughter, Hanna. Born April 6, 1968, became attached to Anton as he to her. They were married on a cruise by the ship's captain on their way to the Bahamas in the summer of 1992.

Sakato Watanabi, Japanese. Jiu-jitsu instructor at the Academy. Later at the University of California in San Diego as judo instructor.

Anton and Watanabi became friends, and Anton visited him in Japan.

Avi Ben Etzioni, Israeli. Cultural attaché at the Israeli embassy in Cairo and an agent of the Mossad. Avi gave Hanna Zapruder Hebrew lessons, which Anton attended, and both became fluent in Hebrew. Avi found in Anton a young and knowledgeable man with sympathy for the Jewish people and Israel. He took Anton clandestinely to Israel where Anton became an agent of the Mossad.

Brigadier Abed al-Hakim Amer. Chief of Egyptian Military Intelligence.

Anton worked for the Military Intelligence and was permitted to travel to Afghanistan for the purpose of seeking out Egyptian Jihad members and, if possible, to assassinate al-Zawahiri.

IN MUNICH AND BAVARIA:

The Schoenauer Family by Koenigsee-Berchtesgaden.

Herr Schoenauer. Industrialist and fomer friend of Otto Nagil.

His wife, Inge Schoenauer, befriended with Rosemarie Nagil.

Their daughter, Betty. A close friend of Anton.

Taxi driver Sepp Kainz of Planegg.

Frau Esther Cohn. Owner of the boarding house Pension Freizeit.

Franz Hamann. Caretaker of Schoenauer's forest holding at Koenigsee.

Ernst Huber of Munich. Taxidriver.

IN ISRAEL:

Nahik Rubin. Shin Bet agent who saw to Anton's arrival and departure in Israel and to his security.

Mordechai Nevot. Deputy director of Mossad. In charge of agents in foreign countries.

Tal Yaron. Shin Bet agent assigned to Anton while in Israel.

Uval Levy. Friend of Tal, lived in Kibbutz Alumot. Later identified as an unwilling agent of the Egyptian Secret Service.

The Ishais. Elchanan and Hanni, with whom Anton became friends.

Eliahu Zamir. Caretaker of the Nagil-Zapruder house in Jerusalem.

ON THE SHIP *PALACE OF THE SEA*:

Arthur and Mary MacKenzie. Arthur was the best man at Anton's wedding.

Captain Montovani.

CHAPTER I

SS COLONEL OTTO NAGIL

When the boy Anton heard the screams of his mother and rushed downstairs, he did not know that from this moment on, his life was changed forever.

The Nagils lived in the northern section of Cairo, called Shubra, on the left bank of the Nile, also known as the German colony. It was part of Old Cairo but it had nice sections, and perhaps the Germans settled there as there were as many Christian churches as mosques. Among them was the Church of Saint Mark's, which Anton and his mother attended. The house they lived in was a villa with a beautiful garden, and they had a pre-war Mercedes.

From the earliest times Anton remembered, he was told by his father about the glory of the *Grossdeutsches Reich*. The greatness of the Fuehrer Adolf Hitler. Otto Nagil told him of his own youth as a member of the Hitlerjugend (Hitler Youth), the glory of belonging, the pretty uniforms they wore with a real dagger in the belt and the Swastika armband. Otto had albums that showed him as a blond, trim boy in the brown uniform. When Anton was old enough, his father had him wear his HJ uniform, which though faded a little, fitted young Anton nicely. Anton, then thirteen, was the same build as his father in his youth.

In fact, his father had indoctrinated him in Nationalsocialism and the glory of the Third Reich since he was just a little boy. Otto had made it a practice to teach Anton once a week. Every Saturday he took the boy down into the recreation room, which was decorated in Nazi paraphernalia, swastika flags and standards, a portrait of the fuehrer with plastic oak leaves around the picture, and in a large glass case, his elegant black SS uniform was displayed. Otto would even wear the uniform proudly for his son, and Anton was impressed.

Comrades from the war years came who also lived in Cairo or Alexandria, and there were festivities in the room on days the Nazis loved to remember the good old times: 9 November, the day of the attempted Putsch (Hitler's revolution); in January, *Tag der Machtubernahme* (Hitler assuming power); 20 April, the fuehrer's birthday; 1 May, Tag der Arbeit (Labor Day); and in fall, Heldengedenktag (Hero Day).

These were regular meetings and celebrations of the Teutonic Order of Cairo, a loosely knit *Kameradschafstbund*—fellowship of former officers of the Wehrmacht, members of the NSDAP, former SA and SS men, and even a sprinkling of gestapo officials. All of them had fled to Egypt shortly before or after the end of the war.

Many of Otto's comrades were sought in Germany as war criminals, as was Otto. In Egypt they lived under the protection—first of King Farouk, and later of President Nasser. Then, when Anwar Sadat became president, they lost the good will of the Egyptians, but were still protected and tolerated. None of them were ever arrested and returned to Germany. During Nasser's regime, all of those for whom an arrest warrant was issued by the new German government were made Egyptian citizens. It was then that Otto Nagil took the name of Omar Nabil and registered his son Anton as Achmed Nabil, and with their Egyptian passports they could easily travel to any country in the Middle East and Europe.

The same group of wanted men could also draw generously from the Deutsche Bank in Cairo, funds which had been deposited after the war in gold bullions and foreign currencies by an unnamed benefactor of the SS. Otto Nagil, who had arrived in Cairo shortly after the end of the war in Europe, could at once draw from this account and became financially independent. Money had never been a problem for the Nagil family.

While there was a school in Cairo that catered to German citizens. and taught lessons in German with Arabic as second language, the wife of Otto Nagil, Rosemarie, had enrolled her son in a private school where he learned in Arabic and English as second language.

By the time Anton turned 13, he was fluent in all three languages. German was spoken at home as neither his father nor mother ever became fluent in Arabic. Many of the pupils of this private school were the sons of Egyptian officials, Army officers and Anton became friends with Ali, the son of a high-ranking government official. Ali's father was a secret member of the Moslem Brotherhood. Ali and his father were always welcome to attend a fellowship at the house of Otto Nagil and his comrades.

Many evenings, Otto had his best friend and comrade Gerhard Lutz and his wife Elke dine with them and then joined Otto in his Nazi retreat. Their children and Anton played the while upstairs.

Neither Anton nor his mother Rosemarie were invited for these intimate meetings but they could hear records of Nazi and soldier songs played, with Otto and his guests joining in, and there were many bottles of beer, champagne and hard liquor consumed. Otto Nagil liked to drink and always had liked his good beer and Schnapps.

Though Anton played with the two Lutz children, Gert and Erika, he did not care for them, perhaps because they were several years younger.

Ali and Anton went to the same class in school and while Ali was a serious boy and devoted to his religion, they had many characteristics in common—both boys of a gentle disposition, friendly to other kids and very loving to their parents, especially to their mothers. They respected each other's religious beliefs and neither found anything wrong visiting a church or mosque together. Ali's father was a strict Islamist, and while he tolerated his son Ali associating with this Christian boy Anton, he was rather reserved toward Anton and his family. Though he was invited to the Nagils and attended these functions remembering the Third Reich, he never became very friendly with the Nagils.

Often father and son sat together in the downstairs retreat where Otto had many books and magazines about the war campaigns, the U-boat war, the *Luftwaffe*, *Kriegsmarine*, and the glorious victories of the *Blitzkrieg*, and victorious battles in Russia. Many of the war books were imported from the New Germany. And there were volumes of the prewar glory of the *Partei*, the SA, the SS, and the Hitler Youth.

By the age of ten, Anton had been imbued with a strong feeling for the former Third Reich, its fuehrer, and its war of conquest. His father explained to Anton that the reason that Germany had lost the war was only the fault of the traitors in the German Army, the defeatist attitude of many army men, and the incompetent scientists who did not produce the *Wunderwaffen* (secret weapons) in time. Or the atomic bomb with which the fuehrer wished to destroy England and force the Americans to make peace on his terms.

As for his own war stories, Otto educated his son in the hard and dangerous work of the SS in the occupied territories where Otto had been in charge of an *Einsatzkommando* (action commando) fighting Russian partisans and Jewish bandits who shot at German soldiers from ambush and then tried to hide in the forests. Anton was shown the many medals for bravery his father received. His uniform displayed the markings of a SS colonel.

He further told Anton that in 1941, he became commander of all forts around Kaunas, specifically Fort IX, where Soviet commissars and Jewish bandits were incarcerated and tried for their crimes against the German Army. After he distinguished himself in action, he became deputy to SS Colonel Karl Jaeger, who was the gestapo Chief in Lithuania. When Karl Jaeger left because of health reasons, Otto Nagil became the gestapo Chief, and shortly after, when the band problem had been solved, he was promoted to regimental commander of the SS Viking division.

Young Anton was impressed with his father's valor and responsibilities as an SS leader. These were happy years for the boy, even more so when he went to school and was old enough to understand and appreciate.

During the hot summer months, the family went to Munich where they had a nice house in Bavarian style of stone and wood in Planegg, a suburb of Munich. There was even a jacuzzi built into the basement and when they came for the Christmas season, it was fun to play with neighbor's children in the snow outside—the boys always built a snow castle and had snowball fights, got all cold and then dipped into the warmth of the hot bath and churning jets. His mother would throw a *Fichtennadel* (a pine scented tablet) into the hot water, which made it turn green and smell of forest.

Anton cherished the visits in summer and Christmas. In summer, his mother would take him to the famous *Tierpark* (zoo). A visit to the Deutsche Museum (the science museum) was never enough to see it all in one day. Walk up the one tower of the Frauenkirche or Sankt Peterkirche and overlook the city—this he had to do himself. Once he counted the steps up the narrow winding wooden stairwell, the steps really high for a boy, and he counted 306.

In summer, his father took them in their car on Sunday outings to the beautiful countryside—much appreciated by the family to see forests and meadows in various shades of green, fields of grain, which were turning into golden waves when the wind whipped through them. Back in Egypt, it was all brown and mustard bareness except for oasis. They visited the lakes around Munich, some large enough to go by steamboats. For lunch they ate at an inn where Anton could order as he wished. He could order his own glass of *Weissbier* (wheat beer) that he liked best in taste, or share a *Radlermass* with his mother, a combination of dark beer and lemonade. His father always drinking beer and Schnapps, reordering until his mother begged him to stop, which made his father angry.

Christmas was Anton's favorite time to visit Munich. He loved the snow and cold. Visit Zirkus Krone and laugh with the antics of the clowns, go with his mother to the *Christkindlmarkt* (Christmas Market) in town and listen to the trumpet trio on top of the St. Peter Church and do their shopping to decorate the Christmas tree. Then on Christmas Eve, they gave each other presents; and he and his mother went to the Catholic Church in Planegg for midnight services. His father never came along.

Anton was less impressed of how his father treated his family—him and his mother. His father was a harsh disciplinarian and demanded total obedience. This was hard on both of them as Anton was as much as his mother a free spirit and did not believe in total submission to anyone. Not in school; and Anton was lucky as there were many foreign teachers from Europe who ruled with persuasion and not the stick. Not at home; but there, when Anton rebelled sometimes against his father's wishes, which were really commands, he was disciplined with a bamboo rod. His father would tell him, "You are in my army and you obey without hesitations."

Once, when Anton was old enough to question his father about the strictness with which he ruled the house, his father explained that this is how he was taught as a boy.

"I had to obey my parents, my teachers, the priest in the church; in fact any adult person. In the army, especially in the SS, the obedience was demanded and given. A soldier either was in command and ordered, or he was of inferior in rank and obeyed. Total."

And he explained that a soldier had to obey even unto death. What he called *Kadaver gehorsam* (to obey as a corpse)!

Anton's mother was a beautiful woman with long dark hair, gentle and kind, rather shy with strangers, though she was a good hostess to the many friends who came both from the German colony and native Egyptians.

Because of their many quarrels, or rather how brutal his father treated his mother at times, Anton had a love-hate relationship with his father but loved his mother dearly—as she loved him, her only son and she saw her likeness in him.

When Anton grew older, he became witness to not only verbal abuse by his father of his dear mother but also beatings. That his father was a brutish man he knew, but the vicious beatings he witnessed intensified his hatred. When he then comforted his crying mother, his father slapped him and called him "unworthy of his nationalsocialist upbringing."

Once, when alone with his mother he asked her, "Mama, why is papa so mean to you sometimes?"

She answered, "Your father has a bad temper."

"I have his bad temper too, you told me, Mama. But I don't hurt anybody then and if I talk back to you or papa, I would never think of hitting you."

"Your father can be brutal at times, Toni."

"Then why did you marry him?" Asked Anton.

"Oh, Toni, I was young then. We girls all flocked to the soldiers and wanted to get married to one. It was the times. Your father looked so handsome in his black SS uniform and he could be so charming. Then I did not know what he was, his bad temper, or what the SS did. I knew so little then, they kept everything secret. It was only after the war that many of us heard about the killings the SS did."

"But mama, it was war then. Papa told me about the SS fighting the partisans who shot at the soldiers after the fighting was over."

"Toni, you are still too young to understand. Once when you are older you will learn the truth. We are family and I don't want to turn you against your own father. At least he loves you and is good to you."

"Tell me mama, why is he so mean to you, is it because you visit that Jewish doctor?"

She smiled bitterly. "Yes, that is one reason. But he always treated me badly, but that is his nature."

"Mama, are Jewish people really that bad as Papa always tells me? You said that your doctor is such a nice man?"

"Jewish people are no different from anyone else. All the stories he tells you are just excuses for him killing so many."

"But mama, papa told me he only killed Jewish partisans when they shot at Germans?"

"You will find out someday, Toni. Let it go for now. We are family."

Anton was 13 years old when the event happened that would change his life and open his eyes to his father's soldiering in Nazi Germany.

He heard his mother's screams in the party room downstairs, and when he rushed down, he saw his father beat his mother, who was cowering on the floor, unmercifully with his riding crop. His father was in a drunken rage, berating his wife for visiting the Jewish bastard doctor again. When he rushed to his father and tried to stop him he was cruelly lashed by him before Otto returned beating his wife. Anton, in his own rage, and only feeling a deep hatred for his father rushed to the desk where he knew his father kept a loaded pistol. Anton called to his father to stop! His father turned to him and lashed at his face—and Anton, from close, shot him. Unconcerned about his dead father, he comforted his mother.

He remembered that they both cried as his mother held him in her arms, the tears not meant for the dead brute.

It was only after his mother changed from her torn dress, washed her swollen and marked face, that she called Dr. Zapruder and told him of Otto's death and pleaded for his help.

Dr. Zapruder rushed to the family's house and when he saw Otto shot, he knew that he could not report this to the police. He called an Egyptian physician whom he knew as being corruptible. Dr. Mustafa Kamel came within the hour and after being given a thousand pounds in English banknotes, he wrote the death certificate as "heart failure," which was true—the bullet had torn his heart.

Dr. Zapruder, dressed Frau Nagil's cuts, bruises and also a cut on Anton's face where he was lashed with the rod, and gave her a sleeping potion. Then he and Dr. Kamel undressed the corpse, washed it, and dressed the dead man in a new suit.

The next day Rosemarie arranged for a private funeral. The funeral home came to pick up the body, and with the proper documentation by Dr. Kamel, Otto Nagil was buried in the afternoon, attended only by his wife and son, neither of them shedding any tears when Father Sebastian, of the Catholic Church, spoke a few comradely words over the coffin, and more sincere comforting words to Frau Nagil and her son as he saw both of their faces marked by lash-like injuries. While the priest did not understand the sudden death of Otto Nagil, he had known the man to be brutal and one who was given to drink and mistreating his wife. He passed the word of Otto's death to his German friends and also the family's wish for a private funeral as they could not appear in public—and he explained why.

The German colony was aghast at the sudden demise of their beloved friend Otto Nagil, but not surprised at the private funeral. They knew the wife of Otto to be a gentle and abused woman, but also a person not indoctrinated with nationalsocialism. When some of them came to call on Frau Nagil to pay their condolences, they were not received. However, Gerhard Lutz was most persistent to speak privately with Rosemarie. When she received him Anton was present. Rosemarie's face still swollen, marked with cuts and one eye discolored and almost shut.

Lutz understood now why there had been a private funeral as Rosemarie did not wish to be seen by anyone in her battered condition. He was surprised to see Anton have a cut in his face. He knew that his friend Otto could be brutal with his wife but dearly loved his son. There must have been a terrible row and it was probably then that Otto had this heart attack—he had seen Otto himself in uncontrolled rage.

Lutz was less concerned with the obvious beating they had received from Otto as with the many documents in Otto's possession which told of their previous lives in Germany, and their work together and he knew included details of their secret wartime work.

Rosemarie wished for her son to see and study these documents as she knew very well what they contained, and hoped for Anton to realize the true nature of his father and therefore never feel guilty for having killed him. When Rosemarie refused to turn over the items, Lutz threatened her with dire consequences, telling her that his group needs to get these documents and will get them even if it means to do so over her dead body.

Rosemarie knew he meant it and told him to give her a few weeks to sort out what belonged to 'them' and what she wanted to keep for her son's education.

"Remember, Herr Lutz," and by calling him Herr Lutz instead of the familiar Gerhard and *du,* he knew that she had divorced herself from him and his kind, "It had been my husband's wish that my son be brought up in the spirit of what the Nazis stood for and this legacy I wish to pass on to him. Therefore, I cannot give you everything that is downstairs."

Lutz snarled contemptuously, "We all know of your sympathies, and they are not for what had been the glory of the Third Reich."

Rosemarie answered, "While this may be so, I nevertheless have to pass on his legacy to my son. When Anton is an adult, he can make up his own mind."

Lutz stood up, and with hate glaring in his eyes told her brusquely, "I give you a week from today to separate what belongs to us and me. Then we come to pick everything up and we will search ourselves that nothing else remains in your house. Else . . ." He made a slash-mark around his throat, turned, and without saying anything, left the house. Anton, who had witnessed the threatening remarks, understood that the Lutzs were now enemies. "That bastard! I'll get him for threatening you, Mother!"

When Rosemarie looked through the things of Otto, she found many bundles of documents, all clearly identified with labels as to their contents. Rolls of 35-mm movies and also the projector to show them. Several metal boxes which she knew contained money, but she had no idea how much or in what currency, though from one box she had extracted the one thousand British banknotes she had given Dr. Kamel.

Rosemarie told Dr. Zapruder of Herr Lutz having visited and given her one week to separate what was hers and of Otto's friends. The important thing was to find personal files of Otto, perhaps of criminal content, to show her son what his father really was and what he did during the war.

Dr. Zapruder knew it was dangerous for him to be in the house of a respected member of the German Colony. Most of these people were ex-Nazis, perhaps even still imbued with Nationalsocialism. For his first visit, he had come in his car because of the urgency of Frau Nagil's request. If he came again, he would do so by taxi, for these people might be interested in a strange car parked outside and could trace it back to him. As far as he knew, Herr Nagil kept his wife's choice of private physician a personal matter. Probably didn't want it known by his colleagues.

In the early evening after the funeral, Rosemarie received a call from Dr. Zapruder. The doctor wished to know how his patients were and that he wanted to come over to apply new dressing to her wounds and Anton's face, or did she wish to visit his office in the morning? Also, he asked if everything went according to protocol at the funeral in the afternoon.

Rosemarie wanted very much for him to come over. There were a number of private and important matters she wished to discuss with him. "And dear doctor," she addressed him with a trembling voice, "yesterday when you came into the downstairs, all the Nazi regalia, that was Otto's doing and had nothing to do with my sentiments. I was never a Nazi."

Dr. Zapruder assured her, "I knew of your anti-Nazi sympathies when you first came to me, you told me then and I believed you. And your son Anton?" Softly she answered, "That is what I need to talk to you about, dear friend."

Avraham Zapruder had been born in Cairo and was the son of a rabbi. He had a distinguished career as a surgeon and had become the chief of the emergency department in the Cairo General Hospital, but had to leave this post when Nasser came to power, and now had his own practice as a general practitioner. He was married to an Egyptian woman named Amal, and she had converted to Judaism. They had one child, Hanna, who was ten years old. Many years ago Frau Nagil had come for consultation for a minor ailment, a friend of hers had recommended Dr. Zapruder as a fine physician. Perhaps she had visited him because he was Jewish.

Otto had only used a German doctor, a former member of the SS, and Anton had likewise only visited him.

Dr. Zapruder came an hour later, only his second visit to the house. After he had dressed their wounds, Rosemarie had a private talk over a glass of wine with him and confided in the doctor her wish that Anton should learn about Otto's life in Germany as commander of the action commando and his role as commander of Fort IX in Kaunas.

She expressed the hope that if Anton would learn about Otto's workings, he would not feel the guilt of having shot his father. She begged him to sort through the documents and movies and explain to Anton the true nature of what was called the Holocaust. Though Dr. Zapruder had reservations of believing that the boy would show sympathies for what had transpired during the war, and that his killing his father was only due to how he abused his mother, he nevertheless agreed to the visits and try to instill in Anton a feeling of concern and compassion for the victims.

As Frau Nagil said, "Otto was a monster and should have been tried for his crimes. Killing him, even by his own son, was a just punishment. And that I wish for Anton to understand."

Frau Nagil took the doctor downstairs into what she called "His Nazi-den." Dr. Zapruder had already been astonished when he saw all that Nazi decoration. The only thing she had changed was to turn the portrait of the fuehrer around. Frau Nagil opened the *Tresor*, which was really a walk-in safe. She left him there.

He found bundles of documents, rolls of film, each labeled by its contents. Several metal boxes, with what? When he opened them he found them stacked with foreign currency. He was only interested in the documents and they seemed to have been categorized by year. Frau Nagil had told him, her husband not only had been a virulent Nazi but also had been a member of the SS and an action commando.

Dr. Zapruder did of course know of the holocaust. He attended services at the big synagogue in Cairo, the Sha'ar Hashamayim Temple and there had been talk. Since he knew English, he read many books on the Holocaust as there was no literature in Arabic on this subject. He knew the misery of the Jews began with Hitler coming to power, intensified with the Nuremberg laws, but the killing of the Jews did not begin until the war started with the Soviet Union. The important thing was to find personal files of Otto Nagil pertaining to his wartime activities in camps or wherever, to show Anton what his father was and did during the war.

Therefore, he picked the two files that read, *SOMMER/HERBST 1941, BANDEN BEKAMPFUNG* (summer/fall bandit elimination) and *MEIN KRIEGSTAGEBUCH von Obersturmbannfuehrer Otto Nagil.* My war diary by SS Lieutenant Colonel Otto Nagil.

When he read the files he knew that this was what he had been looking for. There were also files on SS Major Gerhard Lutz and others and those he put aside as these Frau Nagil had to give to them. He also put cans of movies to the side which he thought were of value. One entitled in German *AUSROTTUNG VON GROSSEM UND KLEINEM UNGEZIEFER.* He could only read the word *ausrottung*, but he knew enough German to understand that what it meant—extermination. He closed the door to the safe, took a brief look around at all the Nazi stuff. Against the wall was a large table, just far enough from the wall so one could walk around it, it was a layout of tin soldiers, or rather brown and black tin figures standing like for a parade, and in front the tin figure of Adolf Hitler. Since in the middle of the large room were about two dozen chairs he surmised that this was a meeting room of the Nazis in Cairo, and Otto Nagil had been their leader or one of the leaders of the group. Even with Mubarak at the helm in Egypt, he knew that these people were not only free to pursue their beliefs but were also under the protection of the Egyptian government. They were still dangerous people and not to fool with.

He returned upstairs and told Frau Nagil of what he had found and thought was important for young Anton to see and read.

The boy Anton and his father had never been a great father and son team. Anton was too much like his mother. Anton however, had loved the stories of the glory of the Third Reich and greatly enjoyed playing in the "SS Hall" as his father called it.

Playing on the big table with the little figures in brown and black uniforms, setting up parades as he saw in the album of the *Reichtstag* in Nuremberg. Playing battles with the tin soldiers in gray, the *Wehrmacht*, against the brown soldiers of the Soviets. Moving little tanks around, the German Tiger versus the crude T-34s. Otto was proud then of his son and played for him soldier songs, Nazi songs and the German Hymn. Then they both stood at attention with a raised arm in Nazi salute. Though the gentle boy Anton was, he nevertheless grew up with militarism and a love for soldiering and fighting. Having been made citizens of Egypt during Nasser's regime, he looked forward to service in the Egyptian Army.

When Ali visited Toni, as he was called by his closest friends and by his parents instead of Anton, they played *Wehrmacht* versus Soviets. When Anton visited Ali in his villa, Ali had also a playroom with a table made to look like the desert, then they played with Egyptian soldiers, with tanks and guns—fighting the Israelis. Anton knew little about the Israelis except that they were Jews who had come after the war and drove out the Palestinians, took their land and homes, slaughtered the Arabs like in Deir Yassin. The Israelis (his father never referred to them as Israelis, but Jewish Pollaks) were interlopers in the Holy Land and must be driven out. Yet, Anton had a certain sympathy for the Israelis as his mother had read to him the Old Testament as part of his Catholic religious education which she gave him. He also attended the Catholic Church in Cairo with his mother and heard sermons by Father Sebastian who spoke of the Jews as Christ-killers, who must be punished for eternity for their dastardly deed.

However, when he asked his mother about the Crucifixion and why the Jews killed Christ, who was a Jew, she told him that it was preordained as God willed it so he would become the Savior, besides it was the Romans who had killed Jesus, and not the Jews.

He knew that Israelis had lived in the Palestinian lands before, had kings and a history as warriors. He knew little of the previous wars except of the glory of the Egyptian Army having re-conquered the Sinai during the 1973 War. He was then eight years old and reenacted the battles with Ali's soldiers and the table showed the Suez Canal. When his father had spoken of the Jews, it was in terms of sub-humans who only won a fight with trickery and deceit. His father showed him school books where Jews were depicted with fat bellies, long hooked noses and thick lips. Even Ali accused the Israelis of having tricked the Egyptians by leading them into ambushes and fighting them only when they had great numerical advantage. The only Jew he knew was his mother's physician and he seemed to be a nice man who looked very much like any other Egyptians and spoke Arabic fluently like any other Egyptian from Cairo. The one trait Anton had inherited from his father was a short temper. Therefore, when he saw his father beat his mother unmercifully with his riding crop, she already beaten down on her knees, in his *Jaehzorn* (rage), he got the pistol, held it against his father, yelled at him to stop and when he turned and gave him a vicious blow across his face he pulled the trigger. He had seen his father jerk backward and fall down. Anton would never remember that he switched the safety off or that he pulled the trigger. Afterward, the boy would only remember the explosion of the gun.

The day after the funeral, Anton's mother took him down into the Hall and told Anton to learn of who his father really was. He must never tell anyone of what happened that day, not even his closest friend Ali.

He felt no remorse. At this time, Anton only knew that what he did was to save his mother. What his father was before was of no consequence to him. To please his mother, he read documents, saw pictures, watched movies and read his father's war diary. For three days, he immersed himself in Otto's history of the war. He did not wish, as his mother had proposed, for Dr. Zapruder to be with him. Then he knew and understood that he had not only killed the tormentor of his mother but had shot a monster who may have been his father, but was no longer.

A week later, in the early evening, Herr Lutz came with two of his colleagues. Frau Nagil gave him everything he wanted. His purpose had been served. Though she did not know the details of what had been brought with them when they fled Germany at the end of the war, she knew that her boy had seen and read.

Together they emptied the many cans with currency of sterling pound notes, American dollars, the new German mark and Egyptian pound. It was close to a million dollars in value. She deposited the money at the German Bank in Cairo.

In his first day alone in the Nazi-room, Anton selected the movies and saw several reels; most of them taken after the war was over by the Allies, showing stacks of corpses the British bulldozers moved into ditches. The camp was called Buchenwald. It held living people, almost walking skeletons. He saw Germans from nearby towns walk by to view the horror, some holding handkerchiefs to their noses, others crying. Anton did not know what to make of what he saw. Propaganda movies? Yet there were so many dead and those people with sunken eyes looking emaciated, wearing the striped cloth of prisoners. How could it have been? Who was responsible? But strangely, these horror movies did not touch the boy. Not until he watched movies obviously taken during the war. There were execution scenes of men, women and children! The victims were showing their backs to the shooters who wore German uniforms. He saw them jerk forward as the bullets hit them and fall down. He saw little children flung into the ditch before they were shot. But why shoot children? If the men and women were partisans and needed to be executed—why the children? They did not harm anybody. He did not understand. There was one short episode, which impressed Anton more than anything else he had seen so far. It came from the reel entitled:

VARMINTS LARGE AND SMALL EXTERMINATED

It showed a square with trucks to the side. Women were climbing into the trucks. One woman came before the camera with a small child holding her hand. A German soldier grabbed the child and tore it away from the woman. He saw the terror-stricken face of the woman as she pleaded with the soldier. He brusquely waved her to the trucks. The little child, a girl no older than perhaps four or five, ran after the woman and took her mother's hand again. The soldier tore the child away and flung the little girl to the side. This terrible scene was repeated three times until the soldier tore the child a last time from the woman's hand, lifted the child high up and slammed it on the ground. One last time the camera focused on the little girl, she no longer could get up but raised her outstretched arms to the woman, her little face of a horror Anton never before saw in a human being, blood running down her face. A child! Anton sat there stunned in shock. Then crying as he understood, though never aware of the tears streaming down his face. Though forbidden to join her mother, the child did what human instinct demanded of her. The child tried to join her mother even after she had been torn away many times brutally by the German soldier. It was only after a while that he noticed that his face was wet with his tears. Anton re-run the reel to see who the soldier was—of the SS? He could not see any insignia, SS or *Wehrmacht*. What this soldier did was against nature!

With the reel was a short document.

It read, *"2.41. Action in Babtei. Movie taken by the Kaunas Gestapo shows 113 Jewesses being transported to the woods to be shot. The scene shows a Jewess separated from her Jew child and clearly demonstrates the filthiness of these people. Twenty-two Jew children were incarcerated in a wooden shack with windows and doors nailed shut to be disposed of later. Through oversight the Jew children were kept locked up for three days until discovered. To save ammunition the shack was then torched and the small varmints destroyed."*

Anton tried to but could not envision the terror of the little children in a small hut, dark inside, kept without food and water, and then burnt alive. He would never forget them. Forget the helplessness and horror in the little girl's face. Was his father involved in the murder of Jews? There was one more short reel Anton decided to see. It was entitled, "The first *Sonderbehandlung* (special treatment) of German Jews. 25 November 1941. 1800 hours. Fort IX, Kovno." There was a label attached to the box, **"Short execution scene filmed by the Kovno Gestapo. Original to be sent to *Reichsleiter* Himmler for viewing by the fuehrer."** It was dusk but the scene lit by spotlights. The movie apparently taken from an embankment. There was no soundtrack. Directly in front a dirt footpath and just beyond was a very long ditch. As the camera moved to either side of the ditch it showed bodies lying. Most were on their stomachs and their backs showed the dark stains of blood. The camera moved level along the embankment and it showed machine guns posted to either side and attended to by two SS men, the barrels pointing down to the footpath. Farther to the right were three men who held machine pistols. The scene shifted to the left, where a line of men, women and children were running past a cordon of SS men who lashed at them with whips and clubs. The people lined up before the ditch and there were scenes of adults embracing their children as if to say goodbye. The camera pointed to the right, where an SS officer walked from the end of the line and shot the younger children with his pistol. The scene shifted to the left, to the end of the line and focused on another SS officer. Before him stood a woman with a child in her arms, with another child holding on to her dress. The little girl in the arms of the woman turned to the officer and offered him a twig. He shot her in the face then shot the woman. They fell into the ditch. This officer then hit an older boy who apparently screamed at him. When he fell in the ditch the officer shot him and the little boy on his shoulder. The camera followed this officer, who went along the line and executed the little children with a shot to their heads.

In the middle the two officers met, then returned. The camera showed briefly the profile of the officer—and Anton was stunned when he saw the face of his father!

The rest of the short movie showed the machine guns in action and the people tumbling into the ditch. Anton saw but it didn't register. Then the film ended. Anton sat there for a long time, his mind numb. He was in shock.

On the third day of his viewing and reading of the atrocities, he found the *Kriegstagebuch,* the war diary of SS Lieutenant Colonel Otto Nagil, his father. Before he began to read it he unfolded an 8-page document attached to the back. The heading on the first page showed a stamp with *Geheime Reichssache*—Secret document of the Reich.

Further:

DOCUMENT 4:

Total number of executions in the area of Einsatzkommando 3a, from 4 July to 1 December 941.

By my order, the following executions were carried out by the Lithuanian partisans and my SS men of Einsatzkommando 3a. Total Jews executed: 137,346.

After establishment of a roving-commando under the leadership of SS Ostuf. Hamann and eight to ten dependable men of the EK. 3a, and the Lithuanian Partisan commando, the below listed actions were carried out.

There followed a listing of executions almost day by day with listings of the day, the place the actions took place and the number of people and children executed.

The first page showed, besides Jews also communists, Russians, Lithuanians and even one German executed. From page 2, the executed were all Jews and listed as males, females, and children. The numbers, staggering—unbelievable. On August 23, 1941 in Pansvesys, 1,312 Jews; 4,602 Jewesses; and 1,609 Jew children were executed.

Anton understood that these executions had nothing to do with fighting partisans but were murder of men, women and children.

He looked at the last page of the report and saw it was signed by SS Colonel Karl Jaeger.

Anton turned to the diary, which began on July 1, 1941.

MEIN KRIEGS TAGEBUCH—von Sturmbannfuehrer Otto Nagil Dachau. 1 July 1941.

Ordered to Berlin to report to Oberstgruppenfuehrer Heydrich. With me my "Kamerad" Hauptsturmfuehrer Lutz. Left with the evening express train from Munich, sleeper provided, arrived in Berlin, Anhalter Station in morning. Proper facilities for cleaning up. Good breakfast in officer's canteen for 1.00 mark. Left our baggage at the station. We took taxi to RSHA and reported on time, ten o'clock, to General Heydrich. Lutz and I in our black dress uniforms. We made good impression, were treated formally by the general. The general told us that we were recommended by Commandant Eicke of Dachau KZ for our strict adherence to discipline in the camp. We were selected for "Bandenbekaempfung" in Lithuania and were to report to Standartenfuehrer Karl Jaeger, chief of the gestapo in Lithuania whose headquarter is in Kaunas. To our surprise and delight, the general gave us our promotion papers—I was promoted to Obersturmbannfuehrer and Lutz to Sturmbannfuehrer. When the general congratulated us and shook our hands, he told us, "Be ruthless with the Bolshevik commissars and the Jewish bandits. Reichsfuehrer Himmler wishes that Lithuania becomes Judenrein *(free of Jews) in short order." His eyes became cold and even threatening as he added in his high-pitched voice, "All your work for the 'Reich' from here on becomes a State Secret!" [My impression of the general. I would not wish to work for him on a personal basis. There was never a smile or a friendly word. He is cold as ice. While I am myself a strict disciplinarian, I am on friendly terms with my comrades. This I find lacking in Heydrich.] In the travel office, Lutz and I received our orders, and the troop train was to depart at one in the afternoon for Kaunas. Lutz and I barely had time to get our luggage. But managed to have a good lunch at the station, bought a bottle of Schnapps, and had a few drinks. There were no sleepers but comfortable second-class compartments. 3 July. Arrived in the afternoon in Kaunas. Taken to our quarters at the SS officers' hotel in town. Lutz and I received our own comfortable rooms. We were to have dinner at six with Colonel Jaeger. Again appeared in our dress uniforms. Felt somewhat out of place as everybody else was in gray. Sat with other officers—at the head of the table Colonel Jaeger. A handsome man with a bushy mustache. After dinner, Colonel Jaeger asked me and Comrade Lutz to an anteroom, offered drinks and cigars. Jaeger of a friendly disposition. Now assigned as head of the gestapo in Lithuania. Also chief of the "Sicherheits und Ordungspolizei." He told us that General Heydrich had recommended us as being strict disciplinarians. His voice then became hard, "We have to be ruthless with this 'Gesindel' (pack) in Lithuania. Who is not for the Reich is against us and has to be eliminated. This includes all Bolsheviks, and there are many Lithuanian communists left who did not run away with the Soviets. They must be ferreted out and shot. Likewise Soviet political commissars captured by our army and brought to us. And Jews. All Jews without distinction of gender or age! "There need not be any trials for this 'Lumpenpack.' Kaunas is surrounded by Forts dating back to the Tsars time. Fort VII is now being used as execution site. Fort IX is being readied for this purpose. Fort IX will be the major site, your department, Obersturmbannfuehrer Nagil. Surmbannfuehrer Lutz will take charge of Fort VII. "Both of you are assigned to the 'Sicherheitspolizei' in Kaunas as 'Kommandants' of your respective forts. The cleaning out of enemies of the Reich in the Baltic countries has been given to 'Einsatzgruppe A.' A smaller group is 'Einsatzkommando 3' for Lithuania. "This is the 'Kommando' you will belong to. In each fort you will have a cadre of reliable SS men and a command of Lithuanian 'Schutzmannshaft' or as we call them partisans.*

"*They will serve you loyally and obediently.*" *At this point Lutz asked, "Are these Lithuanian policemen trustworthy? Do they understand to execute these enemies without mercy?" Jaeger said, "They are former victims of the Bolsheviks and we freed them from the drudgery of studying. Most are university students." He smiled as he continued, "Some may be criminals, but show an aptitude for executing those we wish to eliminate. Most of them also virulent anti-Semites and have proven themselves in pogroms even before our army arrived. They are in uniforms and have a low grade structure of non-commissioned officers." I asked, "Native uniforms?" Jaeger replied, "No. For prestige purpose we dress them in German Gray and as they are attached to the SS, they have runes on the lapels. Most of them have become marksmen in Genickschuss." Jaeger smiled. "Learned that from the Bolsheviks. All executions are carried out by rifle, they are equipped with our standard Mauser rifle when single or in small groups. Mass shootings, 'Sonderbehandlung' or as we call it 'Gross Aktion,' is carried out with machine pistols or machine guns." Lutz asked, "Are we, as higher 'SS Fuehrers' expected to participate in the executions?" Jaeger answered, "Officers are expected to use their Lugers for giving the 'Gnadendschuss' (mercy-killing). If you wish to do so." He smiled. "Might prove to be fascinating. "The SP detachment in Fort VII is led by SS Untersturmfuehrer Eikhart. "SS Obersturmfuehrer Huber is leading the SP troop at Fort IX. When you meet them tomorrow, you will learn of the particulars of all phases of our work here." There were no other questions at this point and we parted with a friendly Heil Hitler.*

4 Juli. I dressed in soldier's gray. The SS motor pool assigned me with a staff car. I also received a map of the city and we drove out to Fort IX. An imposing of medieval complex of high walls, towers, courtyards, and cells. In the main building of brick my office. There I met Obersturmfuehrer Huber. Also from Munich, he was my kind of soldier. Huber was the only officer in my small detachment of SS men. We also had a company of Lithuanian, partisans. And for labor a company of Soviet prisoners who were quartered in the cells of the fort. At the moment we had no other prisoners here. All those to be shot are sent to Fort VII for disposition. At least the main building with offices, kitchen, dining-hall were in tolerable condition but needed painting. I had lunch together with Huber at our table. We reminiscent about our hometown, Ernst Huber is from Schwabing in Munich. The SS noncoms were introduced to me. After we had lunch, the partisans were fed. With Huber, I inspected the fort. The cells were underground, each cell large enough to hold fifty prisoners standing. There were no bunks as prisoners were to be executed the same day they arrived. Similar, we would not be concerned with feeding them. I also inspected the armory where rifles, machine guns and grenades were kept. I found everything in order, only many of the cells were dilapidated and needed more secure doors. Work on those was done by the Soviets, as was the painting and other repairs. When I returned to my office, I received a dispatch from Lutz in Fort VII. He had received a batch of prisoners and invited me over to witness their execution. I let Huber drive as he knew the way. When I entered the large courtyard Lutz received me. There were several hundred Jews, many women. The shooting had stopped when I entered. Lutz led me to a side yard. A long ditch I saw half filled with bodies. A cordon of his SS partisans were lined up from the large yard to the ditch. I saw they carried no firearms only whips and clubs. I told Lutz I didn't have much time. "Just show me the procedure." Lutz said, "Not mine. All Lithuanian partisan action." I asked, "You and your men don't participate?" Lutz replied, "Only with 'Gnadenschuss,' Obersturmbannfuehrer Nagil." I saw why he was so formal. At the end of the ditch stood his own squad of SS men with rifles. Along the ditch ten partisans with their rifles. I then asked, "Anyone worthwhile to see shot, commissars?" Lutz said, "Just Jews picked up by natives. How about the Jew women?" I told him to give the command to proceed. He in turn spoke to one of the ranking partisans standing by us, who gave the order in Lithuanian. I followed Lutz to where the ditch began. I drew my pistol as Lutz had done. I saw the first ten Jew women driven through the cordon of whip and club wielding partisans. I asked Lutz why they beat them. "They seem to be running readily without any resistance?" Lutz explained, "Just following orders. Standartenfuehrer Jaeger was here before and ordered this method to be used. He said the more brutal you are with them the less trouble you will have. He also said, orders from highest up to proceed in an aura of terror when shooting Jews." There were partisans who lined up the women next to each other then stepped back and the riflemen stood behind each woman, perhaps a meter away aiming the rifles at the necks. Their commander gave the order "FIRE!" The staccato of loud rifle shots, ten bodies fell into the ditch, apparently dead. Already the next ten Jew women came in a run. When lined up I wanted to see their faces. Expressionless, perhaps more in shock than in fear, one crying. All looked down into the ditch. "Fire!" Ten more bodies. I saw Lutz point at one. The Jewess was still moving. He raised his pistol. One, two shots he fired into her body, and she lay still. "The next one is yours, Obersturmbannfuehrer?" Nine Jew women came running, clubbed and whipped. The auxiliaries yelling, "Schnell, lauf . . . los Judenschweine." They had learned their proper German. Lutz turned to their commander who stood by us, "Where is number ten?" He pointed back. A partisan dragged one woman by her hair, she laying on the ground, her arms flying—none of the clubs or whips made her get up and run. By the time he dragged her to the ditch the other nine had been dispatched. Lutz pointed to the beginning of the ditch where we stood. The partisan flung her in. She laid there upon bodies on her back looking up—at me as I stood above her with my pistol pointing down. I saw her beautiful face with long hair distorted in hate as she screamed at me "MOERDERER . . . NAZISCHWEIN." I aimed at her face, shot twice, saw her hit and blood spurting from her face. She was dead. My first killing. I felt nothing! Lutz and I left. We drove in silence back to the hotel. My feelings at executing the first Jew? I hated her. Why did she need to be so beautiful? I hated her not because she called me murderer and a "Nazischwein" but because she was a Jew. "Ungeziefer"—varmints that needed to be destroyed. "JUDEN SIND UNSER UNGLUECK"(Jews are our misfortune). Now we were their misfortune. Justice served. I was rather thrilled that my aim had been true. Probably my first shot into her screaming mouth had killed her. But I wanted to be merciful and shot her a second time.

Anton was again stunned, his father a murderer. No—not this father! From this moment on he was Otto. Otto the murderer! He had killed little children and innocent women. Thrilled that his aim was true when he shot her in her mouth, screaming with courage at her killer! His mercy to shoot her again.

He read on. Since the Fort was not ready for executions Otto was writing about his travels with SS Lieutenant Hamann and his ten killers who, together with a company of Lithuanian partisans, went to different villages and towns to execute Jews. There was a remark that Hamann had been summarily discharged from the paratroopers for brutality to the recruits and assigned to the *Sicherheitspolizei* (security police) where his harsh discipline could be better utilized.

The difficulties they had in arresting the Jews but did so with the help of people from the villages who pointed out to the partisans where the Jews lived. Dragging the families out, shooting on the spot those who resisted. Constantly beating the victims with their rifles, clubs they carried and even bayoneting—how cruel and vicious, savages in German uniforms. Otto amongst them with a bull-whip. Otto complaining about the poor food, the miserable sleeping accommodations, but always proudly commenting how he organized vodka. Vodka he consumed and vodka given to the killers.

There was little variation to the method of organizing the killings. The Jews told to come out of the house and bring their valuables and money with them or else they would be shot. Partisans would then enter the house and if they found anything of value they shot these people on the spot, as they also shot those hiding. The victims driven to the market place and gathered there. Then marched; and here Otto added in an amusing by-line how the villagers at once ran to the Jew houses to take what they wanted once the march began; to the execution site which could be an anti-tank ditch or any ditch, ravine or a dip in the farmland, or just at the edge of a wood. If there were just a small number of victims the men and boys had to dig a hole with shovels brought or just with their hands.

For a trouble-free execution the men and boys were shot first. Taken in batches of ten and shot by riflemen in the neck. Then, in the same fashion, the women and children were shot.

Otto wrote that he was detailed as an observer, to learn the business. SS Lieutenant Hamann was in charge. Otto stated that he never shot more then a dozen Jews. That to learn the art of shooting, he used a rifle for that and used his Luger for the merci-killing if he saw victims still alive. Anton realized soon that Otto shot these people out of blood lust, he enjoyed killing innocent victims.

He read one entry in which Otto wrote that he did not personally approve of how SS Lieutenant Franz Hamann handled the executions. *"The man is a true sadist and really enjoys making the Jews suffer before they are shot. I pity the animals he shot as a hunter in Berchtesgaden. Standartenfuehrer Jaeger told me that there was a report from the police that when Hamann wounded a deer he would not kill it before cleaning it out. His license to hunt was then withdrawn."* Anton would remember the brutality of that man.

Otto wrote that he returned to Kaunas on the first of October and was granted a four-week leave after his observing mission in the country. He did not write in his journal about his leave in Munich but began his dairy again on the first of November. The Fort now in action and all his men back. He bemoaned the fact that on the fourth of October, 1,845 Jews had been shot in Fort IX while he was away. He was even more sorry that he was not back for the *Grossaktion* on the twenty-ninth of October when 9,260 Jews had been eliminated, among them 4,273 children. In both cases his comrade Lutz from Fort VII had been in charge and the Jews shot in long ditches dug outside the Fort.

Anton returned to Jaeger's report to see when Otto's first action was in Fort IX, He read: November 25, 1941, Kauen-Fort IX-1,159 Jews; 1,600 Jewesses; 175 Jew children. Total: 2,934. Resettlers from Berlin, Munich, and Frankfurt am.

He returned to the journal to read one last time about Otto. He did not read the account of the resettlers from Berlin and Frankfurt who were shot but turned to the page detailing the Jews from Munich—Otto's people.

At 4:00 p.m., we were finished with the Jews from Frankfurt and Berlin. Standartenfuehrer Jaeger suggested a break for an hour before we dispatched the Jews from Munich. Besides, they were just arriving, having had to carry their baggage from the train. The march past the ghetto, across the bridge and up the hill to the fort had been slower than expected. We saw them dragging through the gate into the large courtyard. Unexpectedly, there were a large number of children. There had been very few among the Jews from Berlin and Frankfurt and no small children. Jaeger, Hamann, Lutz, Huber, and Lutz's assistant Untersturmfuehrer Eckhart and I sat together. Jaeger's chauffeur had brought in a basket of sausages, cheese, breads and excellent Cognac and our kitchen provided the Schnapps, coffee and refreshments for the squad of SS men from Lutz and my people. Huber assured me that plenty of refreshment and vodka were given to the partisans outside who brought the Jews in and guarded them in the courtyard. Jaeger congratulated me for the professional manner the Grossaktion had been conducted so far. 'Wie Paradeschiessen' Jaeger explained. He then voiced the opinion that we shall order the Munich Jews in groups of eighty, instead of fifty. "The ditch is really long enough to stand eighty of them in a row." I answered, "Excellent suggestion, Standartenfuehrer. We brought the others in in batches of fifty as they were incarcerated in groups of fifty." Lutz said, "This way we can finish in less than an hour. It will get dark before we finish." I answered, "I have provided for proper lighting. No problem if we don't finish them before it gets dark." I then addressed Jaeger, "Since there are so many Jew children, should we finish them off first, or last perhaps? In any case separate them from their parents? Otherwise we might have problems?" Lutz said, "We won't have any problems. In the last Grossaktion, there had been over four thousand Jew children. We let them be with parents or adults and my men saw to it that there were no problems." Huber said, "Obersturmbannfuehrer Nagil, I can assure you that our men have trained with Lutz's men. Also the partisans are very good in keeping order." "Good. Then we won't have to separate them." I turned to Eckhart, "What is the head count so far?" Eckhart answered, "We shot exactly one thousand Jews from Berlin. From Frankfurt only 940." Jaeger said, "I have to send a wire to RSHA that the gestapo in Frankfurt fulfill their quota. If a few are missing in each transport, fine. But sixty Jews missing is unforgivable." I excused myself to see to it that two or three extra machineguns were posted for the added thirty people to be shot. I went with Huber to the armory. But with the five guns already posted, there were no more in operating condition. I told Huber to use three machine pistols. He suggested that our own men use them as the partisans were not familiar with the fast firing pistols. He wanted to take one himself. I permitted him. He took three machine pistols with him and had a detail bring extra ammunition. He also said he would attend *to the lighting as it would soon get dark and see to the arrival of the Jews. I returned to the table and found them all in a jolly mood with help of the cognac which had been finished and a bottle of Schnapps was passed around. Jaeger said, "May I make a last suggestion Obersturmbannfuehrer Nagil? Have Eckhart sent in first the adults with children while the light is still good; you and I dispatch the Jew children first, all those under one meter tall. This permits your machineguns to be trained upon the adults without having to deflect their aim." I gave Eckhart the order. It was almost five by the time we posted ourselves; twilight, and the lights were on. The first batch of adult Jews came running with their children, properly expedited by the partisans along the way. Last came a young man with a little boy on his shoulders and a woman with a small Jew child in her arms and one holding on to her dress. All had been told to take their coats off, but these three Jew children still wore theirs. Well, three coats less for the 'Winterhielfe,' too late now. Jaeger was at the other end and I heard his pistol crack dispatching the children. I stood myself behind the Jew woman, the child in her arms turned around to me. A blond Jew child in a red coat, maybe two or three; her face showed fright, her arm stretched out and in her hand a little green twig—she offered it to me? She spoke proper German when she said to me, "Please don't hurt my mommy and me," and tears rolling down her face. I raised my pistol and point-blank shot into her face. Her head disintegrated. Showing mercy, I shot the woman in the neck, and she fell into the ditch upon bodies, in her arms still holding tightly the girl in the red coat, with her the other Jew child who held on to her dress. I stepped close and shot the screaming Jew child. There was this boy with them, maybe fifteen or sixteen. He turned to me and shrieked* Moerderer *at me, his visage full of hate. I hit him with the pistol in the face, and he fell backward upon the bodies of his family with the small boy on his shoulders. It was now shadowy in the ditch, and I shot him twice into his chest. He was still shrieking, but he will soon* krepieren *(die). The little boy tried to stand up on the bodies, was he crying? Maybe, he stood now and the light was better farther back. I finished him off with a shot to the head. "Ein Meisterschuss," well aimed. Afterward, I went along the line and shot all those who were little. I didn't let them turn around anymore as that Jew child did with the twig. In the middle of the line I met Jaeger. We nodded to each other, our work done. We each went back, and the machine guns were in action. Jaeger and I, together with Lutz and Hamann walked along the ditch to dispatch those still alive—screaming, convulsing. One young man raised his hand to show he was still alive. It took less than an hour to complete the execution of the Munich Jews. Jaeger called it again "Paradeschiessen" (shooting drill).*

Anton, in a sudden rage, threw the diary against the wall. Otto was a monster, a mass murderer and a child-killer and deserved to die as he had made those children die. Not they but HE deserved to be shot! And from that moment on Anton never again felt any guilt that he had shot—EXECUTED—his father! No—not his father—Otto!

What he had just read in the war diary and he had seen in the film—it all was true!

CHAPTER II

ANTON'S YOUTH IN CAIRO

Anton visited Munich with his mother every summer vacation and Christmas. During summer, they visited a friend of the family, or rather of Otto, who was a rich industrialist and had a beautiful mountain home on the Koenigsee: *Haus Tanneck*. Anton loved the mountains; and since the daughter of the owner of the house, Betty, was also a teenager and shared his love for nature, they would climb the nearby peaks together. The Koenigsee was surrounded by mountains of which the highest was the Watzmann. This was a difficult mountain and not to be climbed without guides and only by experienced climbers who had to use proper equipment and ropes.

But he climbed the other peaks with Betty—the Jaenner just a walk-up, the Schneibstein not much more difficult. More strenuous and dangerous was the climb up the Brett. There was a sign that read ONLY FOR EXPERIENCED CLIMBERS—ROPED. Higher yet was the Hohe Goell from which they had a beautiful view over the Berchtesgandener Land and into Austria. Betty showed him where to find Edelweiss (the noble white flower) on a wall near the *Stahlhaus*.

The night, they would spend at the *Stahlhaus*, an inn on the border with Austria. Anton knew that Betty liked him and hoped that he would marry her. Anton was fond of Betty and if there hadn't been a little girl with long black hair and dark eyes back in Cairo, he would have considered marrying Betty some day. He was less fond of her father, Herr Schoenauer, who had been a good friend of Otto and was still talking about the Third Reich and its glory, though he had only been a boy then. He always talked about Saukel to whom House Tanneck had belonged until he was hanged in Nuremberg as a major war criminal. The house was confiscated by the government from whom Schoenauer bought it. There was no doubt that Theo Schoenauer was still a confirmed Nazi and that took away from the pleasure of visiting. His mother, Rosemarie felt the same way, though she and Schoenauer's wife, Inge, liked each other and were good friends.

In 1979, Anton entered the Cairo International Academy, a private and prestigious high school which, until the king was disposed by the military in 1952, was called the King Farouq Academy and changed in 1953 to the Gamal Abdel Nasser Academy. After he died in 1970, it was changed to its present name.

The school had an active foreign language curriculum and despite the fact that the new president, Anwar Sadat, had thrown out the Russian military advisers, it was still fashionable to teach the Russian language. Much of the military equipment was still Soviet. Ali Nasr took English while Anton learned Russian.

Anton had learned his Arabic in the private grammar school and spoke it like a native Egyptian.

Anton was intelligent, had a good mind for mathematics and chemistry, and looked forward to a career as a chemical engineer. His friend Ali concentrated on religious studies and wished to become an imam, a cleric. The academy was private and expensive and easily afforded by Anton's mother, Rosemarie.

The Nagils had become friends with Dr. Zapruder and his family. However, it was the Nagils who visited Dr. Zapruder as the family still felt uncomfortable to visit the German Colony. Amal was always treating them to an Arabian dinner and Anton had become fond of their little girl Hanna, now 11 years old. He treated her like his little sister and when he walked with her or visited the city, as her protector.

Hanna was a beautiful girl with long black hair down to her shoulders, dark eyes. She was a bubbly child and full of pranks and liked to tease Anton. If he got angry at her, her mirthful smile and gentle eyes made him at once forgive her teasing. While he thought of her as his little sister, Hanna felt more for him than an older friend or brother.

Her protector he was or tried to be. Both the elementary and high school were in one big complex and Hanna would wait for him after her classes were finished. Anton's mother would pick both up in her car or they would go home by taxi and drop Hanna off at her place first. Hanna's parents didn't have a car then. Once when he came to her, he saw Hanna with some boys from his school who were older than him. He didn't hear what one of the boys said to her but he saw Hanna suddenly cry. Anton rushed over to her, "What is it, Hanna? Why are you crying?" The taller of the boys, whom he knew as Pierre, from a French family sneered at him, "She is a dirty Jew girl."

Hanna said, "He called me a Jew swine."

Anton slapped Pierre, "Don't you ever call my girlfriend that!" Pierre at once slugged him in the face; hit him hard on his nose and he fell on his back. Anton wanted to rush at the boy but Hanna put her arms around him, "Don't Toni, you are bleeding all over."

Pierre walked away, "You Kraut! You are a dirty Jew lover." Anton, quite mad, pushed Hanna away to fight the boy but by then a teacher had seen and came over and held him back. The teacher told Pierre, "I want to see you tomorrow morning at the principal's office." Hanna gave Anton her handkerchief as he bled profusely and his white shirt was all stained. She felt so sorry for Toni but also was quite proud that he tried to protect her. She loved him for that. Anton took her home by taxi and when he came home, his mother saw the bloodied shirt and he told her what happened.

Rosemarie told him that she is glad that he protected Hanna. "But Toni, if you want to fight bigger boys you have to learn to defend yourself. Don't they have a class in school where they teach you how to protect yourself?"

"Yes, they do and I will sign up."

Anton joined Mr. Watanabi's class of jiujitsu.

Anton had developed a new interest, which he kept secret from his friend Ali and everyone else except Hanna. Perhaps it was due to his past discovery that Otto had been a war criminal and killed Jews indiscriminantly or perhaps because he had become friendly with the Jewish Zapruder family and pretty Hanna.

He showed an interest in Judaism, its past history according to the Old Testament, and modern Israel. Her father, who was traditional in his religious belief though not orthodox, wanted his daughter to learn the Hebrew language. There was no hope for Jews in Egypt, not even under tolerant Anwar Sadat. Hanna, as his only child, should have her future in Israel, he believed. To that end he hired a private instructor to teach his daughter the modern Hebrew, or Ivrit as it is called, and for many years he had a music teacher come to give Hanna piano lessons.

Her Hebrew teacher was Miss Levy, who was the secretary in doctor Zapruder's clinic. Her Hebrew was that of the prayers and not the modern language spoken in Israel. Hebrew is a Semitic language with similarities to Arabic in both words and pronunciation though Hebrew writing was different. It was really easier to learn than Arabic.

When Hanna asked Toni if he wished to learn Hebrew, he agreed.

After their lesson, she played the piano for him, Mozart, which he liked and also modern songs of Egypt. Hanna was already an accomplished player.

It was a year later and Anton had become proficient in hand-combat, when once again he picked up Hanna to take her home and Pierre was coming by. Anton wasn't about to start a fight but when Pierre hissed at him, "Kraut, Jew lover!" Anton snarled back at him, "Hey, you snail-eater, come here. I want to teach you to how to behave."

Hanna cried out, "Don't Toni! He isn't worth to get into a fight with."

Pierre rushed at him with his hands clentched into fists and swinging at his face. Anton avoided the fist but hit Pierre hard under his belt. Pierre doubled over and went on his knees. This time it was Pierre who got a bloody nose, in fact his nose was broken as Anton kicked him hard.

The next morning, Anton Nagil had to report to the principal's office. The principal heard about the fight and knew about their previous problem. He admonished Anton that he should never kick anyone. Anton was suspended for a week. But every day, he would be there to pick up Hanna and bring her safely home. Pierre was also suspended for a week for starting the fight and told that if he ever called the girl again names, he would be kicked out of school. Pierre would avoid both Hanna and Anton.

In 1981, after Egypt and Israel established diplomatic relations, Dr. Zapruder hired a new teacher. This private instructor of modern Hebrew was Avi Ben Etzioni, assistant cultural attaché of the newly established Israeli Embassy in Cairo. Etzioni was also a Mossad agent. He soon found a sincere appreciation for Israel in Anton, who was to him a strange boy. Dr. Zapruder had confided in Avi that Anton's father had been a war criminal and was killed by his son, though the reason he had shot his father the doctor did not explain to Etzioni

After Anton had read his father's war diary, he had become sympathetic to Jews and modern Israel. His view of the history of Israel was still distorted by what he learned and read in Egyptian schools, books and newspapers. His family subscribed to the Egyptian daily al-Ahram since the peace treaty with Israel had become at least neutral and no longer spouted inflammatory articles about Israel. The doctor also told Avi, in confidence, that Anton had a close friend whose father was a member of the outlawed Moslem Brotherhood and a high government official.

Avi realized that there was a young man who apparently had an open mind as to the conflict between Jews and Arabs and had learned about it from the Arab point of view. He would try to have Anton see the other side's facts and perhaps influence Anton as to the true history of the Middle East conflict.

As part of his language instructions to Hanna and Anton, Avi told them about the life in modern Israel, its accomplishments in turning the neglected country into the biblical land of milk and honey. And to his surprise, he found the boy quite knowledgeable. It was then that Anton told Avi that after a certain incident in his life, dating back to when he was 13 years old, he had begun his research of both ancient and modern Israel.

In the Academy, they had a larger library with a section of books in English. And there he found books on various religions and not just on Islam. Even the

Old and New Testament were on hand, as were books on Christianity. Anton was a devout Catholic as his mother was and she had taken him to the small Catholic Church in Cairo under the titular head of Father Sebastian who was still blaming the Jews for the crucifixion of Christ. Otto had not been religious, though he too was a Catholic as were most people who were born in Bavaria. Otto had never attended services or High Mass, not even on Christmas. Most of the German Colony were of various Protestant denominations and attended their own services. In fact, there were few Germans who were Catholics, and even fewer Egyptians who professed the Catholic faith. The largest Christian church was that of the Coptic faith.

As part of his religious upbringing, Anton was familiar with the New Testament, less so with the Old Testament. Of course he had become familiar with Genesis and the story of Moses in Exodus.

Anton wanted to research about the land of the Palestinians which the Jews had made into their modern nation of Israel.

So far, he only knew that the Jews had usurped the land belonging to the Palestinians to establish their own nation there. This nation against which Egypt had fought four wars. And as he planned on serving in the Egyptian Army when he finished high school, he wanted to learn more about this adversary whom he might have to fight in any future war. First, to whom did this land really belong to? Anton realized that to understand the very nature of the conflict in the Middle East, he would need an understanding of ancient times and that meant to research the Old Testament and find a book which was more secular and gave the history of the lands and its inhabitants without emphasis on religion. He finally found such a book in English. "Religious and Secular History of Palestine." The author was a professor of History at Cambridge University, Reginald Wallace.

Anton was a firm believer in God and Jesus as His Son and Savior. He also believed that Catholicism was the only right Christian religion and the Protestant denominations were just an offspring, brought about by the rebel Luther. Just as he believed that God did not send Prophet Mohammad and the Koran written by men without guidance by God.

He would never express such thoughts to his friend Ali who was a strict Islamite. Nor did Ali ever use the word infidel toward him and was tolerant of his Christian belief. When Ali tried to proselytize him toward his faith he did it gently, usually quoting a Sura from the Koran and expressing the hope that some day Anton would see the truth and become a Muslim.

When Anton read the Englishman's book, he soon realized that religion and the secular cannot be separated when studying Israel.

Islam, Christianity and Judaism believed in the creation of the earth and man by God. Anton also had been taught evolutionism which made much more sense than the six days God supposedly needed to make the universe, the world and man. However, intelligent as the boy was, he understood the six days meant six periods in time. How else could have God explained to Moses the making of the world, and he in turn taught the people, few of whom could count to a hundred, much less understood the meaning of million and billion.

The making of man, Adam and Eve, surely is an allegory. Man had evolved before as the bible tells of the two sons Abel and Cain. And when Cain slew his brother, God marked him so the people would know him. Anton's studies of to whom the land belonged became more fruitful when he read about Abram or as the Muslims call him Ibrahim.

Abram was an Aramean who lived in Ur of Chaldee, whom God chose to go to the land of Canaan. Canaan, like Abram, was a descendant of Noah, He's a man whom God had favored over all other men. Then, it was the Aramean, Abram God favored and spoke to him, named him Abraham and his wife Sarai, Sarah. God made a covenant with Abraham and told him he will be the father of many nations. His descendants would receive the land of Canaan for perpetuity and God said, *"And I will be their God."* Anton knew that the Jews were descendents of Abraham as were the Muslims. To whom did God promise the land of Canaan, the modern Palestine? According to the Moslem religion, Abraham, when eighty-six had gone unto Hagar, Sarah's handmaiden and servant, and she bore him a child which was named Ishmael. Ishmael revered by the Muslims as their true ancestor and to him God gave all lands that had belonged to Canaan, as Ishmael was the first-born of Abraham and therefore Abraham's inheritance of God belonged to him. However, this Englishman's account spoke of an angel of God predicting that Ishmael would grow up to be a *"wild man: his hand will be against every man and every man's hand against him."* It was only after Ishmael was born that Sarah conceived—Sarah then ninety years old. When he talked to Ali, his friend would not believe that so old a woman could bear a child. Ali believed that the birth of Sarah's son was a tale told by the Jews to legitimize their claim to Israel. Anton, however, found no problem in believing it if God willed it! Sarah's son was named Isaac. Isaac's wife Rebecca was barren, but God spoke to Rebecca, *"Two nations are in your womb . . . the one people shall be stronger than the other people; and the elder shall serve the younger."* Rebecca bore twins, the firstborn was called Esau, his brother, Jacob. According to the narrator of the Bible, the two already fought in Rebecca's womb! Anton read of the treachery of Jacob, as Esau had sold his birthright as firstborn to Jacob. Jacob then deceived his blind father and was blessed by him as the rightful heir. Esau, incensed by the treachery, vowed to kill Jacob, who fled. When Jacob returned with his two wives, during his voyage, at night, Jacob wrestled with an angel and was lamed but was told by the angel: *"Your name from this day forth will be Israel, for as a prince hast though power with God and with men."* The Bible continues and tells that when Jacob arrived in the land of the Canaanites, God appeared to him and told him, *"Your name is Israel. The land I gave to Abraham and Isaac I now give to you."*

It was now understood by Anton that the land of Canaan, of what became Palestine, and now is Israel, belonged rightfully to the descendant of Abraham—Isaac and Jacob, whom God named Israel. Ishmael and his descendant had no part in the inheritance. If one looked at the problem in the Middle East from the religious point of view, the Land of Palestine belonged to the Jews. As a good and devout Christian, Anton believed such.

However, he also acknowledged, as he read further in the book by Wallace, that there was a secular side to the Middle East problem. The Muslims had no case about this religious quarrel with the Jews about to whom God gave the land and promised the land for eternity, but they had a case of possession by right of inhabitants.

He read that in ancient times, the land of Canaan was inhabited by Hebrews (*Habiru*, meaning *wanderers)* and Arabs (desert people). Secular history tells of both living there, and the land conquered by a stronger neighboring tribe and kingdom, the Romans. According to secular history, whoever is in power is the rightful owner of the land. From medieval times, it was the Ottoman Empire, then under British administration. At the present time, the modern Israelites. The Arabs having failed in the war of 1948, 1956, 1967, and 1973 to reconquer Palestine.

When Anton discussed the Palestinian problem with Ali, Ali agreed that the Palestinians lost every war trying to conquer Israel and that therefore, the land belongs to Israel at this time. "The Right of the Stronger," as Ali admitted.

Anton then said to Ali, "I also believe that God gave the land of Israel to the Jews as the bible tells of Isaac, the son of Abraham and Sarah, inheriting the land and not Ishmael."

Ali smiled. "Then you believe that ninety-year-old Sarah had a son?"

"If God willed it, why not, Ali?"

"Toni, you are becoming very friendly to Jews. Is it because of Hanna? I see you leave with her every day after school."

"The Zapruders don't have a car anymore. Mother and I drop her off when we go home. I feel for her as if she is my little sister."

"And maybe more, Toni?"

"Maybe." Anton laughed.

Little Hanna was happy that he sided with the Israelis when he talked to her about religion and no longer felt that there was this impossible gulf between them, he a Christian and she a Jewish girl. Perhaps this was the time when she fell in love with Toni—at this time a one-sided love and affection, or so she thought.

The rights and wrongs of the Palestinian conflict, together with Anton's Christian beliefs and his knowledge of what the Third Reich did to the Jews and his father's involvement in the murders, would lead to Anton's determination to help Israel survive any further conquest by the Muslims. In fact, Anton strongly believed that the Arabs should leave the land of Palestine and disperse among the Muslim neighbor nations of Lebanon, Syria, Jordan, and Egypt—that is, if they did not wish to live in peace under the government of Israel. Therefore, both the Gaza and West Bank belonged to Israel as did, of course, all of Jerusalem, as long as the Jews honored the holy places of the other religions.

When Avi began to speak of Israel, he found the young man well-versed in its history and sympathetic to the land of the Jews. There were questions Anton had. Why the massacre at Deir Yassin? Avi admitted to it and called it a stain on modern Israel, but it had been committed by a Jewish group of terrorists, members of the Stern gang and the Irgun. It was not condoned by the Haganah, the Jewish Army, and the Israeli government under Ben Gurion was abhorred by it and outlawed both terrorist groups. In fact, the Haganah had fought a pitched battle against these groups when they tried to violate the armistice and brought in the Altelena with weapons. Menachem Begin, then the head of the Irgun refused to turn the ship over to the Haganah. The Haganah fired on the ship and killed fourteen Irgunists and wounded sixty-nine. That was the end of both groups, since Israel no longer condoned terrorism by Israelis. But it was still practiced by the Palestinian as their way of fighting now, more so than ever before.

Avi also told him of gruesome terrorist actions by the followers of Arafat, and Anton was especially taken back when he told him of terrorists occupying a school with children in session. On May 15, 1974, a three-man squad of Arafat's PLO went into the school in Maalot and systematically killed children. They executed these children with rifle fire and threw hand grenades among them, murdering nineteen and wounding sixty-eight.

To Anton, anyone who targets children—the most innocent—was on his list of murderers who deserved to be killed themselves. This brought back to him his father's—Otto's participation in the murder of children. And there was still this Lutz, a child-murderer, alive who did not deserve to live. Anton decided that he would execute Lutz for his crimes! He had not forgotten how he had threatened his mother.

Anton was now seventeen, a member of the Teutonic Order, and liked to go there as he had German friends who were not the children of former war criminals or Nazis. There, Anton liked to play Skat, a game similar to bridge, or the English rubber.

By chance he found out that Lutz's family had taken vacation in Germany, probably in Munich. He decided to visit Herr Lutz and question him about the atrocities he had committed during the war. Perhaps Lutz showed remorse. Anton was a Catholic and in his church, if one truly has remorse, it was up to God to judge the man.

Anton packed Otto's Luger in his belt; he kept it in good operating condition. He also wore his short boots, which were fitted, according to Watanabi's suggestion with steel points—a formidable weapon for those initiated in hand combat.

Herr Lutz opened the door and was surprised at the visit. Anton had not been his or his family's friend since the incident four years ago. To show his contempt for Anton, he greeted him with Heil Hitler and gave the Nazi salute. "You, the outcast of the German society here, how dare you come to my house."

"I need to talk to you, Lutz," Anton answered just as contemptuously by addressing him not as Herr Lutz. Lutz wanted to slam the door but Anton already had his foot inside. Lutz, a man in his early 60s and still of good physical health and strength, laughed, "Oh, this is how you want to play the game, force your way into my house. Well, come in and we shall see." He led Anton into his living room and from the wall took his SS dagger and threateningly felt its sharp edge as he sat in the big chair, not offering Anton to sit. Anton stood close to him and glared down at the man. He already knew this man was not one to feel any remorse but he wanted to give him his chance for contrition.

"Lutz! Four years ago when I shot Otto," he saw the man's eyes stare in surprise and then in hatred, "I read his war diary. You and Otto were child-murderers. I wish to know how you feel today about the crimes you committed."

A cynical smile was his answer. Lutz shouted, "You fool, Anton! We were not murderers of children but destroyers of varmint! Besides, we only followed the orders of our fuehrer. If what we did bothers you, then complain to the departed Fuehrer Adolf Hitler and you can join him! And if you really killed your own father then you will not leave this house alive!"

Anton felt rage building up in him, but he controlled himself, unconsciously remembering Watanabi's instruction to remain in control of all his facilities when facing an adversary.

"Lutz, I came here to avenge the crimes you committed but I wanted to give you a chance to confess to remorse for what you have done. I see that it is useless. You are still what you were, a mass-murderer, a child-killer. And I have not forgotten how you threatened my mother."

Anton saw the hand tighten around the dagger; a surprise attack was now needed! And with a swift kick by his steel-pointed shoe he hit the vulnerable throat of the man. Lutz collapsed into the chair, the dagger fell from his hand, he reached for his crushed throat, unable to breath. Anton picked up the dagger stepped behind the man and with a swift motion cut his throat. The man now in his death throes. His eyes bulged out, staring at Anton in fear of death. Anton threw a last contemptuous snarl at the dying man, *"Verreck du Bestie* (Die, you beast)!*"* Soon the wretched groans of the man died away.

Anton used a towel to open the faucet in the kitchen, washed his bloodied hands and worked in haste emptying drawers and cabinets, taking valuables, money and stuffed them into a bag he had found, only keeping the washed dagger. He left all the lights on as he made his getaway as silently and unobserved as he had come. He returned to his home where a block away he had parked his mother's car. He then drove to the Suez Canal and weighing the bag down with chunks of cast iron sunk it into the canal. He had been careful and not bloodied his clothing. He avoided dumping the bag into the nearby Nile and thought no one will ever find it in the Canal. He was back home before midnight, telling his mother good night and what a nice time he had had with Ali.

The next morning at breakfast, he read the al-Ahram. There was nothing about the killing of Lutz. That appeared in the next morning's paper with a headline of

ROBBERY-MURDER AT THE GERMAN COLONY.

Anton read it and showed it to his mother. "He deserved it," was her only comment. Several days later was the obituary, *"Gerhard Lutz, war hero"* followed by funeral announcement—all his comrades invited to honor his memory.

There never was a thorough inquiry into Gerhard Lutz's death. The efficient Cairo police soon announced the arrest of two suspects in the murder and robbery. A few weeks later was a follow up that the suspects has been released due to insufficient evidence.

Then, a few months later, Frau Lutz found an emerald necklace that had belonged to her at a bazaar.

She informed the police who arrested the owner of the jewelry shop. However, all the man could provide was a vague description of the man who had sold it to him. A working-man who had told some story of his grandmother dying and his family needed to sell her heirlooms. And no, there were no other pieces from that man. Frau Lutz found no other shops that sold any of her jewelry. The inspector who handled the robbery-murder suggested that Frau Lutz also check the bazaars in Alexandria, but she never did. The robbery-murder was never solved.

Anton felt no compassion for Lutz. What he had done was serving justice even if he took it into his own hands. He also had formed his own code of what justice is about if the criminal is beyond jurisdiction. He would be a one-person prosecutor, judge and executioner—if the accused was found guilty. No jail time but execution. The defense would rest upon the person. He had given Lutz his chance. Lutz was guilty beyond doubt. Lutz had shown no remorse. There were others who deserved the same fate, foremost the sadistic and cruel Hamann, and no less guilty were the ruthless Jaeger, Huber and Eckhart.

Amal had joined Hanna in learning Hebrew. Amal hoped that some day her family would move to Israel. She knew Hanna wished to live there and that Avraham fully supported his daughter's desire to live in Israel.

Anton still had many discussions with his language teacher, Avi and they had become friends. Avi brought him books to read about Israel and while he still needed an English-Hebrew dictionary, for some words rarely used in conversation, he had become fluent in Hebrew. He read Ben Gurion's autobiography and was truly inspired by the man's vision of a new nation and how he brought it about. And when he read Ben Gurion's account of the Deir Jassin massacre he understood that it was committed by a fringe terrorist group of Jews and not condoned by the Jewish establishment. He read the book "The Edge of the Sword" and was amazed at the lack of weapons and trained soldiers the Haganah had at its disposal when defeating the combined assault of the Palestinian irregulars and the trained armies of the Lebanese, Syrians, Iraqis and Egyptians. Only the Jordanian Legion under the English commander Club Pasha defeated the Israelis in Jerusalem. The Jordanians then kicked out all the Jews living in the Old City and did not let Jews worship at their holiest place, the Wailing Wall. And all he had read before in Arabic were lies and justifications for being defeated by the Israelis. He found that with the exception of the Jordanian Legion, the Arabs, even their regular armies were cowards and ran when they could not hide behind a secure wall or embrasures and shoot at the Jews from safety.

After his execution of Lutz, he gave Avi to understand that he was willing to help Israel against its many enemies.

A war had begun again on June 6, 1982, with Israeli forces moving into the Lebanon to wipe out PLO emplacements that were shelling Israeli settlements. Syrian forces were soon involved though it was not an all-out war between Lebanon, Syria and Israel. The Syrian paper al-Ba'th spoke of air battles between June 9 and 11 when the fighting stopped, at least temporarily, during which the Syrian Air Force destroyed many Israeli Phantoms, Skyhawks and Kfirs. Avi told Anton that on the nineth, the IAF shot down twenty-nine Syrian jets and another fifty on the following day without any losses to the Israelis. Then the war became stagnant, as the Israelis had encircled Beirut and wanted the PLO and its militias out.

Anton discussed the war action in the Lebanon with Ali and he wondered if it would lead to another round of Middle East war. Ali confided in him what he had learned from his father, who had connection to the top people of the Egyptian Government, that the PLO and its collaborators, the Hezbollah, which was supported by Iran together with Syria, were in it alone. Egypt, after the split-up with the Syrians, who shattered Egypt's dream of a UAR—United Arab Republic, was staying out and hoped the Israelis would teach the Syrians a good lesson.

There was no love for the Syrians under the socialist Baath government of President Hafez Assad who according to the Moslem Brotherhood persecuted, jailed and killed many devout Islamists. Nor was there any chance that any other Middle East country would become involved. This secret information Anton passed on to Avi.

When it came time for summer vacation, Anton, with his mother's consent, invited Avi to visit them in their house in Planegg.

(Avi first flew back to Israel and gave a report directly to the deputy director of the Mossad, Mordechai Nevot. Nevot was interested in the source of his information. When he was told that it came from a young German expatriate and asked who this young man was and how old he is. When told his name was Anton Nagil and he was seventeen, Nevot laughed. But he became serious and interested when Avi told him that Anton Nagil had killed his own father who was a wanted war criminal. Also that the young Nagil had a friend who was in with the Moslem Brotherhood, and it was from the Brotherhood this information came from. Further, Avi stated that he was certain of Nagil's sympathies for Israel. He had reported this before and it must be in the files. When the director suggested that Avi bring the young man to Israel, Avi said that he was certain that he would like to come. It would have to be done clandestinely, but this was no problem.

Avi was invited to their house in Munich and he could bring Anton Nagil to Israel where he would be welcomed by the Shin Bet, and spirited through customs without passport control.)

CHAPTER III

IN ISRAEL

Anton was delighted to be invited to Israel and his mother approved. He could not tell Ali since it would be a secret visit, but he told Hanna and she was very happy and wished she could go with Toni. To visit Israel was her dream. Hanna now more than ever in love with Toni and Anton also felt more for his Hanna than just being her big brother. She even kissed his lips gently when he left, their first, if innocent kiss. Both understood in their hearts that this kiss bonded them.

On the fifteenth of June 1982, Anton and his mother Rosemarie boarded a Lufthansa plane and flew to Munich. Separately in the same plane, Avi Etzioni flew on his diplomatic passport. Then together, they used a taxi from Munich International Airport to Planegg. Avi, who spoke little if any German, became an English tourist with his camera slung around his shoulder. In Planegg, they went first across the small plaza to the Heide restaurant since it was lunchtime and Anton educated Avi in the culinary delights of a German inn. The Heide restaurant/inn was a well-known place by locals, city people and the occasional tourist. It had facilities for weddings and parties, a large beer garden under chestnut trees and a smaller restaurant for the daily menu. For the tourist who wandered in, they had the menu in English, which Avi studied but let Anton order. The special from the menu that day was *Wienerschnitzel* with roast potatoes and green salad, which they ordered.

They were served by Resi, the blond waitress, who knew Anton since he was a boy and called him her *Aegyptischen Liebling* (Egyptian sweetheart), and since he turned sixteen had tried to seduce him but never succeeded. Anton was loyal to his Hanna.

Resi never flirted with him when he came with his mother.

After a good cup of coffee with a nice portion of *Apfelstrudel* for desert, Avi bought a pack of German cigarettes, having left his Egyptian back in Cairo. Then Anton took Avi to his Bavarian style house where Avi was greeted more informally by Anton's mother Frau Nagil, who insisted being called Rosemarie.

Avi was shown the house, the cozy Bavarian furnished rooms, the jacuzzi in the basement which was now, being summer, empty and not used.

Avi had intended to spend a week with the friendly family, but when he called to Israel he had been told that he was expected at once in Israel. The war in Lebanon needed him, as he was a major in the IDF reserves.

After a week's stay in their house, Anton bade his mother goodbye and called their local taxi, Sepp, who took him to the airport, caught a flight to Frankfurt and the late flight to Israel where he arrived at 3:30 in the morning, or rather 4:30 Israeli time.

Anton expected Avi to meet him and avoid having to go through passport control, since his German passport did not have a visa. He did not see Avi, or as he thought Avi did not find him in the throng of people, since there had been over 200 people on the flight. This gave him time to exchange marks for shekels. He had not even filled out the form every foreigner was required to complete. He finally decided to join one of the lines for visitors. When he got to the custom agent, she at once asked in English where his form was. Then reading his name on the passport, she told him to go to the newsstand and buy the German *Spiegel* magazine. He took his bag, went to the newsstand and bought the magazine. It was then that a man approached him, asked him to show his passport and then introduced himself in English as Nahik Rubin and as an agent of the Shin Bet. Anton was familiar with the designation as it was of the Israeli Security Service. "I have my car waiting outside, Mr. Nagil. Avi could not come."

Rubin drove Anton to Tel Aviv, or rather the suburb of Ramat Gan, where in an all-night eating-place they had breakfast. By the time they left, it was light and the streets were filled with traffic. All signs on the stores in Hebrew; this really was a Jewish city. Anton was fascinated. They stopped at a nondescript house on Jabotinsky Street, a safe-house or rather apartment of the Shin Bet Service. Rubin explained, "Your home while in Israel, Mr. Nagil. You have a meeting at eight. You have time to relax now and I make some more coffee for us."

It was now six. Anton shaved and washed up. Then he had his coffee with Rubin who, when not speaking English, had tried his broken German with him. Rubin then left to get a paper and Anton had his second cup and read the *Spiegel*. When Rubin returned he brought the daily *Ma'ariv* newspaper. As Rubin got another cup, Anton picked up the paper and read about the war in Lebanon.

"Can you read Hebrew, Mr. Nagil?" Rubin asked in English. In answer, Anton spoke in Hebrew, "*Ken*, of course." They both laughed when Rubin complained that Mr. Nagil had him stutter in his poor German while he spoke perfect Hebrew.

Shortly after eight, the bell rang and Rubin let in a tall man who was perhaps in his fifties, with receding blond hair. "*Adon Mordechai Nevot* of the Mossad," he was introduced to Anton. Rubin then left to return at lunch.

The deputy director poured himself some coffee. "I understand that you speak Hebrew? My English is rather poor and my German nonexistent." They sat together on the small table in the kitchen. Nevot lit a cigarette.

Nevot then explained that through Avi Etzioni he had learned of some of the background of his life in Cairo and of his interest in Israel.

Anton smiled. "We can freely talk about your interest in me as—well, let's call it as a source of information benefiting Israel," he laughed. "Sounds better than calling me a spy."

Nevot smiled. "Yes, I agree. May I ask bluntly, are you willing to work for the Mossad?"

"With one reservation."

"Yes?"

"My best friend in Cairo is a devout Muslim, as is his father. His father is a member of the Moslem Brotherhood and also a high government official. I have promised my friend Ali never to divulge the names of the members of the Brotherhood. While I cannot give their names, I wish to assure you that if I hear anything through my Brotherhood source that would harm Israel, I will inform the Mossad. Besides, it is the Egyptian Islamic Jihad you must be aware. They are the fanatical fringe group who wish to destroy Israel."

"Yes, we know. Do you, based upon your observation and knowledge, see an increase in this what you call a fringe group of a radical religious movement?"

"Yes, I do, mainly because of the teachings in mosques and religious schools in Saudi Arabia and Pakistan. From there, the poisonous fanaticism spreads, and not so much from the Moslem Brotherhood in Egypt, who now accept a nonviolent brand of Islam."

"Your observation is well taken. Saudi Arabia presents a problem, not only to us but to the Western world. To your knowledge, was the Brotherhood involved in assassinating Anwar Sadat on the sixth of October 1981?"

"That was done by the jihad and without involvement of the Brotherhood. As far as I know, no one in the Brotherhood even knew about the planned assassination. The Egyptian Secret Service knew very well who had done it, and most of the three hundred people arrested were from the jihad. The jihad is very secretive and work in cells, with one cell unaware of what the others are doing, except for their leaders. Therefore, Sadat could not be warned. Interesting perhaps for the Mossad, two of the most radical members of the jihad were released by the Secret Service as not involved in the assassination. One is an imam, Sheik Rahman, who is also known as the blind sheik. He went to America or applied to go there as a fugitive; and if in America he will become the poisonous snake in the bosom of the US, you might wish to alert the CIA to that fact."

"We will let them know. And the other?"

"A physician by the name of Ayman al-Zawahiri. That information comes from a colleague of Dr. Zapruder who knows the man. Zawahiri is an outspoken enemy of Israel and Jews in general. He will cause you a lot of trouble in the future."

Nevot had Anton spell the names for him when he wrote them down.

"Do you have any other reservations of working for the Mossad?"

"None."

"We are at peace with Egypt now. But as a Muslim nation, we must remember that they were at one time, and not that many years ago, our most dangerous enemy."

"I understand and can only suggest to be cautious. The educated and the merchant class in Egypt are not interested in war with Israel, but the others, one may never know."

"And the Egyptian Army?"

"I don't know. There is resentment of having been the loser in every war, even in 1973 they lost the war, though they believe they won as they defeated you along the Canal."

"Yes, that is true. They surprised us. But they also crossed with a hundred thousand men and many tank regiments while our Bar-Lev line consisted of eight thousand men and twelve tanks."

"I shall join the army next year and can give you better information."

"I believe you understand what the value of your working for the Mossad means to us."

Anton smiled. "The silent and observing mole. I can visit ex-Germans or rather former Nazis in many countries of the Middle East. As the son of former SS Colonel Nagil, I would be welcome and perhaps I can hear of all sorts of things. Many of them are close to the military, some are even advisers; others are close to government officials."

"*Ken.* We are interested in the Egyptian Army, in the type of equipment, especially anything pertaining to antiaircraft defenses, missiles, radar, etc. Do you know what branch of the army you will join? Do you have a choice? Perhaps become a pilot? We are of course most interested in the type of plans they will have in the future. So far, most equipment is still of Soviet make. But after Sadat kicked out the Soviets, Egypt is and will become American supplied."

"I had interviews, and because of my knowledge of the Russian language, I am to be attached to the tank forces. Most tanks in Egypt are still T-54s and T-55s."

"We have captured plenty of those and their manuals. But we are interested in any improvements, also in up-to-date antitank weapons. But mainly, we like background information about the Egyptian Army. The mood, any feelings of opposition to Hosni Mubarak, who is not as moderate as Anwar Sadat was, but with whom we can live as a neighbor."

"Mubarak has to be careful in becoming as friendly to Israel. He would be assassinated next." Anton then reassured Nevot that in the present conflict in Lebanon and with Syria, Egypt has no interest to interfere.

Mordechai Nevot smiled. "For your young age, you seem to be a very well informed. Let me ask you, *Adon* Nagil, with your feelings toward Israel and your personal involvement with Hanna, do you intend, in the future . . . to convert?"

"No. I am a good Catholic. If I should marry Hanna, I shall honor her religion. But no, I have no intention of converting."

Nevot smiled. "You are more valuable to us as a good Christian." The rest of the morning Nevot briefed Anton on communication.

"You will be debriefed during your visits to Munich by one of our agents. The Mossad contact you will meet there is a Mrs. Esther Cohn, she has a boarding house and our agents. When visiting Munich, use it as a safe house. The name of her pension is Pension Freizeit, and you will find it in the telephone book. We will let her know that you are a friend of us. She is not a Mossad agent, only a contact. In an emergency, she knows how to get in touch with us. Every so often it would be helpful if you visit us in Israel. Work through Esther if and when you come, and when you arrive here, we will follow the same procedures. You will be expected. We wish to give you a code name, any preference? No? Well, let us call you *Sav* (grandfather), a perfectly innocent name. *Sav* is coming to visit, and we shall know who *Sav* is. Now to another subject. I do not know, but some of our contacts in foreign lands, especially if they are not Jewish, need to be financially awarded. We have a fund for that purpose."

Anton shook his head. "Not for me."

Nevot smiled. "I didn't think so. Yet we expect you to accept expense remuneration."

Anton again shook his head. "Fortunately, my mother and I are well-to-do and financially independent. Our wealth comes from money secreted out by the Nazis before the war ended and also after. How they did it, I don't know. Otto, being one of the more prominent escapees, received a large amount of money, SS money. No, I don't need funds for any reason. My service is one of ideology and to do some right of what Otto has done wrong."

Nevot nodded. "I understand, *Adon* Nagil."

Anton then asked, "You accept me then as an agent of the Mossad?"

Nevot looked serious. "Never call yourself an agent of the Mossad. The very thought of being an agent is dangerous. Call yourself a friend of Israel. And never, not to anyone and not even to Hanna, speak of your connection to us." Anton understood and nodded. They then discussed the war in Lebanon.

At noon, Nahik Rubin came back and they had lunch at a nearby eatery. Then Mordechai Nevot left them, and Rubin took Anton back to the apartment for a briefing of Shin Bet. Basically, when in Israel, whom to trust and whom to avoid, trust no one unless he is a member of the Mossad or Shin Bet.

At four in the afternoon, a young and pretty woman came and was introduced to Anton as G'veret (Ms.) Tal Aron, a Shin Bet agent. As Rubin explained, "Tal will be your guide while in Israel for the next two days and will show you the country or whatever you wish to see. And please, Mr. Nagil, never tell anyone that Ms. Tal is a Shin Bet agent. No one must know." Anton promised. She soon left and said that she would return at eight in the morning.

After she left, Rubin showed Anton where the personal defense weapon was located in the apartment. It was under the kitchen sink in a pouch attached to the underside. A 9 mm Beretta pistol, model 92-compact, with a clip of ammunition. And he brought him a card, a permit to carry a hand weapon.

As Rubin explained, all Mossad and Shin Bet agents are always armed. "It is not only for their own security but in case of a terrorist attack, which can happen in any place at any time." The pistol was to be worn in a canvas pouch shoulder holster. He did not expect Anton to be familiar with the Beretta, and Anton was not. Otto's Luger was the only hand weapon he was familiar with and could shoot with.

Rubin drove him in his car to the Police Academy on the outskirts of Tel Aviv and in their indoor range he familiarized himself with the short barreled weapon and shot off a number of clips until he could hit the bull's eye.

After their return, Rubin gave him a cleaning kit and showed him how to disassemble the weapon for maintenance.

Before Rubin left, he told Anton that he would be at the airport to guide him through security as his passport was without an entry stamp. Back in Frankfurt he would have to tell the German passport control that for whatever reason the Israelis failed to stamp his passport and didn't care that he had no visa.

After a good night's sleep he was up early, showered and had breakfast at the all-night eatery. When he returned shortly before eight, he saw a Japanese Nissan parked in front of the house and Tal smiling at him. He told Tal to wait, went to his apartment and fastened the holster with the pistol and loaded clip around his shoulder, covered with his light cotton jacket to hide any bulge, and with his tourist camera slung over his shoulder, he re-joined Tal.

She smiled at him as he sat next to her. "Where to, Anton?"

"I wish to see Jerusalem."

"What kind of music do you like?"

"If in Rome, do as the Romans do. Native Israeli music." Tal put on the army station, which played Israeli music.

(Tal had familiarized herself with his file at Mossad HQ. Most of it was correct and information supplied by Avi Etzioni, some had been passed on by Dr. Zapruder. He erroneously had told Etzioni that Anton had killed his father when he found out that he was a mass murderer, which if nothing else, gained him the trust of the Mossad. There was also a suggestion reported by the doctor that the mysterious killing of Gerhard Lutz, a wanted war criminal and former colleague of Otto Nagil, might have been committed by Anton.)

When they drove through the canyons of the Jerusalem hills, Tal pointed out the rust-brown wrecks of vehicles along the side the road.

"From the 1948 war?"

"Yes, we leave them here as silent monuments. By the way your Hebrew is excellent with just a hint of a Nordic accent."

"German." He smiled.

"What would you like to see in Jerusalem, Anton? You are Catholic, so the Church of Annunciation, the Via Dolorosa?"

"Yes, and I want to visit Yad Vashem."

"I understand." Tal understood very well of his concern for the victims of Nazism. She had begun to like Anton. He was a handsome boy with almost gentle features, his wavy black hair. As a pretty twenty-one year old, who had just finished her army duties, she was free and looking. Of course, Anton was really just a boy. That he was Catholic; well she wasn't intending to marry him or even become romantically involved. However, now they had to complete religious and moral obligations. Tomorrow was another day and she was detailed for two days to chauffeur Anton to wherever he wished to go. Tal wore a sort of loose beige cotton blouse military style, hiding her holster and pistol. But she knew she was pretty and even in her drab outfit, she turned the heads of many men, especially soldiers.

She drove to the Dung Gate of the Old City and parked there and they first walked into the Christian quarter. There were many tourists visiting the churches. When she asked Anton if he wished to have his picture taken, he told her no. "I can't afford to have any mementos lying around to show that I visited Jerusalem or Israel.

"And what for the camera then?"

He laughed, "To make me look like a tourist."

Tal marveled at his adult ways of handling himself. "Maybe you should pretend to be a tourist and use your camera even if you don't take pictures. Do you even have film in it?"

He smiled. "No." But he played the game and had her take pictures of him by the church, and then when they wandered into the Muslim Quarter and came to a small market, he took pictures of her. Here they spoke Arabic, as Tal came from Morocco. Then his eye caught a tall and bearded Arab, looking magnificent in his long white robe. When he playfully turned the camera to the man, the Arab parted his robe. Anton saw the white shirt and pants he wore, a red belt with a dagger. The man's hand went to the dagger, he met the man's eyes which stared hateful at him. He heard Tal say, "Lower your camera, let's get away." Instead, Anton parted his jacket and put his hand to his holster, but lowered the camera he held in his other hand. He saw the Arab's eyes glaring at him; then he turned and walked away. Anton closed his jacket.

"That was dangerous, Anton. You provoked him trying to take his picture. Some Muslims believe it is against their religion to take images of them. Tell me, Anton, would you have shot him if he came at you with his dagger?"

"No! Of course not! I would have just disarmed him, maybe broken his wrist in the process."

Tal believed him and marveled at his bravery. She remembered that in his file was a note that he took hand-combat with a Japanese instructor. She had no doubt that this is exactly what the boy would have done.

Anton loved the narrow alleys in the Old City, the shops mostly with souvenirs for tourists. You could tell in what quarter of the city they were in by what was sold. The Christian quarter with religious objects and the writing was in European languages. Mostly Arabic in the Muslim section. Now they entered even narrower streets with few shops but many small churches and even monasteries. Tal explained they were now in the Armenian quarter.

"Safe here," she added. From there they came back into the Jewish part that was more lively, with synagogues and long bazaars. One enterprising shop owner convinced him to enter and look at his wares, and here Anton bought the only thing he wished to bring home to his mother. A replica of the Old City made in the shape of a circular candle—holder, showing the type of houses there were, along with churches, mosques, and synagogues. It contained a candle in the middle and was made of sterling silver.

When the owner showed him a package of two, he bought them and gave the man extra money to mail one to his address in Planegg and one to the Zapruders in Cairo, addressed to Hanna. Tal told the man to be sure and mail them or else she will be back.

When they came out of the bazaar that ended in a tunnel, they exited just before the Western Wall, the most sacred and holy place for Jews and also revered by Christians. Anton touched the huge blocks of stone and felt two-thousand-year-old history, the remnant of the Second Temple. He saw Orthodox Jews in their white shawls and books in their hands pray with heads nodding toward the wall. Many tourists were taking pictures. Here he didn't need to pretend.

"I know a lovely restaurant not far from here. Care for an Arabian lunch, Anton?"

She led him back into the Christian quarter, along the Via Dolorosa which changed into al-Khanqa Street—he remembered, they had been here before to visit the Church of Holy Sepulchre. They went into the Café Amigo Emil. Tal suggested the menu, an all-Arabian dinner with pita and hummus before, and Anton had Israeli beer. The dining room was made of walls of rock, but the furnishings were modern. A nice man, apparently the owner, came by and asked them how they enjoyed the lunch; he spoke in Hebrew. Tal said it was delicious. The man then introduced himself as Costandi Bajjali.

"Brother and sister?"

Anton smiled at Tal. "Are you my sister?"

Tal laughed, "Yes, I am your sister, have you forgotten?"

Bajjali raised his brows. "The lady is obviously a Sabra, but you young man, I detect a European accent?"

Anton smiled. "Our family is split up. I live with my mother in London."

Bajjali smiled at Tal. "What a shame and I took you for dear friends. May I have the honor and treat you to good coffee?"

The owner took them downstairs into a vaulted room hewn out of rock with low divans, settees, and tables, with hookas on shelves ready for use by customers; and the waiter brought them strong coffee in little cups and sweetbread. Bajjali asked about London but stated that he had never been there, which pleased Anton, as he too had never been to England.

"Rainy as usual," was Anton's laconic answer.

Apparently the owner did not believe their story as brother and sister, perhaps because he wished to see them as young lovers. However, when they left, he did not let them pay and said that they were his guests.

"Arab hospitality?" Anton asked Tal.

"No, Christian, maybe Italian or Turk, a romantic." She smiled at him. "He believes we are lovers."

They returned to the Dung Gate, and Tal drove them out to the Yad Vashem complex.

At one place, she stopped and showed him the panorama of the city. Jerusalem was a beautiful city, modern in the new part, and there is no other like Old Jerusalem.

Tal drove to the Yad Vashem complex. In the underground where the eternal light to the victims of the Holocaust burned, Anton thought of a little girl in a red coat who had offered Otto the twig of greenery and was shot by him. He said his Christian prayer only thinking of her. The unknown girl represented to Anton all the million of children that were murdered.

When Tal looked at him, she saw tears rolling down his cheeks, yet his face was hard. The boy was not crying, yet his soul was. At this moment, she felt like a dear sister to him and not a romantic.

In the cafeteria, they had coffee and sweets. In a leisurely drive, they went back to city. Tal took him to the Ben Jehuda Mall. And here he was in the midst of Israeli life. Here he would have to bring Hanna. Then they went back to Ramat Gan. Again the highway led them through the hills of Jerusalem, then past the plains of Tel Aviv where they saw green fields, orange orchards, villages, and kibuzim—their small white houses now lit softly up in the evening sun. Before Tal parted with Anton, and seeing his somber mood, she forgot all about her romantic ideas. She asked him what he wished to see the next day.

"All of Israel."

Tal laughed, "Israel might not be as big as Egypt, but there is a north and a south, and in one day we cannot see both."

He smiled. "What do you propose?"

"The south would lead us into Bersheba, a beautiful city in the desert, then the long haul through the Negev where you can see wild camels. King Solomon's mines and Eilat on the Gulf of Aqaba, our southernmost city."

"And the north?"

"I take you to Lake Kennereth, to a kibuz where we can go swimming. Safad is a nice and ancient city. Haifa, our jewel of cities."

He laughed, "Then I can do without seeing wild camels."

"We must leave early, at six, *beseder* (all right)?"

"Where do you live? Where is your home, Tal?"

"In Herzliya, about thirty kilometers north, almost an hour's drive in traffic."

"Why don't you sleep here, Tal? There is a second bedroom."

Tal smiled. "I always have my toothbrush with me." She hesitated.

"As long as my Hanna wants me, you are safe with me, Tal. Besides, remember, you are my sister."

She gave a bitter smile. "Yes, I know. You are a good man. Hell, you are still a boy and safe from me!" They both laughed and Tal stayed.

They had dinner at an Arab eatery nearby, Tal being of Moroccan descent liked Arabian food. They bought a bottle of Carmel wine though drank little of it. Anton told of Cairo, his school, his beloved mother, of little-trusting Hanna. Tal told of her family, who came from Marrakech.

When they said good night, Tal put her arms around Anton and gave him a sisterly kiss on his lips. And when she was in bed, felt somber, remembering the tears the boy had shed—*a boy to fall in love with if it weren't for little Hanna.*

They had breakfast at the all-night eatery nearby. Before they left, Anton wanted to leave his Beretta behind, but Tal advised him, "Rules, dear Anton. Besides, we will travel through Arab villages and towns going north." However, they stashed their weapons in the glove compartment after they left the eatery.

"Tal, we have become friends?" She smiled and nodded. "Good. So please call me Toni as my friends do."

"Shalom, Toni."

They drove east through the town of Petah Tiqva, then headed north where the narrow but asphalted highway often skirted the West Bank. Tal showed him the town of Tulkarm across the border. "Don't want to be caught in that place alone as an Israeli." At the crossing, they saw Israeli border guards and civilian cars. "They are waiting for escorts to travel to their settlements and towns across the border," Tal explained.

"Many Israelis living on the other side?"

"Yes. Over a hundred thousand in guarded towns and kibbutzim. They don't live free as the former Palestinian Arabs do in Israel. You see. Toni, that is the unfairness of the Europeans and Americans too. They want the Israelis out of the West Bank, yet we have over two million Palestinians living in our land. They have the same benefits as Jewish Israelis and don't even have to serve in the army. They are secure in their villages and towns, on their farms. Our people living in the West Bank are always in danger."

"But doesn't that square itself with the over a million refugees who left what is now Israel?"

"No, it doesn't, Toni! First of all, the refugees who are still mostly in camps in Lebanon and the West Bank, in Gaza, didn't have to leave like the Palestinians who stayed and still live here. All right, I admit that some were driven out, especially if they were hostile. But it was the Arab armies who invaded in 1948, who told them to leave until they killed all the Jews and then come back and get it all. At the same time, the Israelis who lived in what was to become Palestinian land had to leave. The Jews in all Arab lands were driven out. Along a hundred thousand Jews were expelled from Iraq, they had to get out quickly and leave all their belongings behind. The number of Jewish refugees from Arab countries is just about the same as the Palestinians who left of what became Israel. We absorbed our refugees. They keep their refugees in camps for political reasons. All dirty politics."

"I didn't know. Wouldn't it be best to exchange the Palestinians living in Israel with the Israelis living in the West Bank? Become a homogenous country."

"You are dreaming, Toni. Arafat would never go for it, or the Arab countries that support him. Arafat and the Arabs want us to take all their refugees back. By now they are no longer seven hundred thousand of them but over two million. One thing the Palestinians are good at is to have lots of children, a dozen in each family. Most men don't even have jobs and let the UNO support them and their kids. For Israel to take the refugees back would mean national suicide."

Anton got an education in Middle Eastern politics.

The road turned west and then continued to the north. When they came to the village of Ara, Tal stopped and they put on their holsters. "Mostly Arab villages from here on."

"Dangerous? Aren't they Israelis even if Arabs?"

"Yes. But many consider themselves Palestinians living in Israel. It is not so much them, though as a Shin Bet agent, I can never trust any. But Palestinian terrorists may come across the border and ambush cars." Tal drove rather fast through the towns and villages.

They took a dirt road going east again. "I want to visit a friend in Kibbutz Alumot, and we can have lunch there. You know what a kibbutz is, and how it functions?" Anton knew, since he had read about this strange arrangement of communal ownership.

They entered the small community of small white stone houses. An armed guard stood before a larger house from which children's voices and laughing came.

Tal explained, "The children's house. All the children live there, go to school, and I guess they are having lunch now. In the evenings, they join their parents, easier to guard them at all times."

"What a crazy world, even here in a fenced compound you have to guard the children," remarked Anton.

They entered the dining hall, which was full. At once a young woman came running, threw her arms around Tal, and greeted her warmly. Tal introduced her as Uval, also of Moroccan descent. "We served in the army together." And she introduced Anton. Uval laughed, "My, what a handsome boyfriend you have, Tal." Tal and Anton laughed at that. Uval came along with them as they went to the serving table, took trays, and had their food given to them. Again salad—salad morning, noon, and night in Israel. Then some sort of stew and potatoes, fresh orange juice or tea. They joined Uval at her table and were introduced to an elderly couple sitting with them, Hanni and Elchanan Ishai.

Elchanan soon observed Anton's accent. "From Germany, Anton?"

"No. From Cairo."

Tal laughed, "Born in Germany, but living in Cairo."

Uval smiled at Tal. "On business or pleasure with Anton?"

Elchanan was looking puzzled. "What kind of business could the young lady have with a boy?"

Tal looked at Anton, smiled, then said to Elchanan, "I met Anton in the Old City. He lost his way; we had lunch together and I offered to guide him around in my car. I wished to show him what a kibbutz looks like. I knew that Uval is here. We became friends."

Hanni finally spoke up, "I have one question. Are you Jewish, Anton?" Tal answered for him, "No, Anton is Catholic." Then changing the subject asked, "I have never seen you here, are you also visiting?"

Elchanan explained, "We used to be members of Alumot. We began with the original *chalutzim* (pioneers) who set up here. We live now in Jerusalem, yes, visiting. Hanni paints, and in a kibbutz you need workers, not painters. Besides I was for many years in America with weapon procurement. The many trips forth and back, it was just easier to work out of Jerusalem. Besides, when we had children, we decided to move permanently. How did you like Jerusalem, Anton?"

"We spent a most wonderful day there yesterday," he answered. Tal then related the little incident at the market in the Muslim quarter. Omitting that Anton had a pistol on him.

Elchanan explained, as Tal had done, that some Muslims object to have their pictures taken. "You were lucky, Anton, that he didn't use his dagger." Anton smiled at Tal.

After their lunch, Uval managed to get free for a couple hours and got swimming suits for her guests, and they bathed in the nice pool of the kibbutz. Tal laughed when she saw Toni look at her in her bikini.

He only said, "You look lovely, sister Tal." Uval didn't understand anything, and to Anton she looked lovely too though he didn't dare to tell her.

Before they left, Uval took them to the edge of the fenced-in village from which they had a wonderful view of the lake and Deganya below them, with the Golan hills beyond.

With a friendly embrace, the girls said shalom, Uval saying, "Be sure to call me tonight, Tal."

Tal answered, "Sure. Tell you all about it." Uval shook hands with Anton, "Shalom, come again and visit."

It was two by the time they left and drove along the large lake, which was known to Anton as Lake Tiberias from the New Testament. They stopped briefly in Safad and managed to visit at least one of the many ancient synagogues.

Taking a dirt road, Tal stopped in a nondescript and barren valley.

"I don't know which crusade it was, but here the knights and their soldiers stopped for the night, tired from their march, they went to sleep and then Saladin came down the hills with his warriors and defeated the crusaders."

Anton marveled at the barren hills, which now, in his imagination came alive with white clad warriors slashing their swords at the invaders.

Then on to Acre which they reached in darkness and it was too late to visit the famous crusader castle.

They looked at the beautiful city of Haifa from Ramat-Hadar, the hill above it. Then the long drive south back home. In Hadera, they stopped for sandwiches and coffee. Tal played music from a classical station. They drove along in silence.

Then Tal asked suddenly, "Tell me, Toni, did you eliminate Lutz?"

After a brief pause, Anton asked, "Why do you wish to know, Tal?"

"I want to help you if there are others. I know you are on a mission of vengeance."

"No one can help me. Also it has become very personal."

"I understand, Toni. But the help I offer is one of the Mossad. Unless you know where they are, the Mossad can help you find those killers."

"How?"

"If you know their names, know where they lived, they might have returned to their homes. Mossad agents have access to sources you might not have. Not just telephone and address books but city archives, the German *Bundesamt* in Koblenz, and the War Crimes Commission in Wiesbaden."

They got back to Ramat Gan around midnight. Before Anton went to sleep he wrote down what he knew.

> *SS Colonel Karl Jaeger, I believe from Munich.*
> *SS First Lieutenant Ernst Huber. Munich.*
> *SS First Lieutenant Franz Hamann. Berchtesgaden.*
> *SS Second Lieutenant Joseph Eckhart. From Saxony.*

Anton had set the alarm for three. He returned the Beretta to Tal who placed it back under the sink. Tal made tea and he gave her the slip with names.

"You have a Mossad contact in Munich, Toni?" He nodded.

They drove in silence to the airport. She stopped by the terminal. He got his little handbag, and they stood before each other. This time Anton put his arms around Tal and kissed her gently.

"Will I see you again, Toni?"

"Yes, I promise you, dear Tal."

"Rubin will be at the entrance."

"Shalom, Tal."

"Shalom, Toni. Please be careful."

Anton watched her drive away in the darkness. He walked into the terminal and found Rubin by the door. Rubin took him through a side door into the departure terminal and they said good-bye. When time came to board the plane, Anton took his seat in the comfortable business class. He was asleep when the plane left. When he woke up they were halfway to Germany. Having missed the big breakfast, the steward brought him a plate with rolls, cream cheese, lox, juice and coffee. He had to smile, a Jewish breakfast. Jews apparently didn't know that Germans were just as fond of lox, though usually not served with cream cheese and bagels.

By noon he was back in Munich, took a taxi to Planegg and was home where he had a lot to tell his mother, but not all.

Anton kept in shape by running each morning, lifting weights and karate exercises. They went for walks, drove to nearby lakes and picnicked in the forests. Or they went into Munich and visited museums, the Englisher Garten, theaters, and went to the opera.

It was a week after his return from Israel that his mother received a call from a Mrs. Cohn who invited them for Sunday dinner. They lived in a nice apartment; she and her husband Moritz were good hosts. Once alone in the kitchen with Frau Cohn, she gave Anton a letter, "from the M people," she said. He stashed it in his pocket.

Later, alone in his room he read the letter. No heading, signature or anything personal. Just the information he was looking for.

> *SS Colonel Jaeger, Karl. Arrested in Munich in 1959, committed suicide in prison.*

> *SS Sergeant Huber, Ernst. Born in Munich 12 December 1920. Listed as having served in Kaunas with the Einsatzkommando 3a, from July 1941 to 1944. At that time at grade of first lieutenant. Demoted to rank of staff sergeant in 1943 for drunkenness. After 1944, served in the Viking Division. Sentenced in 1952 to six months prison for belonging to an Einsatzkommando. Never tried as war criminal, probably due to his low rank. Nor did Karl Jaeger's deposition ever mention him or Hamann in 1959. Released after three months imprisonment in Landsberg. Returned to Munich and works there as a taxi driver. Married. Two children, adults. Address: Schleissheimerstrasse 190. Rgb. III.*

> *SS Corporal Hamann, Franz. Born in Rosenheim, 13 August 1917. Served from 1938 to 1941 in the First Parachute Regiment as captain. Dismissed from the army for brutality toward his men. Served with the Einsatzkommando 3, in Kaunas from July 1941 to 1944. At that time as SS First Lieutenant. Demoted to corporal for disregard of orders of superiors and*

slapping an officer. After 1944, served with the Viking Division. Sentenced to one year prison in 1952, for belonging to an Einsatzkommando, and due to disciplinary problems served the full year. Not tried as war criminal. After the war he returned to Berchtesgaden and worked as Jaeger (hunter) for the forest service. Married, no children. Dismissed from the forest service for poaching in 1950, worked then as a logger. After imprisonment, his wife divorced him. Hamann went to Schoenau/Konigsee, where he was employed taking tourists around the lake. Dismissed from that job for rudeness and fighting with tourists. Became an employee of the industrialist Schoenauer and is presently the gamekeeper for Schoenauer's forest holdings. He has a room at the Edelweiss Inn in Schoenau but spends the summer months at the cabin, somewhere in the forest of the Watzmann massiv. Hamann is known as a dangerous man, usually armed when in the forest. Be careful and good luck.

SS Second Lieutenant Eckhart, Joseph. Born 5 May 1919 in Breslau. Member of Einsatzkommando 3a. in Kaunas from July 1941 to 1943. Then with the SS Totenkopf Division, where he was killled at the battle of Kursk in July 1943. M

CHAPTER IV

THE AVENGER

"Mother, let's visit House Tanneck."

Rosemarie was surprised that Toni wished to go there. They hadn't been there for a few years since Toni did not get along with Herr Schoenauer, nor did she care for the man. Though she was friendly with his wife Inge, and of course, there was Betty.

"How about Hanna, Toni?"

"Oh mother, you know I love Hanna but I can be friends with others, can't I?"

"Of course you can. If you really wish to go, I will call Inge."

Later she told Anton that Herr Schoenauer was in France on business. Inge and Betty would be happy to have them visit. "Other good or bad news, Betty is engaged."

"Great, I just want to romp around with her in the mountains."

They left the next day, a Saturday. It was June, and for a change it was hot in Munich. They traveled by train to Berchtesgaden and took a bus to Schoenau, the small village that sits by the Koenigsee.

From there it was a pleasant walk to House Tanneck, which was by the lake. Anton carried their suitcase and Rosemarie a small carryall. They planned for a week's stay, since it would be nice without Herr Schoenauer around. They were greeted warmly by Inge and Betty and two guestrooms were prepared for them. Later, Anton walked with Betty down to the lake.

"Did my mother tell you that I am engaged, Toni?"

"Yes, and I am happy for you. Nice guy?"

"Yes, Josef is a wonderful man. I want you to meet him." She looked at Toni. "I am so sorry, Toni. But you, so far away."

He smiled. "You wouldn't have liked it in Cairo anyhow; it gets brutally hot in summer." They were, as they always had been, good friends.

Sunday morning, they took the boat over to Sankt Bartholomew and attended Mass at the small church. For lunch, which Inge and Rosemarie prepared, Josef came. Anton got along fine with him. In a way he was glad that Betty had found a man she loved, spared him to disappoint her. However, like him, only seventeen, she would have to wait a year before marrying Josef.

It was two days later that the women went to Berchtesgaden on an all-day shopping trip. Anton said that he would just go on a long hike around the lake and visit the Obersee, a smaller lake behind the Koenigsee. He could use their faltboat going up the lake.

When they had left, Anton went into the office of Schoenauer and there on the wall he found what he was looking for, a map of the forest region at the foot of the Watzmann. The X he found marked on the map he hoped was the location of the cabin. He couldn't help seeing the gun cabinet and his first impulse was to take one of the rifles with him. There was a short one, what is called a *Stutzen* which could easily be hidden under a coat, but then he knew about ballistics, a bullet in Hamann might be traced to one of these rifles. Also he realized that whatever one plans, it usually goes awry. He might not even find Hamann.

Taking a last reading of the map, he set out for the forest. He was not about to follow the road, which led along the lower fringes of the mountain. He must not be seen by any tourists and there were plenty during the summer. Instead, he cut across the road and walked through the forest leading straight up where he would meet the path. When he did after an hour's walk, he tied plastic shower caps over his mountain boots that left no clear imprint where it was still wet from the thunderstorm the night before.

He followed the path and soon saw a sign NO TRESPASSING—PRIVATE PROPERTY. He knew he was now in the private forest of Schoenauer. When the path became rocky, he took the coverings off again. The path led up to higher reaches in the forest in a serpentine manner. He had encountered no one so far. By his watch, he had walked another hour and soon spotted the cabin in a clearing, surrounded by lush alpine grass.

He walked boldly up to the door and knocked. A voice behind him said, "*HALT*," which made him turn around and there stood a man with a full gray beard in the breeches and green jacket of a hunter.

"What do you want here, boy? This is private property. Didn't you see the sign NO TRESPASSING?" the man growled at him.

"Sure. Are you Herr Franz Hamann? I came to visit you."

"I am Hamann. Who are you?" His face unfriendly as was his voice.

"I am Otto Nagil's boy. You remember Otto?"

While he spoke friendlier, Hamann's face remained stoic, threatening, "Sure I remember Nagil. He died a long time ago I heard, lived in Egypt somewhere. But I still want to know what you are doing here and what you want from me?"

"Otto told me about you and the others in his unit. Lieutenant Colonel Lutz, Lieutenant Huber, and Lieutenant Eckhart. He told me about the difficult work you all did in Kaunas. Fighting bandits, getting rid of the Jews. He said if I ever come to Berchtesgaden I should look you up, since you were good friends."

"I haven't lived in Berchtesgaden for a long time. So how did you find me up here?"

"We are friends with Herr and Frau Schoenauer, and I am a good friend of Betty. When I mentioned Otto having been a high ranking officer in the SS to Herr Schoenauer, that Lutz was his deputy, and Eckart also working with him, he said that you were now his hunting-master and taking care of his *Revier* up here. I thought I would visit you and we can talk about your comradeship with Otto and the others. Kind of re-establishing old ties."

"Did he tell you to come up here?"

"Sure, how else would I find my way up to you."

"He promised not to tell anyone. I guess you are an exception because you are Nagil's son. And you are good friends with Betty, she is pretty and nice and full up here," and he put his hands to his chest and bounced them up and down.

"Oh yeah, that she is my dear Betty."

Hamann's bearded face showed a grin, "Wouldn't mind getting into her panties myself. You getting any boy? What was your name again by the way?"

"Anton."

"Well, come in Anton, and we have a drink and talk."

The door was unlocked and Hamann led him into a typical Bavarian style living room and kitchen. He took a seat at the table around which were wooden benches. The whole place was rustic but primitive without electricity or a real stove. There was an open hearth and on a movable iron holder hung a kettle. In the back a bed.

Anton watched Hamann as he went to a shelf with many bottles, "*Kirsch, Enzian, Kuemmel,* or you don't drink? How old are you, Anton?"

"Seventeen. Like father like son, sure I like a Schnapps here or there. But more so beer, but I will try an *Enzian,* I never have had one before."

Hamann poured two glasses. Anton raised his glass, "To the fuehrer."

"Our fuehrer! He let us down committing suicide. And he was stupid starting this war with the Soviets, a war we could never win. The only good thing he did was getting rid of the Jews."

Anton took a sip, it was strong stuff and tasted of herbs.

"Like it, Anton?"

"Brrrr, give me a beer anytime."

"No beer up here. I would have to lug it up. You still live in Egypt?"

"Yes, in Cairo. Many good Germans still live there. You know, former gestapo, SS, people who can't come back."

"Yes I know. After they arrested Jaeger, all our necks were in danger." He then told Anton about his life, most of which Anton already knew from the brief he received. And Anton told him of his life in Cairo, his upbringing in the spirit of nationalsocialism.

Anton had managed to finish his glass of *Enzian,* and Hamann refilled both glasses. But he didn't seem to be a heavy drinker. Getting him drunk as Anton hoped was not possible.

"Otto told me about the work you, Lutz, and the others did in Kaunas. Was it difficult getting rid of the Jews?"

Hamann laughed, "Otto and the others had it easy, they worked out of the forts. The Jews were brought to him and all he had to do was line them up and boom-boom, finish. Jaeger called it *Paradeschiessen* and he was right. I had the dirty work of going into villages and towns, rounding up the Jews, but had to find them first. The locals helped us, and they were eager to get their belongings. Still, the screaming and yelling. I didn't have enough SS men helping me and had to rely on the Lithuanian partisans. Though I must admit they were good. They knew how to handle the *Gesindel* (pack)."

"Otto told me of the most difficult work he and Jaeger did. When they lined them up at the ditch, he and Jaeger went first along the long row of Jews and shot the little ones so the machineguns would not have to deflect."

"We didn't have machineguns, just rifles and machine pistols. Took longer that way, but we had fun with their children. Make the bastards suffer, I mean the adult Jews."

"So, what did you do? I mean having fun with the children?"

"Oh. Like in the evening when it got dark and we were late in taking them to the forest or ditch. We needed lighting, so we just tied some of the rabbis to trees, poured gasoline over them and lit them, made nice burning torches. For fun? We took their little children, as long as they were old enough to walk or run, poured gas over them and lit them up. Then while they were running around burning and squealing, we shot them. I used my machine pistol for that at night. Drove their parents crazy, wailing and screaming. We couldn't even line them up by the ditch and had to beat them to death. Did that with shovels, some used spades, just cut them apart." Anton felt his rage building up . . . this was an even worse monster than Otto!

Hamann looked at Anton, the boy's face distorted and pale. "You don't like that? They were just vermin we had to destroy."

"But this sounds cruel, lighting up the children."

"No stomach for that, boy? Ah, your new generation, nothing like we were. We need the Hitler Youth back to teach you the real spirit. The SS to take care of what's left of the Jews. Your Egyptians and all the other Arab countries don't know how to fight. Let the Jews take over. Beat the shit out of you. Give me one SS Regiment and we take care of Israel. Wipe them clean off the map, drown them in the seas."

"Are you in any way sorry for what you, Otto and all the others did?"

"Sorry? What are you? Besides being one of the new German generation, all weaklings, are you sorry that we got rid of that plague, the Jews? You—a son of Otto Nagil?"

"I am asking you, Hamann!"

"I am only sorry we didn't get all of them."

Anton knew it was hopeless. Once a killer, always a killer, like Otto and Lutz. He even managed a grin at Hamann, "I guess we are of the new generation, all weaklings."

It was time to act. He had spied a weapon hanging on the wall, a crossbow. He got up and went to it, took it down, "Look Hamann, we all are what we have become. I am not trying to change your way of thinking. I just wondered, now with Germany being sorry for what it had done that you might have different feelings. I see that I am wrong. This is an interesting weapon; can you shoot a deer with it?"

"All right, Anton. You are not like me or your father was. He failed you. As you said, we are what we are. Forget it all. I am just sorry for you. You will never know how great the movement was. Uniforms, flags, the songs, the spirit of comradeship, now all gone.

This crossbow, well at least I hope you can keep your mouth shut. When I shoot a deer outside the regular hunting season I use the crossbow. Silent."

"Can you show me how to use it?"

"You really don't deserve my showing you anything. But you are still Otto's boy. Here, I will show you." He took the crossbow and from a box a steel arrow, really a pointed metal shaft with feathers at the end. He took Anton outside, worked the bow back and inserted the shaft, and pointed it at a nearby water barrel, "Try it, just don't miss, I'd hate to lose an arrow."

Anton took the crossbow, pointed it at the Hamann's stomach and pulled the trigger. There was only the sound of the bowstrings recoiling and the thud of hitting. Anton looked at Hamann, his face expressing surprise, fury and agony . . . "You stupid idiot!" And then a piercing scream as the pain registered, his hands went to his belly and felt the bolt sticking in his stomach.

"I didn't know I pulled the trigger, Hamann. Let me help you to your cot and I will take it out carefully." Hamann was bent over, the pain excruciating, he let Anton help him into the cabin and lay on the cot, groans of pain and heavy breathing showed his suffering. On the cot he pulled his knees up, lying flat hurt even more.

"Do you have any first aid stuff around?"

"In my night table, by the bed," Hamann whispered, and again began his groans alternating with whimpering. Anton found the box and brought it. He opened Hamann's belt and drew the pants halfway down, the same with his shorts. The steel shaft was deeply imbedded just above his groin. Anton knew that this wasn't a fatal injury. He pulled slightly on the shaft and Hamann yelled, "It hurts, oh it hurts badly."

"You have to drink some Schnapps, else you won't be able to stand the pain when I extract the shaft."

"Give me some, give me lots."

Anton gave him the bottle and between groans and whimpering Hamann drank most of it, then dropped the bottle. Soon he was in a drunken stupor. Anton sat by the cot and looked at the beast. He felt no compassion or for that matter hatred for this man. Otto, Lutz and Hamann were outcasts of society. He would make him die as he made the rabbis and children die. He grasped the shaft and with a swift movement pulled it out. There was just a small hole with blood spurting out. Hamann gave a shriek and sank back again. He whimpered half conscious, "Pain, pain . . . oh it hurts, like fire in my belly." Then when Anton wrapped the comforter tightly around him that the man became like a package he stared, "What are you doing, boy?"

"Just keeping you warm so you won't go into shock, try to relax."

The whimpering intermixed with groans became less as the stupor diminished his suffering. It also helped that the shaft was taken out and the loss of blood weakened him. With Hamann drunk and tightly ensconced in the heavy blanket, really unable to move, Anton worked fast. In a water bucket he washed his hands and the arrow and put it back into the box and hung the crossbow on the wall. He didn't have to worry about fingerprints.

The bottle of Schnapps was now drained on the floor. He took a can of kerosene he found and poured it over Hamann, soaking his blanket, poured the rest along the bed and a trail to the puddle of Schnapps. He then lit the oil lamp on the table and closed all the window shutters from the inside.

He stood before the prone man: "*SS Obersturmfuehrer* Franz Hamann!" The man looked up. "It is so dark in here, I can hardly see you . . . ohhh, the pain is killing me," he murmured.

"Yes, the pain will kill you soon enough, Hamann. You are going to die."

"I don't want to die. You plucked the hole, boy? Go run down to the valley and get a doctor." Hamann, despite his drunk stupor and weakened state, still seemed to be able to think and hear.

More to himself than addressing the man, Anton said "How could you ever become such a savage. You are not even a man, just a foul thing in human form. You are without anything that makes a man civilized. You came from hell, spit out by the devil and you will return to hell. You will burn as you burned the rabbis and children."

Did Hamann listen? Understand? "Hell, devil? What are you talking boy? Burn? The children burned and squealed like pigs."

"Soon you will burn Hamann, and when the fire consumes you maybe it will purify your rotten soul."

"Burn? Fire? I have a fire in my belly . . . you goddamned boy put it there."

"My mother always told me, those who damn God are damned themselves." Anton took the oil lamp and smashed it on the floor by the puddle of Schnapps. There were bright flames with little smoke as the kerosene burned its way up to the blanket . . . in a moment the man was engulfed in flames and his screams filled the cabin, he had come out of his drunken stupor, the agony of burning alive and the terror of it overcoming his drunken weakness. He tried to get up but the blanket held him tightly enshrouded. For a short while he sat, trying to free himself, his beard already burned off, the skin in face peeling, his eyes no longer seeing . . . he burned like a sitting torch. His shrill screams piercing the room, until his lungs inhaling the fire no longer functioned and only animalistic groans came forth.

Anton left the cabin and opened the door for a good draft. He watched from nearby in the forest as the cabin was burning and when everything was engulfed in flames and smoke, he left. It was noon. He rushed back, off the trail as he expected people to come to see what all the smoke was about. When he reached the road, crossed it and went through the forest down to the lake. Nobody had seen him though he saw people running toward the upper reaches of the forest. He got into his boat and rowed along the shore to the end of the lake, found some tourists there and took a boy his age back in his boat. Then slowly rowed back and stopped at the little church. There he found the deacon and talked to him. From the church he could see just little wisps of dark smoke high up in the forest. He paddled back with the boy and arrived at the house around four. They already had come back from their shopping trip. Anton invited the boy in for some refreshments and introduced him to the women. His name was Bernard.

"Where did you two go?" asked Betty.

"We were at the Obersee," Bernard answered. He soon left to go to the hotel in Schoenau and await his family who had to walk back.

Anton washed the two caps he had used and returned them to the shower.

It was then that Inge came in, "The cabin burned down. The forest manager just called. They found Franz dead, burned. They think he drank himself senseless, broke the oil lamp and it started the fire. They found him on his cot. They think he died from the smoke before he burned. I have to call my husband."

Anton asked, "Where is the body now? Are they going to bring him down or bury him up in the mountains?"

"They have removed him and are taking him to the coroner's office. If he died of natural causes, meaning he was drunk and killed himself, they will let him get buried here. My husband is coming back tomorrow then we will give Franz a Christian burial."

It was Rosemarie who then wanted to leave at once but Inge talked her into staying till the next morning. In the morning, when the Berchtesgadener paper came, Anton read the short notice of the fire up in the Watzmann forest and the demise of the caretaker Franz Hamann.

CABIN BURNED AND CARETAKER DIED.

The police from Schoenau report the burning of a cabin in the forest of the Watzmann Mountain, and the death of the caretaker Franz Hamann. It is suspected that Hamann was intoxicated and accidentally dropped an oil lamp which caused the fire. Burial of Franz Hamann in the cemetery of Schoenau will take place Saturday at 10 a.m.

Anton and his mother returned to Munich before Herr Schoenauer arrived back from France. (There was no further inquiry about the fire. Herr Schoenauer, who knew that Hamann liked his drink but was never a heavy drinker or intoxicated, asked about any strangers. Inge told him that Rosemarie and Anton had been here. On that day all the women had gone shopping in Berchtesgaden. "And Anton?" Betty supplied the answer. "He was with a boy at the Obersee that day. They both had come back in the afternoon.")

For Anton it was three out of six, Otto, Lutz and now Hamann. Eckhart had been killed in Russia in 1943. Jaeger had committed suicide in prison.

The last of the six was Ernst Huber and he lived in Munich. As Otto's deputy and usually in charge of the killings, he was as important a person to have him account for his crimes as the other three.

With Lutz it had been easy, he surprised him at home alone, faked a robbery, which was believed. Anton realized that he had been overly cautious in disposing the carryall in the canal where it was dredged up instead of just throwing it into the Nile. Hamann was also relatively easy, he alone up in his cabin.

Huber presented a more difficult problem. He could not visit him in his home as there was a wife and children. Huber was sixty-two by now, and his children grown up and probably living somewhere else. However, there was still the wife. He could not visit and be seen by her, nor get in touch with Huber. As Otto's son he was probably welcomed, but again he would surely tell his wife about the visit. He looked for his name in the telephone book. Ernst Huber. There were many Hubers, even a few Ernst Huber, but none living in the Schleissheimerstrasse 190. He found his name and address in the Munich address book. For telephone number it was written **Funk-Taxi 22 33 33**. His number was unlisted.

With this information Anton made his plan. First he needed to research the destination where he wanted to take Huber to. He was familiar with the forests to the south of Munich, Gruenwald and Grosshesselohe. Gruenwald was farther from the city, but he found it all built up, no isolated roads leading into the forest. At least not in walking distance from the streetcar stop.

In Grosshesselohe he found what he was looking for; a dirt road leading into the forest and a sign directing to the picnic grounds and 00 facilities—meaning outdoor toilets. It was noon when he walked along the gravel road for about fifteen minutes. There were tables, the toilets in a small brick structure—and many people picnicking. Some apparently had come on bicycles, most by streetcar. He read the sign posted, about removing trash, that the picnic ground is open from 8 until darkness. No camping permitted—*verboten*.

Next he went to a convenient location near where Huber lived. He chose the *Nordbad*, a public indoor pool a short distance from Huber. Outside was a convenient public telephone booth. He returned to midtown; and in the Hertie Department Store, he bought a rucksack and plastic gloves, stashed them at the Bahnhof train station in a locker. His plan was made.

At home he got the Luger and cleaned it. He did this while his mother was out shopping.

He then told his mother that he would spend the night with a friend in Munich. When she asked him with whom, he smiled. "You don't want to know. Don't worry, I am going picnicking with someone tomorrow, I'll be back before evening." Though it surprised her, she knew better than to pry. Toni was a strong willed boy, did what he wanted to do and never got in trouble. And while she suspected it had to do with romance, she knew how attached he was to Hanna. When he left, he was dressed for a picnic, in his leather shorts, jacket, and even took his rainproof coat.

He left Planegg late in the afternoon and took a room in a hotel near the station. He had himself woken at four in the morning and checked out at five, just as it was getting light. He then walked over to the station and got his rucksack. He had to wait for the right streetcar for a half hour, which took him to the *Nordbad*. It was now close to six o'clock. It was cool and he put on his coat. From the booth, he called the Funk-Taxi and asked for a pickup at the *Nordbad*. His name: Hans Schmitt; destination: Gruenwald. The operator told him that it would be about fifteen minutes before she could have a cab, and gave him the cost of the fare when he asked. All his plans were now dependent that the closest driver was Huber, who lived just a few blocks away.

He saw the taxi come from the north, the right direction. It made a U-turn at the *Nordbad*, and stopped. The elderly driver asked "Herr Schmitt?" Anton threw his rucksack in the back and sat next to the driver.

"Are you Herr Huber?"

The driver looked at him, "How do you know my name?"

"The operator told me that she would wake up an Ernst Huber who lives nearby."

"Oh, yes. That is me."

The driver then called in, "Picked up party, a Herr Schmitt, to Gruenwald. Out." He hung up the microphone.

"So early, Herr Schmitt. A *Wanderung* or camping?"

"Both." They drove in silence. Huber was not very communicative. From his pocket he took a small bottle and took a drink, "*Staerkung* (nourishment)," he said without smiling. He did this several times before they left the city and drove along the main road to Gruenwald. Anton could now leisurely look at Huber. He knew he was sixty-two, but looked perhaps older, an elongated face with thin lips, sparse blond hair. He didn't care to make conversation with this man and his silence just suited him. He would talk later.

Before they reached Grosshesselohe, Anton gave a sigh, "Look Herr Huber, I have to go, there is a picnic ground off the road in Grosshesselohe."

"I am not supposed to take you any place except to Gruenwald."

Anton gave a laugh, "You don't want me to shit in my pants?"

"You know what—I have to go myself. So where is this picnic place?"

Anton showed him, just past the streetcar stop to the left into the forest. A five minutes drive and they were at the empty grounds. Huber was the first to exit, finished the small bottle of liquor, threw it down and headed for the building marked with 00, and disappeared behind the door. Anton followed. Inside, the man's toilet was a tiled washroom with two stalls. Behind the closed half-door he saw Huber's feet. He heard him groan, then sigh.

He took the Luger from his coat pocket and kicked the door open. Huber sat there with his pants down, looked up at him "What the hell . . . ." then he saw the Luger in Anton's hand. "What is this? A robbery?"

The next moment Huber jumped from his seat, his head hit Anton in the lower torso and also his hand which held his pistol and knocked it away, but not before Anton pulled the trigger and the bullet deflected into the wall. The force of hitting Anton into the groin made Anton collapse in agony and then Huber was upon him; his hands went around Anton's neck, the man's finger tightening around his throat. With a last maximum effort, Anton brought his knees up and hit them into Huber's groin. The hands loosened their grip and Anton smashed his head into Huber's face, this freed him of the man as he now doubled over in pain. Anton stood up and shoved Huber back down on the seat. His face a bloody mess, his nose a pulp of raw flesh. Anton picked up the pistol and stood before Huber a good distance away.

"Huber! Do you remember when you killed Jews in Fort IX? When you gave those not dead yet the *Gnadenschuss* (mercy shot) into their bellies . . . *die verrecken schon!*" Huber stood up, wanted to pull his trousers up.

"SIT DOWN!"

Huber sat back down. "Why? Why now after so many years . . . who are you? Are you a Jew?"

"No, I am not a Jew. Why did you kill these people, murder them? So many, even children?"

Huber stared up at Anton. "Now he asks, forty years later . . . *Befehl* (orders). We had to obey orders."

"Then why did you shoot them in their bellies, which made them even suffer more?"

"They were just Jews. You don't know, you are too young, but they were responsible for the war. Our fuehrer told them, if you start another war, we destroy you. We were told to make them suffer, they were just animals, you don't know what kind of people they were, *Untermenschen,* filthy, human garbage. So what do you want from me? Who are you?" He licked the blood that ran from his nose.

"I am Otto Nagil's son. I already killed Otto, Lutz, Hamann and you are the last of the evil six. Now you will die in agony as you made them die!" He pointed his Luger at the stomach of Huber and fired. The shot sounded again like an explosion in the small building. He saw Huber thrown back against the water closet—a round hole spurting blood on his bare belly. Huber, his face distorted in pain slumped forward, Anton kicked his body back. He held his hands to his belly. Huber went into shock and slid off the stool. He was not dead and still breathing. Anton pointed the pistol at his mouth and shot him a second time; the bullet jerked his head. He had stopped breathing. Careful so he wouldn't step into the puddle of blood, Anton extracted the billfold from Huber's jacket then took his watch. The door to the toilet was sturdy and muffled the sound of the shots, too far from the trolley stop to be heard.

He went to the cab and got the pair of gloves from his rucksack, then opened all the car doors. Anton went through the glove cabinet and threw the contents out on the ground. Opened the trunk, just a spare tire and in a small bag another bottle of Schnapps. He found a rag, which he used to wipe the door handle on the car and the door knob of the toilet. He took the money out of the billfold and threw the billfold on the ground. The money and watch he put into the rucksack. He knew he had not touched anything else. In between he checked the road—no one coming. It was only seven in the morning and if anyone came it would not be before eight, if that early.

He put his coat, the three empty shells, the rag and gloves into the rucksack and the Luger into his jacket. A last look around. Nothing forgotten.

He made his way through the forest walking to the north. He had to walk slowly with his legs spread apart, he was hurting badly. At some distance he climbed the lower branches of a tall spruce and hung his rucksack on a knob so it was hidden. He continued north in his slow stride until he came to Harlaching, many miles through forest and got there before noon.

He crossed the bridge over the Isar River and walked to Thalkirchen, another couple hours walk. There he took the trolley into town, by then it was afternoon. He went into a movie theater to pass time, here he could relax in his agony and by seven he was back home in Planegg. His mother smiled as she asked if he had a good time. "And where is your coat?" He left it at the camp. "Then it is lost."

When his mother commented that he walked funny, he told her that he had a heat rash at a certain place and she gave him Calamine Lotion to put on 'the certain place.'

When he lay in bed, he kept his legs parted, but the agonizing and benumbing pain had diminished. He thought about the incident. He had been careless, he stood too close to Huber and so gave him a chance to attack him. 'Shoot, don't talk' Watanabi had instructed them when confronting an enemy with a weapon. However, he needed to talk to Huber first. Anton had learned his lesson and would not forget. (The next morning there was a column in the *Sudeutsche Zeitung*. It made the front page. The murder and robbery of taxi driver Ernst Huber. It said that most likely the murder was committed by a local as the call in for the taxi showed. His name was supposedly Hans Schmitt. It continued: 'if anyone saw someone getting into a taxi at six in the morning by the *Nordbad*, to call the police, or anyone who was near the picnic ground in Grosshesselohe or heard the shots.'

There was a witness who saw a man in a long coat and a rucksack get into the cab but after that no one in or near Grosshesselohe, where the robbery-murder had occurred, had seen such a person.

All the drivers and conductors of the streetcars going to Grosshesselohe and Gruenwald were closely questioned but they too could not report having seen any person in a long coat or anyone going into town during that morning with a rucksack.)

Anton had completed his mission. He neither felt good nor bad about it, just something he needed to do. The little girl in the red coat had been avenged.

At the end of August, Rosemarie and Anton flew back to Cairo. School started again in early September and Anton was now in his last year of the academy. Before they left, the little package arrived from Jerusalem with the silver candleholder. Rosemarie was very pleased with the memento from Jerusalem. She left it in the house. Hanna would have received hers by then too.

By the time Anton finished the academy, he was an A-student in all subjects and proficient in Russian. He had even picked up a smattering of Japanese from Mr. Watanabi, but never attempted to learn to read or write. Anton had found favor in the instructor and learned from him a love for Japan and its culture. He also belonged to a smaller group of students Mr. Watanabi taught both self-defense and attack-by-hand combat, which Watanabi-san called "The Code of Samurai." In effect, how to immobilize an opponent and even kill him with bare hands. He taught this select group how to fight someone who has a knife, a sword, a bat or even a lance as he taught them how to use these weapons if available. "Everyone is vulnerable to a lightning-fast attack, and then immobilize or kill."

Hanna was also pleased with her gift from Jerusalem. A treasure, as Toni was her treasure. She was so happy that Toni went secretly to Israel. How she longed for that land, to live there. However, wherever Toni took her someday she would be happy—to be with him!

They sat together all afternoon while Anton told Hanna about what he had seen and experienced, well, almost all. Especially about the Ben Yehuda Mall and Israeli life there.

Hanna had turned fourteen in April, too young to think of marriage, yet these were her thoughts, her hopes.

Chanukah came and though the Zapruders were not very religious, they always lit the candles and went for services to the synagogue. For the first night, and the first candle lighting, Anton came with his mother and they celebrated together. Amal had made chicken soup with Matzo balls which Anton was so fond of. The two Jewish holidays the Zapruders always invited Anton and his mother were Passover and Chanukah. As Catholics they found nothing wrong to celebrate Jewish holidays, especially since Passover was part of the Old Testament.

Then came two weeks of Christmas Holidays which the Academy observed since many of the students were Europeans, as were some of the teachers.

This year, Hanna and her mother Amal accepted the invitation to visit Munich with the Nagils. It was Hanna's first time out of Egypt and her first time flying.

They sat in the comfortable seats of business class, Hanna and Anton were together and he held her hand when the plane took off. It was strange to Hanna to be suddenly flying—so unnatural for people to fly like birds, though she was not afraid. The plane arrived in Munich before lunch.

It was overcast when they landed and the taxi took them to the house in Planegg. Rosemarie proudly showed them the house and their room was like the others in Bavarian style of antique wooden furniture.

During the afternoon, it began to snow and Hanna was thrilled since she had never seen snow.

What they had brought were warm clothing but nothing for a walk in the cold of winter. Rosemarie had plenty of warm things and while they were too big for Hanna she wrapped her into a warm coat, a scarf and gloves and out she went with Anton. Like a child she was enchanted with the flakes, which came down heavy and soon covered everything in white.

Hanna took her glove off and let a snowflake lay on her hand, marveling at its star-like shape. Then licked it off, she tasted snow. Anton told her that no two flakes were the same and she believed him. In the nearby park, she ran around catching more flakes, just joyfully being a child—the wonder of it all. The wind brushed snow into her face and when she opened her ruby lips, she tasted more of the cold miracle. Soon, they both were covered with snow and after playing for hours, in what had become a snowstorm, they went home into the warmth of the house and the fireplace in the living room that was lit.

Hanna, who had been told to bring her swimming suit, changed into it and went with Anton, he wore his trunks under his robe, downstairs . . . and there was the jacuzzi bubbling with green scented pine. The two, still shivering from cold, immersed themselves into the hot water and sat side-by-side holding hands—and exchanged sweet innocent kisses.

These were wonderful days for Hanna. Almost every day, they went into Munich, going to museums, eating lunch somewhere, the circus and afternoon plays. Viewing the Christmas displays in store windows and shopping for presents. Vacationing in Munich in snow and ice was a wonderful experience for the girl from Cairo and she was with her Toni.

Hanna helped Toni set up the Christmas tree and attached with him the many colorful bulbs, decorations and the silvery strands of tinsel.

Every day, coming home cold and tired, they would frolic in the churning water of the jacuzzi. Rosemarie and Amal left the kids alone and went their own ways. Amal was also delighted with the wintry weather and snow and the many elegant stores in the city.

And then came Christmas Eve. For Amal and Hanna it was something new—Christmas.

You can be Jewish or Muslim and still enjoy these festive times. Rosemarie, with Amal's help, was baking cookies and the *Stollen*, a special cake. A goose was roasting in the oven. Just when it got dark, they heard children singing outside. When they all came out, they saw a bunch of children holding lit lanterns and caroling Christmas songs. A few adults were with them and Sepp, their taxi driver—his doing surely, showing the guests from Egypt what a Christmas was like in Planegg. To Hanna it was all so magical, the children all bundled up in the brisk cold wind of snow flurries, singing happily and spreading kindness and good will to all. Rosemarie and Amal got the plate with cookies and made the children happy.

Then back into the warmth of the house. Dinner with roasted goose and dumplings, red cabbage, a spiced hot punch of tea and red wine, *Gluehwein,* glowing wine as Rosemarie called it. Then they opened their presents.

Later they watched the Nutcracker Ballet on television. It was a wonderful Christmas Eve and the next day a long walk in the snowy forest.

"They make such a lovely pair," Amal sighed as they trudged behind the kids.

After Christmas they returned to Cairo.

There would not be any more visits soon to Munich by Hanna and Amal. Amal was deadly afraid of flying, every shudder of the plane made her panicky. The four-hour flight had been a mental torture, a phobia she understood she could not cope with. And Hanna was too young to go alone on such a long trip, even if Amal fully trusted Toni—she did not trust the airplane.

CHAPTER V

ANTON IN THE EGYPTIAN ARMY, UNIVERSITY OF CAIRO, SAN DIEGO

In 1983, at the age of eighteen and as a citizen of Egypt, Anton joined the army; and since he was proficient in Russian and the army was still equipped with Soviet armor, he was assigned to the tank force and their T-55 tanks.

Though he was soon promoted to tank commander, Anton had to learn all the positions of driver, loader, gunner of the 100-mm cannon, radio operator, maintenance and repair, then was promoted to lieutenant, commander of a squadron of tanks. After his obligatory two-years service, he accepted a promotion to captain and the Special Forces. There, with his academy knowledge of chemistry, he became proficient in demolition work and handling explosives.

The Egyptian Secret Service also became aware of this foreign-born multi-talented officer and linguist, and offered Anton membership in their Secret Service as an undercover spy in whichever country he should visit. They also knew that he was a close friend of Ali Nasr, whom they knew to be a member of the Moslem Brotherhood.

Though Anton made it clear to the Service that he would never spy on his friend, the Service accepted him under these conditions. He was to be an "ear" to be used whenever the Service needed him. However, the army managed to have him assigned to Army Intelligence.

In this one year with the Special Forces, Anton had learned the tricks of the trade as a combat specialist. He furthered his hand-to-hand combat and became a marksman in various weapons; demolition expert for land and underwater exlosives.

Anton had become an agent of the Mossad in 1982, and of the Egyptian Army Intelligence in 1986. He was less of an active agent but rather a mole for both services.

To the Army Intelligence he supplied names of Egyptian Jihad members if he found their names through Ali and gossip he picked up while traveling to Middle Eastern countries.

To the Mossad he supplied brief reports of a general nature in regards to the Egyptian Army. At this time there was no movement in the army in any way to disturb the friendly, if cool, relationship between Egypt and Israel. These reports he gave to Mrs. Cohn during his visits to Munich.

When Anton Nagil was recruited by Military Intelligence he had a personal interview with the head of the department, Brigadier Amer. Anton came as Major Achmed Nabil in uniform as he was now in the reserve. Anton saw the brigadier open a drawer in the large filing cabinet and take out a folder, lay it on his desk, open it and read from it—Anton's service record. He then looked at Anton and said, "Impressive! Tank corps, then special forces and left active service as a captain, a specialist in demolition work. Also you speak several languages fluently. We might even need you when we buy military equipment in Germany. Since the Secret Service has cleared you, we just transferred your papers to Army Intelligence. We will carry you, you have both Egyptian and German citizenship? Yes, of course, I placed you in our German agent's designation." He closed the folder. "We were able to take you away from the Secret Service because you are a major in the army reserve. We work with them but we have our particular needs, mainly pertaining to the military of other countries and specifically Middle Eastern countries we have less than desired relations with. We are not trying to make you into an active agent going to Syria or Iraq or wherever, but in the course of visiting your German acquaintances, anything you can gather about the military, weapon procurement, and terrorist groups, we will appreciate."

There was a knock and an officer opened the door, "Your wife to see you, Brigadier." The brigadier excused himself, "I will be just a minute, Major Nabil." He took the folder with him and placed it on the cabinet and left.

This was an unexpected opportunity. Anton quickly went to the filing cabinet, opened the drawer where his file had been taken from. This was dangerous, what would he say if the brigadier or anyone else came in. He opened his file as if browsing but did not look into it. The files arranged by countries . . . Germany, Ghana . . . a few files back, Israel. He looked into it, there was a cover sheet typed with names, most Arabic names . . . a non Arab name, Patriarch Christopolis Alexi . . . Levi Uval . . . Vanunu Mordechai. He closed the file and returned. A few minutes later the brigadier returned and smiled. "Are you married? No? When a wife comes at noon, she wishes to be taken out to lunch. You will hear from my office. Ma'as salaema (Goodbye, Major Nabil)." Anton saw how the brigadier put his file back and locked the cabinet. He saluted the brigadier and left.

Anton had to see Nevot urgently. If these three names were Egyptian agents, the Mossad and Shin Bet had to know. It was the name of Uval Levi that disturbed him most of all. Uval was the friend of Tal, he met in Kibbutz Alumot. Uval was just a first name but . . .

Anton told his mother he must go urgently to Germany and no, he could not tell her why, it was army business.

He took the next flight out to Munich, and at once went to the boarding house to see Frau Cohn. He explained to her that it was an emergency, that he had to see Nevot and would take the evening flight to Frankfurt and the late flight to Tel Aviv. Esther Cohn assured him that she would at once contact the Mossad. He told her to tell them that "sav" is coming with the early morning flight on Lufthansa. Buying first class tickets Anton needed no reservations and arrived early in the morning in Israel where he found Nevot awaiting him. He explained the significance of the three names. Nevot assured him that they were aware of the Patriarch being an agent for Syria, but had not known he spied also for Egypt. Vanunu was in prison. Nevot understood the problem with Uval Levi. If she was Tal's friend, she might have compromised Nagil. They drove to Tel Aviv and roused Tal, though it was her husband who sleepy-eyed and in his shorts opened the door. It was barely after six.

They sat with Tal in the kitchen and the first thing Nevot asked was the last name of her friend Uval.

"Uval Levi." Tal looked puzzled when she heard Anton groan and Nevot shake his head.

"What is it, what has Uval done?"

"Is she still in Kibbutz Alumot?" asked Nevot. "Yes, she was."

Tal then added, "Strange, whatever it is you want from her, a few months ago Uval asked me get her an application to join the Shin Bet. I gave her references and her application is pending. Please, can't you tell me? We were together in the army and we are both from Morocco."

Nevot said "No, not at this point. Anton wishes to ask you something."

"Remember, Tal, four years ago when we visited the kibbutz, we met Uval. We sat with the Ishais. They wondered what business we could possibly have. You told them I was born in Germany but lived in Cairo. Uval asked you to call her when you get back and let her know. What did you tell her?"

Tal gave a sigh but looked relieved, "I gave the story she wanted to hear. I met you in the Old City. You asked me directions in Hebrew, which surprised me as you were obviously a tourist with a German accent. That you were a good-looking boy and I told you I would show you around. The places we went to. That I took a day off to show you the North and visited the kibbutz." Tal smiled. "Uval was more interested if we became lovers, you a good-looking young man. I told her yes." She smiled. "You don't mind, Toni? I mean it was a good cover story. And it could have happened if there wasn't a cute little girl waiting for you back in Cairo."

Anton smiled. "Yes, it could have happened." Tal seemed pleased.

Nevot said, "Then there was nothing about Anton coming at the invitation of Mossad, secured in by the Shin Bet?"

"Of course not!" After a few moments' hesitation Tal continued, "When I went steady, Uval asked me if I was still in touch with that handsome boy, she had forgotten your name."

"And you told her what, Tal?" asked Nevot.

Tal smiled. "No, just a one-night affair. I didn't remember his name. Nothing more about you, Toni."

Nevot exhaled deeply. "Looks like Uval bought Tal's story. Still, did she pass on anything about the young man from Germany and living in Cairo? We have to squeeze Ms. Levi. It is so rare for an Israeli to spy on us, unheard of. May I use your phone, Tal?"

When he came back from the living room, he said that he has a helicopter take them to Kibbutz Alumot and an officer of the Shin Bet would come along.

Nevot drove with Anton to a small military airfield outside Tel Aviv where the helicopter and a Shin Bet agent awaited them. An early morning flight of about an hour took them to a grass field outside the kibbutz. At the gate, they were met by some of the elders who were surprised by the unusual visit, and everybody else who was not at work in the fields were outside their houses to see. Nevot asked to see a *g'veret* (Ms. Levi) and when she came from kitchen duty, she was taken to the office by Nevot and the Shin Bet agent. Anton waited with the pilot in the dining hall and was served a late breakfast.

It was several hours later that the two and Uval Levi came into the hall. Uval had been crying, but she smiled bravely at Anton and slightly shook her head.

After the pilot was asked to return to the plane and get it ready for departure, the three sat together with cups of tea, and Anton was told what was behind the affair.

The Levis had wished to immigrate to Israel and had flown to Cairo to continue to Cyprus and then Tel Aviv. In Cairo, when they changed planes, their luggage was searched; and undeclared currency was found in the luggage of Uval's parents. All three were arrested. There was a trial, and while Uval was found not guilty, her parents were sentenced to ten years' imprisonment. Uval was made to understand that if she reported from Israel, her parents would receive good treatment and their sentence reduced.

She was to send her reports to her old address in Casablanca, which was used by the Moroccan Secret Service as a letter drop, and the reports were forwarded to Cairo. Letters to her came in the same manner. Sometimes a handwritten note came along from her mother that all was well. However, the other letters often contained information "they" were seeking which Uval could never supply. Then about a half year ago, she was warned that if she did not give more useful information, her parents would have to serve the full ten years. Uval then tried to give something important by writing that she was befriended with a girl whom she met in the army who was a Shin Bet agent. She was then advised to apply for service in Shin Bet, which she did. The promise was that if she became a member of the organization and reported first of all names and addresses of agents and other useful information, her parents would be freed.

"Of course," as Nevot explained, "once she did that, she was compromised and blackmailed."

She had reported during the past four years such mundane things as the armaments in the kibbutz. During her army times, what weapons she was trained with and who were her superiors, what rank they held. "Nothing of what she ever wrote was of any importance until their request for her to join Shin Bet."

When Anton asked what would happen next, Nevot suggested that most likely she will be turned as a counterspy, able to write that she was admitted to the organization. Giving them tidbits of real information to wet their appetite to get the release of her parents.

"We know how to handle such matters," Nevot assured Anton. "Uval's mistake was to try to handle it all by herself instead of coming to Shin Bet immediately. And we are grateful to you in daring to look in the file of Israeli agents. Uval was a make-believe agent on her own terms, Patriarch Christopolis was already known as an agent of many other countries besides Egypt, and the same with Vanunu. He is everyone's spy who is anti-Zionist. However, he is still in prison and has eighteen years to serve. As far as the Arabic named agents, most are probably known to Shin Bet. Perhaps the most important item in the cover sheet you read was the absence of any other Jewish Israeli names."

At the age of twenty-two and after his three-year service with the army and Special Forces, Anton entered the University of Cairo in 1987. Hanna was now nineteen, and her parents gave their permission for Hanna to visit Israel with Anton. They both flew with Rosemarie to Munich where Anton made contact with Esther Cohn. The date was confirmed that Anton and Hanna would arrive in Israel on the early morning of June 21. They spent one happy week together in Munich. Anton rented a car, and they visited the castles of King Ludwig.

He stayed away from his favorite former playground, the Koenigsee, which was now just bad memories. Hanna, the romantic girl she was, loved Neuschwanstein, the dream castle; and the Linderhof at Chiemsee, they visited them all. Lastly, Anton took her to the nearby Stanbergersee where he showed Hanna the end of King Ludwig II, a large mausoleum and cross in the lake where the king had committed suicide.

The evening of the twentieth, they took a plane to Frankfurt and then to Israel. They arrived again early in the morning, and this time, Rubin was awaiting them and guided them through passport control. He drove them to Ramat Gan, the same safe house apartment. Did he need Tal? Not for the next day, Anton wanted to show Jerusalem to Hanna by himself. But after, if she was available, he would appreciate her as a guide.

First, before he was free, the debriefing by the Mossad; and it was again Mordechai Nevot who came at eight and sat alone with Anton. Rubin returned at noon to take them to lunch.

Anton decided that they would go to Jerusalem in the afternoon and stay there for two nights then return early in the morning of the twenty-third of June. Rubin promised to have Tal at the apartment in the morning.

Anton didn't bother with the Beretta and left it where it was. This time he could wear a short-sleeved shirt with his shorts. Hanna was dressed summery in blouse and skirt. The few things they needed for overnight—pajamas, toilet articles. Anton carried in a small handbag, and Hanna stuffed in a frilly negligee. Rubin took them to the main bus station.

At a coffee stand, Anton bought two cups, and at once the vendor asked if the bag he had left in a corner was his. With suicide bombers blasting innocents in cafes, bus stations, and in buses, everyone was careful.

Hanna was thrilled to speak Hebrew, though she got strange looks because of her Arabic accent. When they didn't wish to be overheard, they spoke Arabic. This might not have turned people's heads in regards to Hanna, she could very easily be a Palestinian, but because of Anton looking European and speaking Arabic.

Then on the long bus ride to Jerusalem, and Hanna could finally relax, so far she had been full of tension. She hadn't slept a wink in the plane, too excited of what lay ahead. Anton had slept, and she rested in the wide seats with her head on his chest, feeling secure.

It was only later in the apartment that she napped. While Anton and a tall man were in the kitchen, drinking coffee and talking. And now she was refreshed and looked out at the land of Israel. How she longed to live here, among her own people. She knew her mother would come at once, and even her father had always said that she belonged in this land, Erez Israel—yet he did not wish to go. He was born in Egypt, and it was his home.

At the main bus depot in Jerusalem, they got a taxi and Anton told the driver to take them to the Ben Jehuda Mall; and when he asked for a hotel near the mall, the driver took them to the Ron Hotel. It was a small hotel, built of Jerusalem stone which at night, when lit up, gave it a soft warm beige color.

They went down into Ben Jehuda Mall. This was a delight for both. The broad street, like a mall, was buzzing with life, shops, one after another, vendors on carts, cafes, clubs, restaurants, and the people in their summer attire. Hebrew was spoken by all, though they heard many speak Russian.

He smiled when some young men conversed in Russian and talked about the beautiful girl with the long black hair—Hanna. This time his tourist camera had film, and he took pictures of Hanna to show her parents, and she took pictures of the mall and its people. They went from one end of the mall to the other and back again. Only then did they stop at a café to have dinner. Then sat with a glass of sweet wine and just enjoyed looking as it got twilight, and all the stores and places were lit up brightly.

"This is where I want to live, Toni. My country, Jerusalem my city, these are my people."

"And Munich, my city?"

For a moment there was a sad shadow in her eyes; then they sparkled again. "Winter in Munich, summer in Israel."

Anton laughed, "Spring and fall?"

"Spring comes after winter, part of winter then. Fall is the cooling of the summer here."

"And Cairo?"

"Cairo is for the Egyptians."

"And your parents, Hanna?"

"Mother would be happy with me here. I have to begin to speak with her in Hebrew. Father? I don't know. He wants me to come here, no future for the Jews in Egypt. Yet he wishes to remain in Cairo. His practice, his life is there, his friends. Mother will of course stay with him."

Anton smiled. "We don't have to worry about it now. It has already been decided."

"You mean preordained, Toni? How? You mean God decides, and we have no say into what will happen to us?"

"No. What I mean is that it will all come to pass. We have a choice, of course. We don't know what choices we shall make. Ten years from now, we can look back and it has all happened, like a script we followed. Only now we don't know what is written."

Hanna smiled. "I know what is written in my script. That wherever you will be I shall be too, Toni." He put his hand on hers and pressed it gently. Hanna accepted it as a sign of love, just as when he kissed her lips softly.

They wandered up and down the mall again, now with an even a greater throng of people in the mellow evening.

When they returned to their hotel, they saw it lit up brightly like a small palace—their palace. When he kissed her lips good night, and she returned to her room, she was very happy. Toni was such a gentleman, and she was full of passionate longings. She showered, put on her negligee, knocked on his door. "Toni, I come to be with you," her voice trembling yet sure—their first night of love and passion.

They slept late and breakfasted in the hotel cafeteria. They were at their second cup of coffee when Hanna looked at Toni, saw his smiling eyes and giggled. Anton nodded his head, like asking "what is it?" Hanna giggled again and then burst out in laughter, "Oh no, I can't tell you, Toni."

He took her hand. "Please, Hanna?"

"It is my secret. Wives have always little secrets, Toni."

Anton smiled. "But you are not my wife yet, Hanna, so?"

"If you must know, but you asked for it. You know, Toni, you are a friendly person but also typical German."

"In what way, Hanna?"

"I don't mean it insulting, dear Toni, but you are always the perfect gentleman."

"Straight you mean?"

"Like a palm tree."

Anton replied, "But palm trees sway in the wind."

"Last night, you bent like a storm hit you."

Now he laughed, "Yes, a storm of passion hit me. I had a wonderful time."

"Is that the best way you can explain, our storm?"

"Hanna! Our first night of love . . . OUR NIGHT WAS STUPENDEOUS!" He shouted and then softly added, "You were the greastest sex kitten, Hanna."

"Shhh, Toni. People are listening."

"You asked for it, Hanna darling." He smiled. But turned around and looked at the laughing faces of nearby guests.

"This morning you are like a different person, Toni, all shining and smiling eyes."

"I guess you showed me there is more to love than loving."

"Did you like it, Toni?" she whispered.

He just nodded emphatically.

Hanna whispered, "Did you notice that I was a virgin?"

"No, I never did."

"Oh, Toni!"

He took her hand. "Hanna, how would I have known the difference?"

"Yes, you better didn't know the difference." They laughed.

They finished their coffee, and hand in hand they went to the taxi waiting for them.

The full day in Jerusalem, they spent retracing Anton's steps with Tal. Only this time their first visit was to Yad Vashem. In the dark chamber of the eternal light, while he thought of the girl in the red coat, the child was at peace now; he needed no longer to shed tears for her. However, Hanna wiped hers away when they left.

Anton took her to the Old City, and they took pictures like natives. They had Arabian lunch at Amigo Emil's café.

In the bazaar, he showed Hanna where he had bought the Jerusalem candles, and she made some purchases for her parents.

That night, Anton had Hanna sleep in her own room. It was his sign to Hanna that he loved her and not only lusted for her. Hanna understood his gesture of deep love for her.

Early in the morning they returned by taxi to Ramat Gan. When Tal came at ten, they were ready for her. Anton had his holster under his shirt and summer jacket.

Tal and Anton did not greet each other with a kiss but shook hands. Tal embraced Hanna and kissed her cheek. She at once told Hanna that on his last visit, they introduced themselves to all as brother and sister, and Hanna was pleased.

Anton wanted to show Hanna what he had seen, and this time they spent the night in Kibbutz Alumot where they were received as welcomed guests. Uval Levi no longer lived in the kibbutz but in Tel Aviv. Hanna was delighted by the life in this communal village, and in the evening the villagers sat together with their children in the dining hall and had a sing-along, accompanied by an accordionist and then couples formed a circle dancing the *Hora*.

Wonderful days and evenings followed. With Tal they toured the north during the day and visited Safad, Acre, Haifa, and Netanya. They spent the night in a resort hotel in Herzliya, but first dined with Tal's family.

They spent two days touring the south—Beersheba, which suddenly appeared in gleaming white in the brown desert of the Negev. Anton saw wild camels as they neared the southern tip of Israel. They toured the copper mines of King Salomon. In Eilat, Tal took them to one of the old small hotels she always liked to stay in. Tal and Hanna, who had become good friends, took one room together. This hotel used the same air-conditioning as had been used for thousands of years. In front of the open windows was a large wooden box, really a frame filled with reeds from the sea. Water was continuously dripping from a pipe in the top, wetting the reeds, and the hot desert wind from the north was cooled by evaporation. At night it was comfortably cool, the town being by the sea.

They swam in the Gulf of Eilat and went in a glass-bottomed boat to see the corals and fish. Tal pointed out the Jordanian city of Aqaba, farther south was Saudi Arabia, and to the south-west, in the distance, was Egypt.

One happy week was spent exploring and sightseeing. Hanna knew that some day she would call Israel her home. That is where her children must grow up—her and Toni's children, just as her father wished for her, his child, to live in the land of the Jews.

After four years at the University of Cairo, Anton graduated with a degree in chemical engineering.

Anton and Hanna were deeply in love. Hanna now a beautiful woman, gentle in nature and yet passionate. As for marriage, he had one more obstacle to overcome before he could marry. He wished to complete his studies in chemistry at an American university and chose the University of California, San Diego, mainly because Mr. Watanabi was now a judo instructor there.

Two more years and he would return home and marry. Hanna would wait for him. There was a dark shadow over their lives—Hanna had been told that she could not have children, and she had not told Toni.

Anton also was no longer the cheerful youth he had been until—when? The year of avenging when he did what he had to do, it had scarred his soul. Not that he regretted executing those three, what he called "savages in human form," but their revelation of how inhuman man can be.

War criminals, violent criminals, drug pushers, wife beaters, rapists, and children abusers were all the same types of human savages, and so were terrorists. There were authorities whose job it was to find, try, and incarcerate them or kill them.

But let none of these outcasts, these scum of society, ever cross his path!

CHAPTER VI

JAPAN

Anton liked to learn and was fascinated by chemistry. This was graduate work, and his specialty was the behavior of gases and plasma. The University of California in San Diego, or UCSD, was to the north of San Diego in La Jolla, a prestigious teaching institution. Watanabi-san was overjoyed when Anton visited him in his house off campus.

Anton lived on campus in one of the small private houses together with three other students.

Anton joined the judo class of Mr. Watanabi and, when awarded the black belt, became his assistant. They spent many evenings together, sipping warm saki; and Watanabi-san, as Anton called him, enjoyed his water pipe which he had learned to appreciate in Egypt. Anton was also trying it and, liking to smoke a pipe, bought him a good briar so he could smoke at any time.

During the next summer, Watanabi-san wanted to return to Japan and invited Anton to visit him. Anton learned more appreciation of Japanese culture and, with Watanibi's help, increased his knowledge of spoken Japanese.

Anton and Hanna stayed in constant touch with letters of love and devotion, and very private. These were not erotic letters but of longing for each other, of two souls who belonged together. While they had written to each other weekly, her letters came more at random, often a month in between. To any questions he had, she would only assure him of her undying love and devotion to him.

He knew he had to see her. He had been almost a year in San Diego, and soon summer recess would begin. They had to be together again and remove anything that had come in between during his absence. Anton invited Hanna to join him when her school was out for the summer. Hanna was in the university to become a pediatric nurse. She would finish her school next year as he did his graduate studies.

Yes, Hanna would come, and she would join him on his trip to Japan. Hanna knew, for his and her sake, she must tell Toni. Then—whatever!

Watanabi-san was ending his contract with UCSD. He had enough of world traveling and wished to return to Japan to his family in Tokyo and, in his old age, take a wife and write his memoirs. Too late for children, he would be a grandpa to them and not a father.

Hanna came as soon as her school was in recess. It was long flight from Cairo to New York, and on to Lindbergh Field in San Diego. Anton was there when she came from the plane, and he took Hanna into his arms and kissed her gently. They were together again, but to Hanna it was a painful reunion, not knowing what the future held. She would tell Toni as soon as—when was the best time? Not now, they were happy to be together. Anton took Hanna to a nice hotel in Del Mar, just north of the university.

He still had a few days of school. Hanna walked along the beach in Del Mar. Solitary walks among the throng of happy tourists and natives who braved the cold water of the Pacific. Those who saw the pretty woman could not understand why there were tears in her eyes. But in the evening, she was a happy young woman being together with her Toni.

The time was never right to tell him. Anton felt that something had come between them, but he was certain that it had nothing to do with their love for each other. Even before Hanna came, she had written that her father had been diagnosed with cancer. The Zapruders were a close-knit family, and her father's illness must sadden her.

At the beginning of July, they boarded the comforts of first-class JAL for the long flight to Tokyo from Los Angeles. Chasing after the sun, they arrived in Hawaii shortly after they had departed, time-wise, then on to Narita International Airport in Tokyo. Watanabi-san welcomed them and, in his new Toyota, drove them to his house near Ueno Park.

It was a small and old house, one of the few standing after the war and the firestorms and only saved by its location on the edge of the park. As is custom, they took their shoes off, and Watanabi-san gave them cotton slippers to wear. All rooms were covered with matting, and the rooms sparsely furnished with delicate carved pieces of mostly brown lacquer, except for the living room, which had European- or American-style furniture and the TV. There was a kitchen, seldom used as their host preferred to eat out instead of cooking for himself. Though once he cooked the traditional sukiyaki dinner for them.

If the house was traditional Japanese, so was the garden out back—the garden is the pride of every Japanese house, with gravel paths around green plants, flowers, a waterfall that emptied into a small pond with goldfish lazily circling and various sculptured stones in the form of bells, lanterns, and animals.

Tokyo was a huge city, and best to get around was in a taxi—there were few places to park. Watanabi-san showed them all the sights to see, took them to a Kabuki play, to his favorite Chinese restaurant in the Ginza, the main shopping district, and the palace grounds. For Hanna and Anton, the most impressive dinner they had was in an out-of-way place where the specialty was tempura. For that, reservations had been made, and they were expected. In the foyer they were shown a large book with the signatures of famous people who had visited. The only person Hanna knew was Charlie Chaplin; Anton knew of General MacArthur. In a small anteroom, they sat on cushions and were served tangerines and green tea. The three were then led into the dining room, a very private affair, as they were the only guests admitted. There was a flower display with a waterfall, and they sat before it in a recess, a step down into a half-ring where perhaps a dozen people could sit. Then the display turned, and a kitchen appeared with the cook in white who bowed several times and greeted them in English. Before them in hot oil canisters, the cook fried tempura of delicate vegetables and morsels of fish already prepared in batter. It was eaten hot off the grill and given with steamed rice, green tea, and saki was served.

In the evening, they sat with their host who put together an itinerary for the next seven days and explained to them what to see and visit. Seven days were not long enough to see all of Japan, neither the far north of Hokkaido nor the south to Kyushu.

Watanabi-san took them to the station where they parted from their friendly host with promises that he would visit Anton in Munich some day.

Nikko was a small town, and a taxi took them to the Kanaya Hotel. At the desk, Anton used his Japanese for the first time to the surprise of the clerk.

Arriving at midnoon, they at once set out for the temple city—a complex of myriad temples in the forest. Walking across the regular bridge of the Daiya River, they were told that the ornate bridge in black and red lacquer next to it was reserved for the emperor. Temples were small and large, and from some gongs, bells sounded. As it was Sunday, they saw a parade of Samurai warriors and officials in elaborate dress. At one insignificant temple, really just a small carving under the overhang of the roof, someone pointed out to them the famous carving of the three monkeys, "see, speak, hear no evil."

They had such a wonderful time wandering in the complex that they were still there when dusk came, and low clouds of fog enveloped the forest and temples. By then most visitors had left, and hand in hand they walked alone. The beauty of a Tori, a large wooden gate, appeared suddenly in the mist; and the temple behind emerging black in the fog. It became chilly, and they returned to the warmth of the hotel and a good dinner.

The next day they took a tour and visited Lake Chusenchiko and the Kegon Waterfall. They even found time to take a sailboat out into the lake and almost had a mishap.

Anton had never sailed before and was therefore, unfamiliar with boats. Once away from the dock, he turned the sail properly into the wind; but whatever he tried, the boat drifted to the end of the lake and the waterfall. He already told Hanna that soon they would have to swim to shore. Then a rowboat came along, the Japanese climbed into their sailboat and lowered the keel. Anton and the man bowed to each other a few times, and when Anton thanked him in good Japanese, the man was as surprised as happy to have helped the novices. Anton now could sail wherever they wished to go. Across the lake to a small temple where they swung a wooden beam into the big bronze bell, the brisk wind carrying the sound over the waters; a custom of both natives and tourists was to ring the huge bells. The third day, they traveled by train to Kinugawa, a small village in the hills famous for its hot springs and many geisha houses.

The hotel they stayed in had its own hot spring, a beautiful indoor pool surrounded by rocks and plants. They had been advised to shower first or have attendants "bathe" them. They showered and wore their swimming suits, and with provided bathrobes, they went to the downstairs pool. They laughed when they realized how right they had been to shower first as they saw both men and women being soaped and washed by attendants in wooden tubs, then rinsed with buckets of water; and once they stepped out of the tub, the person was nude, as were all the men and women in the hot pool. Hanna avoided looking at anyone and admonished Toni by waving her finger at him when he gazed at one of the younger women; then they both laughed.

In the evening they attended a real geisha performance, with several geishas in their silken dresses, around which was fastened a different-colored obi, dancing gracefully while others played string instruments and sang.

The next day, they returned to Tokyo and then by fast train to Kyoto. They could see Mount Fuji in the distance. Then flooded green fields of rice, alternating with forested hills, pretty villages, solitary temples—Japan was a beautiful country.

From the station, they took a taxi; and when Anton spoke Japanese and wished to go to one of the native hotels, they were taken to the Kori Hotel where they received native cotton frocks to wear, as did all guest. Since their hotel was in the center of the city, they walked around in their native attire and wooden sandals. They had dinner in a small restaurant and later signed up in the hotel for a trip down the Hozu rapids.

Dressed again as tourists, they were driven up the hills in a bus and entered with a dozen other tourists, all natives, into one of the wooden longboats. They shot the rapids down into Kyoto, and everyone got a little drenched as the runoff made the river wild.

One day was spent visiting Nara where deer roam freely in the large park. They visited Osaka and the famous castle in the afternoon. And the last day took a tour to Takurazuka where they saw a beautiful musical and dance show of the all-women cast.

They returned to Tokyo and their flight back to the United States. The plane stopped again in Hawaii, and since it was daylight, they could see most of the islands like green jewels in the blue of the sea. Night and day alternated fast as they were flying into the sun.

Hanna spent a few more days in San Diego. There was much to see. A trip to Sea World was fun for both. Hanna especially enjoyed visiting the Wild Animal Park, with the monorail around the park, which was like an African savannah with rhinos, giraffes, buffalos, and other animals roaming around freely, and with African huts interspersed.

A day to Los Angeles and Disneyland where Hanna's happiness was shadowed again when Anton told her that someday they would have to bring their children here. She had still not told him and could not bring herself to do so. Anton noticed her change from a happy girl she had been in Japan but did not pry. One more year, no less, and they would be together forever.

Then a last embrace of love and kissing at the airport, and Hanna was gone.

Anton concentrated on his studies. Every week he received a letter from Hanna as she did from him. Hanna had decided that one day she would find enough courage to tell Toni in a letter—but she never did.

CHAPTER VII

HANNA GETTING MARRIED TO ANTON

Anton took his last year of graduate studies in organic chemistry and the study of plasma, part of his nuclear energy course. He had persuaded Hanna to join him in Miami for a final last trip together on a cruise to the Caribbean Islands. He had made reservation on the *Palace of the Sea* to visit Jamaica, the Virgin Islands, and Bahamas.

To see more of America, he left San Diego in a rental car that had been driven from Florida and needed to be returned to Miami.

In Yuma, it was 111 degrees, it was like being back in Cairo. He stopped overnight in Tucson. The long drive through California and Arizona had been more interesting than the flatlands of Texas. But he found San Antonio fascinating and spend half a day visiting the Alamo and downtown with its shopping centers and river crossing through.

Louisiana was not much different though there were more green with isolated plantations along Highway 10. In New Orleans he stopped, garaged his car near the Mississippi, and walked around the French Quarter, listened to authentic Jazz ensembles, ate spicy Cajun food, and spent the night there.

The drive through Mississippi would be short, along the coast, past Biloxi. When he stopped for a hamburger in Kreole, he got into one of those rare incidents he hated to get into. As he came out of the restaurant, he saw a commotion across the street. Some teenagers were pursuing a black youth, who was just a kid, maybe thirteen or fourteen. They yelled something about "Don't you go looking at my kid sister, you damned nigger" and other racial slurs. The kid fell, and they were beating and kicking him. Then a car came by, stopped, and the black driver yelled to the kid, "Get in!"

The kid got up, freed himself, got into the front seat, and was just about to draw his legs in and close the door when a beefy white youth ran up to the car and, holding his baseball bat level, jabbed it into the crotch of the kid. The kid screamed and collapsed and the car, with the door still open, raced off. The teenagers all laughed and patted the beefy youth on the back. One laughed, "Well done, Georgie, I hope you crushed his b—"

They walked off; and Anton, in a rage of what he had witnessed, the brutality of the beefy youth, crossed back to the other side and followed him. Kreole was really just a one-street town, and by the last house, the youth followed a footpath away from the road into a field and toward a cove of trees and a farmhouse, swinging his bat happily. Anton was still behind him. Just as he reached the trees, the youth must have heard footsteps and stopped. He saw Anton and waited for him. When Anton walked up to him, he grinned. "I showed that nigger kid, didn't I?"

Anton had regained his composure but was still quite angry. "What did you show him?" he asked with remarkable control of his voice.

Again the youth grinned. "I guess I crushed his b—"

"Why did you do that?"

"Because he is a nigger kid. They were all beating on him, so he deserved it, I guess."

"You know, even though you are big bully, you are just a little sonafobitch. And I am gonna crush your b—, Georgie."

The grin vanished, and the face turned red and mean. Georgie advanced on Anton, his bat held high up to swing it down on him. Anton was glad he wore his low boots with the steel toes. His sudden kick caught the youth in his crotch, and the bat fell out of his hand. Georgie doubled over, and only then the pain registered. By then Anton had given him a powerful jab against the side of his neck, immobilizing the youth. He fell on his knees and then crumbled, breathing torturously. No, he wouldn't die from the chop, nor would his paralysis last. But he had been punished enough, and his manhood would never be the same.

Anton walked back to his car and drove off. He came soon to Mobile in Alabama where he turned his car into a rental agency and paid the extra money to have it delivered to Miami. Then he boarded a bus for Miami. He took a taxi to a downtown hotel and stayed overnight.

It was good that he had traveled light. Most of his things he had sent on ahead to Cairo. He had a taxi take him into town where he bought a white tuxedo, black tie, and proper white dress shirt. Then on to the airport, and soon the plane came from New York and brought him Hanna. Both were overjoyed and happy.

He gathered their luggage, hailed a cab, and drove to the pier where the *Palace of the Sea* was docked—a big white sparkling ship. They were one of the last passengers to board the ship; it was four in the afternoon. A steward took them to their stateroom on promenade deck, and Anton now relaxed, took his beloved Hanna in his arms. And they kissed more passionately than at the airport.

Shortly after, the ship was gliding out of the port and into the canal that took them out to sea. Then they heard the alarm for boat drill, and when that was completed, they could finally relax and just enjoy themselves.

Their cabin was beautiful and spacious and so was the ship, which they toured before their call for second sitting. Decent but comfortably dressed, as the guide book suggested, they went into their elegant dining room and joined the table for eight, met and introduced themselves to their fellow passengers. People or couples really from all over the world.

One couple was from Scotland, one from Las Vegas, and one from Germany.

All spoke English except for the couple from Scotland whose English was brogue, but understandable. Everybody was of course interested in Anton and Hanna, speaking rather British English, and yet they were from Cairo. They wanted to know if they understood Arabic.

"Any other languages?" asked Mr. MacKenzie from Scotland. Anton turned to the Schmitt couple. "Und etwas Deutsch." Mrs. Schmitt smiled. "Ach wie schoen, then we can speak German together." Soon she wondered how he learned his Bavarian dialect. In fact the handsome man from Cairo, looking so American in his clothing, speaking with a British accent, and the beautiful Hanna, looking very much Egyptian, also speaking British English, would be a mystery couple to the guests from beginning to end.

The menu was rich in exotic dishes from around the world and would be every day for lunch and dinner and always different. Only breakfast would be with same choices. That Hanna and Anton would order toasted bagel with cream cheese and lox was another one of their mysteries. They couldn't be Jewish, with Anton wearing a small cross on a gold chain and Hanna something in Arabic on her necklace which actually was Hebrew script and said *chai* (life) bought for her by Anton in Jerusalem.

The *Palace of the Sea* was a beautiful ship, and only one of few ships that had a complete eighteen-hole miniature golf course on deck. They bought tickets to become lifelong members and almost every day had fun playing the course. There were outdoor swimming pools, a library, and a game room and at night shows. But their favorite place was the indoor pool built in Roman style. Around the circular pool were fountains, which all came together in the middle; and in the swimming there, you got drenched, like a waterfall hitting you. And there they played like happy youngsters. The water was salty—seawater pumped in, always fresh and cool. Then when they had enough in the pool, they immersed themselves in one of the big jacuzzis. Then laid in comfortable reclining chairs and held hands.

They visited Kingston in Jamaica for the day. That evening was Captain's Night, and they had to dress up. Anton in his white tuxedo and Hanna in a black pantsuit, they made a pretty couple. Mr. MacKenzie, the Scotsman, looked especially attractive in his black kilt and white jacket with a red sash. The next day they were in St. John. The following day they came to the other Virgin Island of St. Thomas. Here the large ship couldn't dock, and they had to ferry the passengers to shore. They had signed up for Moonshine Beach, and a van took them there on the other side of the island. But first the van stopped on top of the mountain, and they had a wonderful view of the harbor below, and their white ship anchored in the bay.

The beach was beautiful with clean sand and shaded by palm trees; the lagoon like a horseshoe in shape and the water crystal clear. Swimming here in the warm water and the beauty all around them was a delight.

Anton took his Hanna into his arms. "Here we have to bring our children some day." He smiled and saw her happiness wane and tears were in her eyes, and then she lay in his arms crying and finally telling her love about their fate of never having children.

When two people love each other with their whole being, their souls like one, nothing can mar their happiness—and of this Anton convinced Hanna. Besides, if they so desperately wanted children, they can adopt one. Anton was glad that he finally found the shadow that stood between them. And when he gently kissed her tears away, Hanna understood his unselfish love for her just as she felt about Toni. And now with her life free of hidden sorrow, she was bubbling with joy, especially when Toni went to a jewelry store and bought two golden rings.

He did not explain, but Hanna thought that they would become engaged on the ship. When they returned to the ship, Anton had some business to attend to at the purser's office. He needed urgently to speak to the captain of the ship. The purser wished to know for what purpose. If Mr. Nagil had any complaints, he would gladly take care of it. When Anton told him that he wished for the captain to marry him, the purser made a call to the captain who was on the bridge but came at once.

Captain Montovani was delighted with the request. It was rare for him to marry a couple, and he had the authority to do so in international waters. He told the purser to make all the arrangements and prepared the necessary papers.

The purser asked Mr. Nagil to be in his office the next morning after breakfast, and they would complete the paperwork, to be sure to bring his bride-to-be and their passports. Did they wish to make it a public wedding? Anton wanted it very private. Then it would be at three in the afternoon in the captain's cabin, and for him to bring two witnesses. The next day they would be at high seas on their way to the Bahamas.

At dinner that evening, Hanna saw how Toni and Mr. MacKenzie left the table for a few minutes; and when they came back, the Scotsman was beaming and ordered champagne for all of them. She knew that something had happened that made them both so joyful, but when she asked, neither Toni nor Mr. MacKenzie would explain. The Scotsman only said, "Anton and my secret, you will find out tomorrow." When his wife, Mary, asked if she could know, he told her he would tell her later and he did. He and Mary would be the witnesses together with Arthur MacKenzie, also Anton's best man.

At breakfast, a smiling Anton said to Hanna, "Get your passport, Hanna, we have important business to conclude." He had his already on him. They went to the purser's office where at last Hanna was told that she would be wed to Toni this afternoon, with the marriage performed by the ship's captain.

Shortly before three in the afternoon, Anton already in his tuxedo and Hanna in a white summer dress, the Scotsman came with his wife—he in his kilt and jacket. MacKenzie put his red sash over Anton's jacket and fastened it with a diamond clasp. "Mr. MacNagil it is, a proper Scotsman."

"Call me Toni, please."

"And I am Arthur, and my wife is Mary."

"And I am Hanna." And they laughed as everyone already called her Hanna. Mary gave Hanna a bouquet of artificial red roses from the gift shop. They proceeded to the captain's cabin. Captain Montovani was in his dress uniform, and the purser was also in his best.

Anton and Hanna stood hand in hand.

"By the authority vested in me . . ." Captain Montovani read from his book, followed by the ceremony of rings.

"I now pronounce you, Mr. Anton Nagil, and you, Hanna Zapruder-Nagil, MAN AND WIFE."

They all signed the proper document, which was in the form of an elaborate scroll, and there were drops of tears on the scroll after Hanna signed. The captain gave Hanna a small silver replica of the ship, the purser a box of the best pralines, and took a picture of the newlyweds. Hanna had become the wife of Toni. It was 3:15 p.m., the fourth of July 1992.

Their marriage registered under international law in Nassau, Bahamas, in the headquarter office of the shipping line. Less elaborate but more formal documents would be sent to them in Cairo.

At the purser's desk, they composed identical telegrams to Hanna's parents and Anton's mother:

> *Dearest, today, on the high seas, nearing Bahamas* (stop) *we were married by the ships captain* (stop)
> *Toni and Hanna Nagil.*

Dinner was spectacular as it was the American Independence Day. Anton ordered champagne for all, and he and his wife Hanna were congratulated by the Schmitts and the couple from Las Vegas. The purser brought a fancy wedding cake to the table, and when the orchestra played the Wedding March, the waiters all came and surrounded the table and sang along, and everyone in the dining room stood up and applauded them.

The night was long as there was the midnight buffet with all types of food and pastries, with beautiful ice sculptures in between. Though the wedding had been very private, the night's celebration was with many.

CHAPTER VIII

BACK IN CAIRO

Anton and Hanna had returned to Cairo, and Hanna lived now with her husband and Rosemarie.

Anton was welcomed at the Academy as a teacher in chemistry and also taught Russian and, when that was no longer in demand, joined the athletic department and taught judo. Hanna, who had completed her nursing training, was hired in the pediatric department of Cairo General Hospital.

His good friend, Ali, had become an imam at the Great Mosque in Cairo. They were still the best of friends; and when Anton told Ali that he married Hanna, a Jewish woman, Ali had only smiled. "You Catholic, she Jewish, what does it matter, you are both infidels." And they had a good laugh. Ali, of course, sported a dark beard as is proper not only for a devout Muslim but also for an imam. They went on many outings together, to other mosques—and there were many in Cairo—museums, and even sport events, but rarely to places of entertainment like movies and never to bars. Nor was Ali interested in women, though he was good friends with Hanna.

Anton had joined the Egyptian Army Reserve as Major Achmed Nabil. Every spring, he had to fulfill his army obligation and attend a camp for three weeks with his unit where he taught the use of explosives and defusing of bombs.

He was still with the Army Intelligence, but except for attending periodic meetings with his contact officer, he was not needed. And then only when he was sent to one of the Middle Eastern countries like Lebanon, Syria, Iraq to make contact there with German expatriates and get information which intelligence could use. Many of these Germans were also former escapees, and some had contact with government officials, army people, and even terrorist groups. As a son of Otto Nagil, he was always welcomed.

Christmas was spent by Hanna and Anton in Munich; however, Amal could no longer join them as Avraham's incurable cancer prevented her from leaving her sick husband. How long did he have left? Amal was told at most a year.

Finally, Anton could provide a real service to Army Intelligence instead of the tidbits of information of rumors and hearsay he picked up from his German acquaintances.

It was on one of his trips to Beirut, visiting a former SS officer and friend of Otto, an Alfons Berger, a merchant, that he was introduced to a Lebanese, Yusuf Khawwash. Berger introduced him to Khawwash as an explosive engineer of the Egyptian Army. As Berger explained, Yusuf Khawwash was an important member of the Lebanese Hezbollah, their explosive expert; and he wanted a professional opinion on a structure to demolish.

Khawwash looked at Berger. "I can trust Nagil, fully?"

Berger replied, "I told you, Anton Nagil is the son of a former colleague of mine, a high-ranking SS officer. Anton Nagil is still one of us."

"What structure?" Anton asked Khawwash.

"It is a bridge. I just want your opinion if the explosives I place are at the right position to bring the bridge down."

"What kind of bridge?" asked Anton. "Of wood, concret, metal? How long and wide is it, how many supports does it have? I asked because it is a matter not only where the explosives are placed but also how much to use. I expect that you use plastics?"

Khawwash answered, "Yes of couse. We use RDX-4. Which bridge? It is a secret, and I must not tell you. It is of metal with concrete supports."

Anton said, "All right, then make me a drawing with rough dimensions and show me how you will place the explosives and how much."

Alfons Berger brought a sheet, and Khawwash drew the outline of the bridge with its concrete supports and wrote the approximate dimensions. It was really a trestle-bridge, about a hundred meters long with sidewalks on either side, a two-lane highway, and three supports.

Khawwash said, "I plan to place two hundred kilograms of RDX under the center span. Will that be enough to blow up the center of the bridge?"

Anton chuckled, "More than enough. You demolish the complete center, right up to the two other supports." He smiled. "Now if this is meant just to blow a big hole into the bridge, it will do. However . . ."

Khawwash interrupted, "However, what?"

Anton continued, "If I would do it and it was meant to, for example, to blow up a car crossing the bridge, this arrangement might fail."

Khawwash asked, "How, why?"

Anton explained, "I would do it of course with remote control, being close enough to see when the car is in the middle. However, if for example the car is speeding across the bridge, let us assume that I wish to assassinate an important person, perhaps the bridge will be even cleared of traffic. A car, then going fifty miles an hour, you would be lucky to catch him in the middle. The car would be closer to either end of the bridge, and there is a good chance the car might escape."

Khawwash said, "So you suggest that I place the charges at all three supports? I might not have that much explosives."

Anton said, "First of all, you don't need two hundred kilograms to bring any of the three supports down. Half of that would be enough. If you know from which direction the car comes, you need to place your charges only in the middle and at the end support."

Khawwash continued to ask, "Then if I use one hundred kilograms for each support, it would demolish the bridge from the middle to the end?"

Anton assured him, "Yes, it would. And also demolish any car crossing." After thanking Anton Nagil for his guggestions, Yusuf Khawwah soon left.

Anton asked Alfons, "What is it all about?"

"Khawwash wishes to assassinate the vice president of your country, Anton. He was the one who conducted the peace agreement with Israel. Hezbollah has never forgiven him for that. He is supposed to visit the president of Lebanon and then drive out to the main army camp to see some of the Lebanese military big shots. I guess he will bring some of his military men with him. You don't mind, Anton?"

Anton smiled. "No, of course not. I did not know that Hafez was doing the negotiations. He was not vice president then to President Anwahr Sadat."

"No. But he was Zionist friendly as was Sadat, of course. Sadat they got, Hafez they can get now visiting Lebanon. Tell me, Anton, where are you going from here?"

"I like to visit Schuler in Damascus. If you call me a taxi, I would be grateful." Anton flew at once back to Cairo. At the airport, he called Brigadier Amer and asked for an urgent meeting with him. With a speeding taxi, he went to Military Ingelligence where the brigadier awaited him. After Major Achmed Nabil told the brigadier what he had learned, the brigadier made the necessary phone calls; and as Anton found out later, the trip of Vice President Hafez to Lebanon was cancelled. There would have been several high-ranking military men with Hafez.

(At a ceremony to honor Brigadier Amer, who was received by Vice President Hafez and several generals who would have been with Hafez, Brigadier Amer was awarded the Order of the Nile for his intelligence work which prevented a catastrophy. The chief of intelligence received full credit for aborting the plot, but Amer would remember Achmed Nabil fondly.)

Summer vacation came; and Anton with Hanna went to Israel by way of Cyprus and, in Tel Aviv, was welcomed by Rubin. The safe house apartment was theirs to use. There was the debriefing by the Mossad deputy. Anton's information provided more of background knowledge of Egyptian policies in regards to Israel. Since President Mubarak's relationship with Israel was hot and cold, the why of it became important. Under what pressures was he—the army, Brotherhood, jihad? Or Saudi Arabia? Always Syria and Iraq. Terror acts had become common in countries other than Israel. After members of the jihad shot a bus full of tourists visiting the pyramids, tourism suffered greatly. Egypt had warmed to Israeli's efforts to combat its brand of terrorist. They adopted similar restrictions Israel used to safeguard airports and planes, as at last, Israeli and Egyptian security services were cooperating. The information Anton had learned in Lebanon and Damascus was really gossip from German sources. Yet both rumors and gossip have nuggets of truth and facts in them if you can corroborate with other information. Once Anton had established a trusting relationship with the German businessman Alfons Berger in Beirut, he was introduced to others. The refugees from Germany were getting old; and many had died, their offsprings, in most cases, had gone to Germany to live. However, many of the ex-Nazis remained, having established business and becoming ingrained in the countries they sought refuge in and were always welcomed and protected. Few were still sought in Germany, and those who were wanted remained. Almost all ex-Nazis remained true to their faith in the lost Third Reich, and their beloved though departed fuehrer.

Mordechai Nevot had a pleasant surprise for Anton. After the debriefing, he took Anton and Hanna to the Tel Aviv office of the Mossad where Israeli passports had been prepared for them. They only needed to have their pictures taken and included, and while neither of them was an Israeli citizen, they now had passports and needed no longer to enter Israel under the guardianship of Shin Bet. From Egypt, Hanna could use her Egyptian passport to fly to Cyprus and use the Israeli passport from there. Similarly Anton could use his German passport to Germany or Cyprus and switch to his Israeli when arriving in Tel Aviv.

Then they were free; and while they called Tal, who was now married and living in Tel Aviv, they were on their own. His carrying the pistol had become optional, and he declined to take it along on most trips.

They had come on a special mission. Hanna's father, Avraham, knew he had a half-year to live and wished to move to Israel. Though never very religious, he wanted to die in Israel. And more important, this was a good reason to establish the family in Israel, for Amal and Hanna to live there as he had promised both a long time ago. He had sold his practice and was selling his house in Cairo. Money was no problem. Hanna and Anton came to look for a nice house for the Zapruders, and someday also for themselves when the time came. Avraham, more than any of the others, regretted not to have a grandchild. Hanna promised that they would adopt a child someday—he knew it would be too late.

Neither Avraham nor Amal had any preference where they wished to live as long as it was in Israel and near good medical facilities. Hanna and Anton knew it had to be in Jerusalem. Tal could not help and suggested a real estate office to guide them. It was Anton who remembered the Ishais on his first visit to Kibbutz Alumot. He called the kibbutz and got from them the address.

They stayed again in the Ron Hotel where the same desk clerk smiled knowingly when they showed their brand-new Israeli passports and congratulated them when he saw her passport listed as Hanna Nagil. This time they needed only one room. They had arrived late in the afternoon and went at once in the Ben Yehuda Mall and to their favorite restaurant which served Arabian food. They called the Ishais from there, and Anton spoke to Elchanan who remembered them fondly and asked them to come by in the morning. He was now retired.

The Ishais lived in a section called Mahanavim and had a nice apartment. The top floor of the small apartment house had a big picture window where Hanni did her painting. They were invited for a late breakfast and had a warm welcome. The Ishais were sorry about Hanna's father's condition but assured them that at the Hadassah Hospital, he would receive the best of care. Elchanan and his wife listened to the happiness of the couple and their story of how they got unexpectedly married on the ship. As to a house, neither knew of one for sale that was suitable, but they told them of places in Jerusalem that were nice to live in. Elchanan gave Anton a map and circled those sections. He suggested they take a taxi and walk around and, if they found a place they liked that was for sale, to call the real estate office.

When G'veret Ishai asked if they also would some day move and live in Jerusalem, Hanna looked at Toni. "On and off," he said. "My mother will move back to Munich during the next few years to live there in her house. For various reasons, with some important business I have in Cairo, I am tied down. It is only a short hop to Cyprus and Tel Aviv from Cairo. If not weekly, then monthly we would visit. Christmas vacation, we'll spend in Munich, summer in Israel."

At that, G'veret Ishai smiled. "This sounds strange that you would spend the hot summer month in Israel. In winter, it is lovely here."

Elchanan laughed, "Yes, when the rains come."

"Hanna," Elchanan suggested, "When you come here to settle, you can become an Israeli citizen and get a passport, then you won't have any trouble coming into Erez. You need a visa now every time you come from Egypt."

Hanna replied, "Look, Elchanan, it is no secret that I have an Israeli passport. But I only show it when we register in a hotel. We need it to open a bank account, but we don't broadcast it, too many questions."

Elchanan looked surprised. "That I don't understand. How is that possible, Hanna?"

Hanna looked annoyed. "I just knew the right people."
Elchanan still was puzzled. "Someday?"
"Someday," Hanna answered.

First and most important, they had to open a bank account. Elchanan had told them that the IDB (Israel Discount Bank) on King Shlomo Street would be best as they dealt with foreign accounts and currencies.

This is what Anton and Hanna did. With their Israeli passports and their address listed as the safe house on Jabotinsky Street in Ramat Gan, they had no problem. However, they could not make it into a joint account with the Zapruders as Avraham and Amal needed to be present and sign. The bank accepted the bank draft of the Zapruders for a half million dollars for deposit in the Nagils' account which however, would take a month to clear. To have cash available, Anton deposited ten thousand dollars—ten notes of one thousand dollars, which also needed a couple hours to clear. The bank officer had never seen a thousand dollar note. Then, after lunch, they took a taxi to the place and circled on Elchanan's map, the area he said was the most beautiful to live in. It was in the southern part of Jerusalem, the area called Givat Masua. Elchanan had explained the name, "In very olden times, communities were informed of *Rosh Hodesh* (the new moon) by torchlight signals emanating from mountains tops around Jerusalem. *Givah* means hill, and *Masuah* torch." Anton already understood that just about everything in Israel was history.

When they left the taxi and walked, they soon spotted "their" house. A two-story house with stone of a rose hue from a Jerusalem quarry, a gated entry into the driveway and garage, a lush garden behind. There was a For Sale sign in Hebrew and English. As they walked along the stonewall, looking here and there, an elderly woman came out of the house and to the gate. She smiled at them; Hanna and Anton walked back to her and greeted her with a friendly, "Shalom, ma shlomech (And how are you)." She returned their greeting.

"What a beautiful house and really for sale?" asked Hanna.
"Are you interested?
Hanna smiled. "I just love the view from here. Yes, we are."
The lady invited them in to see the view from the large balcony on the second floor. And when they stood there, they saw before them the Ya'ar Hashalom (the Forest of Peace) and a breathtaking view of the wide valley called Emek Refaim, leading to the City of David. The lady pointed out in the distance the Old City and the Temple Mount, and they could see far to the north. "A three-minute drive from here is the lovely Biblical Zoo. Five kilometers to the south-east is the city of Bethlehem, and three kilometers to the south-west, the modern Hadassah Hospital."

Hanna looked at Toni, her face radiating her joy and happiness. He knew this was the house she wanted.

Hanna had marveled at the large living room with the French doors that opened to the balcony and already knew where her piano would go. From the master bedroom, they could look down into the beautiful well-kept garden, a large shade-giving palm stood in the middle. A couple of basket chairs were under the palm. "We like to sit there in the shade," the lady said.

She offered to call her real estate agent who could talk to them and did so while she offered the young couple a glass of cold lemonade and let them sit on the balcony.

When the agent came, he asked them first where they where from.

"Cairo."

He smiled at Hanna. "Yes, you must be of Sephardim descent, but Anton Nagil has a European accent?"

"German descent." He looked at the small cross hanging from Anton's gold chain. "I thought so. Egyptian Jewish and German gentile, *nebich,* why not?" He told them the price would be four million shekels, close to a million dollars. They had thought in those terms, with each family providing half. The agent then toured the house and garden with them.

The money Anton had deposited in cash was immediately available for holding the property. The IDB Bank certified the deposit of two million shekels and promised the clearing of the draft as soon as possible. Anton said that the other two million would be transferred immediately from their Deutsche Bank in Cairo to the IDB. The house would be theirs in less than four weeks.

They returned to Cairo and arranged for the transfer of the funds. It would be the house of the Zapruders and Nagils.

In the middle of August, they received a notice from the bank that the money was available and at once returned to Israel and concluded the purchase. The lady of the house had her things packed and taken out and shipped to Haifa where her son lived.

Then in the dusk, with the sun settling behind the hills, Hanna and Anton were in their empty house all alone and stood on the balcony overlooking the city bright with myriad lights.

The real estate agent arranged for a trustworthy caretaker and a contractor to begin at once with the painting and changes they wished to make, foremost modernizing the kitchen and bathrooms, and also to put the swimming pool in order and install a thermal hot water heater on the roof of the garage to heat the pool The Zapruders had decided to leave all their furniture in Cairo and sell them together with the house.

Anton and Hanna were ready to buy furnishing, or rather, Hanna did the buying with a bemused Anton making rare suggestions. Her most treasured buy was a white grand piano. However, it was Anton who bought the car, an American white Ford with the latest gadgets, good air-conditioning and heater, with the seats of gray leather.

Their driver licenses from Egypt were legal in Israel, but they also got Israeli licenses which they decided to leave in a bank deposit box when not in Erez.

At the end of August, still living in the Ron Hotel, as the furniture had not all arrived, they left the house in the care of their caretaker Eliahu Zamir and returned to Cairo.

The Academy started school in beginning of September, and Hanna returned to her hospital duties. Shortly after the Zapruder's house was sold, they moved with their personal belongings to the Nagil's house. By the end of September, they received a wire from Eliahu Zamir that all was ready.

Anton received a one-week emergency furlough from the Academy, as did Hanna from the hospital. Most of their belongings the Zapruders sent by freight. In October, after Yom Kippur, the two families flew to Tel Aviv. Amal, calmed with a couple Valium pills, was still afraid but not in panic. Eliahu Zamir awaited them and gave Anton the keys to his car and house; he would return by bus.

It was late in the afternoon when they left the airport and, in the sinking sun, drove to Jerusalem. Hanna sat with Anton in front, her parents in the back, with Amal crying softly. She was leaving her beloved Egypt and moving to another country with a dying husband. Amal soon began to smile again as she listened to the exuberance of Hanna who sang along with Israeli folk music the radio played. Amal's Hebrew was good enough to converse; Avraham's Hebrew was that of the prayer. He would never have enough time to learn.

When darkness fell, they arrived in Jerusalem; the beautiful city all lit up. Then on to their house with the gate open. Hanna showed her parents the house, decorated and furnished according to her tastes, and the white piano. There were three bedrooms upstairs, and the parents' bedroom had a balcony overlooking the garden. Eliahu had placed a vase with flowers in the large living room, and the refrigerator was full as was the freezer with precooked meals. The bread box had bread and rolls. Even the bar was stocked with Carmel wine and flavored brandies from Israel.

Eliahu was not only a good caretaker but would become a trusted friend and of course was generously paid for his loyal services.

Amal and Avraham were impressed and happy to live in this beautiful house. The next day, Hanna would show them the garden and pool.

Amal prepared a light evening meal with cold cuts, and then they sat together in the comfortable living room, and Hanna entertained them on the piano. The first song she played, which she and Anton sang the lines, was the Hatikvah, the Israeli national anthem, "The Hope." Hanna then told the story of the composer, Naphtali Imber, who was born in Galicia, Poland. He supposedly wrote the song while in Ukraine, inspired by the founding of the village Petah Tiqvah. However, as Hanna explained, the Hatikvah did not become the national anthem until it was sung at the opening of the ceremony to declare the new State of Israel on May 14, 1948. Then she played Mozart and Chopin, and when she played Brahms's "Lullaby," it was time for bed, and the happy family spent their first night in their new house.

The garden was beautiful, and they liked to sit together under the palm. Anton took Avraham to the Hadassah Hospital and brought along his bundle or medical records, albeit all in Arabic. An oncologist examined him and ordered new tests. The bad news was that his cancer of the pancreas was incurable. The good new was that with proper treatment, they could give him more than six months. After a week, Anton and Hanna returned to Cairo.

Things were turning nasty with terror attacks in Israel, in the Middle East, and in Europe. The Mossad needed Anton badly as a listening post in Egypt and so did the Egyptian Army Intelligence who appreciated his travels to Middle Eastern countries.

Through his Brotherhood connection with Ali, he was even permitted to visit Saudi Arabia and the city of Mecca, but there were no German expatriates to gather information from. Ali joked with him upon his return that he had become an infidel Hajj, one who has made the pilgrimage to the holy city of Mecca.

Anton asked Ali, "Now that my in-laws live in Jerusalem, would you like to visit the city and be their guest?"

"With you, Toni? Gladly. Jerusalem is the third holiest city for us Muslims. It is every Muslim's obligation to visit Mecca, Medina, and Jerusalem. My father went there when it was part of Jordan. Since then it is under Zionist occupation . . ."

Anton interrupted, "Please, Ali, when Muslims use the word *Zionist*, they mean it negatively. Israeli occupation."

"I am sorry, Toni, I do not wish to hurt your feelings. Israeli occupation then, I undertand. Hanna and her family are Jewish. But since the Israelis conquered Jerusalem in 1967, very few Muslims visit the city. Yes, I am certain my father would approve. I have been to Mecca, I have also been to Medina. To visit Jerusalem would be for me to fulfill my dream. And I am honored that you invite me."

Anton smiled. "The honor is on our house if you come and visit. You know and you are liked by the Zapruders. I too wish to visit Jerusalem. As a Catholic, I would fulfill my Christian obligations. For you it is the visit to the Haram al-Sharif, and for me the praying at the Church of the Holy Sepulture, the Via Dolorosa and other holy places."

"And for us, there is also the Mosque Al-Aqsa."

Anton said, "Let us apply for a visa at the Israeli Embassy, and when the opportunity presents itself, we go. I should go soon, I have promised Hanna. Her father is very sick; he has cancer of the pancreas and will not live much longer. We should pay our respects."

Christmas came. Anton and Hanna spent it with Rosemarie in Planegg, and before returning and accompanied by Rosemarie, they visited for a week the Zapruders in Jerusalem. It was Rosemarie's first visit to Israel, Jerusalem, and its Christian holy places. While still in Munich, Anton had called Ali and told him that the family would visit the Zapruders and this was a good opportunity for both to see Jerusalem. Ali had his visa and promised to come to Israel. Anton had never told anyone, not even his best friend Ali, that he had visited Israel.

Anton picked Ali up at the airport in Tel Aviv in his old Ford.

"Now I am in the Land of the Jews." Ali smiled. Ali received a cordial welcome from Amal and Avharam and an even warmer welcome from Hanna and Rosemarie. The guestroom downstairs was his to stay as long as he wished. Avraham was confined to his bed and looked haggard and in pain. He had not long to live.

Ali could only stay for three days and wished to spend the next day visiting the Haram al-Sharif and Al-Aqsa.

Anton took Ali there in the morning. With them came Rosemarie as Hanna wished to stay with her father. Anton took Ali to the Lion Gate, the entry to the Dome of the Rock.

There was a checkpoint where all had to show their idenfication before permitted to enter. After Ali had disappeared through the gate, Anton took his mother to the Dung Gate where they entered the Old City, visited the Christian places, and had lunch at Emil's Café. They picked up Ali late in the afternoon, and Amal had prepared an all Arabian dinner.

The next day, Anton showed Ali the new city of Jerusalem and also drove him out to the Yad Vashem complex and the underground memorial.

In the cafeteria drinking coffee, Ali asked Anton, "Tell me, Toni, did the Holocaust really happen?"

"Yes, it did, Ali. The Nazis executed, shot, gassed, or just burned alive over a million children."

"Your father, he was in the SS, was he involved, Toni?"

"I am sorry to say, yes." Ali remained silent. They sipped their coffe.

"Tell me, Toni, why did the Germans kill the Jews? Was it because of their religion?"

Toni smiled for a moment. "Ali, you use all the wrong terms. Don't ask why the Germans killed, I am also German, Egyptian-German. Call them Nazis. No, it had nothing to do with religion. At one time, before the war, Europe was very nationalistic. The English thought themselves to be better than the Italians, the Italians better than the Greeks. The Germans believed they were better than any other people. The German national hymn had these words, 'Deutschland ueber alles' (Germany above every one else). Hitler furthered this superiority complex. The Germans thought of themselves as the super-race. The other nations were of lesser value. The Jews, the Slavs, and Gypsies the Nazis thought of as *Untermenschen* (inferior beings). They made laws that a German could not marry such an inferior because it poisoned their blood. Their children would be half-breeds."

"But humans all have the same blood, Toni."

Anton smiled. "Decent and educated people know this. Ali, it is of human nature to believe you are better than anyone else, superior even if only by birth. The Nazis tried to get rid of the Jews by having them leave Germany; few could leave, nobody wanted to take them in."

"Why didn't they go to America?"

"America had a quota system. They let in a certain number of Germans each year, and it didn't matter if they were Jews or Christians. Amazingly, countries like China, Australia, and Cuba let many come in. Arabs were against them coming to Palestine, their ancestral land."

"Remember, Toni, it was Ishmael to whom Allah promised the land of Palestine."

"Ali, do you believe in the Old Testament?"

"The book of Abraham? Of course, but it was his son Ishmael who inherited Palestine."

Anton smiled. "I know, it is because you don't believe that old Sarah could conceive. Ali, you believe everything else that is of the Abrahamic tradition, so if Allah willed it, why not? The Old Testament, as also the new one, clearly gives the inheritance of the land of Palestine to the descendents of Abraham and Sarah's son, Isaac, his son Jacob whom Allah named Israel and promised his descendents the land forever. It is written such, Ali. To come back to the Nazis, Hitler then decided to get rid of these, what he called inferior beings, by killing them. He murdered most Jews, Gypsies, and many Slavs. The rest of the Slavs he decreed that they become slaves to the Germans. Ali, you asked before if my father was involved. I said yes. I let you read his war diary, and you can see for yourself how the Nazis massacred the Jews, from the old to the babies. After I read his diary, I no longer considered him my father but a mass-murderer, a child-killer."

"Is the diary in Arabic?"

"Oh, Ali, I forgot. It is in German. I can show you a movie taken by the gestapo in Lithuania where Otto was the commandant of the fort where they killed the Jews. It shows a long ditch filled with many Jews already shot. A long line of men, women, and children are lined up before the ditch; and they kiss each other for a last time. Machine guns above them. There is an SS officer who shoots a little girl in the arms of her mother then walks along the line and shoots all little children in the head. When he walks back, the movie shows his face. Ali, it was my father! Let us leave and return to the Zapruders." The next day Ali had to return to Cairo.

Anton and Hanna received the news that Avraham had died. Together they flew to Israel to attend the funeral. Hanna spent an extra week with her mother.

In 1995, Rosemarie made the big move and left Egypt to live in her house in Planegg. She was now an elderly lady and rarely visited Israel. Every winter, Anton and Hanna would visit her, sometimes joined by Amal, who with her panic pills, could bravely fly.

During summer vacation, the couple lived with Amal in Jerusalem. The evenings in Jerusalem were cool and, even more so, on the balcony with a breeze coming over the hills.

Ali also came to visit during many summers. He no longer considered the Israelis as occupiers, but sincerely wished that the Israelis and Palestinians would unite into one nation. As he told Toni, one has to believe all that is written in the Abraham tradition, or none of it. As a faithful Muslim, he believed.

BOOK 2

FLIGHT FROM AFGHANISTAN

CONTENTS

NEW CHARACTERS

IN AFGHANISTAN:

Sidqi Suliman. The young friend of Ali who wished to become a warrior.

The Swede Jihadist Sven or Mohamed.

The German Jihadist Heinz or Hassan.

Amir Haq Khan. Taliban commander of the al-Qaeda training camps near Khost.

Omar al-Hamza. The Egyptian Deputy of Commander Haq.

Fawzi and Abdullah. Two British Jihadists, Comrades of Mohamed and Hassan.

Husayn Sabre, Abd al-Hamed, Zahi Abu Shanab. Three Egyptian Jihadists, protectors of Achmed Nabil.

Mohamed Atta. Childhood friend of Ali.

Saleh al-Moqrin and Talib al-Moqrin. Two Yemeni brothers.

Ahmed Shah Massoud. "The Lion of Panjshir." Warlord of the Northern Alliance.

Sasha Tokarev. Russian prisoner of war. Accompanied Anton & Sidqi on their flight.

IN UZBEKISTAN:

Boris Sokolov. A Russian driver.

IN RUSSIA:

Natasha Tokareva. Sasha's mother.

IN MUNICH:

Head Inspector Wagner. In charge of the anti-terrorist unit.

Chief Inspector Kirsch. In charge of the criminal investigation division.

Head Inspector Keller of the CID. Inspector Nagil's boss.

CHAPTER IX

AFGHANISTAN

It was in the beginning of July 1998 that Ali proposed to go to Afghanistan to attend an al-Qaeda training camp there.

Ali was torn beween his nonviolent belief and the young radical students who came to the mosque and wanted him to take part in the movement to overthrow Egypt's tolerant and western oriented government of Hosni Mubarak and forcefully introduce the *Sharia*.

Anton had seen a change came over his friend. That he was a devout Muslim, had studied to become a clergy and was now an imam, one of many at the Al-Azhar Mosque, had never interfered with their close friendship. However, when Ali spoke of his religious work at the mosque and his teaching, and quoted from the Koran to Anton lately, he had the feeling that Ali was proselytizing him. When he questioned his friend about it, Ali smiled "It is because you are my best and dearest friend that I try."

Ali was always frank and open with him which hurt Anton as he harbored secrets he could never tell Ali. The only secret he had confided in Ali was that he had married Hanna, the Jewish girl he had loved for many years and of course that her family had moved to Israel and Anton with Ali had visited the Zapruders. Lately, Ali had quoted him from the Koran about martyrdom. That a Muslim who dies in the Holy War, the jihad, will sit by the side with Allah.

Anton had replied with a smile, "And don't forget the many virgins." Poor Ali, he had actually blushed—he who had never touched a woman. "So let's forget about the virgins," Anton offered and Ali nodded. When Ali asked Anton if Jesus would not welcome a Christian who gave his life in martyrdom, Anton was frank when he told him.

"Jesus would send me straight down to hell. Remember, Ali, we Christians are told to love our enemies, to turn the other cheek," which caused Ali to laugh. "You Christians don't believe in that commandment."

"It is true," replied Anton. "We Christians in the past two millenniums have not followed the scriptures. We warred upon Muslims, Jews, heathen, and ourselves. Very few of us are saints. I am not a saint."

"But you are a good man. You could become a devout Muslim."

It was when Ali said that he needed to go to Afghanistan and wished for Anton to accompany him. "They need you to teach them bomb making." To which Anton replied, "They would tear me apart as a Christian." "No, they will not!" Ali told him that if he went, he would be under the special protection of the jihadists. "Also I have been told that the Taliban would protect you, and I have it from a source I can not reveal, that bin Laden himself invites any Christian who could teach bomb making, especially right now as they lack an explosive expert in the camp." Anton asked Ali to give him three days to think it over—how could he refuse his best friend's request, yet it was madness to accompany Ali.

It was three days later that Ali came to visit Anton. Ali was always welcomed in the Nagil's house as a friend of the family, and Hanna knew of their close attachment. Anton and Ali went downstairs into what had a long time become a recreation room, every bit of Nazi regalia removed and discarded.

To Anton, the visit to Afghanistan was fraught with unknown dangers. Teaching terrorists the arts of bomb making, God forbid! He had not even told Hanna—they were happily married, and he did not wish to risk it. Besides, he a Christian, an infidel in the midst of a bunch of crazy terrorists—lunatics.

He talked to Ali, "Why risk it all and for what?"

Ali admitted he had mixed emotions. "You know, I am a nonviolent person. I don't believe in terrorism, hurting or killing innocents. There is tremendous pressure brought upon me by the young faithful and also by some of the elderly imams. I need to see for myself what motivates the many young jihadists who go to the training camps. If I understand their thinking, their self-sacrifice, I believe I can help them to see the Koran as a nonviolent message from the prophet. It has been suggested that if I wish to have my own mosque, I should go. Being an imam is not only to guide the faithful in prayer but also to teach. You don't understand the hierarchy of the clergy here in Cairo. It is like a corporation, all politics. If you wish to advance, you have to cater to the top people. I have already an inside track as a member of the Brotherhood. Going to Afghanistan will enhance my standing, and once I become the leader of my own mosque, I can teach the young faithful that there are ways to achieve grace before Allah without resorting to violence."

"But me, why should I risk it?" Anton asked.

"Perhaps, I need you to protect me," replied Ali.

"From danger? If they wish to kill you and I, we can't stop them."

Ali smiled. "Not that kind of danger. Rather that I do not become involved in their thinking and methods. I always value your judgment, you will be my conscience. As to the risk to you as a Christian? I have it from the jihad that first of all, there is a desperate need for explosive experts—theirs have gone to Africa on a mission. I have a close friend, you know him, Sidqi is to me as a faithful as what you are as a Christian. I trust him as I trust you. Sidqi not only is a member of the Brotherhood but has ties with the Egyptian Islamic Jihad. Sidqi will go with us. You are needed, and I have their assurance that they will protect you. Three members of the jihad will travel with us and attend the same camp and are sworn as your protectors."

Anton knew he could not refuse. There was this deep bond of friendship he felt for Ali nutured by so many characteristics they had in common. In fact, more than once they had referred to each other as brothers.

Anton took Ali's hand. "For you and to protect you, yes, I will go."

At once, he stopped shaving to grow a beard. Suntanned as he always was he wanted to look like an Egyptian.

Anton wished to learn about the country of Afghanistan before he went there and from the library of the Academy, he got some books. This was a fascinating country with an ancient history; and it seemed, at the crossroads between the Middle East and Asia, in constant strife. However, first, he studied the maps and its topography.

Afghanistan was surrounded by many nations, which seemed the cause for its violent history. To the north, the former Soviet Republics: Turkmenistan, Uzbekistan, and Tajikistan. To the northeast, a finger touched on China. East and south was Pakistan, and to the west Iran. The principal cities, or those Anton was familiar with, were the capital Kabul and to the south Kandahar. Situated to the north of a vast desert was Herat, and the city of Mazar-I-Sharif. The mighty Hindu Kush mountain range began at the northeast and curved to the southwest with a range extending above Herat. To Anton it looked like a most inhospitable country, if not mountains then it was desert. A wild country with violent neighbors.

The history was like its topography, untamed and yet warred over by many nations and civilizations, last conquered—which was the wrong word to use as Afghanistan was never conquered for any length of time by anyone—by Britain. He found the famous Khyber Pass every schoolboy had read about, if not in geography class, then perhaps in Kipling or Tennyson books. The Khyber Pass was the gateway to Afghanistan.

He read: "A wise man once said, 'When God made the world, whatever He had left over in parts and pieces, He threw down on earth and that became Afghanistan.'"

Population: 20 million, perhaps less with many having fled into Pakistan and Iran during the war with the Soviets.

Language: Afghani, Urdu, Pashto, Dari/Persian, Turkic and tribal dialects.

Currency: The Afghani—but as Anton was informed, American dollars, English pounds, and German marks were also used and the Afghani was worth little.

Forty percent were of the Pashtun ethnic group who had ruled the country for the past three hundred years, but lost some of their power during the war with the Soviets and were again the ruling group. Most of the Taliban were Pashtun with one-eyed leader, Mullah Mohammed Omar. At this time, there were a number of factions under the Northern Alliance who opposed the Taliban and were supported by all its neighbor countries with goods and weapons, except for Pakistan and Saudi Arabia. Pakistan sent many young fundamentalists from the Madrasses to fight with the Taliban. Both of these nations were playing a dubious game of supporting these Islamic fundamentalist Taliban while combating their own brand of jihadists at home.

Before the war with the Soviets, the British had tried to conquer Afghanistan for many hundreds of years, never ruling but rather bribing if they couldn't subdue the various tribes. The Soviets fared even less well in their ten-year war from 1979 to 1989 and left defeated.

Afghanistan always defeated those who tried to conquer it; those who came and destroyed existing civilizations, kingdoms, religions, and tried to supplant with their own brand of rule—never benign, always by the sword. Warriors and traders carried Buddhism over the Silk Road to China and Japan. In the seventh century, Arab armies swept through the land and brought their new religion of Mohammedanism, promising justice and equality, but never peace.

There is an endless warring across Afghanistan. The Afghans are a proud people and fierce warriors. Then, from practically nowhere, the Taliban appeared and ruled.

In 1998, when Anton went to visit Afghanistan, the Taliban were in power except for the northeastern part of the country and the Panjshir Valley.

Anton told Army Intelligence of his plans. His contact man there wanted Achmed to go and report back on members of the Egyptian Jihad who might be attending. There was one more briefing with Brigadier Abd al-Hakim Amer, who wished to see Anton. The brigadier warned him that this was a most dangerous undertaking. "You are dealing there with fanatics, religious zealots, who, if they find out you are a Christian, might kill you as a damned infidel."

Anton replied that he was under the protection of both the Taliban and the jihad.

"All the same, there will be some extremists to whom it doesn't matter under whose mantel of protection you are. Bin Laden might welcome you as you have the skills of a bomb maker, al-Zawahiri might welcome you as a native of Cairo as he is from here. They have declared war on all infidels and did so in a fatwa by the newly formed World Islamic Front for a jihad against the Jews and infidels. This fatwa was signed by mullahs who could issue such a document, including al-Zawahiri for bin Laden. However, the style of writing, the pronouncements, it is bin Laden's."

Anton took the document and read it.

Since Allah spread out the Arabian Peninsula, created its desert, and drew its seas, no such disaster has ever struck as when those Christian legions spread like the pest, crowded its land, ate its resources, eradicated is nature, and humiliated its leaders. No one argues today over three facts repeated by witnesses and agreed upon by those who are fair. They are. Since about seven years ago, America has been occupying the most sacred lands of Islam: the Arabian Peninsula. It has been stealing its resources, dictating to its leaders, humiliating its people, and frightening its neighbors. It is using its rule in the Peninsula as a weapon to fight the neighboring peoples of Islam. The most evident proof is when the Americans went too far in their aggression against the people of Iraq. Despite major destruction to the Iraqi people at the hand of the Christian alliance and the great number of victims exceeding one million, Americans are trying once again to repeat these horrifying massacres as if they are not satisfied with the long blockade or the destruction. Here they come again today to eradicate the rest of these people and to humiliate its Muslim neighbors. Although the Americans' objective of these wars are religious and economic, they are also to serve the Jewish state and distract from its occupation of the Holy Land and its killing of Muslims therein. The most evident proof thereof is their persistence to destroy Iraq. All those crimes and calamities are an explicit declaration by the Americans of war on Allah, His prophet, and Muslims. Based upon this and in order to obey the Almighty, we hereby give all Muslims the following judgment: The judgment to kill and fight Americans and their allies, whether civilians or military, is an obligation for every Muslim who is able to do so in any country. We also call on Muslim scholars, their faithful leaders, young believers, and soldiers to launch a raid on the American soldiers of Satan and their allies of the devil.

Anton looked at the brigadier after he read the fatwa. "This is unheard of, to explicitly declare war on civilians. The Koran forbids this."

"It does!" The brigadier answered, "It is not Islamic to kill civilians."

"The fatwa certainly reads as if written by bin Laden in his quest to expel the Americans from the Arabian Peninsula," suggested Anton.

"Exactly. There is not even a clear justification to declare holy war on the Americans who are in Saudi Arabia. They are there as guests of the government and not invaders. The Koran—here let me quote from the Holy Book. 'Permission to take up arms is hereby given to those who are attacked, because they have been wronged.' Here is a quotation in the Koran which bin Laden uses to justify his jihad." He read, "'But when the Sacred Months are past, then kill the idolaters wherever you find them.' However, this verse is taken out of context. Islam, the Koran taken as a whole, teaches tolerance of Christians and even more so of the Jews, whom the prophet acknowledged as the People of the Book." He closed the Koran.

"Also, Major Nabil, the true meaning of jihad is the struggle of oneself, to overcome one's own shortcoming and evil desires. The lesser jihad is the battle against the infidels, especially the godless ones like the Soviets were. As far as his call for killing civilians, the Koran is very clear that civilians must not suffer during battle, or for that matter at any time. Mohammedans are just as horrified by this fatwa. As you so rightly suggested, Major, it is his, bin Laden's."

"Now let me suggest something else, Major Nabil."

He proposed to Anton that if possible, he should assassinate Ayman al-Zawahiri. The man had become a central figure in al-Qaeda and bin Laden's right-hand man, planner of terrorist attacks in many countries including Egypt. "He is also an embarrassment to our government. Short of strapping on a belt, but IF AT ALL POSSIBLE, you would be doing the greatest service to Egypt." He added, smiling, "Your country also, Major Achmed Nabil. And please, don't be too expert in teaching them bomb making."

Anton smiled. "I have no intention of teaching the terrorists anything of value."

He then gave Anton a press card that he was a correspondent for the Cairo newspaper al-Ahram. "Might come in handy, Major Nabil, one never knows." The brigadier also gave him a code name, *perach*, to use when calling by phone or e-mail

If he needed any funds, they could be sent to him to a bank or one of the moneychangers who had a phone or Internet connection. It would be forwarded by a Cairo bank.

"I will receive all communication sent by you under this code name." He had Anton memorize the addressee. Anton was taken aback when he said the word *perach*, which in Hebrew means "flower." Without showing his surprise, he asked, "What does *perach* mean?" The brigadier smiled. "As code names, we use foreign words. It makes it twice as difficult to decipher. It is the Hebrew word for *flower*. I doubt very much that anyone you meet knows Hebrew. Please, do not wear your cross, Major, or have anything Christian-like with you. If they see that cross on your neck, it is like a red cloth would be to a bull. You might as well say ole, and they come at you."

"If I go, Brigadier, and come back, I wish to resign from the reserve."

The brigadier agreed, especially as Anton would still belong to Military Intelligence and wished to do so.

Anton still had a week before they went. His face showed a sprouting dark beard. There was no time to fly to Israel to see what the Mossad was interested in or to visit his mother in Munich. He did not tell Hanna where he was going; only that it was in a foreign country and for Army Intelligence. He would be back in less than a month, and it would be his last assignment. He would resign from the army reserve and be free of any obligations. It was for that reason that Hanna abided and looked forward to their lives free of anything that could mar their happiness and keep them apart.

On the first of August, Anton packed the few things he would take in a backpack and a small handbag. He took his Egyptian passport and his credentials as a reporter. He would now be known as the Egyptian Achmed Nabil.

For traveling, he chose a sort of khaki uniform but without any insignia. He also took his pair of stout army boots, sandals, and extra underwear, socks. A turban he would buy in Pakistan. For money, he took Egyptian currency, but as the brigadier had advised him to take American dollars, he secreted those in ten, twenty, and hundred dollars bill in his money belt.

When they met at Cairo International Airport in the early morning for the flight to Karachi, they were a band of six. Besides Anton and Ali, there was Sidqi Suliman, the young Brotherhood member and good friend of Ali, and three young men from the Islamic Jihad. All, except Sidqi, bearded men, though trimmed and Anton's was still rather short; only Ali and Anton were in their thirties.

Sidqi was a quiet, young, faithful, and together with Anton and Ali, sat in one row; and they kept to themselves, as did the three jihad members. Sidqi was the youngest, barely eighteen and handsome. He had tried to grow a beard but couldn't manage and had a smooth face. Maybe because of his young and handsome looks, almost with girlish features and yet a devout Muslim, he had chosen to go to a training camp to become a warrior for Allah. He was also the contact to the jihad. Why his parents had let him go to Afghanistan into the rigorous training of a *muj*, he never explained. But Ali told Anton that he promised Sidqi's parents to watch over him and that no harm befall their son and even made Anton promise that if anything should happen to him, he should protect Sidqi and bring him safely back to Egypt.

In Karachi, they changed to a PTA plane for the flight to Islamabad. Here they were already in the Asian world as the hostess wore a sari and headscarf and served curry dishes.

At the airport in Islamabad, they were met by an agent of the Pakistani ISI, the Interservice Intelligence, who spoke English and Arabic. He had a van with a driver waiting, and the six piled in for their long drive to Peshawar. The agent preceded them in his own pickup.

The Grand Trunk Road to Peshawar was poorly maintained, as witnessed by the many wrecks along the road.

Halfway there, the van crossed the Indus River, which begins in the mountains of Tibet. Anton remembered Otto's teaching that the Aryan Nordic Race came from the Indus Region. Was it true or just another fanciful idea of the Nazis?

They stopped at the largest *madras* (religious school) in Pakistan, the Darul Uloom Haqqania, for lunch of rice and mutton. Here, they were joined by a dozen Pakistani faithful who wished to go to bin Laden's training camp. These were impoverished students and a few exiled Central Asian Islamic radicals. They traveled in their own van also sponsored by the ISI. The two vans made their way in a many-hour jolting ride to the city of Peshawar, the capital of the North-West Territory. They spent the night in a safe house of bin Laden which bore the innocuous name of beit al-Salaam (House of Peace) where they also had a simple meal.

Early, after morning prayer and breakfast, they were driven to the Khyber Agency. They were ushered into a large office and introduced by the agent as jihad warriors to the officials and each had to show his passport, and the Pakistani students their ID cards and, after scrutinizing their documents, received an entry stamp into Afghanistan. Then they were taken to the waiting room where they met another three dozen jihadists and their leader who would take them to the camp. Anton could at once see that some of the *muj* were Europeans by their light complexion and lack of beards. The agent, who knew of Anton being an Egyptian of German descent, had these four Europeans join Anton's van. The leader sat in the front with their driver, and their van was the first of their small convoy, right behind the pickup, which made it nice traveling over these dusty roads.

These four did not recognize in Anton a European, especially as he spoke Arabic. However, when Anton listened to their conversation, he heard one speak German to another who spoke German poorly. The other two spoke English. The two German-speaking men were surprised when Anton joined their conversation in German. They introduced themselves, though they had Arabic names; one was Heinz, the German, and the other Sven, a blond Swede and a giant of a man. All four were Muslims, Heinz and Sven had converted some years ago to

Islam. Among themselves they would call each other by their Christian names. Anton was pleased when Heinz told him that he would have never thought of him as anything but an Arab.

They were now a convoy of five vans, still preceded by the agent. Shortly after they left the outskirts of Peshawar, they came to a checkpoint where the ISI agent cleared them and then left the convoy to return. Their leader was now their guide into Afghanistan. By the checkpoint were large signs in several languages, also in Arabic and English: ENTRY OF FOREIGNERS IS PROHIBITED BEYOND THIS POINT. They were now in the northwestern tribal territory where even the Pakistani government had little, if any, jurisdiction.

They came to the town of Darra, where they stopped for an hour of leg stretching and getting something to drink. There were many shops and vendors selling food, tea, and stores that sold just about any type of weapon. They also saw vendors who openly sold hashish. Anton, who was with Ali and Sidqi, bought a Colt 45 pistol for thirty dollars, the only currency accepted. He checked the weapon, working its loading chamber back and forth; it was well-kept. The price included several full magazines, and Anton inserted one and chambered a round. The gunsmith spoke a little Arabic, "You kill *muj* . . . he *shaheed,* martyr . . . meet Allah . . . much virgin."

"And do what?" Anton asked, and they laughed, even Sidqi.

Anton stashed the pistol in his belt under his shirt, Ali smiled and Sidqi looked pleased. Anton explained, "We never know what or whom we meet."

As Ali felt himself the protector of Sidqi, so did Anton of Ali. Anton and Sidqi had become good friends since they left Cairo. Sidqi was of a gentle nature even though he was very religious. As Ali would explain to Anton later, Sidqi suffered greatly because of his beardless and generally unmanly appearance. That he was always the object of seductive leers and comments by so inclined men and had been raped as a boy by a mullah of the mosque he had belonged to who told him that it is Allah's will that he serve men. Ali knew, and so confided to Anton, that the main reason Sidqi went to a training camp was to prove his manhood.

No one paid any attention that he bought a weapon since many men were seen with a rifle slung over their shoulder. Most carried the AK-47, and some old men had ancient muskets.

They had hot tea at a shop and then returned to the van, and soon they were on their way to Khyber Pass, the gateway to Afghanistan.

The road went uphill toward the pass. The Khyber Pass was not the traditional pass of up, over the top and down, but a 48 kilometer long stretch of road, some serpentine, and at a height of 3,500 feet. It led between mountains which at this altitude were mere brown, treeless hills. Except for its violent history and the sight of fortresslike houses of tribal families, the long stretch afforded little of interest. After they came through the small town of Landi Khotal and higher up in the pass the fortress of the Pakistani army, they stopped at the border post, which was manned by the Taliban. Their leader talked to the guards, and they were passed through freedom fighters for bin Laden, they were in Afghanistan. Soon they came out of the pass, and in the clear air, they saw the brown plains of the Kuna River Valley that led to cultivated fields and orchards toward the city of Jalalabad.

Their guide took them through the center of the city and its busy bazaars to a walled compound. They drove through the open gate and entered the large house built of mud bricks, the house called by the Arabic name of beit al-Shuhadaa (House of Martyrs), bin Laden's welcome center for freedom fighters. Their room was poorly furnished, metal beds with straw sacks, blankets, but they would only spend this one night here. Their large room would be shared with the four Europeans. It was after lunch and prayer time, and they were free to spend the afternoon in the city.

Anton, Ali, and Sidqi took this opportunity to explore the city. First, Anton wished to buy native clothing as he stood out in his khaki type uniform. In a bazaar, he found a store and bought loose-fitting pants, a cotton shirt, a brown sweater, and a type of flat turban, which could be worn like a cap. Ali paid for him in Pakistani rupees, neither one having any Afghani money. In the back of the store, he changed, bundled his khaki clothing with string "like a native." Ali laughed when he saw Anton.

"A native who cannot speak the language," replied Anton. Of course, neither of them could speak Pashto, Dari, Urdu, or one of the Turkmeni or tribal dialects spoken up in the north, except for the little Sidqi knew. He had studied Pashto and Dari and could speak French, which was of no use here, a country of many ethnic groups and as many languages.

In a teashop, they had rice with vegetables, nan—the large round flat bread baked of unleavened dough—and tea. At a money exchange, they traded rupees for Afghanis; the Afghani currency was worth little and came in hundred and thousand denominations.

They strolled along the bazaar and then followed a large crowd streaming to a soccer stadium which was full. What they saw was Taliban justice, a gruesome spectacle. A thief had his hand amputated by a mullah and was then attended to by a doctor. It was even more grizzlier when a robber had his hand and opposite leg cut off. The cheering and enthusiasm of the crowd sickened them. Anton thought how brutal people get in their religious fanaticism. The Roman circus in modern times—no, not modern but back to medieval times.

"This is barbaric," he said to Ali who was embarrassed by it all. Sidqi averted his eyes from the cruel proceeding. "Misinterpretation of the Koran," answered Ali, "Yes, *Sharia* recommends this type of punishment. But new laws, edicts by imams, such as incarceration of thieves and robbers, supplement this sort of old-fashioned and barbaric punishment. Prison has been approved by commentaries in Egypt, but remember, Achmed, these are wild tribesmen. And with the Taliban in power, they regressed. The jihad supports these laws but not the Brotherhood or modern Islam."

They left before the judgment day was over. There were a few more who were to lose their limbs. The cruelties inflicted, the cruelties watched—Afghanistan was truly a strange country—or was it just where the Taliban reigned? Why did so many people come to watch? Again the savagery in man.

They returned to the bazaars, the more human form of life in Jalalabad. There were few women to be seen, and those they saw were dressed in their all-encompassing *burkhas*, which must be most uncomfortable in the afternoon heat. There was lots of traffic in the main streets, Japanese pickups racing with white banners flying from the antennas. On the back, fierce-looking men in white or black turbans, all with AK-47s in their hands, some were even manning machineguns though there was no enemy. They were young men, mostly Pakistani students and Talibans.

Men, young and old, wore baggy trousers and cotton shirts, *shalwa kameez*, as Sidqi called their attire.

After they returned to their quarters, they had a simple evening meal and sat together with the Europeans in a community room. They told each other their reason for attending the camp. Sven, the Swede, explained that he was drawn to Mohammedism by reading stories of Arabia and the deeds of Lawrence in the First World War. He had converted to Islam after college where he earned a degree in civil engineering for the construction of sewage and water piping. He spent a year in London, where he found jihadists and was invited to the camp as his expertise was badly needed. He spoke English well. Anton found in the blond giant a well-educated man and sincere in his Islamic belief and not a freedom fighter who was about to become a martyr. However, he did not like the way he leered at Sidqi with staring eyes that told of lust for the handsome young man.

Heinz confessed to have been a neo-Nazi and was attracted through the violence of the Islamic Jihad. He had converted to Islam in Hamburg and had participated in discussions with jihadists and was invited by them to attend a training camp. He had been jobless, and they paid for his trip and gave him spending money. "All in good marks. I changed it all to Afghanis here in Jalalabad. Look, I was a fighter in Hamburg, I might as well use my fists for a good cause."

Anton asked, "What kind of a fighter were you, a boxer?" Heinz laughed, "No, well yes, I boxed, but I was more the bully type of fighter, getting into brawls all the time."

The two Englishmen told of their being born in England to Muslim parents and of their frustration in a country that discriminated against Muslims. Their wish was to become fighters for Islam. The imam in their mosque had guided them to a man in London who arranged for them to fly to Afghanistan. The same was true for the Swede.

Anton explained that Otto, his father, had been a war criminal and fled after the war to Egypt, where he was born. Which caused Heinz to exclaim, "Then you too are a Nazi, Anton?" Anton smiled. "Nazis are in the past, we are jihadists here."

Sven asked, "When did you convert to Islam?"

"I am not a Muslim, I am still and always will remain a Catholic."

"How could you come? I thought that all foreigners have to be Muslims to be accepted in bin Laden's camps?" asked Sven.

Ali explained, "Achmed came at the invitation of bin Laden. He is an explosive expert, and they need him, Muslim or Catholic. He is needed to teach bomb making."

"And you, Sidqi?" Sven asked.

"I came because I belong to the Egyptian Brotherhood, and I am willing to become a warrior."

Sven sneered, "Just be careful that one of the martyrs doesn't think of you as one of the virgins that are awaiting him in paradise." They laughed, except Sidqi who looked embarrassed and Anton who shot a dangerous glance at the Swede, which Sven did not see. They soon retired to their straw mattresses.

Fourth of August—DAY ONE IN AFGHANISTAN

After morning prayer and breakfast in the community hall, they were introduced to a bin Laden representative who would take them to their camp. He spoke first in Pashto for the Afghans and Pakistanis and then in Arabic as many of the jihadists were from Arab countries and had been here in Jalalabad waiting to go to the camps. When he spoke in Arabic, he began with the usual call for Muslims, "Allah is Great, Allah is Merciful" and intoned the Sura of Mulk, "Blessed and Most Gracious is God, Whose goodness and glory shine everywhere: His is the true Reality: His promise of the Hereafter is true." Then followed by a propaganda speech of why the mujahedin needed to fight for the Glory of Allah. "Slay the infidels, the satanic Americans." He must have taken his cue from one of bin Laden's pronouncements, Anton thought. Apparently, he was not aware that one of his muj was an infidel.

He then told them that they were destined for the Al-Badr camp, about 300 kilometers southwest from Jalalabad. The camp was one of the many satellite camps of the Zawhar Kili complex near the town of Khost.

They soon left in a long convoy of vans and pickups for the daylong ride to the camp, only stopping for prayer time.

The dirt road was in bad condition. They saw many ruins, few standing structures. This region had tasted the Soviet war and again the civil war between the Taliban and Dostum's legions and Massoud's fighters. For a year now, the fighting had stopped in this part with the Taliban in control.

It took them eight hours to get to the camp. Camp al-Badr consisted of two close villages, called al-Badr 1 and 2. They stopped in Camp 1, for Arabs including foreigners. Pakistani students, Kashmir Jihadists, and Afghans continued to Camp 2, a kilometer away. Both villages had been roughly handled during the wars and the villagers had left. With bin Laden's money, the destroyed houses had been rebuilt with mudbricks from the ruins and new concrete structures erected. Most of the villagers had returned and worked now as laborers; they did the housekeeping chores and their women did the cooking and washing. All women and even girls older than ten wore *burkhas*. For them a tent city had been erected between the two camps and they were well paid.

They unloaded at an open square in the middle of the camp with their belongings. They were again a band of six as the three Egyptian Jihadists had joined them.

Fronting the square was a concrete house, which obviously was a mosque as it had a small minaret. To one side was a large rectangular structure with smoke coming from a chimney in the back, the kitchen and dining hall. To the right of the mosque was a smaller concrete structure with signs in various languages including Pakistani, Pashto and Arabic—the headquarters. There were more solid structures around the square.

It had been now four weeks that Anton had not shaved and his dark beard, while not bushy, looked presentable. Ali too had a trimmed beard and not the full beard of Taliban, nor did the Arab Jihadists.

It was late in the afternoon, and the August sun still burned mercilessly. At last a man in a camouflage uniform, a full beard, and a belt with a pistol strapped to it, strutted out from the HQ and stood before them. He introduced himself in Arabic as Amir Haq Khan.

He said that he was a Tajik by birth but a Taliban and the commander of the camps, so designated by Osama bin Laden, "Our leader, and may Allah grant him victory over the apostates and infidels." He welcomed them as freedom fighters, "In the cause of Allah and the true religion as given to us by His Prophet Muhammad." After some more propaganda phrases—he was a fiery speaker—he told them that they volunteered to come here for training in weaponry, combat, attack tactics, and bomb making. They were a new group of 48 jihadists and would join the one hundred from the previous group who remained behind to learn bomb making as the explosive experts had gone on a mission.

There would be nightly religious sessions after evening prayer, except tonight. He further told them that after evening meal they would be assigned to their houses by his deputy, Omar al-Hamza, and had the evening off and could freely wander around the camp and its environs. If they wished, they could visit Camp al-Badr 2.

"And as a welcome present from our leader Emir Osama bin Laden, you will each be given a prayer rug. Further, you will be issued camouflage uniforms in the morning after breakfast and then detailed to your various squads for training."

He then asked them to gather around the mosque for a personal greeting by him. The commander went to the door of the mosque where prayer rugs had been piled and from a list given to him by the guide he called them individually by name.

Each man was personally greeted by the commander who spoke a few words, took a prayer rug and went into the mosque.

When he called "Achmed Nabil," Anton stepped to Commander Haq, was greeted and surprised that he was recognized, "Achmed, my explosive expert, German? You look more like an Arab than a foreigner. Welcome. We have great need for you." When Anton asked if he wished for him to take a prayer rug, as he was not a Muslim, Commander Haq replied, "Yes, I know. Take one; it makes you less conspicuous as a non-Muslim. Just remain in the back. Pray to Prophet Jesus if you wish. And please be in my headquarters after you have eaten."

Ali followed Anton, and one of the last to come into the mosque was Sidqi Suliman. Anton went with them when the call for prayer came from the minaret, the faithful knelt and the mullah led them in worship. No one paid any attention to Anton, who stood in the back with his rug in his hand unused.

After prayer, the dining hall was opened and all went in to eat, holding their prayer rugs under one arm and in the other a wooden dish they had picked up. They then moved by the kitchen where each received a large nan bread, a bowl of rice with spiced lamb stew and fruit. It was the beginning of the harvest time in the orchards and fruit was available, if no fruit, a handful of sweet dates were given. They had choice of tea or coffee. At least in this camp with many Arabs, coffee was served three times a day. Men served but women cooked in the back of the kitchen. Food was always plentiful and brought from Khost daily by pickups. The main staple was rice but always given with spiced vegetables and meat, most often mutton but also chicken and duck.

Anton, Ali and Sidqi sat together on a table for four. They made light conversation, talking mainly about what they had seen and their Commander Haq, he seemed a pleasant man and not a firebrand terrorist.

Suddenly, Ali jumped up and happily pointed at a table where four uniformed men sat and announced, "I know this man. It is Mohamed Atta, a long time friend of mine. We went to school together, I have to meet him." He went over to the table, the man got up and the two embraced and as is custom, kissed each other on the cheek. He soon returned and told them that he will bring Mohamed Atta over later to meet them all, "He was in Germany to study and speaks fluently German."

After they had finished their meal, the deputy assigned them to their quarters. Anton left his belongings in the care of Ali and Sidqi and went over to headquarters. He came to a door marked in both Pashto and Arabic as office. He knocked and heard Pashto words and then in Arabic, "come in."

He met Commander Amir Haq Khan who was a tall slender built man in his uniform of camouflage; his face with a bushy black beard, as he was a Taliban.

Men who wear beards, especially the full beards of Taliban, are hard to judge as to their countenance with part of the facial features hidden. It is their eyes that tell of what type of person they are. Haq's eyes were friendly and pleasant to see as he smiled at Anton and greeted him with "My German Arab from Egypt" and offered Anton a chair before his large desk. The office, which was well lit, as it had become dark outside, was of concrete with the walls whitewashed, the floor was also of concrete though in the middle and behind the desk were large rugs. Filing cabinets were along one wall, a computer was on a table and in a corner a radio, which was attended to by a uniformed Taliban. Telephones and files lay on the desk, perhaps what were missing for a modern office were pictures on the wall. There was a wooden bowl on the desk from which the commander ate dates, and when Haq offered Anton some he also munched on the sweet fruit. Haq began the conversation by saying that he understood that Achmed was an explosive expert, "Which we are in great need as our experts Rifia Ahmed Taha, Abdel Rahman and their crews have gone to Africa on an important mission for our leader, Emir bin Laden. We should hear soon about their work. By the way, Taha is the leader of the Egyptian Islamic Jihad. You don't belong, as you are not a Muslim. Do you belong to the Brotherhood, Achmed?"

"No, because I am not a Muslim."

"Ah yes, your faith, you are Christian. Better do not tell anyone, we have faithful here who might harm you if they knew. Who knows about your Christian faith?"

"Of course, my friends Ali Nasr, Sidqi Suliman and the group of foreigners who came with us, there are four, the Swede, the German and two British Muslims."

"You have to give me their names and I will call them in and make them swear not to reveal your Christian faith. Taliban command most of the camps, except the Arabs ones. All training, except for certain experts like you, is conducted by our Taliban warriors who are well versed in combat and weaponry of any type. We even have Russian tanks available for training, though that training is conducted in another camp."

"I am a expert in Russian tanks. In the army, I was in a tank regiment."

"The Egyptian Army, of course? Yes. I will have you take a look at one T-55 tank that is at our range, it runs all right but the cannon is defective, it was hit once by a self-propelled grenade and damaged. Well, now to you Achmed, as one of our instructors, you can sleep with the others with somewhat better accommodations."

"May I stay with my Brotherhood friends?"

"Yes, if you wish." He turned to the radioman, "Khalid, see that the deputy assigns Achmed and his two friends and the four foreigners they came with, to house number twelve. Write down the names of the jihadists." Anton gave the man the names. "The house I give you is more comfortable, also at the end of the camp. It has its own shower and toilet, as few houses are connected to the water and sewage line. I believe a Swedish man came with you who is a sewage engineer?"

"Yes, his name is Sven or Mohamed. He is a Muslim."

The commander smiled. "Yes, all are except you. Tomorrow after breakfast I will show you the magazine-bunker where we keep our explosives. As for you and your work, there is a schedule posted by my door. All training in explosive matters is conducted here in al-Badr-1. You will have a small group of men, perhaps a dozen in each group, for a week to teach them. In three months, you should be able to teach all of those who are now in our camp, about 150 warriors. The main emphasis must be on car and truck bombs and explosive belts for martyrs to use. Those are for the Arabs, none of my Afghan Taliban wish to blow themselves into paradise, they want to fight like warriors. No need for you to build them, we have plenty on hand. But their circuitry must be faultless. Are you familiar with those delicate mechanisms?"

"Yes, but more in the form of repairing and dismantling them."

"If you can do that, then you can also make them work."

Anton smiled. "To make them work is easier than to repair them."

"I expect so. The explosives we have on hand are mostly plastic RDX-3 and 4, TNT and some dynamite and powders. We have plenty of fuses, detonators, equipment for wiring, batteries and manuals in Arabic."

"Fresh explosives? Some deteriorate over time."

"Most are new and from our brothers in Pakistan. We get a shipment every month from Peshawar."

"The ISI?" The commander's eyes looked serious. "That is none of your concern, Achmed. Do you have any other questions?"

"I just wondered, you said you are a Tajik. I thought only the Pashtuns are Taliban, the Tajik, Uzbeks and Hazaras are from the Northern Alliance?"

The commander smiled again. "Ah, you know about our country, or its politics. Yes, you are right; those you named belong mostly to the Alliance. I did too. Massoud, the warlord up north, is a personal friend of mine. We went to school together, are from the same village and I fought with him. Politics here in Afghanistan are difficult to explain. It has little to do with religion. Massoud is a faithful Muslim and even in politics he can be trusted. Some of our other warlords like Dostum and Hekmatyar shift their flags with the winds. However, when the Taliban emerged in 1994, they had only one goal and that was to unite Afghanistan under one banner. I then switched my allegiance to the Taliban and Mullah Omar. I do not agree with some of their extreme religious philosophies and their treatment of women. My wife is still up north and I don't wish for her to be treated like a second rate citizen. But most important is for Afghanistan to become one nation and that I can see happening only under the banner of the Taliban."

"Then you fight your friend Massoud and his warriors from the north?"

The commander laughed, "I can live with my enemies, in fact I can trust my enemies. It is our friends I have to beware of, like Dostum and Hekmatyar. Most of Afghanistan is now under our control, from the east to the south to the west and even north. After our warriors captured Sharif, we control fourth-fifths of the country. Massoud is now holed up in his fortress of the Panjshir Valley. We don't disturb him as long as he doesn't come down to Kabul again. In fact, we let his supply trucks come from Uzbekistan thru the Salang tunnel as long as they don't carry weapons and ammunition. The rest of the Northern Alliance I do not fear. We have the tanks, the planes left us from the Soviets and all the weapons we need. It is only a matter of time that Massoud and the Alliance will join us for the good of Afghanistan. Once we are united, the religious fervor will subside. Afghanistan is, as it always has been, a country that does not bow to any conqueror, not even a religious one. You understand Achmed that what I tell you here are my personal feelings and must not leave this office!"

The commander's eyes were now penetrating and threatening.

With just as serious a demeanor, Anton answered, "Commander Amir Haq Khan, you spoke in confidence to me. I shall not violate your honest opinion. Besides, I do not wish to mix in Afghan politics. I came here because my father was a German SS officer and fought the Soviets as you did. I respect the Muslim religion. I am an Egyptian and though Egypt at this time is American friendly, but we still have the same enemies my father fought against."

"Yes, the Americans and British, the same enemies, you are right. The Germans under Hitler understood who the foe of Germany and the Muslims are. They could have smashed the Soviet colossus had they not had to fight the Americans and British from the other side. I am truly sorry that Germany, the Aryans, lost against the Slavs and Jews and their imperialist supporters."

For Anton, the discussion with the commander became a painful experience. Yet he knew that to have Haq friendly and to see to his, Ali's and Sidqi's safety, he must cater to Haq's expressed beliefs. "You know Commander Haq, you, from Afghanistan and the Pakistani, are the true Aryans. The Aryans originally came from the Indus Region. There was a Muslim division who fought under my father's SS."

The commander seemed pleased, "Then I would have been welcomed by your father's legions. He was a general in the SS?"

"A very high ranking officer in the SS, a close associate of both Hitler and Himmler. He had to flee Germany after the war and became a martyr. He was assassinated in 1978 by his enemies."

"I hope there is a Christian paradise where he has many Christian virgins."

Anton smiled. "Surely, a legend."

Commander Haq laughed, "Yes, you and I know. But don't tell the faithful. Let me warn you, Achmed, there are fanatics here, if they knew of your religion, they would kill you, not openly but in ambush, one dark night with a knife in the back. You are under my protection. If you are threatened, come to me at once."

"I thank you, Commander Haq, and I shall heed your warning. We might have one problem which has nothing to do with my or anyone's religion. Have you met my friend, Sidqi Suliman?"

"The young, handsome jihadist, the beardless one? Yes, I met him." He smiled, remembering.

"I believe the Swede has erotic designs on Sidqi."

"If he does, you must have proof! If you should catch him in a lewd act toward Sidqi, kill him. We have killings sometimes. I call a *jirga*, a council of tribal elders, and we debate the circumstances. If it is of that nature, you are permitted to kill and will be spoken as justified. But beware Achmed, you need a witness who is a Muslim as he must swear by the Beard of the Prophet."

"My word is not good?"

"Not the word of an infidel."

"Well, Sidqi then if he is attacked."

"If he is still alive. It he harms him in lust, he will kill him to leave no witness. And now good night, Achmed. Tomorrow after breakfast, come with the Swede Mohamed to my office."

"One more thing commander, I brought a pistol."

"We normally don't allow anyone to have a weapon on him except knives. Those who bring one, we store them in the armory where we keep all weapons. I will make an exception with you, being a non-Muslim and having concern about Sidqi. Hide it somewhere safe, don't tell anyone."

"Good night, Amir Haq Khan. I am very pleased to be under your command." He left.

It was dark outside but all the houses had lights, and directed by deputy al-Hamza, Anton found house number twelve, at the very eastern end of the camp. From a concrete building nearby came the humming sound of a generator. He entered the small house and found his compatriots sitting around two tables, the room lit by a bare light bulb. Mohamed the Swede, Hassan the German, and the two British Fawzi and Abdullah sat at one table. Ali and Sidqi sat together at the other. Hassan and Mohamed were smoking cigarettes, so Anton filled his pipe and sat with his friends.

Sven called over, "A private audience with the commander, you rate high here, Anton."

"Not any more important than you. And we might as well get used using our proper names to fit in."

"All right, Achmed. You are dangerous to live with being a *Kafir*, an infidel. I hate to get blown up by a bomb."

Anton laughed, "Nobody here knows how to make bombs until I teach them. Besides, the explosives are under lock and key."

Just then the door opened and deputy al-Hamza came in and asked all except for Anton to accompany him to the commander's office.

Anton now had time to look around. There was one window and besides the two tables and eight chairs, their packs and bags were laying around. There was a shelf on which laid a Koran.

He went into the second room, which was their bedroom. The floor was concrete with an old hemp rug in the middle; it was all very primitive. Eight hammocks hung suspended from stout ropes and on each a heavy blanket of wool and a pillow. Another door led into the primitive toilet. A rusted flush toilet of iron, a small metal sink with a cold-water faucet, cut paper hung on a nail and an open shower stall. The opened blankets told him which hammocks were taken. Where to hide his pistol? He had it in a canvas pouch in his belt. With his sewing kit, he fastened the pouch under his hammock, placed the colt into it with the two extra magazines. It was well hidden.

He heard the others return and joined them, but not Ali. Sidqi told him that Ali went to see his friend from Cairo. They had brought a bag of dates, courtesy of the commander. Mohamed explained, "We had to swear that we won't tell anyone that you are not a Muslim, Achmed. Here, have some dates."

"Yes, I know. Thanks for the dates, but I had some before." Anton relit his pipe.

Just then the door opened and a man in camouflage uniform came in followed by Ali. Ali introduced the man as Mohamed Atta. Atta then spoke to them in German, which he spoke fluently with just a slight middle-eastern guttural accent, "Ich kann Deutsch. Ich lebte fuer acht Jahre in Hamburg (I can speak German, I lived for eight years in Hamburg)." Hassan, the German, got up and embraced Atta, as did Anton. Atta was a tall and handsome man, though looking so serious, but then smiled. "My German comrades." He sat at the table with Ali, Sidqi and Anton. He did not smoke but ate dates. Ali explained in English to the others, and then continued their conversation in Arabic, which all of them with the exception of the Swede and the German understood, their knowledge of Arabic was poor.

Ali told, "Mohamed Atta and I were from the same neighborhood in Old Cairo, Mar al-Qadimas, you have been there Achmed. We went to the same primary school until my people moved to al-Ahmar so I could study at the al-Ahzar University."

Atta looked surprised, "You did? Then you became a jihadist because of your studies?"

"I became an imam and teacher at the al-Azhar Mosque, next to the university. I am a member of the Brotherhood as my father is. Sidqi is too."

Atta frowned, "I am glad you came. It is rare for Brotherhood members to come here, I am told. Most of the Egyptians are of the Islamic Jihad. I know about the split, but I don't believe that the Brotherhood will succeed by persuasion to change the alien government, for they are secular and American friendly."

Ali replied, "Don't forget our teaching the young, if by persuasion or by violent means, we all have the same goal. And don't forget that Egypt is a poor country; it doesn't have the oil of the Saudis or United Arab Emirates. We are overpopulated and need help. Better from the Americans than the Soviets or Russia now, the Godless ones. So tell us, Atta, how come you are living and studying in Germany?"

Atta spoke to Ali, "Do you remember my father? He is a lawyer. When we were little, my two sisters and I, he was strict that we learn." Ali said, "Yes, I remember your sisters, they were older."

Atta continued, "They are both successful. One became a physician, the younger one a botanist. I was frustrated in Egypt, first Sadat who made peace with the Zionists. Imagine, an Israeli Embassy in Cairo! Finally, the jihad eliminated that Jew lover. Mubarak is dealing with the Israelis, though he keeps his distance from them, it all disgusted me. I was not doing well in school. My father pestered me to learn and sent me to Germany. Since I learned drafting, I worked in Hamburg as a draftsman and learned German. When I knew the language well enough, I attended the technical university and majored in urban planning. We, my group of four from Hamburg, visited the Sheikh in Kandahar and pledged our martyrdom to his cause. The Sheikh sent us here for combat training and how to use explosives."

Ali asked again, "Living in Hamburg, with western culture, how did you become a jihadist?"

"I had been religious since I was a boy. The social structure in Egypt that left the poor to stagnate; it was injustice. The decadence of western culture I witnessed in Hamburg confirmed my Islamic beliefs. I searched for truth in the Koran. I attended the mosque near where I lived. There I met Ziad, Marwan and Ramzi who thought like I did. We formed a cell to serve our faith and Zammar, a Syrian Jihadist, financed our travels to Arab countries to see and learn. He then sent us to the Sheikh. After Achmed has trained us in explosives, we return to Hamburg, finish our studies and next year we return to the Sheikh to await his instructions." He turned to Anton, "We are to begin with you as our instructor tomorrow."

Anton replied, "Tomorrow I have to go with the commander to inspect the explosives, the day after, we begin."

"Will you be able to teach us everything in a week's time?"

"Not everything, but whatever you need to know. How to put on a belt."

Atta smiled. "Not a belt for us. We have other work in mind."

"Like what?"

"You will find out when we are with you. It must be kept a secret from everyone else."

Atta soon left them and it was time to go to their hammocks. Prayer and sunrise came early. Tired as they were from the long drive, they soon went to sleep in their primitive beds.

Fifth of August—DAY TWO

After morning-prayer, they had breakfast in the dining hall, coffee or tea, a bowl of mush with fruit cooked into it. Afterward they received their uniforms and dressed. Anton went to the commander's office and soon were on their way to the bunker, a good size concrete structure without windows which was near the firing range, a mile away from the camp. He also gave him a large key for it; the lock was old fashioned but strong and secure. He told him "Wear the key on a string around your neck and never take it off. Not even when you sleep." The commander then left him and Anton checked the contents. Most were plastic explosives still in their original packing with Pakistani writing. There were also cases of TNT and some smaller boxes with dynamite, along with containers with black and smokeless powder. None of the material was chemicals of nitrates and chlorates, so at least he would not have to prepare explosives, nor was there any nitroglycerin as he had feared, as it was dangerous stuff to have. Plenty of boxes with detonators of various make, fuses—some in the form of bundles of prima cords, plenty of wiring, and a box with Casio watches. He also found a co le wooden boxes with Chinese writing and when he opened them he found them to contain shaped charges, which must be thrown. He had seen them with the Special Forces in Egypt. They looked like the German potato-masher handgrenade and when thrown, the granade tumbled end over end, a small parachute would pop out at the end to stabilize it and the front part would fly off and expose the shaped charge which, when it hit an armored vehicle, would burn through and kill everyone inside. A wicked weapon but also a suicide weapon as the thrower would have to approach as close as five to ten meters. He saw ready-made explosive belts. On a shelf were a number of manuals for instruction on making bombs, booby traps and the like, all in Arabic.

He browsed though one and quickly found errors in making and connecting fuses. Most of the book was for making explosives from basic materials, which was not needed here with ready made explosives on hand. He soon left, locking the heavy metal door securely.

Nearby was the ammunition and weapons bunker, a similar secure structure that was open now as jihadists were firing on the range with their AK-47s under the instruction of a Taliban soldier. He spotted Ali and Sidqi among them.

Anton returned to camp. An empty, brown and muddy-beige landscape of hills, just here and there a few desert bushes; except near the two al-Badr Camps, which were once villages in an oasis of water wells, orchards and grassland where sheep and goats grazed but did not extend to the range and hills.

Anton checked in headquarters for listings and found his name under the heading of EXPLOSIVE TRAINING and those of the twelve Arabs who had been detailed to him for one week, Atta among them.

When he returned to his house he found Atta waiting. They greeted each other in a friendly manner; Anton lit his pipe and sat with Atta. "You are not an observant Muslim, smoking," Atta remarked. Anton ignored the comment.

"Achmed, what I tell you is a secret and you are not permitted to tell anyone, not even Ali." Anton promised.

"This comes from the Sheikh to whom I and my three jihadists have pledged as martyrs. We will crash small, explosive leaden planes into targets of importance to our common enemies."

"What enemies?" Anton asked.

Atta frowned, "That you must not know. What we need from you is first of all the type of explosive that is best to use and secondly the proper fuse to rig to the plane. Can you teach us?"

"The only explosive that would work is plastic. Will they be available to you?"

"That is not of your concern, Achmed."

"How heavy an explosive load can a small airplane carry?"

"How much do you need to destroy a large building?"

"You need at least five hundred kilogram. A bomb that size dropped from an airplane would destroy a good size house but not a large structure. The plane has to be at least a four-seater for that size of a charge."

"I understand. Can you make a fuse that explodes on impact?"

"A single engine plane is not suitable because of the propeller sticking out you cannot attach a fuse to it. If you put the detonator in the back where you carry the explosive, the detonator might become defective by the crash. You are more certain if you have a two-engine plane and then attach the fuse to the cockpit in front. That is no problem."

"I guess you are right, Achmed. This type of plane could also carry more explosives. Can you make us fuses that would work?"

"Certainly. Can you fly, Mohamed?"

Atta smiled. "That is also not of your concern, Achmed. Just make us a dozen fuses and demonstrate their effectiveness."

"First thing tomorrow morning I will work on them. I saw enough material here." Atta then left.

That night, when they had retired, Anton lay awake for a long time thinking how he could make these fuses and not have them work properly. He would have to show them that the fuse worked and that all of them were alike. Yet they must not detonate.

He remembered a book he read about American submarine warfare in the Pacific. How during the first war years, the subs had many failures with torpedoes not exploding. The ordinance department insisted that the torpedoes were effective and some exploded properly. He didn't remember the sub commander's name, but after many failures, he found the fault. This commander had realized that with a straight shot at a ship, the torpedoes did not explode, even at a short distance. He found that when a torpedo hit the plate straight on, the force of the impact bent the firing pin before it could fire the detonator. The solution was simple enough, which was to attach a stronger firing pin. If he could make a fuse with a weak pin, it would bend or break before it detonated the charge.

He wished he knew what target they were thinking of . . . in what country? Small airplanes were available in many countries. The availability of explosives was another matter. Flying a small airplane, even a two-motor plane was easily enough to learn.

But he also realized that apparently, Atta was to be one of the suicide pilots and as far as he knew he had no flying experience. There was time, but it certainly was something they were planning. The most likely target was Israel. He had to warn the Mossad when he got back.

Sixth of Augus—DAY THREE

After prayer and breakfast, Anton cancelled the morning session of his group and told Commander Haq, that he had to work on something for Mohamed Atta.

The commander understood as the Sheikh had informed him by messenger that Atta had special requirements and was to be given every accommodation to complete his training in explosives.

Anton went to the bunker and knew what he wanted. The Chinese shaped charges that needed to be thrown by hand had very delicate fuses. He extracted a number and climbed upon the concrete structure, dropped one and it exploded nicely. He took several back to camp and to the machine shop, which really was an auto repair shop from which the cars, vans and pickups were serviced. From several fuses, he separated the detonators.

He put one fuse into a vise and gave it a good bang with a hammer. When he checked it, he found that the pin had penetrated and would have exploded the detonator.

How fast would a plane go in a dive to a target? It could not go straight down as the dynamics of a small plane could not take it, it would disintegrate. It could only dive at an angle; small planes like Piper Cubs were not fighters. He estimated 180 km/hr, a two-engine plane perhaps up to 250 km/hr. He put another fuse in the vise and smashed down with a larger hammer, this could be the force of crashing at 150 km/hr.

He found that the firing pin had broken off. He tried a third fuse and hit it with a sledge—hammer at full force. The firing pin was demolished and never penetrated to the detonator. This type of fuse would never work in a plane that crashed itself.

After midday meal, he took Atta to the bunker and this time, his three conspirators were with him to watch. Anton climbed to the top of the bunker and with the four standing nearby he dropped several fuses and they all exploded nicely. Atta was satisfied. He helped him during the afternoon to prepare a total of twelve fuses, which Anton then packed firmly into a wooden box with plenty of straw.

Sevent of August—DAY FOUR

When Anton wanted to gather his twelve jihadists in the morning, he found that there were only eight. Atta and his three compatriots had left with their van to return to Kandahar. The box with the useless fuses was with them.

He gathered his eight men in the dining hall; they were all Arabs from different countries in the Middle East. The eight, like most of the other Arabs he had met, had sullen faces, and were unfriendly. Mohamed Atta had been an exception. Atta was like a civilized man, though serious and determined as a jihadist, a man obsessed!

Anton had worked out his lesson plan. He wanted to teach the mujahiden as little as possible about bomb making during the week he was their teacher. Therefore, he began with a basic background of the chemistry involved, something they had no need for, as they were not expected to make the explosive material but learn how to use it. He had writing material which he distributed and told the men to take notes.

"Before you use explosives, you must have a basic understanding of the how and why material can be made to explode. Anytime you have a question, please interrupt me and I shall explain. I want you to understand that when you work with explosives you are handling dangerous stuff, so be careful, pay attention or else you will get hurt if you are lucky, otherwise killed before you put your knowledge into practice. This will be especially true when you attach the detonating device to the material. If it is just a prima cord which you light, you are fairly safe, regardless if you wish to get away or become a martyr. If you made the proper connection to the initiator, a prima cord it is almost guaranteed to work."

Somebody asked, "What is a prima cord?"

"It is a detonator cord, a cord impregnated with combustible or burning material. There are different cords, some burn fast, some slower, some even under water."

Anton then began his basic course in chemistry by telling the men that all explosives contain just a few basic chemicals in various combinations."

Another jihadist asked "What is black powder?"

"We have plenty on hand and it is used in pipe bombs. I will teach you how to make pipe bombs or similar contraptions which are very useful in car bombing, or sending someone a gift package. It is even used in letter bombs and you can add enough material in the letter to kill, but it takes a delicate detonating device."

Anton then told of the history of black powder, invented a couple thousand years ago by the Chinese and used primarily for fireworks.

"Black powder was really the first material used to cause instant explosion. In medieval times, it was brought by our Arab brothers to Europe who used it in cannons as the explosive charge to propel the stone or iron cannonball at walls of fortifications. Then it was used in a metal tube to propel a small ball to kill, and the musket was invented.

Black powder is an effective explosive material and if no other is available to you, it can be bought in any sporting store or from a gun club."

Another question was asked, "You need a license of sorts to buy black powder?"

"In most countries, no. If you cannot buy black powder, you can always buy the ingredients freely. They consist of basic chemicals, such as sulfur, charcoal, ascorbic acid, sodium benzoate, starches and sugars. For oxidizers, you can use potassium nitrate also known as saltpeter, sodium nitrate, and if you can get it, potassium perchlorate. I will distribute flyers in which these ingredients are listed and the manner they have to be combined to make the black powder. If you can buy black powder it comes in little chunks or granolas.

The other basic explosive you may use in pipe bombs, packages etc, is the smokeless powder. It is not really smokeless but less so than black powder. You can ignite both types of powders with a flame or heat, or spark of an electric wire."

Anton then went into the construction of a pipe bomb, that it requires a robust container, preferably, of metal to contain the charge for as long as possible. "The rest of the pipe is filled with fragmentation objects, such things as ball bearings, nails, nuts, bolts and even marbles. An initiating system could be a burning cord, or a spark from a power source like a battery. More elaborate systems may be designed such as a complex timing apparatus or a triggering device that operates remotely. Then you have an effective and deadly pipe bomb. For cars the triggering device can be attached to the ignition system."

By then, and with his students writing things down diligently, it was time for noon—prayer and since they were next to the mosque, when the call for prayer was announced, they went into the mosque and after prayer to the dining hall.

Anton was just about to depart with his eight men for the range when Commander Haq came in with important news. Others had been called in and the dining hall was full again.

Haq raised both arms and all fell silent, "Alluhah Akbar—God is Great, I just heard over Al-Jazeera radio station that two American embassies have been bombed. The first around 10:30 this morning; that is 12:30 our time. The American embassy in Nairobi in Kenya was destroyed by a truck bomb driven by two martyrs. Hundreds of Americans were killed. Nine minutes later martyrs drove a truck into the American embassy in Dar es Salaam, Tanzania. Again many of the American infidels were killed and wounded. These are the most punishing attacks against the Americans since our Shiite brothers of the Hezbollah bombed the Marine barracks in Lebanon. Let Allah's Grace shine upon our *amir-ul mominin* bin Laden (commander of the faithful) for slaying the enemy."

There was pandemonium in the dining hall with many cries of "Alluha Akbar and Allah-o-Akbar" and other words of devotion to Allah, until the commander raised his hands again for silence.

He told the jihadists to continue their work of learning to become warriors for the true faith and honor the martyrs during their afternoon prayers.

The muj all cleared out and Anton walked his eight students to the range and magazine, distaining the pickup available to him, to demonstrate the effect of black and smokeless powder.

He spent the afternoon with his students packing pipe bombs, later crates with powder, using generous portions of powder and prima cord to, if possible, deplete what was stored and letting them explode the bombs. For targets, he used ruins of houses, or wrecked cars, armored cars and old tanks that were on the range.

After evening-prayer and dinner, all muj were again called into the dining room and Commander Haq had his radio on to tell about scenes of utter destruction by Al-Jazeeraa. The casualties were said to be in the thousands in Nairobi.

His deputy then came in with an e-mail from the Emir, which told that most likely they can expect a response by the Americans in the form of bomber attacks or missiles. However, as the message read, the Americans are slow to respond and any retaliation by them was at least one week away. That is after the fourteenth of August, or any time thereafter, some of the camps might be bombarded and the Emir advises that after the fourteenth, they should beware and if they wish to sleep away from camps they can do so. Most likely such attacks would come at night. At this time there are no bases near Afghanistan where planes can fly from nor are missile ships in the Arabian Sea or Indian Ocean. Training must continue without interruption.

Eight of August—DAY FIVE

Again Anton had his muj assemble in the dining hall for more lectures on the chemistry of explosives.

"Yesterday we talked about the simplest explosive you can use, black and smokeless powders. You learned to make pipe bombs, and larger detonations for destroying cars and small structures. You saw how effective these powders are, simple to set off with a prima cord. For the more elaborate detonation devices you have to use available apparatus like timing, or remote control. You will learn how to use these devices later. To make them is a complicated affair and you will be shown how to construct them at the end of our lesson when we use more modern explosives. Black powder was replaced in the past century by nitroglycerin which comes in liquid form. It was mainly used in mining, and by railroads to clear a path through mountainous terrain.

It was the Swede Alfred Nobel who invented dynamite by dissolving the sensitive nitroglycerin in absorbent material like sawdust. Dynamite was more stable and safer to handle."

Someone asked, "Is this the Nobel the awards are made for each year?"

"Yes. In Norway and Sweden."

Someone shouted, "Arabs were never awarded the Nobel prize."

"Well, Arafat received the Nobel prize."

Another shouted, "Arafat is a traitor. He made peace with the Jews."

"Well, this is not true. He never made peace with the Israelis.

"You should never call them Israelis, they are Zionists who occupy the land of Palestine and kill our brothers and sisters and their children!"

Anton understood that he had to be careful with these religious fanatics. "It is true, they are killers and occupiers, but nevertheless they are there now and made it into their country. Remember the saying, the Right of the Stronger."

"Teach us how to use explosives and we blow them all into the sea!"

"Another explosive invented later was TNT and PENT. But we are mainly concerned with the modern explosives freely available to us from our Pakistani brothers, the plastic RDX. These we call HE, or high explosive material. RDX is fairly insensitive to friction and minor impact and very stable in storage. Small amounts of RDX are also used in detonators and blasting caps. But we can also use inorganic substances for detonators, mercury fulminate and better yet, lead azide, which is also very sensitive stuff and it works well."

Anton wondered if they understood what he was teaching them . . .

A question was asked, "What did that American hero use to blow up that building in Oklahoma City? I read that he used just fertilizer?"

"This was in 1995, and his name was McVeigh and he was no hero. He blew up a kindergarten of little children too."

"He killed infidels!"

"He will always be remembered as a child murderer. There is nothing in the Koran that tells us to murder children. This is not Islamic."

"The new fatwa permits us to kill civilians of the enemy."

"But it does not say children."

"They will become adults, enemies of the faith, so why not kill them now?"

"If your faith in Allah and the Prophet tells you to kill children, do so. But I don't think this is what the sheikh has in mind. You will find out later if you can sit with Allah in paradise or be forever dead. But to come back to what McVeigh used in his truck bomb. Yes, he had tons of commercial fertilizer, which is mainly ammonium nitrate. It is not a good explosive and he needed large amounts. However, fertilizer alone will not give a big bang, he had to add fuel. In this combination, ammonium nitrate becomes a devastating explosive. All in large quantities and it takes a big detonator to set the mixture off. He used a timing device as he was not a martyr, but it was very effective."

"Why did this American do it? He was not a Muslim?"

"He had a grudge against the FBI because of their involvement in the attack of the Davidian compound. There was an FBI office in the federal building, so he blew it all up."

"Who were the Davidians?"

"Some religious cult, not Muslims."

"They were all Americans. He did the work for us."

Some more shouted, "We should blow up the White House!"

"All synagogues and churches!"

There was laughing.

Anton thought, *Fanatics, what can you do with them except put a bullet in their heads.*

He continued lecturing on the use and effect of plastic explosives, explaining to them the basics of the chemicals that are used; that they come in various forms of pressings and castings. "We are mainly interested in putties which can be shaped like modeling clay and retain this shape.

A similar material we have here is rubberized RDX and it comes in sheets and can be cut in any desired size and glued to whatever. We have some of these sheets that come from the American Du Pont Company and supplied to the Pakistani military. Its name is "Deta Flex" and it is 6 mm thick, which is very useful for our purpose.

Dynamites are mainly nitroglycerin in mixture with a moderator to handle them more easily." *Was he repeating himself?* They didn't seem to notice

"Plastic explosives make good truck bombs?"

"Yes, they make a big bang."

"In American movies, I see that they use sticks of explosives with a burning cord?"

"In cowboy movies? These are sticks of dynamite and set off with a prima cord, a burning fuse. Dynamite, if you remember, is mainly nitroglycerin and can be set off with a hot flame."

"You have all taken your notes. This afternoon we will go on the range to use plastic explosives, both in putty form and sheets. I had laborers set up thick wooden poles which you might find supporting bridges. Wrap plastic sheets around and blow them up. Tomorrow morning in class I will teach you about the initiation of explosives, types of detonation devices and how they work."

After the noon-prayer and lunch, Anton took his group out to the range and exploded a lot of material that was on hand. However, the deputy al-Hamza came to inventory and new material was sent from Peshawar. Inexhaustible supplies. Along with the explosives sent, came new boxes of ammunition for the Kalashnikovs, machine guns, rocket propelled grenade launchers, mortars and whatever else the muj used.

In the evening during the meal, Anton sat together with Ali and Sidqi and they told about the firing on the range at paper targets, the use of rifle grenades, and during the cooler mornings they had combat training. Sidqi liked the firing and according to Ali was good at it, hitting the bullseye even firing automatic. He said he was bushed from the combat training and would lie down.

After evening meal, the commander drove Anton out to the T-55 tank on the range and had him examine the cannon, which had been damaged. He told the commander that the mechanism to close the breech was damaged and could not be repaired. Haq then drove to Camp 2 where another tank was, that could not be driven anymore. From it Anton removed the breech mechanism and promised the commander he would repair their T-55. Since it was dark by then, he would repair the tank the next afternoon.

When he returned, the room was empty. Anton lit his pipe, there was nothing to read except for the Koran. He prepared notes for tomorrow, more talk to keep them from the range and learning. A short while after, Ali came in. He was alone; he looked at the bed, "Where is Sidqi?"

"Wasn't he with you Ali?"

"No. He lay down and was asleep when I left for the mosque." Ali looked around, "No British, no Mohamed and Hassan."

"And no Sidqi!" Said Anton.

"The Swede got Sidqi!" Ali cried out.

Anton got his Colt from under the hammock and his flashlight, "I think I know where they are," and ran out followed by Ali. Anton went to the supply house where he knew Mohamed had a key since his supplies were kept there. The door was locked, but a soft light came from the small, high window. Anton had Ali climb on his shoulders.

"Achmed! THEY ARE DOING IT TO HIM AND I THINK SIDQI IS DEAD!"

Anton ran to the door, fired at the lock and burst the door open . . . in the candle light he saw Sidqi stripped, laying over a sawhorse, his upper body hanging down . . . Hassan was crouching before him and holding his arms down . . . the Swede with his pants pulled down was sodomizing Sidqi who appeared lifeless, blood running down his face. Anton ran to the Swede who apparently was in the throes of discharging, mindless of him.

Anton raised his pistol to his head and pulled the trigger . . . the Swede fell off Sidqi.

Hassan looked up, his face distorted with fear as Anton held the pistol to his head. He yelled in German, "Bitte nicht schiessen, ich bin unschuldig (Please don't shoot, I am not guilty)." Anton was still in rage and kicked Hassan in the face. Lying on the floor, Hassan still pleaded for his life. Anton's rage began to subside, but he still held the pistol pointed at Hassan. Ali was examining Sidqi's lifeless figure, his head, which was bleeding from the back, on the floor a hatchet which apparently was used on Sidqi. At last, Ali looked up at Anton, joy in his eyes. "He is alive, Achmed."

Anton snarled at Hassan, "You testify to what happened and you better tell the truth!" He wrapped Sidqi into a blanket and carried him to the infirmary which was behind the HQs. Men had come when they heard the shots, among them Haq. Ali explained what happened. Haq had someone call Ismael, the medic; then unlocked the door. Anton placed Sidqi on the table and Ismael came and examined the head wound. He cut some of the hair off, separated the deep wound, blood still running out. "I don't think the skull is split open," and applied a pressure bandage, wiped the blood off Sidqi's face.

The commander told his deputy to examine Mohamed, and then have his body buried at once. "Since he is a Muslim, you say the prayer for the death over his grave. Lock up Hassan, he was a participant and safeguard the hatchet. I will take Sidqi to the hospital in Khost."

He soon came back in his pickup. Anton carried the still unconscious Sidqi to the pickup, sat in the middle and held him in his arms; Ali to his right. Haq raced over the dirt road and soon they were in Khost and the hospital. Sidqi was at once taken to surgery.

The commander slapped Anton on the shoulder, "Don't worry my brother, your friend will live. I call the *jirga* tomorrow and we will hold a trial. You have Ali as your witness and the German. Good that you didn't kill him even if he deserved it. Two witnesses and all will be well. And Hassan better tell the truth or I will kill him." The commander soon left to see to order in the camp.

They waited for word from the surgeon. Ali was distraught; he had promised the parents of Sidqi to watch over him and now this. Anton consoled his friend that Sidqi was alive and would survive.

When the surgeon came, he told them that Sidqi would be all right. The skull had not been fractured but he had a severe concussion. The wound was stitched up and Sidqi would have to remain in the hospital for a few weeks. He had lost a lot of blood and was given a blood transfusion. Ali and Anton promised to come back the next day, then returned to camp. They woke the two British Fawzi and Adbullah and asked where they had been when Sidqi was taken by Mohamed. They said that Mohamed had told them the deputy al-Hamza wanted to see them. When they found al-Hamza he knew nothing about it and when they returned the house was empty.

Ninth of August—DAY SIX

Before Anton and Ali left for Khost they saw Haq. The commander said that he would cancel the morning session for Achmed and would distribute flyers to the muj so they can study more about pipe bombs. He would call the *jirga* for the afternoon and Ali must be present. Hassan was locked up and would have to testify.

Haq gave Anton permission to use a Toyota Land Cruiser and to get the key from the deputy who was in charge of all trucks and cars. "You should consider it your car while here in camp, Achmed. Your men complain that they have to walk so far to the range. Pack them into the Toyota, you are wasting time by making them walk."

"I am sorry that I killed your sewage engineer," Anton apologized. The commander laughed, "We have been without proper sewage and water for so long, the muj are used to use our common latrines and wash rooms. I shall ask for a new engineer. Go in peace my friends, give Allah's blessings to your comrade."

The Toyota was an old beaten up vehicle but ran well. Soon, Anton and Ali were in Khost and at the hospital. They found Sidqi in brown pajamas in a room with many other patients, a heavy bandage around his head. He smiled at them and stretched out his hands to greet his friends. His face was so white; then a light blush appeared when he said, "I feel so ashamed of what Mohamed has done to me."

"Don't call him Mohamed, call him monster, that is what he was. I have met his kind before and they all deserve to be killed like mad dogs," Anton said.

Ali asked Sidqi, "How do you feel, my friend?"

Sidqi smiled. "I have a terrible headache and sore in my rear." They laughed. Sidqi then told how it happened. "Mohamed and Hassan had come in, asking where Achmed and Ali were. When I told them, Mohamed said to the British that the deputy wished to see them and they left. I was sitting at the table reading the Koran. Mohamed then told me that Ali was in the shed and hurt himself. I ran with the two to the shed. I didn't see Ali and then I was hit from behind and I knew nothing until I woke up in the hospital with this bandage around my head. Only this morning did the doctor tell me that I had been raped."

Sidqi then asked, "What happened to the Swede?"

Ali told him that Achmed killed him.

"You must flee Achmed. You killed a muj."

Anton replied, "It was justified. This afternoon the commander will call a *jirga* and Haq said that in this case, killing the rapist is justified. Don't worry Sidqi, everything will be all right, you get well and we will return to Egypt. You have to stay at the hospital for a couple of weeks."

Sidqi said, "I want to finish my training first."

"You learned how to shoot. And you did well. The rest we learn here is not important," Ali said.

But Sidqi pressed on, "I must learn how to defend myself, not just with a rifle."

Anton assured him, "When we get back to Egypt, I will teach you judo."

They don't even have a nurse here, all men," Sidqi said.

Ali answered him, "Taliban."

A medical attendant in a white gown came in and told them that they should leave and when they saw that Sidqi was drifting into sleep they left and returned to camp. Anton drove to the range and let Ali join his troop.

Since there was still time he replaced the breech assembly of the tank cannon. He got one round for the 100 mm gun and fired the shot at a nearby hill. It worked.

After lunch, he took his troop out to the range in his cruiser. Then he drove the tank to the ammunition magazine and had the muj hand him the shells to fill up the tank. With his eight men sitting on the tank, he drove the T-55 closer to the ruins and wrecks. They were cheered by the other men on the range as they drove by them.

Anton detailed one man as the loader and first fired several rounds to show them how accurate the cannon was blowing up wrecks. Then he took one man at a time into the tank, taught him how to aim and fire the cannon, he doing the loading. This is how he spent, or rather wasted, the afternoon instead of teaching them bomb making. No one complained as they all had a great time shooting at the wrecks, interrupted only by prayer and a rest period when the water carrier came by with large plastic containers of water and metal cups. In August, it was very hot but the nights were refreshingly cool.

Anton drove them back to camp for supper and evening prayer. In the house, he met Ali who told him about the proceedings of the *jirga*. "Haq conducted the proceeding as accuser. He told them of who was involved in the killing. Mohamed from Sweden and Hassan, a German, both Muslims. Sidqi from Egypt and a member of the Moslem Brotherhood. I was a witness. And you, Achmed who killed Mohamed, the rapist. Haq explained what and how it had happened. He showed the jirga the hatchet. He further explained that Mohamed and Hassan then stripped Sidqi who was unconscious and believed to be dead and then Mohamed raped Sidqi. You and I entered the shed and witnessed the abomination of rape and you shot Mohamed in the head and killed him. The commander then explained that you are Egyptian, that you are here to teach bomb making to the jihadists at the invitation of the Emir himself and therefore under his protection. I then gave witness, swearing by the Beard of the Prophet that it all was true.

Next Hassan was called and Fawzi, the British interpreted from Hassan's English into Arabic and Haq into Pashto.

When asked why he helped Mohamed to commit the dastardly deed, Hassan confessed that he did it under duress as Mohamed threatened to kill him if he did not comply. Commander Haq then reported that Mohamed had received a proper burial and the sura for the dead was read.

The eldest of the *jirga*, who was also a mullah, then read from the Koran the scriptures forbidding rape, the sura forbidding homosexuality, and the laws against befouling the body as both believed Sidqi to be dead. Their judgment was that the killing had been justified and Achmed Nabil declared free of any crime against a Muslim. Since Mohamed had received a proper burial under Muslim law, he had been dealt with according to the customs for the dead. Hassan was found guilty as being an accomplice and the *jirga* decreed his immediate expulsion from

Afghanistan. The commander ordered Hassan to be kept locked up until supplies came from Peshawar and he could be taken to Pakistan.

"That was it, Achmed. You not being of the Faith was never mentioned or discussed."

There were now four hammocks unused in house 12 and the deputy assigned the three Egyptian Jihad members to join Achmed and Ali. Husayn Sabre, Abd al-Hamed and Zahi Abu Shanab brought their things. Husayin Sabre, their leader, told Ali and Anton that if they had lived with them, the deed would not have happened. "Remember Achmed, we were told to protect you. This also includes Ali and Sidqi. From now on, I will join your class."

When they drove to Khost after the evening meal, Husayn joined them. Sidqi was doing better, though still very weak and unable to walk yet, but he was cheerful. The food was not very good in the hospital but there was plenty of fresh fruit, which he liked.

Ten of August—DAY SEVEN

When they had assembled in the dining room and some writing material was given out, Anton briefly summarized the types of explosives used for the benefit of Husayin, explaining in more detail the use of plastic explosives, repeating what he had already taught.

A question was asked, "How modern are plastic explosives, when were they invented?"

Anton was happy to explain.

"In the 1960s by Czechoslovakia, now the Czech Republic. Invented in 1966 by Stanislav Brebera, a chemist. They were first manufactured by the Semtin factory; therefore, they called the explosive Semtex. Pakistan can still get it freely from them for military application and we have it here. It became at once a favorite of our brothers as it was difficult to detect, easily obtained and as little as 250 grams could down an airliner.

However, the new Semtex has an additive, a detection taggant which produces a distinctive odor and can be smelled by dogs. We cannot get it through airports where they have dogs sniffing the baggage. The explosive constituent of Semtex is RDX."

"What is RDX?"

"A complicated chemical formula, which we cannot make."

"Please tell us the chemical and spell it?"

"It is: c-y-c-l-o-n-i-t-e or c-y-c-l-o-t-r-i-m-e-t-h-y-l-e-n-e t-r-i-n-i-t-r-a-m-i-n-e. Our modern plastic explosives contain 91% of RDX, that makes it very powerful. The rest is binder, plasticizer and now a marker or taggant chemical to help detect the explosive and identify its source."

"How far away can you be without getting hurt?"

"It depends on how much is used. You might see in Hollywood movies how bombers seem to run away from such an explosion. If you know that the explosion expands at a velocity of 1,000 meter per second you realize that unless you use a timing device you become a martyr."

"How does an explosive belt work?"

"Very simple. You push a button and you go to paradise." There was laughing.

After lunch, Anton took them out to the range in his cruiser. They pleaded with him to let them shoot the tank cannon again; besides, Husayin wanted to learn. Anton gladly let them shoot off the cannon and also taught them how to drive the tank—another afternoon wasted.

In the evening, Anton with Ali and Husayn visited Sidqi. First they went to a food market and bought for him edibles. Sidqi was still confined to bed and looked haggard, and pale.

Eleventh of August—DAY EIGHT

After their early morning visit to Sidqi, Anton had his class again assembled in the dining hall for a lecture on detonators, time fuses and remote control. He first distributed mimeographed copies from the Arab textbooks so they could follow his explanations. These included the faulty descriptions on how to connect detonaters to the explosive charge and completely missed to mention the induction of static electricity. It was technical instructions he gave, which he was certain they didn't understand.

In the afternoon, at the range, they preferred to drive the tank around and shoot the cannon at distant targets until all the anti-tank, HE, and shrapnel ammunition was used up. Then Anton let them throw the Chinese shaped grenades at wrecks and they could witness the force of a hot jet burning through steel.

Twelfth through Fourteenth of August—DAY NINE TO ELEVEN

The fourteenth of August was the day the eight jihadists ended their instructions in bomb making.

Anton commended them on their skill and daring—though he knew that they had learned little about bomb making. He had made all of the connections to fuses, timers and remote controls and then had let them explode the charges. As far as they understood, they had become explosive experts. He doubted that any of them could even make a decent pipe bomb. He was satisfied with their progress and so were the men and the commander.

He had learned from Haq that the two explosive experts and their crews had returned from Africa and were in Kandahar with the Sheikh. There was no date of when they would return to the camps. Anton hoped soon so he, Ali and Sidqi could return to Egypt.

That evening after prayer and supper, the commander called everyone in and told them that as of this night, they could expect at any time American bombers and missiles and they can take tents and sleep with the Taliban in their village. Nothing else would change, training during the day would continue, and during the day all facilities were open including his office.

After Ali, Anton and Husayn returned from the hospital they found Haq in their house. He chose it for sleeping since his room was at headquarters. There was an extra hammock in house 12 and he had brought his warm sleeping bag. The house was located at the extreme end of the camp. None of the jihadists chose to sleep in a tent that night.

Haq had brought his AK-47 along and a pistol in his belt, a basket of fresh fruit, a bag of dates, and small cakes, which were a welcome addition to their frugal meals. He told them, as they sat around the two tables from which they made a large one, that another e-mail had come from Kandahar telling of a number of warships seen in the Arabian Sea.

"American?" Husayn asked.

"Who else would have ships there now?" Haq laughed. "There are also reports that B-52 bombers had been spotted at Diego Garcia Island. I must insist that those who live in houses near the center of the camp move into tents. Tomorrow morning, all will help to erect tents, large ones for my headquarters, the mosque, the messhall and infirmary."

Ali asked, "Commander, do you really believe they will come?"

Haq shrugged his shoulders, "Allah knows, I don't. In Kandahar, they believe the Americans will come, and they will come by night. I don't know how they can find us, even with their cruise missiles. I understand, they have cameras on board to see and find their way, so?"

Anton smiled to himself. The commander had never heard of infrared devices and radar bombing. Soon they sought out their hammocks. First prayer came before sunrise.

Fifteenth of August—DAY TWELVE

After breakfast, deputy al-Hamza formed work details to erect the tents, both for the men and larger ones for facilities. Ali and Anton worked with the two British and the jihadists. When Anton walked back to camp to get some more pegs, he walked by a group of Yemenis. They stopped working and looked at Anton in an unfriendly manner. One hissed *kafr* (infidel), and his dark eyes were like two daggers staring dangerously at him. His being a non-Muslim was no longer a secret. Anton guessed that it was Hassan who had broken his pledge of silence.

That evening, after they had come back from visiting Sidqi, and they were sitting together, Anton told the commander about the incident. Haq looked worried. He asked the British if they had told. They said no. Then Husayn spoke up that it was now common knowledge that Achmed was a non-Muslim. "I heard that Hassan told the guards."

Haq asked, "Aren't you three jihadists pledged to protect Achmed?"

Husayn answered, "Yes, though we did not know that he was not a Muslim."

Haq continued, "You will still protect Achmed?"

Husayn said, "Yes. We talked about it and since we gave this pledge to our leader of the Egyptian Islamic Jihad, we will still honor it. We also understand the importance of Achmed being here. We will protect Achmed with our lives."

The commander smiled at Anton. "You see how important you are to us? However, be careful. The six Yemenites are fanatics, especially their leader Saleh al-Moqrin. He has a vicious temper." He turned to Husayn, "I will issue you a Kalashnikov, carry it with you at all times. My deputy, Omar and I are always armed. So together with you, and you being always close to Achmed, we should be able to safeguard him. I will put all your names on this week's explosive training. The Yemenis I will post for the last week. We'll see what happens three months from now." Anton knew he would not be here for three months.

Sixteenth through Twentieth of August—DAYS THIRTEEN TO
SEVENTEEN

Anton taught the new group of twelve jihadists in the same way. In the morning, classroom instructions and in the afternoon they were on the range. He was able to get new ammunition for the T-55, and they had fun driving the tank around and shooting with the cannon. Otherwise, he wasted precious time teaching them the construction of pipe bombs which were the least dangerous bombs in a terrorist's hands. And when he taught them the more potent explosives of plastic bomb making he showed them, but did not let them do the connections of fuses, timers and remote controls. Then he let them set the charges off. They were satisfied learning to explode charges.

Ali, who was now in his group, took him for a walk later. "Achmed, you are not teaching them, you are showing them."

Anton chuckled, "You have noticed? Ali, you a nonviolent person? Do you really wish for me to teach these fanatics how to blow up innocents?"

"No, I do not."

Anton was glad that even if Ali noticed he understood why he showed and did not teach.

Twice a day, early in the morning and in the evening, Ali, Anton and Husayn, who now always carried his AK-47 with him, went to see Sidqi in the hospital. Sidqi was making good progress; he not only walked without getting dizzy spells but even did some jogging and exercises to get his strength back. Ali had brought him his loose fitting uniform; as small as he was, even the smallest size uniform hung loosely on him. His head wound was healing nicely but it was still bandaged. The doctor thought that in another week he could leave the hospital, though he was still worried about the effects of his concussion.

It had been now over two weeks after the embassy bombings occurred and there was no sign of any retaliation by the Americans. Some of the warriors had returned to their houses, which were farther from the center, including the Yemenis. The commander said he too would return to his room at headquarters.

The commander told them that there were rumors that not only the Yemenis but others looked upon Achmed as a cursed infidel and he suggested that even Achmed should carry his pistol at all times in a holster under his jacket. Anton said he would do so the next day.

It was around ten o'clock at night; Anton, Ali, the British and the three jihadists were already in their hammocks. Only the commander was still out there, as usual, making the rounds with his deputy to check on the guards. Anton was still awake and thinking of his Hanna—he sent her letters from Khost but received none in return and did not know if his letters arrived.

He then heard a strange sound he could not identify, he thought it sounded like an express train rushing . . . followed a moment later by extremely loud and near explosions . . . the walls shook, the earth trembled . . . the window exploded, the blanket covering it saving them from the shards of glass. In quick succession, more explosions followed, debris hit the house—they all had thrown themselves on the floor, and then it was still.

Since they slept in their uniforms, all they needed was to put on their boots.

Anton turned on his flashlight and followed by the others rushed out. It was utter destruction, especially in the center of the camp. The mosques, HQs, dining hall, in fact every structure around the square was totally demolished. Fires were everywhere.

They saw a pickup approach. It was the commander and deputy. "The Americans have arrived," Haq said. "These must be their missiles as we heard no motors of planes; at least six of them hit us. I heard many hit the other camp and more distant explosions."

The deputy voiced, "Allah be Praised that you told the men to sleep in tents away from the camp."

"The Yemenis moved back in!" Followed by the others and shining their flashlights around at the destruction, the commander and deputy went to the house of the Yemenis. It had not taken a direct hit but it was half blown in. They heard voices from the crumbled house and dug out three men, all of them wounded and bleeding. The other three were dead. The two brothers, Saleh and Talib al-Moqrin, were mainly injured by glass shards as they had not affixed the blanket to the window. They found a third Yemeni, Wasfi al-Jundi, lying by the back wall and unconscious. He had been blown from his hammock. They carried him to the pickup, wrapped him in a blanket and lay him in the back. With Saleh and Talib sitting in front, the deputy drove them to the hospital in Khost.

Others had arrived from the tents. All damaged houses and ruins were searched, but they found no one else.

Casualties in Camp 2 were also light. Several Afghans and Pakistanis were killed, some wounded. Also, almost all of his vehicles were undamaged as they had them parked away from the camps. Like in Camp 1, the missiles hit the center and utterly destroyed every structure.

Anton and the others returned to their house and cleaned up. Then affixed a blanket to the window to keep the wind out. The generator was not damaged and they had light. There was no thought of sleeping, and when the sun finally rose and the call for prayer came, they knelt on their prayer rugs, intoned the customary prayers and thanked Allah for being saved.

Twenty-first of August—DAY EIGHTEEN

The commander and deputy had work details erect the large tents in the middle of the square. One for their their new dining hall; one would be the mosque, and one the headquarters. Other details searched through the destroyed structures to save anything salvageable for a kitchen like tables, chairs and any unspoiled food. Others were salvaging items from the workshops or houses. He dispatched pickups to Khost to bring in fresh food and medical material; one tent would become the new infirmary. Many of the Taliban laborers were at work clearing the rubble, to build new houses. The few houses at the fringe, and relatively undamaged ones, were re-occupied by their owners. No one believed that there would be a second strike. The three Yemenis were buried with customary rites.

By evening, things had gotten back to almost normal, the mosque-tent was ready for prayer, the dining hall-tent was used, though the food they had were cold dishes. Tomorrow, hot food would be cooked in the Taliban camp and brought to them. New cooking equipment was bought in Khost and was to be delivered in the next few days.

Ali, Anton and Husayn drove to the hospital in the evening and Sidqi, worried about his friends, was joyful to see them unharmed.

Sidqi asked if they saw the "BAN" posted in the waiting room. "With the many injured coming from the camps, they want to impress the jihadists with their devotion to *sharia*."

"Who are they?" asked Ali.

Sidqi smiled. "The Taliban, of course. Taliban laws, not *Sharia*, though they claim it is."

When they left they saw the bans printed large on many sheets and posted on the wall of the waiting room. Written in Pashto, Urdu and Arabic. They read:

1. UNDER THE LAW OF SHARIA, THIS BEING A HOSPITAL FOR MEN, WOMEN ARE FORBIDDEN TO ENTER.
2. BAN ON WOMAN BEING TREATED BY MALE DOCTORS.
3. WOMAN DOCTORS AND NURSES ARE PERMITTED IN HOSPITALS IN KABUL TO TREAT ONLY WOMEN.
4. SICK WOMEN MAY TRAVEL BY BUS TO KABUL IN BUSSES DESIGNATED FOR WOMEN ONLY.
5. BAN ON WOMEN WORKING OUTSIDE THE HOME.
6. BAN ON WOMEN DEALING WITH MALE SHOPKEEPERS.
7. BAN ON WOMEN STUDYING IN SCHOOLS AND UNIVERSITIES.
8. REQUIREMENT FOR WOMEN TO WEAR THE *BURQA*.
9. WOMEN WILL BE PUBLICY WHIPPED FOR HAVING NONCOVERED ANKLES.
10. PUBLIC STONING OF WOMEN ACCUSED OF EXTRAMARITAL AFFAIRS.
11. BAN ON WOMEN USING COSMETICS. PUNISHMENT IS CUTTING OFF FINGERS.
12. BAN ON WOMEN SHAKING HANDS WITH NON-*MAHRANM* MALES.
13. BAN ON WOMEN LAUGHING LOUDLY.
14. BAN ON WOMEN RIDING IN TAXI WITHOUT A *MAHRAM*.
15. BAN ON WOMEN PLAYING SPORTS.
16. BAN ON WOMEN WEARING BRIGHTLY COLORED CLOTHES.
17. CHANGING ALL NAMES OF PLACES INCLUDING THE WORD WOMAN.
18. BAN ON WOMEN APPEARING ON THE BALCONIES OF APARTMENTS OR HOUSES.

19. ALL WINDOWS OF HOUSES AND APARTMENTS WHERE WOMEN LIVE MUST BE PAINTED BLACK.

Ali and Anton both shook their heads in disbelief. Husayn Sabre, the fundamentalist and jihad member spoke for them all when he said softly, "These Taliban are mad."

When they returned, they sat together with the others and Commander Haq said that he had toured all the camps. Besides the two Al-Badr camps, many of the other camps had been hit. Casualties were light, twenty warriors had been killed, but not many wounded. Then he said in a more somber tone that he felt a deep tension in the camp here. He, being an Afghan, was not close to the men, but his deputy al-Hamza was an Egyptian and was a confidant of many and he told that there was deep a bitterness against the Americans for the missile strike, against Westerners in general, and against Achmed as a non-Muslim. "Achmed, I think it best if you leave and return to Egypt. Take Ali and Sidqi with you. I understand that Sidqi is ready to travel. I will send a message to the Sheikh to send his explosive experts back to the camps."

Anton agreed. He had fulfilled his obligation to his friend Ali. His mission was done as he knew the names of five other Egyptian Jihad members who were in camp. He told the commander that he also believed it was best to leave and not to cause problems.

His heart pounded with happiness at the thought of returning to his beloved Hanna.

Twenty-second of August—DAY NINETEEN

Anton noticed the stares of hatred by many. The commander brought him news that he should stay one more day and teach. The experts would arrive that afternoon.

He took his group including Ali and the three jihadists out to the range and blew up lots of plastic explosives, the same after lunch. During the middle of the afternoon, a messenger came from the commander for all to return to camp. They did and they stood in the square waiting for what no one knew, not even Haq. He had been told by messenger from one of the camps which was not attacked that an e-mail arrived for the camp to assemble.

The two Yemeni brothers Saleh and Talib al-Moqrin had returned, both with sticky-plaster on their faces and hands where they had been cut with glass shards. The third Yemeni, Wasfi al-Jundi, was severely injured and remained in the hospital.

Then some pointed to the distant road; a caravan of vehicles was seen trailing a big dust cloud. They all stopped outside the camp and a warrior in uniform came and spoke to the commander, who then gave orders for them to move into the large mosque-tent, and were told to sit down. The deputy came to Husayn Sabre and told him to take his rifle to his house and remain there, which Husayn did.

The deputy then placed Haq's sleeping bag with a woven rug over it in front of the gathering. Commander Haq then faced the warriors and told them that the Emir had arrived to view the camp and would come in to address them. There was much jubilation and cries of Allah is Great among other praises.

After a while, in strode a lanky figure in a white robe, a camouflage jacket over the robe, a white turban and a Kalashnikov rifle in one hand. All recognized him at once as Osama bin Laden; and dressed in a white robe and turban and following him came Aymen al-Zawahiri together with many heavily armed warriors—their bodyguards. Bin Laden sat on the prepared seat and to his right al-Zawahiri, and when bin Laden motioned to him, the commander sat to his left. As they entered, all the cries and chattering of the excited men stopped and there was complete silence. All eyes directed in devotion at the Emir as if he was the Prophet himself, clinging to every word he uttered as if they were revelations from the Koran.

"My faithful, I greet you from the peaks of the Hindu Kush mountains," he began his oratory.

Anton did not pay much attention to bin Laden's words but studied the man. He was a tall and imposing man. His camouflage jacket hung loosely over his ascetic figure. He had laid the rifle next to him—bin Laden the warrior. He sat with his legs crossed on the makeshift cushion, sometimes raising his hand to emphasize a point. His eyes dark, impressionless; his lips soft, sensual. His long, bushy beard was rather shaggy and sprinkled with gray.

The speech he made was mainly directed against the Saudi government, who were in evil conspiracy with the Western nations, especially the satanic American government and the godless Russians. He told how his Mujahedin had defeated the Russians and those warriors who had fallen had become martyrs and were honored sitting with Allah—quoting the Koran: *"Blessed and Most Gracious is Allah, Whose goodness and glory shine everywhere; His it the true Reality; His promise of the Hereafter is true."*

After reveling against the Saudis, he began a harangue against the Americans, Clinton and his three Jews who controlled him, Cohn, Berger and Albright. He described them as arrogant, criminal, hideous, inhuman and barbaric. The Americans were the sons of Satan who occupied Arabia, the most scared land. "For this and other acts of injustice against Muslims, we have declared jihad against the Americans. It is our sacred duty to make holy war against them so that Allah's words, as given to us by Prophet Muhammad, Exalted be He, are fulfilled and we drive the enemy from all Muslim lands." He added this terrible pronouncement of his, which Anton would never forget. *"We do not differentiate between those dressed in military uniforms and civilians. They are all targets."*

Bin Laden spoke without raising his voice in anger or passion, like a storyteller.

Anton wondered, what was the charisma of bin Laden that put these people under a spell like a conjurer? He was nothing like Hitler, whom Anton had seen in movies and seemed to hypnotize the masses that saw and listened to him. Why that reverence for this man? Bin Laden appeared cold, his eyes radiating nothing. Anton felt it was rather self-hypnosis of the men around him, religious fanatics to whom bin Laden was a leader, advocating the violence they were seeking, even the need of self-destruction in the cause of the call for jihad. All in the name of Allah and his revelations passed down by the Prophet, and a good dose of half-truth, misinterpretation and outright lies. Then, at last he raised his voice and pointed at the warriors, "Divide their nations, tear them to shreds, destroy their economy, burn their companies, ruin their welfare, crash their planes, sink their ships and kill them on land, sea and air. May Allah torture them by your hands."

Commander Haq stood up and told that all must leave and can accompany the Emir on his tour of the camp. Only those who are Egyptians should remain to be greeted by Mullah al-Zawahiri. The Mujahedin jumped up and offered their praises to Allah; went toward bin Laden, just to touch his hand, his clothing, his Kalashnikov, then followed him and his bodyguards out of the tent.

There were nine who remained behind: Ali and Anton, two jihadists pledged to protect them and the five other Egyptian muj of the Egyptian Islamic Jihad. They sat down before al-Zawahiri with bodyguards standing behind him. He asked each one his name and where in Egypt he was from. He was a squat man sitting in his white robe and white turban. He too had a full beard flaked with gray. His thick lips had mirth as he spoke with the men of places they came from and he was familiar with, most were from Cairo. At times, he looked stern when he spoke about the jihad they had pledged themselves to. He did not have the aesthetic bearing of bin Laden, yet he spoke with more conviction and raising his voice to emphasize a point he wished to make. To Anton, he appeared as a school teacher or a mullah giving religious instructions as he too cited from the Koran and praises to Allah. Or, as a sheik with his almost sensuous lips and friendly smiles who was ready to enter his harem for worldly delights. He was a poised and good speaker but looked even less than bin Laden as a terrorist leader.

When al-Zawahiri directed his gaze at Anton, who stated his name and where in Cairo he came from, al-Zawahiri knew not only about him and that the commander had praised his skill and devotion but also about the tension in the camp. "Please, Achmed Nabil, understand the emotions of our jihadists. After this barbaric attack by the Americans who are afraid to attack us with their soldiers, but murder with their cowardly missiles, and even though you are Egyptian, they see in you as an enemy, not one of their faith. Yes, as Commander Haq suggested, it is best for you to return tomorrow. We have returned our bomb makers and they will continue to teach our warriors." He then shook hands with Anton, but embraced with all of the Egyptians. Even al-Zawahiri regarded Anton as an outsider not being of the true faith. Al-Zawahiri then left to inspect the camp with bin Laden. They soon departed with the convoy of bodyguards without inspecting Camp 2, the camp of the Afghans and Pakistanis.

Anton, Ali and the two jihadists returned to their house. On the way, Anton took Ali with him to find some tools to clean away the debris around their house. They found a shovel and a rake and when they returned to the house, they started to work clearing away stones, dirt, bricks and wood the explosions had thrown against and around house 12.

Ali wondered if he should get the three jihadists to help them, but Anton thought to let them rest in the house, for they could finish the work by themselves.

The door opened and the two Yemeni brothers came out, in the hand of Saleh a rifle, the AK-47.

What happened then was all over in a flash, though Anton would remember it clearly and sorrowfully. Saleh came toward Anton, yelled in a high-pitched scream, "*Kufr*—you directed the Americans to bomb here, die and go to your Christian hell!"

Saleh pointed the rifle at Anton, the shot cracked and Ali who had quickly stepped before Anton fell mortally wounded. Anton enraged, rushed at Saleh, swinging the shovel. Saleh pointed the rifle at him and fired. There was the sound of clicking as the hammer hit but the firing pin did not explode the cartridge. The next moment the flat of the shovel hit Saleh, the force smashing his face into his head . . . he collapsed.

Anton cradled Ali in his arms . . . his face so white, blood running from his mouth. His eyes opened and recognized his friend. His lips tried to form a smile. Ali whispered, Anton moved close to him, "Achmed . . . bring Sidqi back to Egypt." Eyes that no longer saw, his chest no longer rose to breath—Ali was dead. Anton held his dearest friend close to him, his heart broken. "ALI . . . ALI . . ." he whispered and kissed the lifeless lips stained with blood.

Men had come running when they heard the shot. The commander came holding his Kalashnikov, al-Hamza came, in his hand his revolver. Ismael, the medic, attended to Saleh who was held by his brother Talib. Talib yelled to do something, Saleh couldn't breath . . . his face unrecognizable, where his eyes had been liquid like from broken eggs was running down, the nose just flesh, his mouth caved in and his teeth smashed. Ismael cut an opening in his throat and inserted the hollow tube of a pen into his trachea—Saleh would survive but never see again.

Anton lifted up his dead friend and carried him into the house followed by Haq. He laid Ali on his hammock and sat by him holding his hand, on the floor the three jihadists dead with their throats cut.

The commander shook Anton by his shoulder, "Achmed, you must flee. The Arabs in the camp will revolt, they want vengeance, they will kill you!" When Anton did not respond, Haq said, "Think of your family, your mother!" Anton awoke like from a bad dream, HANNA! New life surged through his being, he must not fail Hanna and his mother.

"Ali!" He looked at the commander. "Ali gave his life to save me!"

"We will bury him in our cemetery but you cannot help him now. Ali sacrificed his life so that you may live. Honor him by staying alive and flee."

"How, where to?" Anton was still immersed in his pain and anguish, he could not think clearly.

Deputy al-Hamza came in, and saw the dead.

Haq gave him his rifle, "The Yemenis killed the three Egyptians and then took the rifle. I have to get a few things for Achmed. Achmed has to flee, guard the house until I return."

Al-Hamza said, "They all gathered in the tent. I am certain they plan to kill you, Achmed." The commander said, "You have the rifle, you can keep them off, they only have knives. I shall return in a few minutes." He drew his revolver and rushed out.

When he returned in his pickup, he had a backpack with food and one more Kalashnikov, a wooden box with twelve dynamite sticks, and unloaded four cans of gasoline into the back of the Toyota. "Go and see what they are up to friend Omar, they trust you. But take the rifle with you," the deputy left.

Anton had cleansed the lips and chin of his dead friend, and a last sorrowful look at the face he had loved; he put a blanket over Ali's body.

Anton was now again a man of action. "I am ready, commander."

Haq instructed him how to flee. "The best road out is to go east from Khost into Pakistan. Make certain that you pick up Sidqi; they will come after him as he is with you, just as they killed the three Egyptians sent to protect you. The other road is back to Jalalabad and then to Peshawar. There is a third possibility, to go up north to Kabul and make your way through the Salang tunnel to Mazar-1-Sharif and into Uzbekistan. This is a long way and fraught with many dangers, but it is all Taliban territory. You will be stopped many times by guards, asked what you are doing in Afghanistan, if you tell them that you were an instructor they will want to know why you are away from the camp. Better to go into Pakistan."

It was getting dark and Haq turned on the light, the blanket in front of the window guarded them from unfriendly eyes. Anton got his things ready, took the pouch from under his hammock with the pistol and extra magazines.

The deputy returned. He had bad news. The muj had united to kill Achmed and Sidqi. Some had already left in pickups to block the roads to Pakistan, to Khost, and some would go farther past Khost and make roadblocks on the road to Jalalabad. Others had gone to the nearest Arab camp to get weapons and more Arabs to help them ambush Achmed.

Haq asked if any were setting up roadblock on the way to Kabul.

Al-Hamza said, "I don't know, they are not thinking that he would go north,"

"Then you have to take the northern escape route, Achmed." Haq then extracted boxes with ammunition from his backpack for Anton to take along with the rifle. In addition, he had a burqha, "For Sidqi. They will not bother him as a woman and you must be his *mahram,* his male relative, so he can travel with you. Sidqi speaks a little Pashto and Dari; I don't know how you will explain having a female with you as an Egyptian from the training camp. Whatever you tell them, if they won't let you pass or threaten you, use the rifle and pistol. If you do, others will follow you, it is all dangerous; and your chances of escaping become less if you have to shoot your way past. Here is one more suggestion, if you make it north past Kabul and toward the Salang tunnel and you are followed, they will radio ahead that you are coming and the roadblock by the tunnel is strong and you won't be able to fight your way past. About sixty kilometers north of Kabul is the town of Jabal os Sarar. The bridge there leads across the Panjshir River into the town of Golbahar. If you make it there, you are in the territory of the Panjshir Valley ruled by my friend Ahmed Shah Massoud. If you are not killed by either the Taliban on one side or when you cross the bridge by Massoud's warriors, you are safe. Tell them to take you to Massoud."

Haq then took a prayer rug out of the backpack, "Achmed, this rug was given to me by Massoud. He presented it to me as a sign of our everlasting friendship. Give it to him with my regards and my wish that he helps you to escape to the north and he will do so."

"One more thing," and the last item Haq took from his backpack was a white banner.

"Affix it to the antenna of your Toyota and in most cases you will be seen as just a Taliban and they may not even stop you. Now let us rush to Khost and get your friend Sidqi, unless they have already killed him. I come with you to Khost. Maybe if we are stopped by the Arabs, I am still recognized as their commander. If not?" He patted his rifle, "Achmed, you also may be able to bribe your way past guards. Do you have plenty of money?"

Anton had already taken his pouch with the credentials as a reporter from the al-Ahram newspaper, his Egyptian passport and the dollars in his money belt. "I have plenty of dollars, Commander."

His backpack and handbag were ready; he had also stuffed all of Sidqi's things into handbags. It was quiet and dark when they went outside. Anton loaded everything in the Toyota and Haq fastened the banner.

Haq was driving the Toyota cruiser, his rifle next to him. Achmed carried his in his hand.

Halfway to Khost the road was blocked by pickups; uniformed men stood by them. Haq could not drive around as one side was a ravine on the other side the steep mountain. The commander leaned out of the window and ordered the men to move the vehicles. They were unarmed except for knives. They did not obey the commander but also did nothing to attack him, they knew he was armed and Anton showed his Kalashnikov.

Haq gently nudged against a pickup, then gunned the motor and pushed the vehicle away and they raced along the dark road.

"I am afraid they got to the hospital for Sidqi, the ones they left at the roadblock were the more timid from Somalia."

Haq left the main road and took a side road to the hospital. Before the narrow road exited to the hospital, they were stopped by uniformed men with AK-47s. They were Arabs from the bodyguards of the sheikh. They asked what he wanted. The hospital was closed as the sheikh was spending the night there. They also told Haq that some of his men had come by before and wanted to enter the hospital, but all entrances had been blocked, they had returned to the main road. The leader of the guard then asked if there was some trouble.

The commander explained briefly what had happened.

The guard wanted to know the name of the injured. When Haq told him it was Sidqi Suliman, the guard left and promised to bring him. Shortly after the guard returned with Sidqi. Sidqi was in his loose uniform and wore his boots. His head was still wrapped in bandages and without a hat. Sidqi got into the cruiser and Haq returned the way they had come. They continued north until they came to the main road out of Khost.

Haq got out, "Allah be with you two. If the Emir had not decided to spend the night at the hospital, they would have killed Sidqi."

"What will you do, Commander Haq? Come with us. Your life is also in the hands of these Arab fanatics," said Anton.

Haq smiled. "If it is Allah's will, so be it. No, I have unfinished business. I am pledged to the Emir and he will protect me. Once you are gone from the camp, their tempers will cool down and their wrath will diminish. They know that you were under the protection of the Emir and they went against his promise of safety for you. I cannot advise you to do anything but go north. They are still manning roadblocks to Pakistan and Jalalabad and by now have alerted other Arabs and they soon will be armed."

From the *SURAT ad-Dhuha* the commander recited:

In the name of Allah, Most Gracious, Most Merciful.
By the Glorious Morning Light, And by the Night When it is still,—
Thy Guardian—Lord Hath not forsaken thee, Nor is He displeased.

"Go in peace, my friends and may Allah protect you from harm here and up north."

"From Khost to Kabul, it is about 170 kilometers. The road from here is good and you should make it in about three to four hours. Try to get into Kabul with sunrise, not at night. No traffic is permitted into the city during the night." The commander walked back into the dark town.

CHAPTER X

FLIGHT

Driving along the dark, unfamiliar road Sidqi asked, "Achmed, where are we going? And where is Ali?" Anton did not answer, his heart heavy with sorrow. Ali and Sidqi had been as close friends as he was with Ali.

"Achmed . . . . Ali?"

"Ali is dead, my friend."

The warrior Sidqi became the gentle boy he really was . . . sobs of pain shook him; he cried uncontrolled and unashamed. Anton said nothing.

"How did it happen, Achmed?"

Anton told him. "His last wish was for me to bring you back to Egypt, Sidqi."

"Ali was your best friend too."

"Ali was my best friend as he was yours."

"Achmed, I am sorry I cried like a child."

"You loved him. Your tears were like greetings of your affection for Ali."

"Will you be my friend now, Achmed?"

"I am your friend, Sidqi. We belong together."

"Can you help me get back to Egypt? My parents did not wish for me to leave, I am their only son. You have Hanna waiting for you."

Anton smiled. "You know about my Hanna?"

"Yes. Ali told me. Also that she is Jewish. It was hard for me to believe that you, the son of an SS man had married a Jewish woman. I don't care anymore. I just wish to live among good people like my parents. I don't care who they are. I am a Muslim and read and follow the Koran. It does not say that we should hate believers of other faiths or kill them."

"Then why did you join the Brotherhood? To go to Afghanistan?"

"Because I am a sincere believer of the Koran. I thought . . . the way some mullahs spoke and taught us was to fight for our religion."

159

"Is this the only reason, Sidqi?"

Sidqi remained silent for a few minutes . . . "No. I was raped. The man told me I was like a girl and had to serve men. I wanted to become a warrior to . . . ."

"To prove that you are a man?"

"Yes."

"You have proven that you are a man."

"I will no longer be an extremist, Achmed. I saw what these fanatics can do."

"Sidqi, you were never an extremist but I am glad you say so. My Hanna told me that the essence of Judaism is moderation in everything. It is fanaticism for anything that leads to strife and hate, and murder. All your things are in the handbag on the backseat, including your passport, money, a warm jacket for it might get cool later. Also your small turban which will cover your bandage, no questions then by anyone. One more thing, the commander thought it will help us if you put a burqha on, because it covers your head completely. I am to be your *mahram*. He thinks the Taliban road-guards will just wave us on if they see a woman in the car."

Sidqi gave a bitter laugh, "Again! I try to prove that I am a man and you want me to be a woman. Only in an emergency to protect you, I rather use this, Achmed," and he padded his rifle. He took his bag, put on his turban and jacket.

"Now you look like a warrior again, Sidqi. How do you feel by the way? No more dizzy spells?"

"No. I am fine. They took the stitches out, the wound is almost closed and the bleeding stopped. They just put the bandage on to protect the wound. They cut my hair off and gave me medicine against an infection."

They drove in silence through the steep mountains rising on either side of the dirt road like dark shadows. At midnight they reached the town of Gardez, the houses all dark and silent, no one to be seen, and no roadblocks. When they left the town they saw a sign in several languages—100 kms TO KABUL.

The road was less hazardous here, asphalted and the mountains not as steep. Anton saw that Sidqi was sleeping.

Twenty-third of August—DAY TWENTY

The commander had warned Anton that entering Kabul at night was forbidden; they had roadblocks to stop anyone. After a couple hours driving, the odometer showed that they had traveled close to eighty kilometers. Anton pulled off to the side. It was past midnight. He then woke Sidqi.

"I never asked but do you drive?" Sidqi answered, "No."

Then Sidqi asked, "How did the two Yemenis overpower the three jihadists who were to protect you, Achmed?" Anton told him. "The rest you know. I should have been more careful. When Bin Laden left and the jihadists followed him, I did not see the two Yemenis. I should have become suspicious but did not. If I had, Ali would still be alive."

"You got almost killed yourself if the rifle had not misfired. Allah protected you, Achmed."

"Maybe so. But it was Ali who took the bullet."

"In the *Surat Al-Ahzab*, it is written: '*Nevertheless do ye What is just to your closest friends: such is The writing in the book.*'"

"And in the *Surat* it continues: '*And remember: We took From the Prophets their Covenant: And from thee: From Noah, Abraham, Moses, And Jesus the son of Mary: we took from them A solemn Covenant . . .*'"

Sidqi interrupted, "You quote Jesus to me, Achmed, are you trying to make a Christian of me?"

"No, Sidqi. We are all the children of one God. How we serve him is only important. Be it by the Old Testament of the Jews, by the life and death of Jesus and His resurrection, the scriptures of the apostles, or by the Koran. And the most precious gift God has given us are true friends." Anton then told Sidqi that he will sleep until morning prayer and he must stay awake and guard.

"Wake me up at once if you see or hear something. Taliban we need not be afraid of, but there are also bandits around."

Sidqi asked, "How can I tell the difference between Taliban and bandits?"

"Taliban carry a white banner or flag. Just don't permit anyone to come too close to the cruiser. You know how to yell stop in Pashto and Dari?"

"Yes. Sleep, Achmed. We have a long drive ahead to go north. Where are we heading to?"

"If we can go north through the Salang tunnel it would lead us to either Tajikistan or Uzbekistan."

"And if not?"

"Then we shall see. It is in God's hands."

Anton woke up as he was pulled down in his seat. "Pssst, someone is coming." Anton glanced in the rearview mirror, a white pickup with its lights off and motor cut was slowly passing them, then pulled in front of their cruiser and stopped.

"They are probably thinking we are sleeping," whispered Anton. "Is your Kalashnikov ready?" He heard Sidqi chamber a round, the soft click of the safety off.

"I have it on automatic."

"Roll your window down slowly. When I give the command, fire at them."

"Who are they?" asked Sidqi.

"I don't know. They are stupid to stop in front of us, probably to prevent us from fleeing. We will know in a moment when I turn the lights on."

Anton had his window down; in his left hand was the Colt. He looked over the dashboard. He could only see the dark shade of the white pickup in the deep of night. He heard a door open . . . then a second door; he sat upright, his hand with the pistol out the window, "Are you ready Sidqi?" "Yes," came the return whisper.

Anton turned on the headlights . . . in the brightness of the sudden illumination, they saw one man approach from the driver's side, a dagger in his hand; two men, the first holding an AK-47, on the other side. Anton recognized the men in uniform from the camp. "FIRE!" His Colt cracked and the men near him fell, then the staccato of the Kalashnikov of Sidqi and both men crumbled.

Anton flicked the headlights off, told Sidqi to stay in the car, turned his flashlight on and approached the pickup. There was no one else. He held the light on the three; all were dead. He took the AK-47 back to their Toyota; now they had two rifles. He checked the road. Off to the side was a dry creek bed.

He started the pickup, put it in neutral and had Sidqi help him sit the three back in the front seat. Anton turned the wheel and they pushed the pickup down into the creek. Using his flashlight to see, he climbed down and crouching low fired two shots into the gas tank. He lit a match, threw it and soon the pickup was aflame. They watched until the gas tank exploded, "There won't be much left of them. Charred, they might not even see that they had been shot. Just an accident," Anton said. He had seen a side canyon a couple kilometers back, and drove there, got off the road and there they waited for sunrise.

When it got light, and after Sidqi prayed, they drove on. The pickup was now just a smoldering wreck as they passed by.

The sun had come up and lit the big valley below them, the city of Kabul. All around were mountains. Now in late summer very few of the higher peaks showed the white of snow and ice. 'From the peaks of the Hindu Kush Mountains' bin Laden had said, and here they saw the high mountains to the west, north and east.

Driving down into the city they hit a roadblock, flying their white banner they were waved through. Coming from the south on the main road they followed it through the center of town. There were many big buildings and most were heavily damaged. Destruction everywhere as the city had been shelled mercilessly after the Taliban captured it. There was traffic now, lots of pickups and vans flying the white banner. People walked, few women seen in their dark or black clothing, men in their loose fitting trousers, shirts and jackets, wearing a cap or turban; most in sandals, and all with beards. They saw a few policemen directing traffic but no one paid any attention to them and their Toyota cruiser flying the white flag on the antenna. Following the main road northwest they soon came to the outskirts. All houses here were of the mud-brown brick, most with walls around, a few with trees and gardens with vegetables. It all looked very normal; a city come to life in the early morning sun. They passed mosques with men going in or coming out.

"I am hungry, Achmed. I didn't have supper last night."

"And no breakfast this morning. We will stop when we are away from the city. We have plenty of food in the backpack and there is a bag with water."

"You thought of everything, Achmed."

"No, it is all from Commander Haq. He really helped us."

"A good Muslim." Sidqi smiled.

"There are many good Muslims."

Anton pulled off the road at a level place and they ate. There was nan bread and chicken in the backpack, and they drank water from the skinbag. It should be another one hundred kilometers to the Salang tunnel. The driving was slow through the mountains of the Kush, with many curves and serpentines; these were no longer barren hills but really high mountains, some with white tops. After a three-hour drive, they came to a town which was Jabal os Sarar as they could see the Panjshir River. There were many Taliban soldiers, even armored cars and tanks. In the middle of the town, they saw a road to the right with barricades of sandbags blocking the way to the bridge and more soldiers. Again because they wore turbans, and Anton had a proper beard and the white banner flying, they were not stopped. They were now close to the tunnel.

"If we make it through the tunnel, we'll be all right Sidqi. Then to Mazar-I-Sharif and north into Uzbekistan. We should get to Sharif tomorrow."

After another hour's drive they came to the tunnel. The entrance was blocked and fortified with concrete structures and many Taliban soldiers around. They were stopped. Sidqi tried to speak in Pashto but he knew not enough to converse. He told them that they were Egyptians and spoke Arabic. The Taliban then brought someone who spoke Arabic. The Taliban wanted to know who they are, what they were doing here and where they were going. Sidqi showed his passport and so did Anton, along with his credentials as a reporter for the al-Ahram newspaper.

The soldiers then brought someone in charge of the roadblock, they showed him their passports, told him that they were reporters from Egypt and that they wished to travel to Mazar-I-Sharif to report on the Taliban's victory there.

They were told that without a permit from Mullah Abdul Shakor in Kabul they could not go through the tunnel and they must return to Kabul.

"You will find him in the Foreign Affairs Ministry in the center of town."

Achmed turned around and drove back.

"We have to make our way through the Panjshir Valley and go north into Tajikistan."

"Over the bridge? Achmed, they have barricaded it and many soldiers there. How can we get through?"

"We have to wait for darkness. Late at night, or even early in the morning when most sleep and they have fewer soldiers at the roadblock."

Anton drove back and turned off the road where a house once stood, now in ruins. He drove behind it and there stopped, out of sight. They ate some more nan and chicken. Anton and Sidqi gathered bricks and built a wall in the back of the cruiser to protect them from bullets. They sat in their seats to await the night; Anton smoked his pipe and felt relaxed.

"Achmed, you are married to Hanna. You love her. What is love?" Anton mused, how to explain love. He sorted in his mind how best to tell. "I have never been with a woman," added Sidqi.

"I could give you the definition of love and sex from the psychology class in the university or even from social sciences. However, they teach it in a complicated and far out way. It isn't all that difficult to explain and understand. Love and sex are two different feelings. Love is emotional; sex is physical. Let me first try to explain love and do it in a common sense manner and the way I think what love is.

First of all, it is how we feel toward others. It is affection. Even animals feel that kind of affection especially those who live with people, a dog, a cat and even a little bird."

"We had a dog once when I was just a boy. It was always so happy when I came home from school, it just jumped up on me and its tail wiggled," said Sidqi.

"Yes, I believe you. The dog had true affection for you and probably for your parents too. This love of affection is even more so in a human. We have a soul."

"What is the soul, Achmed?"

"It is something in humans that is not in animals. There was a philosopher by the name of Buber and he called it the "I," the consciouness. We, Christians believe that when we die, while our physical form returns to dust, the soul comes before God on Judgement Day.

To return to love. It is an emotion that encompasses many human traits, some of which we share with animals such as trust, happiness, friendship, and loyalty. Some emotions are human feelings we don't find in animals, not even in dogs that are closest to us; mercy, compassion, gratefulness, sacrifice and the caring for other's feelings. There is the beautiful saying in Christianity, 'Do unto others as you wished them do unto you.' All these emotional feelings together make us human. The lack of them makes us inhuman.

Take the suicide bomber, like I am certain that Atta is or will become. He has traits of devotion to Allah, is loyal to those men he believes in and he trusts them. He even has the very human emotion to sacrifice his life for them or the cause they espouse. However, when he explodes the belt, or crashes a plane laden with explosives, he will kill innocents, children, women, men. He does it without any mercy or compassion for their rights to live. His way of love is to hate; hate is the curse of mankind."

"They will go to paradise."

"Will they? A child torn apart sit next to him and Allah? Most likely all those he killed are Christians who don't believe in his God of Mercy, in his paradise. Perhaps there is nothing but this one life given to us by God. They all have a right to live in happiness and he tears them asunder, takes their God-given right to live from them. In Christian thinking and beliefs, he is not a martyr, but a monstrous killer, a murderer. There is nothing in the Koran that permits him to kill indiscriminately. A fatwa written by a hateful mullah does not make it right if it is against the basic teachings of the Prophet as written and commented on in your scriptures or in ours by our Prophet Jesus.

"Love is an all-encompassing feeling of goodness. When two people meet, and this is only my personal thought, we radiate our personality of what we are as human beings. The other person receives and acknowledges these feelings; therefore, we become attracted. I also believe, that you can see in a person's face, the facial features, expressions of gentleness, goodness and kindness or brutality and evil.

"Often we meet someone and think, I would love to know him, become his or her friend. Then we part, our wish unfulfilled. Sometimes we unite, we become attached to each other, we become friends as you were with Ali, and I was. We find love for another. This ultimate love was for Ali to sacrifice his life for me.

"This is also the love we might find for a woman. If we then share common interests or are willing to learn to share, we become deeply attached to each other—we fall in love.

"Then there is sex. It is a natural gift, a desire of the flesh. It is given to us by God to propagate, to have children. The moment of uniting is sweet with all its affection for another, as part of what is called making love, the embracing and kissing and touching. This tender affection is human and not given to animals. The final release, as powerful as it is, is purely lust. When the Swede raped you, he was in the throes of his lust. When I held the pistol to his head he didn't care, he was consumed by this sexual instinct.

"Love is good, and yes, sex is part of it. Again let me quote what my Hanna believes in and taught to her by her religion, the essence of Judaism. *Everything in moderation*. It makes for a happy and lasting marriage.

"Now let us sleep in peace until midnight. We are safe here as nobody can see us from the road."

Anton dozed while Sidqi stayed awake contemplating how Achmed expressed love.

Twenty-fourth of August—DAY TWENTY-ONE

A gentle shaking woke Anton. "It is midnight, Achmed."

"Check your rifle, Sidqi, and have a full magazine loaded, keep more in your pocket."

They both armed their Kalashnikovs. Anton had his pistol loaded and put it in his pocket. He also extracted a half dozen dynamite sticks from the box and checked their cords then cut them short to explode within five seconds after he lit and threw them. Three sticks he tied together in a bundle.

They drove back to the town of Jabal os Sarar.

"How do you plan to get over the bridge, Achmed?"

"We have to see how many men they have guarding the bridge and barrier."

By Anton's watch, it was three in the morning when they reached the town of Jabal os Sarar, a dark and silent town. Before he turned into the street leading to the bridge, he turned off his lights, cut the motor and coasted until they stopped close to the barrier of sandbags. There was a fire burning in a metal trashcan and they saw a number of Taliban by the can, their bearded faces lit up by the light of the fire.

Anton could see a similar fire burning at the other side of the bridge. It was like Commander Haq had told him, Massoud's warriors stayed on their side of the river and the Taliban on this side. He opened the door quietly and hugging the side of the buildings moved closer. In his dark camouflage uniform, he melted into the black of the houses.

He saw there were six soldiers with rifles slung over their shoulders. Off to the side stood a tank; a man was visible standing in the turret and talking with the soldiers. Was there anyone inside the tank, ready to use the machinegun and cannon? The building next to the tank had a light burning, more soldiers on guard? He had seen enough and returned to the Toyota. He tore off the white banner; they were no longer Taliban.

"Ready, Sidqi? When I come back and start the car, begin shooting at anything that moves." He took the six sticks of dynamite and slowly moved along the houses. In the back of the tank, he took a sheet of paper and crumbled it, then lit it with a match and dropped it on the ground. He lit one fuse, rushed up at the back of the tank, gave the turret man a chop in the neck which immobilized him and threw the stick down the turret, jumped off and the explosion came. He lit another stick and threw it at the soldiers, one through the window of the house. He lit the bundle of three sticks and threw it at the sandbag barrier; there was a terrific explosion; he ran back to the car, jumped in, started and drove for the opening in the barrier. He heard the automatic fire of Sidqi's rifle shooting at the soldiers; only a few had been killed by the explosion. One Anton shot with his pistol as he drove by.

They were on the bridge racing across without lights; he headed for the fire on the other side. Anton did not see soldiers coming out of the house, but it didn't matter, he was halfway across. He heard the rapid fire of automatic rifles behind him. Bullets hit the back of the Toyota, smashed into the wall of bricks, which crumbled. Anton pushed Sidqi down to the floor. Another volley hit the back; one bullet went through the front seat, Anton felt as if he was hit with a club as the bullet tore into his shoulder. The cruiser crashed through the sandbag barrier. They were across the bridge, Anton pushed the brake, skidded by soldiers who fired across the river, and blacked out.

When Anton came to he was in a bed, daylight shone through the window. He saw Sidqi sit by the bed dozing. *Where was he?* He felt his left side in pain, a bandage around his torso. "Sidqi?" His friend woke, his eyes lit up as he saw Achmed awake.

"Where are we?" asked Anton.

"You are in a hospital in Barak. Massoud's warriors brought you here. You have a bad wound in your shoulder. The bullet had flattened out and made a hole but it did not go deep, a doctor removed it this morning. You lost a lot of blood and they gave you a transfusion. My blood, for we have the same blood type. We are blood brothers now, Achmed." Sidqi smiled.

"How are we received, friendly?"

"I don't know. I told them we were Egyptian reporters. They took everything from us, our passports, money, everything."

"Our car? Is it damaged at lot?"

"It is air conditioned."

"Well, it was. Only it didn't work."

"I don't mean that one. It is so full of holes." They laughed. "Just in front where you hit the sandbags, it is a little dented. I guess we can forget about the car, our money, for it seems we are imprisoned in this valley."

"Well, as long as the natives are friendly. We'll get it all back, Sidqi. Don't worry."

"I am not worrying, just so you get well. The doctor said, and he spoke Arabic, that most likely you would get wound fever. He said he did his best cleaning out your wound and gave you a shot of penicillin."

"What language do they speak here?"

"Few Arabic, some know Pashtun, most speak Dari. They even have female nurses here. A nurse told me when you wake up she will bring you food."

"I am starving."

Sidqi knocked on the door, "We are locked in here."

Someone opened and Sidqi asked in Dari to bring food. Soon a nurse came, accompanied by a guard, she was in a long white dress and headscarve. She brought a bowl of mush and a small nan bread. Anton ate, "Did you eat, Sidqi?"

"No. I guess they just feed the wounded." He smiled. Anton pushed the bread over to him. When she returned to get the empty bowl, Anton asked Sidqi to tell the guard that he needed to see Ahmed Shah Massoud. He wondered if the guard understood and would give the message.

It was an hour later that the door opened and in came a man, his beard black and trimmed, he wore a short turban, a shirt, loose trousers and army boots. In his hand, he held the prayer rug from Commander Haq. He looked neither friendly nor unfriendly, but held the rug in front of him, "How come?" He spoke Dari, and at once his eyes became piercing awaiting the answer.

Anton looked at Sidqi, "Ask him if he speaks Arabic, you don't know enough Dari to explain." When Sidqi asked, the warlord shook his head, looked at Achmed.

Anton asked, "English?" Then, "Sprechen sie Deutsch . . . pa ruski?" Each time Massoud shook his head. Then Massoud asked, "Parlez-vous francais?" Sidqi at once smiled surprised and answered *oui*; and they both continued speaking in French, Sidqi interpreting to Anton, addressing Massoud as Shah.

Sidqi said, "The Shah wants to know how did you come by this prayer-rug?"

"Tell Massoud that I bring the prayer rug to him with greetings from his friend Amir Haq Khan, from the village of Jangalak," Anton said.

The warlord's face showed genuine surprise and delight, his lips gave a mirthful smile and then he broke out in laughter, "My friend Amir, my enemy Haq Khan! How is the devil? Wait . . ." And he walked to the door, opened and spoke to the guard standing there, then moved the chair next to Anton's bed and motioned Sidqi to sit on the bed.

Sidqi translated, "The Shah wants to know everything, and not the phony story of us being Egyptian reporters."

Anton looked at the still smiling warlord, "It is a long story and if our cover story of being Egyptian reporters is not good enough I will tell you the truth as Haq told me to do."

"Tell the truth and tell all, I have time," the warlord demanded.

Anton began with their friend, Ali Nasr who wished to go to Afghanistan to show jihadists that there was another way to bring true Islam to Egypt without violence. That he asked his friends Sidqi and Achmed to accompany him.

The interpretation was long. Anton was soon interrupted by the guard bringing in a small table, glasses and a carafe of tea with small cakes on a dish.

Anton told his story from the day they came to the camp until he left with Sidqi, with occasional interruptions by the warlord to clarify an event. He repeated what Haq had told him about his friend and enemy Ahmed Shah Massoud, "And as a sign of his everlasting friendship and love for you, Commander Haq gave me his prayer rug to give to you."

The warlord gently stroked over the rug, "It is mine. I gave it to Haq, now I have to return it to him and I hope it is in peace."

Another pot of tea was brought, "Eat Achmed Nabil, you need to get your strength back, I'll see to it that you get nourishing food. When you are well, we will get you safely up north into Tajikistan. From there, you won't have any problem getting back to Egypt."

Anton wondered if there was no chance to get through the Salang tunnel with one of his supply trucks returning up north.

The warlord laughed, and told him that the Taliban no longer permit him to use that tunnel as a supply route. "Like all the agreements the Taliban make, they violate it. I hate the Taliban as much as the Arab Jihadists who come from other lands to do their terror in our land. My friend Haq is wrong when he believes that we all must join the Taliban to unite Afghanistan. We have support from the countries in the north, from Iran and help from America will come. It is us, the Alliance who will unite Afghanistan as a country free of religious oppression and traditions. I say this as a devout Muslim but not a fanatic. But you Achmed, it is to the north you must return, for the Taliban will be waiting for you and so will the Arabs. You killed theirs and you are a non-Muslim. Even bin Laden, may the devil devour him, cannot help you anymore."

Anton asked, "One question, Shah Massoud, our car, our belongings?"

Through Sidqi the warlord answered, "All of your belongings will be returned to you, everything is at my headquarters which is here in Barak." He then shook hands with Anton and Sidqi and then left.

Twenty-fifth of August to Twenty-first of September—DAY TWENTY-TWO TO FORTY-EIGHT

Anton lay with wound fever for several weeks, with only his health and stamina overcoming the infection. Every day, his wound was cleaned and sulfa powder sprinkled into it, and he received more penicillin injections. Sidqi was with him and even sleeping in the same room, cleaning his friend and bathing his feverish body with cool water and feeding him broth of chicken with finely cut meat. He cut fresh fruit and put small pieces in his mouth. Anton could not have had a more dedicated nurse than Sidqi. While his infection and wound fever lasted, his injury finally healed, though a deep scar would remain.

When his fever was gone and Anton could get up, clean himself and learn to walk again, the kitchen served more solid food: *Pilau*—rice mixed with meat and vegetables; *Bolani*—spicy vegetable pies; *Korma*—side dishes of vegetable, as there was little meat available in the valley. *Jelabi*—pieces of wheat bread fried and basked with syrup or molasses, and fresh fruit from the orchards. Anton also learned to sip his black tea with a piece of sugar held between his teeth, as was the custom here.

Sidqi was sleeping in the other bed in the room. They had let them use the hospital room as their quarters and both ate in the dining hall with patients. Anton was served his special diet of rich food. Sometimes he would share a sweet dessert with children patients to their delight. Neither of them had seen the warlord since, though he had left word with the nurse that whenever Achmed was ready to travel to let him know.

The past week Anton had exercised again, gaining back his strength. Most of their things had been returned and his uniform washed and a patch sown over the jagged bullet hole. Their car was in the shop and ready to be used, the inside cleaned out. They went for walks in the town and sat by the river in the evening which they both enjoyed.

Then one sunset, as they sat looking into the mountain stream rushing by, a cold wind whipping down from the mountains which made Sidqi shiver and pull his jacket collar up, Anton asked, "Sidqi, what are you dreaming about?"

Sidqi smiled. "You know, Achmed."

"Cairo and your parents."

"Yes, Achmed. And you about Hanna?"

"Hanna, how I miss her. She doesn't know where I am. Sidqi, it is time to go home. Let us give word to the Shah."

CHAPTER XI

SASHA AND THE BANDITS

The next morning Sidqi told the nurse that they were ready to leave. That afternoon a warrior came and took them in his pickup to the warlord's headquarters. Ahmad Shah Massoud was waiting for them and greeted them with friendship.

"I have been busy but I received reports of your getting well, Achmed. You must have heard helicopters fly over. They come from the north, from Tajikistan. Even the American CIA visits me. However, their planes are filled when they come and go; therefore, I cannot get you flown out from here. You have to take the land route. There are a number of roads from the valley north, good enough for walking and mules. When they stopped us from using the Salang tunnel, we worked on one road and made it passable for 4-wheel drive vehicles. Your Toyota is a 4-wheel drive, so you can make it. I sent for a guide who will take you. His name is Sasha, a Russian prisoner of war. He has been with us for the past nine years and was most helpful in reconditioning weapons and repairing tanks left behind by the Soviets. He was loyal and I wish to reward him by sending him back. He has been many times over the mountain road and knows the way to Taloqan. From there it is only eighty kilometers to the Amu Darya River, which is the border to Tajikistan. There will be boats to take you across. But there is nothing, no towns or villages or roads. You better hire a boat and have them take you to the town of Panz from where a road leads up to Dusanbe. There is an airport with flights to Russia. And be careful, the north is in the hands of the Alliance but there are bandits roving and killing. Always be prepared to be ambushed. Talk it over with Sasha, he will know best. I will give you a letter for Commander Malik, who commands the Northern Alliance, to help and protect you. Ah, here is Sasha."

The man who came in was big, with curly blond hair as he took his cap off. He had Slavic features and smiled cheerfuly. The warlord introduced him to Anton and Sidqi. Then Sasha turned to Anton, "Panimyety poruski?"

"Da," answered Anton and Sasha was beside with joy that someone could speak Russian with him. The warlord continued to speak in French to Sidqi, who translated.

"I have explained the different options to Sasha and you must see what is best for you three when you get to Taloqan. He will stay with you this night in your room. In your Toyota, you will find sleeping bags for both of you, warm jackets as it will be cold up in the mountains and provisions the hospital will provide for you. You will have your rifles and ammunition back and your American pistol. I kept the dynamite, as we are short on explosives." He gave Anton an envelope.

"Here is the letter for Commander Malik and passes that will give you safe passage through our controls. I had the extra gas from your cans emptied into your car. We have to bring the gas over the mountains and you can fill up when you are over the pass in Warsaj, Sasha knows and he has a map. May Allah protect you."

Then he gave them the two Kalashnikov rifles, ammunition and pistol, their documents and money pouches which he had in his office. He embraced each of them and the friendly warlord bade them a safe journey.

They left headquarters and in front stood their Toyota. Sasha explained that he had serviced the car and it is in good condition, also he had a metal plate welded to the back where the van had been holed, "Many holes the crazies shot in your car." Sasha said and put his bag in the car. Anton drove back to the hospital.

They went to their room. Sasha spoke Russian with Anton and he translated to Sidqi. Sasha came from St.Petersburg, which he called the most beautiful city in Europe. The river Neva and canals crossing the city, its bridges with statues better than in Paris, its churches and museums, the Hermitage grander than the Louvre. Everything was bigger and more beautiful in St. Petersburg. He told that he was in the Soviet Army and had to fight in Afghanistan. Nine years ago, when they stormed the Panjshir Valley, he was wounded and left behind. They treated him well and he helped them with the equipment, for he was in ordinance and knew how to repair. He is very happy that he can go back to St. Petersburg and his mother. She knows he is alive and here, and somtimes he received letters and wrote to her.

Then Anton told their story, but only that he and Sidqi are correspondents from Egypt and got in a fire fight with the Taliban when they crossed the bridge into the Panjshir Valley to visit the warlord.

Sasha said that he heard the story of the two Egyptians getting in a fight at the bridge, killing many Taliban, "the crazies" and blowing up their tank. "You are heroes!"

They told him about Cairo, their city and how beautiful it was. They exchanged addresses, Sasha inviting them to visit him in St. Petersburg. "My mother has just a small apartment but you will stay with us. The Russian way is to sleep all together in bed, sofa, on the floor. Guests are important to our custom. Mother will cook Russian food for you, you will like." They could see how happy the Russian was to return home. He had been lucky as during the Soviet war they killed each other's prisoners.

Then they looked at the map Sasha had. He showed them the road they would travel on over the mountains. He was adamant they should try to drive with the Toyota into Tajikistan and to Dusanbe. There, sell the car, so they will have money to fly home. He said that he has lots of Afghani money but it is only good here and not in Tajikistan. Only Russian rubles and American dollars are good.

Anton told him that he has dollars and promised Sasha that he would pay for his ticket home. They could see how happy Sasha was to go home, just bubbling with joy and enthusiasm. He would make a good travel companion. At once they both liked the big Russian.

Twenty-second of September—DAY FORTY-NINE

They awoke when the call for morning-prayer echoed through the hospital, sunrise.

They had breakfast in the dining room, then they received a bag with bread, cooked vegetables and fruit.

They loaded their backpacks and handbags into the Toyota. Anton had his pistol in his coat pocket and gave Sidqi and Sasha the rifles. When the sun came over the mountains and warmed the valley they were off.

Anton drove deeper into the valley. Twice they had to cross the Panjshir River until they came to the village of Anjoman. There a fairly good road branched off to the north into the mountains. Now they were in the highest peaks of the Hindu Kush.

After about twelve kilometers, the road became narrow and steep and Anton had to shift into low gear and 4-wheel drive. At noon, they reached the mountain village of Kurugah, where they stopped next to the creek. Sasha at once built a little fire with gas he extracted with a hose from the tank. He made hot water for tea and they ate and filled their water bag with the fresh water from the creek. The road continued to go up higher, to the right a peak, which was over 4,700 meters high and covered in snow and ice. They were glad they had warm jackets as neither the air conditioning or heater worked. They had problems with occasional pickups coming their way, the mountain road never wide enough to pass, and a few times they had to back down until they found a place to let each other get by. On one side always the steep rise of the mountain and on the other side the depth of a gorge.

Then suddenly the road tilted down. They were over the highest pass. Driving slowly over the makeshift road, they reached the village of Warsaj as the sun set.

Here was a control of warriors by a fort-like structure. They showed their letter and pass, were waved on and directed to the guesthouse where they were given a room with straw mattresses on which they placed their warm sleeping bags. Sasha made his obligatory tea for them and they ate by candlelight and lay down. Sasha cleaned their metal cups and prepared to build a fire in the morning. As a Russian, he could not do without his black tea.

Twenty-third of September—DAY FIFTY

With sunrise, and after Sidqi completed his prayer, Sasha had made hot water and brewed tea and they ate from their provisions. They drove to the fort-like compound where the soldiers were. This was the supply point where the trucks came from Taloqan and the north, were unloaded and then shipped by pickups into the valley of Panjshir.

There were stacks of gas cans and paying with Afghan money they filled their tank and their extra two cans. The other two had been punctured by bullets and left behind.

Here they also bought bread and cans of beans, hash and stew, fruit and even cake in cans, made in Russia, which made Sasha happy, though he had them also in the valley. One step closer to home for him.

From here, the road was good enough even for trucks. They had no problem with oncoming traffic, only closed their windows as each vehicle raised a cloud of dust.

They were even treated to Russian songs by Sasha. He was one happy man going home and in him they had found a good companion and friend. He taught them how so accompany him singing the song *Vercherniy Zvon* (Evening Bells), with Anton making the sound of deep resonating bells and Sidqi the jingle of high bells. After a few tries they did fine imitating bells. They were cheerful and going home.

In the evening, they reached Taloqan and found an inn where they could buy warm food, hot tea and a room with bunks and straw mattresses.

Twenty-fourth of September—DAY FIFTY-ONE

In the morning they drove to the militia. After showing their pass and letter, they were taken to an officer with whom Sasha spoke in Dari, since no one here spoke Arabic. Again the officer read the letter and scrutinized the passes. He explained to Sasha that Kondoz was still in the hands of the Alliance and they would have to drive north from Kondoz to the village of Qezel Qala, about seventy kilometers distant, and find a boat to take them across the river to escape into Tajikistan. He permitted them to buy gas from the compound.

When they reached the town of Khanaba, they were out of the Kush Mountains and in the plains and arrived in Kondoz at noon. They found an inn that served a hot meal of rice and chicken. From there they took the road to the north. To the right is was still mountainous and to the left the flat land with orchards and fields near Kondoz and then wide-open scrub land, desolate. By late afternoon, they reached the village of Shir Khan and had only ten kilometers to their destination and the river.

Past the village and about halfway to Qezel Qala, they saw a wrecked van in the ditch and two people lying nearby and more people slumped over in the van. Anton stopped a short distance past. Something didn't look right, though one of the people lying there was obviously a woman. "I don't like it," Anton said to Sidqi, "It all looks staged." They looked back, the woman was raising her arm, waving to them then tried to get up and fell back again. "We should help," Sidqi answered, disregarding Anton's comment. Sasha was already out of their cruiser walking toward the wreck. Anton called, "Come back, Sasha!" The Russian was all enthusiastic to help these unfortunate people, came back. "The woman is bleeding, she has blood all over her face. The people in the van look like they are dead."

"Take your rifle with you and be careful, Sasha."

Anton told Sidqi to stay in the car and also walked toward the wreck. He saw how Sasha laid his rifle down and bent over the woman, trying to help her up.

The woman sat up and suddenly raised her arm, a pistol in her hand and shot Sasha. He came stumbling back, holding his hand to his chest . . . "I am hit." Anton supported him and helped him into the back seat, Sasha collapsed. Anton saw the dead ones in the van tumbling out; one had a AK-47 in his hand.

There is a time to fight, and to run. This was time to run to get away and see to Sasha. He gunned the engine and raced away, heard the rapid fire behind him. Their cruiser lurched as both rear tires were hit; the metal plate was hit but stopped the bullets. Anton sped on until they were out of range. By then he had to slow down, as both tires were flat and burning off.

He stopped and they looked at Sasha who had slumped in his seat, foamy blood running from his lips. Anton knew Sasha had been hit in the lung, Sasha was dying . . . his face turning white from shock, his breathing stertorous.

Anton sat next to him and held him, another friend dying in his arms. Sasha's blue eyes looked at him, he tried to smile a painful grin. "Skaji moey mame (tell my mother)," he whispered. A cough and blood spurted from his mouth, and he stopped breathing—his eyes lifeless, Sasha was dead.

Anton took the thin metal chain with the Russian-Orthodox cross from Sasha's neck, he had only put it on when they left the last village, so close to freedom and home. With his knife he cut off a lock of hair. In his pocket he found letters from his mother and a picture of her. The picture, cross and lock of hair he put in his coat pocket.

By the side of the road they buried their Russian friend who would never see his beautiful St. Petersburg again. They had nothing to dig a grave for him in the hard ground; they made a pile of stones over his body. As they did, a motorcycle drove past them. Too late for Anton to shoot at him with his pistol even though he knew he was one of the bandits.

Anton spoke the Christian prayer for the dead over Sasha in Russian. Sidqi knelt on his rug and said the prayer of the Muslims. Twilight had set in and soon it would be dark.

Anton said to Sidqi, "The bandit who drove by will alert other bandits from the village ahead. We can expect to be ambushed on the road; we have to get off. But first we have to avenge Sasha. I expect the bandits to come to the car to see if we are still here, kill us too and rob us of our possessions. Having taken the rifle from Sasha, they expect us to be unarmed."

They quickly took from the car their most necessary things, sleeping bags, some food and their water bag. The Toyota, now useless to them with two tires burned to the rims, was set on fire. Then they walked away from the road far enough to see the burning car but not be seen themselves, and sat behind some scrub bushes. They waited in silence in the darkness. The motorcyclist returned and stopped by the burning wreck, then drove on.

It was about an hour later that they heard voices and saw men by the car which was still visible, albeit by then no longer burning bright but smoldering with just flames from the inside illuminating the men around it.

Anton told Sidqi, "Stay behind the bushes, have your Kalashnikov ready," which he gave him as the boy was not familiar with the Colt, and told him that if he didn't return to make his way to the river and look for a boat to get across into Tajikistan.

Keeping himself low and silent, Anton advanced on the men. There were five of them. In the flickering light he only could recognize one for certain—the woman, though obviously, it was a man, now with the headscarf off. It didn't matter, they were all bandits. With his pistol in his hand, safety off, he crept closer, then stepped out into the road and shot the one masquerading as a woman, then the man next to him, they fell. The other three were on their knees, blubbering in their native tongue, their hands together praying for mercy.

Anton called for Sidqi, who came running with his rifle. "Sidqi, cover the three bandits while I check the two I shot." The beardless bandit, a young man who was obviously the one who had masqueraded as the woman—he still showed red color in his face, was alive. He was the one who had fooled Sasha. "This bandit is still alive Sidqi, he is the one who was dressed as a woman and shot Sasha."

"Kill him, Achmed or I kill him!"

"Can you do it, Sidqi?"

In answer, Sidqi emptied his Kalashnikov into the wounded bandit who had shot Sasha.

Anton was surprised at the ferocity of his gentle friend.

Anton had just turned his head for a moment to see Sidqi fire, the three bandits had risen . . . to do what? Rush him or try to escape? Anton did not wait to find out; three times in rapid succession his Colt-45 cracked and the bandits, shot between their eyes, were flung backward and lay dead.

They returned to the bushes and picked up their bags.

Keeping off the road but near it, they walked in the darkness. When they saw the lights of Qezel Qala they walked around the village and to the river; there they found the boats of the villagers tied up. From the nearby village, they heard dogs yelping.

None of the boats had a motor; one was just a small rowboat with oars folded inside. Anton had Sidqi get into the boat and gave him their things and the rifle, "You take care of it. I have the pistol." Then he untied the others and pushed them into the river which was wide and flowing at a slow pace.

Anton pushed the boat off and jumped into it, rowed with the flow of the river to the west. Soon they overtook the other boats gliding slowly along in the rivers current.

How far should they go and where to get off into Tajikistan, Anton did not know. He knew from the map that there was a village on the other side, but if these people here in Afghanistan practiced banditry they could not expect the people on the other side of the river to be anymore friendly. It was a long way to the bridge where a road would take them north. They would have to wait for daylight. For now they were safe in the darkness of the river. The river was flowing with the speed of someone walking, much faster as long as he rowed. He couldn't change seats with Sidqi as the boat was too narrow to risk it.

By his luminous watch he could see that it was midnight. When he grew tired he just let the boat drift, holding to the middle of the river.

Twenty-fith of September—DAY FIFTY-TWO

With first twilight, Anton was still rowing. He knew they had to get off the river in daylight. Villagers or bandits might have found the boats, some surely had drifted to the side and they might follow them.

When they came to a confluence, where a smaller river drained into the Amu, he saw the northern banks covered with reed. Anton woke Sidqi, then carefully slid the boat in between and had Sidqi in the back upright any reed that had been displaced. Completely hidden, the boat hit land. Nothing could be seen in any direction, just the river between low banks, flatland on the south side and reeds all along the northern bank and behind a forest of cedars. They carried their belongings to the trees and in a well—hidden cove they placed their sleeping bags. Since there was nothing to do until darkness, they crawled into their sleeping bags. They were sleepy yet still excited from their encounter with the bandits.

"Achmed, why did you kill those three men? They pleaded for mercy."

Anton smiled. Did his gentle friend feel sorry for the bandits?

"How did it feel to kill Sasha's murderer, Sidqi?"

"I was full of hatred, Achmed. I behaved like a madman."

"Are you sorry now that you killed the wounded bandit?"

"No! He deserved to die for what he did. I was full of vengeance, but I was wrong in pumping him full of bullets. One would have been enough and for that I feel bad."

"Why I killed the three begging for mercy? I could say that they were rushing at me, a good excuse to kill them. But Sidqi, I would have shot them anyhow. They were bandits, as guilty as the woman-bandit who shot our friend, Sasha. Who knows how often they have pulled this trap of a wreck and people came to help and were killed and robbed. I am certain they come from either or both villages. In this part of the world, banditry is like a profession. Like pirates, these men show no mercy to those whom they ambush. They did not deserve mercy from us or anyone else who can stop them. For whatever reason I killed them, it had to be done for our safety and self-preservation. To let them live would have meant to alert the village. Once we killed one or two of them, it became a blood feud, their way of life, seeking revenge. Coming to their village meant we were trying to get across the river into Tajikistan. They would have guarded their boats and looked for us with their dogs. Now let's sleep." Anton slept, watched over by Sidqi.

In the late afternoon, when Sidqi awoke Anton, he told him that he had seen boats pass by. As Sidqi explained, "The first one was rowed by four men and moving fast; later boats more slowly searching along the banks." None had ventured into the reeds as it was a sea of greenery and impossible to search. They ate their food.

Anton was sorry that he had not saved the map. It was not on Sasha, he must have put it into the glove compartment. How far to the bridge? He estimated another forty kilometers, three—four hours rowing. When it got dark, they loaded their things in the boat, breeched the reeds and once back in the river, Anton rowed at a good clip.

They saw a campfire along the southern bank and many men sitting around it; the dark outline of boats. They must be the ones who had been looking for them.

Apparently, they had guards who watched the river and one must have seen their boat, or more likely a dark shadow gliding along in the middle of the river. There was a crescent moon and stars shining in the clear night, or perhaps their campfire illuminated them. Anton heard their cries and saw them jump up and reach for their weapons. He could see the flashes of one firing his automatic and saw the splashes nearby in the water. Anton fired his colt at the flashes and they stopped coming. Already Sidqi was firing his AK-47 at the men who were lit up by the campfire. Some dropped; others ran away into the darkness.

Anton told Sidqi to put another magazine in and fire at their boats, which he did. Then he rowed fast. Darkness engulfed them and they went past.

Anton laughed, "The fools! Shooting at us standing by the campfire."

"This was the last magazine, Achmed."

It was close to midnight when they saw the lights.

Twenty-sixth of September—DAY FIFTY-THREE

As they came closer, they saw the bridge and soldiers on it shining with a spotlight over the river. They also saw lights before and after the bridge. The Taliban were looking for them, probably alerted by the men they had seen in the boats, though Anton couldn't imagine how they got to the bridge, not in boats.

He steered the boat to the side and they waited. About two hours after midnight, the lights went off. The moon had set; it was the black of night now Anton went back into the river and staying in the middle, he let the current move their boat along; they safely drifted under the bridge. They could see lights at both ends and soldiers but no one was on the bridge. He rowed again to get away.

When it was getting light in the east, they looked for a good place to hide during the day.

It was all flatland on either side but he knew the north side was in Tajikistan and they were safe there. It was all desert and scrubland and not knowing where they are, and in which direction to walk, Anton decided to continue their journey on the river until they found some habitation to the north. At a small inlet with bushes, he stopped and they pulled the boat on land and hid it behind bushes and there they stayed during the day.

Anton opened some of the cans of food with his knife. They ate it with bread, drank water and Anton went to sleep while Sidqi guarded.

As soon as darkness came they continued, trying to get away from the Taliban as far as they could. There was nothing they could see to the north, no road or lights of villages. How long had they been on the river? It seemed such a long time and yet it was only the third night.

Anton rowed well, they made good speed, rowing or drifting they must have covered a good distance. They spoke little, both feeling the loss of their Russian friend. Anton told Sidqi that since he had saved the cross he would send it to Sasha's mother with a letter.

Sidqi answered, "Perhaps we should go to St. Petersburg and give the cross to his mother and tell her about her son." Sidqi was so very much concerned about parents.

"Maybe. Now sleep, my friend. Who knows what happens tomorrow. We should try to get off the river and go north." Sidqi rolled out his sleeping bag in back of the boat, lay on it and slept.

Twenty-seventh of September—DAY FIFTY-FOUR

During the night, Anton had seen occasional cars drive by on the southern bank in Afghanistan where a road paralleled the river. Later, he saw a few cars pass by to the north. There must be a road in Tajikistan along the river. He let the boat drift and when it got light, it was time to leave the friendly river and make their way along the road to wherever it took them.

CHAPTER XII

UZBEKISTAN, RUSSIA AND RETURN

With first light, Anton stopped at the riverbank as he could see the dirt road nearby. He awoke Sidqi and they decided what to take and how to dress to look more like natives.

They took off their uniforms and dressed in just baggy pants, shirts, kept their jackets and their turban-like caps. Sidqi, with his wound closed and hair growing back took his bandage off. They went through their things and Sasha's bag; there was nothing of value to send home to his mother. The Kalashnikov rifle Anton threw as far as he could into the river, he kept only his pistol with one magazine left.

They checked their money-belts under their shirts; Anton had close to one thousand dollars, his passports and reporter's credential. Sidqi had only Afghani money. Everything else, their packs and sleeping bags they put back into the boat and then pushed the boat out into the river were it slowly glided away. If they were still followed no one would know where they exited the boat.

Since Sidqi's jacket had an inside pocket, Anton had him stash the pistol with the last clip inserted. He would get rid of the Colt as soon as they came to a town or city and they were safe from Taliban and bandits. They hoped they would just appear as Tajikistani workers on their way to their jobs. Unhindered by any baggage, they walked along the road to the west.

There was hardly any traffic and the few cars or trucks going by did not stop when they waved to them, but then it was just after sunrise. Without a map they had no idea where they were—in western Tajikistan?

At last a driver in a small truck came from the east and stopped. When they approached him, the driver exited and spoke in a strange tongue to them. They shook their heads and with their hands indicated that they wished to go with him. Sign language seems to be universal as the driver made gestures with his hands as if counting money—he wanted to be paid. He was a big man, of coarse features, unshaven but without a beard and his clothing was native-like. Only his headgear was unusual, a round cap of smooth fur. Sidqi, as told by Anton, offered the driver a handful of Afghanis. The man shook his head. Anton extracted two 20-dollar bills from his pouch and showed it to the driver. He nodded, apparently familiar with dollars, took the money and stuck it into his pocket. Then suddenly reached down and took a dagger from his boot.

His dark eyes became threatening. He made a gesture to Anton as if he wanted more, or all of his money. A spasm of laughter shook Anton, a man threatening him with a dagger, he a judo expert, trained in disarming just such a man. He went into the attack posture with his hands open and stared dangerous at the driver. At the same time, Sidqi had taken his pistol and held it loose, pointing down. It was again universal sign language as the driver held his hands palm up and moving them from side to side—he wanted no part from either one. Since he saw Anton still laugh, the driver grinned and showed his bad teeth, some missing. But there was also fear in his eyes and he said something in Russian, "Don't kill me." And then with obvious relief. "As salam olekum (hello)." Anton took his dagger away and put it in his pocket. Anton spoke to him in Russian and the driver explained that he was a Russian living in Termez and returning with a load of fruit from a farm. They piled into the front seat of the truck, Anton sitting in the middle to keep an eye on the driver and Sidqi still held the pistol. Anton spoke with the driver, asked him if he had been more afraid of him or his friend's pistol.

The driver answered grinning, "I was not afraid of the pistol, the way he held it he was not a shooter, or of you in your fighting stance. I am, or was a good boxer. It was your eyes I was afraid of, fierce, the eyes of a killer."

"I am glad you didn't try anything, I can be a killer though I rather not hurt or kill anyone," Anton answered smiling.

The driver then told his story. His name was Boris Sokolov and he was originally from Kiev in the Ukraine. He came here as a Soviet bureaucrat to Termiz. Anton asked in surprise, "Are you an Uzbek now? Where are we?"

"In Uzbekistan, man. Where did you think we were?"

"Oh yes, I remember seeing it on the map, Termiz is in Uzbekistan. How far are we from the town?"

"About forty kilometers. Where did you come from?"

Anton turned to Sidqi and in Arabic said, "We are in Uzbekistan, Sidqi. Better yet, we are close to the town of Termiz. From there we should have good transportation to the north." Sidqi was just as pleased, "We came a long way during these three nights on the river. Is the driver really a Russian?"

"Yes, he is just telling me his story. His name is Boris."

Boris continued explaining, how he decided to stay in Termiz after the Soviet Union became Russia and the republics became independent. He married a woman from Termiz and had four children. He had bought a fruit store and brought fruit and vegetables from farmers.

"Then you are not a bandit?" Asked Anton.

"Oh, no. I have never robbed anyone. My wife is sick and I have a child in the hospital, business is bad. When I saw the money belt and dollars I, being desperate for money, decided to take it from you." Anton wondered how much was true. The big Russian seemed more meek than vicious and his smile genuine friendly. Anton was sick of violence.

"Why did you carry a dagger in your boot?"

"To defend myself from bandits, they prowl both sides of the river." Anton asked Boris if there was good transportation up north.

"Yes, a bus is going to Samarkand every morning. From there the train leaves for Tashkent. Are you an Arab? I heard you speak to your young friend in Arabic."

"You speak Arabic? I heard you say *as salam olekum?*"

"No, that is Uzbek. Maybe also Arabic. Look, emir . . ."

Anton interrupted, "Don't call me emir, my name is Achmed."

"Thank you, Achmed. After I unload my wares, I can drive you to Samarkand."

"How far is it? And how much do you want Boris?"

"Samarkand is about 400 kilometers from Termiz. Some roads are good, some narrow, some through plains, up mountains. I take you for free; you were good to me even though I tried to take your money."

"What money do you use here?"

"Not the Afghanis your friend showed me. We use the som. If you have dollars, you get thirty-five som for a dollar. You can buy anything for a dollar but locally in restaurants and hotels, on the bus or train you need som. If you need to change money, I take you to a money changer and watch that he doesn't cheat you."

"I will pay you a hundred dollars if you take us safely to Samarkand."

"You are very generous, Achmed. My wife will be pleased even though I spent the day and night away from home and will again if I drive you to Samarkand. May I ask where you come from?"

"We are Egyptian reporters and come from Afghanistan. We had some troubles with the Taliban and decided to go north; we thought we are in Tajikistan."

"Ah yes, the Taliban bad people. Fanatics. Not good for Afghanistan. You came by car, walking, by boat?"

"You don't need to know, Boris."

"Yes, Boris is nosy. Don't need to know everything."

Soon they came into the town of Termiz and saw small houses with gardens. Boris stopped by a market store with vegetables and fruits. A very healthy woman came out and helped him unload. Anton said to Sidqi, "He was lying about his wife being sick, probably his child is not sick either. It doesn't matter. Hide your pistol and we will move on to Samarkand.

After Boris and his wife unloaded the baskets and he explained to her, they left and Boris stopped at a money-changer. The man wanted to give only thirty som for the dollar. Boris bargained with him and he finally offered thirty-three som, which Anton accepted and changed five hundred dollars. Then Boris drove to a gas station and Anton paid to fill up.

It was eight in the morning when they left Termiz for the long ride to Samarkand. At noon, they stopped in a village and at a small inn, ate *plov*, a mixture of rice and meat. Boris had some arak, Anton and Sidqi had black tea, drinking it with a cube of sugar between their teeth as they had learned.

They continued their journey and drove through the Hissar Alai Mountains. The road narrowed with many serpentines and the driving was slow. Then out of the mountains the scenery was barren and dotted with hills, only near villages or irrigation canals were there fields and orchards, some grassland with cattle and horses grazing.

It was already dusk when they reached the fabled city of Samarkand. It had taken them longer than Boris said. Boris dropped them off at the Zarafshan hotel, near Central Park, and Anton paid him his money. Boris was now the friendly Russian, as he embraced and kissed both, and bade them *khiyr*, goodbye in Uzbek and *do svedanya* in Russian.

First a long hot shower, and how they had missed taking a hot bath since they left Egypt.

After a frugal evening meal of bread, cheese and tea they walked around the block where the hotel was. The buildings were small, usually just one or two stories high. There were stores and the writing was in both Arabic and Russian alphabet, though Anton couldn't understand either, as the language was Uzbek. Then behind the hotel, he found trashcans and in one he buried the pistol under garbage, the last of their armory.

Twenty-eighth of September—DAY FIFTY-FIVE

They decided to stay an extra day in Samarkand and explore the fabled city.

From their window on the second floor and with the hotel on a rise, they could look over Samarkand. It was a beautiful city and they saw many mosques with blue cupolas, tall minarets, even a few churches, but also drab apartment houses interspersed with parks and trees. In the far distance lay brown plains, desert land and beyond barren hills.

The clerk at the hotel spoke Russian and told them, "The city has a population of 350,000. It has an old history dating back to the Common Era. Samarkand was destroyed by the Mongols under Genghis Khan in 1220, later the Mongol warlord Timur rebuilt Samarkand, and you can find many mosques, madrassas and mausoleums." He also told them what to see, foremost the Registran, a madras complex of four beautiful buildings, which was built during the fifteenth to seventeenth centuries.

They decided to see the Registran first and took a taxi there. It was beautiful, with dazzling tilework of oriental designs, a large courtyard with gardens and a small fountain. Each building of the complex had big doorways pointing almost to the roofs. There were towers, the half-round cupolas again in blue tile and slender elaborate minarets. Whatever the Soviets used it for, it was again a Madras; a school for religious training. Very impressive was the Shakki-Zinda Mausoleum, the tomb of an Arab missionary who was responsible for bringing the Islamic faith to Central Asia and Samarkand. In a park they saw the famous sculpture from Uzbek folkore—the figure of Nasredin Hodja teaching a monkey to read the Koran.

"If that sculpture had been in Afghanistan, the Taliban would have demolished it," Anton said. While much of the city was old, there were many modern structures and besides the newly built apartment houses, many one story dwellings with plain wooden fences around and gardens inside and not the fortress-like or walled compounds they had seen in Kabul and other towns in Afghanistan.

They visited the bazaar outside the Bibi Khanym Mosque and here they could see the people of Samarkand; a mixture of Uzbeks and Tajiks in their native clothing, some in robes and turbans, others modern dressed, women in headscarves or their dark hair in braids. Anton could spot the Russians with their fur caps and elderly women in a scarf covering their hair, babushka style. They would have to buy decent clothing.

In a bank by the bazaar, Achmed changed the rest of his dollars into som, as they needed money to get to Tashkent and buy airline tickets. Here he received the full worth of thirty-five som to the dollar.

They had lunch at the bazaar and later visited the central outdoor market. Then walked to the train station and inquired about the train to Tashkent. The morning train would leave at seven. The distance to Tashkent was another 400 kilometers and they should arrive at two in the afternoon.

Twenty-ninth of September—DAY FIFTY-SIX

The train compartment was second class and comfortable; the seven hours ride less interesting than their ride from Termiz to Samarkand. Without rivers, the land was dsolate and anything cultivated was done with irrigation.

Since they had no baggage, they quickly left the station in Tashkent and when Anton spotted a taxi driver with a fur cap, he and Sidqi used his cab and told the driver, who was Russian, to take them into the city and a comfortable medium priced hotel. They stopped at the Hotel Orzu and had to show their passports when registering. The room was modern; it had two beds and their own shower and toilet. First again a long hot shower.

At once they took a taxi to the central post office, as the hotel clerk had adviced them that from there they could make calls to any place in the world. He also wrote down the name of a bank, which dealt in foreign currencies. The post office was huge, of white stone and on top still the Soviet Star and writing in Russian CENTRAL POST OFFICE AND TELEGRAPH. Anton found a clerk in the telephone center who spoke Russian and soon he was in the booth and connected to Cairo and the hospital where Hanna worked. It was four o'clock in Tashkent, two hours ahead of Cairo. When the ward nurse answered he asked for Hanna Nagil, Anton was back with Arabic.

"*Na'am*—yes?" Antons's heart filled with joy when he heard his Hanna's voice.

"*Es salaem* alekum (hello), Hanna!"

"TONI! Toni . . . oh, Toni, where are you?" He heard her sob.

"Are you crying, Hanna?"

"Yes, I am, I am sooo happy!"

Anton told Hanna he was in Tashkent, in Uzbekistan and on his way home. He told her little of his stay in Afghanistan, nothing about having been shot. But, that Sidqi was with him.

"And Ali?" Anton had to give Hanna the bad news that Ali was killed. He would visit his parents and tell them.

"Toni, you were in danger! I had this feeling that things were bad for you wherever you were; I had this intuition. I haven't heard from you since you left."

He told her that he had written several times from Khost; but none of the letters had ever arrived. He added "I have to give similar sad news to the mother of a friend of ours, a Russian. Sidqi and I will travel first to St. Petersburg and visit her, then from there we fly home to Cairo.

"I am so sorry about Ali, but you are safe and coming home Toni. WHEN?" Hanna shouted into the phone.

"In three days we should be back. Tomorrow we will fly to St. Petersburg, one day there and the next day to Cairo."

He then asked her to send five thousand dollars to a bank here in Tashkent and he gave her the name of the bank and address. Hanna said that she would at once go to their bank and have the money transmitted by wire, and asked how to reach him in Tashkent. He gave her the phone number for the hotel. She promised to call in the evening and have him tell her all about his adventures in Afghanistan, and why he is in Uzbekistan.

"Ma'as salaema, Hanna."

"Goodbye, Toni, until this evening."

Then Sidqi went into the booth to call his parents.

When Anton saw tears roll down his friend's face, he knew that his parents were just as happy as his Hanna had been.

Later they drove to the World Bank, a squat, white one-story building sitting along a broad avenue, but the money had not arrived.

Driving through the city of Tashkent, they saw the typical large Soviet apartment houses along wide avenues and government buildings, big edifices. At a traffic circle was a huge monument of a woman and man commemorating the Soviet workers who helped rebuild Tashkent after the disastrous earthquake of 1966. The streets were wide and there were many parks, mosques and churches. Tashkent was a modern Russian city and had nothing of the charm of ancient Samarkand. There was even a subway but since they did not know their way around and all signs were in Russian and Arabic but Uzbek language, they had to rely on taxis.

They returned to their hotel. Anton spoke again to the clerk and gave him ten dollars worth of som. He needed a flight schedule to St. Petersburg. The clerk called to Aeroflot and wrote down a number of flights to Moscow. From there, they could continue to St. Petersburg. He also advised them that he saw in their passports a lack of an entry visa to Uzbekistan and they would have trouble boarding a flight to Russia without proper documentation. When Anton asked the clerk about an Egyptian embassy or consulate, he said there was an Egyptian legation in Tashkent and he made the connection on the phone.

Anton spoke to an official about the visa they lacked. The official told them to come by and they could apply for an entry visa but it would take several weeks to get it.

It was only after Anton told the official that he was traveling for the Egyptian Army Intelligence and had to flee Afghanistan and to call Brigadier Abd al-Hakim Amer in Cairo and give him the code word *perach*, that the man told him he would and call him at the hotel. They went to their room and fifteen minutes later the phone rang. The legation head Mustafa Said Nosair called and brought greeting from Brigadier Amer. He told Anton to come by at nine in the morning and he would take their passports to the foreign office and have the visa secured.

It was already evening when the phone rang, it was Hanna. Anton had a long conversation with his wife and told some of what had happened; omitting that he had been shot, Sidqi's rape and the trouble with the bandits. After an incident with the Taliban, they thought it best to go north into Uzbekistan and arrived here in Tashkent. Hanna spoke about her work in the hospital and that her mother in Jerusalem was fine. His mother called a few times and she told her that he was on a trip for the army and she had not told her that he went to Afghanistan, as she didn't know either.

"But mainly I am lonely, alone in the big house and only thinking of you."

"Misae el kher, dear Hanna (have a nice evening)."

"Good night, my darling," she replied.

Thirtieth of September—DAY FIFTY-SEVEN

Early in the morning they checked out of the hotel and gave the clerk a generous tip. A taxi took them to the Egyptian legation where they met Mustafa Nosair and gave him their passports. Anton also asked him to procure a permit for Russia and told him why they needed to go to St. Petersburg.

They went to the bank; their money had arrived and he took it in dollars. From there they went into town to a clothing store where they bought themselves decent clothing to look like journalists: shoes, a small bag to carry their things in, and tobacco. They discarded their own clothing. Nearby was a jewelry store and Anton bought a necklace of semi-precious stones for Hanna, as did Sidqi for his mother and a gold ring for his father.

From there they went to a café and had breakfast and in a barbershop Anton had his beard shaved off. After, they returned to the Egyptian legation. They had to wait until afternoon for Nosair to return with their passports and stamped permits. Nosair told them that he had already ordered their tickets to St. Petersburg and they were paid for, courtesy of the legation, as requested by the brigadier.

A driver from the legation took them to the airport where they had to wait for the evening flight to Moscow. In the bar, Anton had Russian beer, Sidqi just tea. Anton smoked his pipe in leisure; it seemed that all was going smoothly for a change.

Later in the restaurant they ate a light meal of baked sweet cakes with honey, served by a waiter who understood Russian. When they walked in front of the terminal they spotted a beggar women and her little wretched looking boy. Sidqi looked at Anton and then at the woman in her shabby clothing. Despite their giving baksheesh—tips to everyone who helped them and their purchases, Anton still had a large sum of som left. He gave it all to the woman and Sidqi was pleased. The woman, after thanking them in her native language and with many bows of gratitude at once hurried off with her boy—Christmas had come early for her. Then they checked in for the flight.

The flight arrived in Moscow past midnight. This time there was no problem with their passports and Anton could speak to everyone in Russian. The Sheremetyevo airport was rather primitive and all facilities were closed. With many others, they took a seat in the waiting room for their early morning flight to St. Petersburg.

First of October—DAY FIFTY-EIGHT

The flight arrived in St. Petersburg before noon.

They took a taxi to the address Sasha had given them. Since it was Sunday, they expected Natasha Tokareva to be at home. Both with a heavy heart, Anton rang the bell. A blond, middle aged woman, in simple clothing opened. "*Da?*"

"Are you Natasha Tokareva?"

She smiled. "At one time if I received a visit from two strange men I would have been afraid it is the KGB, asking me if I am Tokareva. You look like friendly men. So, yes, I am Tokareva. What can I do for you? Now you look serious, I must be in trouble?"

Anton nodded, "It is about Sasha." Maybe it was his demeanor or the sadness in his eyes, at once the woman turned away and they saw her cry, her shoulder heaving in distress . . . without turning she asked, "Is Sasha . . . is he dead?"

"Yes, Natasha. I bring you his last greetings. May we tell you?" She turned and gestured for them to come in. They came into her sparse living room, she left them. They sat down on the old sofa. Anton took the little plastic bag with her picture, the lock of blond hair and the necklace with the cross and laid it on the table.

There was only silence from the next room. Anton asked Sidqi, "Should we just leave?"

Sidqi shook his head, "She wants to know."

After a while later Natasha returned carrying a tray of tea and cookies. She poured two cups and motioned them to sit at the table with her. Anton was stunned, even in her grief, she wished to show hospitality. With the back of her hand she wiped tears away, then looked at Anton, "Tell me, please." Then she saw the plastic bag . . . her picture, the cross and the lock of golden hair, "From Sasha?"

"Yes." She took the little package and held it dear to her chest, tears rolling down her cheeks.

Anton told her how they met Sasha in the Panjshir Valley, their trip together, his good heartedness to help the people, how he was shot, died in his arms, "His last words, 'tell my mother that I love her.'" They sat in silence and let Natasha cry.

Anton took two thousand dollars and laid it on the table, with his address in Cairo, bent over the woman and kissed her head, padded her hand that held the bag, "Natasha, come and visit us in Cairo and I tell you all about your son, Sasha," and they left the grieving woman. There was nothing else he could say or do for her.

By taxi they returned to St. Petersburg's Pulkovo airport, neither one in the mood to visit the sights of Sasha's beautiful city. There was an afternoon flight to Frankfurt in Germany and from there flights to Egypt.

Once in Frankfurt, a modern airport, they took a taxi to a hotel. Here in Germany, Anton could speak his native language.

At the restaurant he treated Sidqi to a culinary German dinner: stuffed beef roulade, followed by *Sachertorte*—a sort of Black Forest cake—and ice cream. Anton had a glass of beer, Sidqi had his tea. They sat in peace with themselves,

Anton smoked his pipe and they reminisced about the past two months. About Ali, to both the best of friend. They avoided the violence and tragedies they had seen and encountered.

But there had been some good times when the three had been together, especially the evenings in the camp after training.

Sidqi remembered the time in the Panjshir Valley, the weeks when he had nursed Anton, then when he could walk, their visiting the town of Barak. "I enjoyed the evenings when we sat by the swift flowing Panjshir River until the sun set behind the mountain peaks and it became chilly and we returned to our quiet hospital room."

Anton thought he enjoyed most of the times after they met Sasha, who was so exuberant and sang Russian songs in the car.

"Remember when he taught us how to sing the song of the Evening Bells? How he laughed when we couldn't get the right resonance to imitate the bells?"

"Sasha said you sounded like an old frog croaking," chided Sidqi.

"And you Sidqi like a duck squawking." They laughed remembering.

"But you know, Sidqi, once we did it right, got the proper tone and came in at the right time, it sounded good. His voice was so beautiful, so clear and full of joy. He should have become a singer. Russian folk songs are really wonderful."

"But also melancholic, Achmed."

"Yes. It shows the Russian soul."

Anton, who had a fine baritone voice, began to sing "Evening Bells" softly in Russian.

> *Vecherniy zvon* (Evening Bells ringing)
> *Kak mnogo doom Navodit on* (bringing thoughts of memories)
> . . . *boom* . . . *boom* . . . *boom* . . . *boom.*

And Sidqi chimed in with the higher sounding bells, and the restaurant was suddenly silent, and then others accompanied them with the sound of bells until Anton had finished the inspiring song. Everyone clapped their hands and looked at the two, which made them feel embarrassed. Anton was surprised that so many in Germany knew this Russian song.

After a couple minutes of silence while they remembered, Anton added, "And Sasha was always ready to brew tea for us, fix something to eat, then clean up, and talking about his big, beautiful St. Petersburg."

"I never understood what he was talking about" Sidqi said, "But I saw the happiness in him, his eyes sparkling, smiling and laughing. He was a good man, tried to please us all the time. He wanted us to like him."

"He was a good friend to us, and we liked him. He knew and felt it."

"So happy to go home. But it was written in the book that he should never return, Allah willed it."

Anton felt that they were getting into the sad part of their flight from Afghanistan and he treasured their being together in this fine restaurant, and going home.

"Tell me Sidqi, what are your plans for the future. You finished high school; wouldn't it please your parents if you went to a university?" And smiled knowingly at his friend, he added, "You accomplished what you set out to do, my friend."

"I believe; I know, I have gained my manhood. My parents always wanted me to become a doctor. I shall go to medical school."

"I almost have the urge to go to Munich and visit my mother. I have to show you the city; it is beautiful, maybe not as grand as St. Petersburg as Sasha believed. I would like to take you into the mountains and climb some of the peaks as I used to do when I was a teenager. Have you ever seen or felt snow?"

"I saw the white peaks of snow and ice in the Kush Mountains."

"No, there is more to it than to see from a distance. My Hanna is enchanted with winter in Munich, each Christmas we vacation there with my mother. Hanna just loves to get all bundled up and walk out into a snowstorm, feel the cold, with each breath exhaled into a white cloud. She takes her glove off and lets a snowflake fall on her hand and then tastes it. She is like a child in winter wonderland, frolicking around. Then home into the warmth of the house, the fire crackling in the hearth, or we go downstairs into our hot jacuzzi."

"I would love to visit with you, Achmed."

"You will. In summer, we can vacation with Hanna's mother in Jerusalem. I will show you the Old City, we will visit the Haram al-Sharif—the Temple Mount and the Holy Sanctuary and we can see it from our house up on the hill."

"I will come, the Haram al-Sharif is the third holiest place for Muslims to visit. Maybe it all comes true."

"Insha'allah (If Allah) the most Gracious One, wills it."

Sidqi smiled. "You speak like a Muslim, Achmed."

Anton laughed, "Don't I have Muslim blood in me?"

"We are blood brothers."

Then Sidqi asked, "Should we go to Munich and visit your mother?"

"Hanna, my wife, is waiting for me."

Sidqi smiled. "Oh yes, love."

"Someday you too will find love. She is already waiting for you, dreaming of you, wanting you to hold her in your arms."

"You are a romantic, Achmed."

"So are you, Sidqi."

Second of October—DAY FIFTY-NINE

They took the morning flight to Cairo and arrived five hours later. The custom inspector scrutinized their passports—"Afghanistan, Uzbekistan, Russia, you had a nice vacation?"

Sidqi exhaled deeply, showing his reservation to having had a nice vacation.

Anton only said, "Fantastic."

At the taxi stand they looked at each other, "I don't even know the names of your parents, Sidqi or where you live, your phone number."

"My father is Saleh Suliman, my mother's name is Rudenah. They will welcome you, Achmed." He wrote down his address and phone.

They embraced. "Ma'as saleama (go in peace), Sidqi."

"And peace be with you, Achmed."

Anton took a taxi to the hospital. And there, in the children's ward was his Hanna singing with the children. He was glad—then their getting together would not be so emotional. Anton should have known better, when Hanna saw him she screamed out and flew into his arms, and as he held her dear, she cried tears of joy.

That night, when they lay together and they touched each other in their embrace, and her hand went around his shoulder she cried out in horror "Toni! There is a hole in your shoulder!"

He kissed her gently, "It is nothing Hanna, just a dumb bullet that ricocheted off the seat." Then they united in love.

In the days to come, there was much to tell. Anton would never tell her how Sidqi was violated, how close he had come to being killed if the rifle had it not misfired. How he had killed all the bandits, except for the one who had murdered Sasha, nor that Sidqi had fired his whole magazine into the bandit.

CHAPTER XIII

THE YEARS 1998-2004

Anton had been gone for two months and one of his first duties was to visit with Ali's family. For this sad event, he called Sidqi who knew the family better than he did. Ali's father had been proud of his son's becoming an imam and had encouraged Ali to go to a training camp in Afghanistan. He knew that Anton was accompanying Ali as an explosive expert to teach the jihadists bomb making and also that Sidqi Suliman was with them.

At Anton's suggestion, Sidqi called Mr. Nasr and told him of his son's death, and if he wished we would visit with him. Nasr asked Sidqi to bring Anton as he was present at his son's killing.

At the arranged time, Anton and Sidqi visited the house of Nasr and it became a formal occasion as Zahi Nasr was rather reserved and did not even show the normal hospitality of having refreshments or coffee served. To Anton, it seemed as if he blamed both for the death of his son. He only spoke to Sidqi and rarely asked Anton for an explanation. Anton thought that Sidqi did right by not telling that Ali stepped before him and received the bullet, but instead said that there was a dispute about religious matters that enraged the Yemeni al-Moqrin and he shot Ali. He seemed pleased when Sidqi told him that Achmed then hit the Yemeni with a shovel in the face that blinded him and when he briefly looked at Anton his eyes were less unfriendly for a moment.

He asked about the burial and nodded in agreement when he was told that it was with proper Islamic ritual. He wanted to know the exact location of the grave, which Anton supplied. When the interview was over, he disappeared without saying anything and had the servant take Anton and Sidqi to the door.

Anton and Sidqi became close friends, or rather continued their close friendship and visited each other. Sidqi's parents welcomed Anton in their home and he visited him and Hanna. Though devout Muslims, they were friendly with nonbelievers. Whatever Sidqi had told them, they saw in Anton as his protector in Afghanistan.

Anton had called Brigadier Amer and was invited to visit him in his office. He spent the afternoon with the brigadier as he had much to tell, and he told Amer the truth. He also supplied the names of the five Egyptian Jihadist which was important to the Chief of Army Intelligence as even one Islamic Jihad member could supply much information about their cell and other members; having five members was that much more important. While the brigadier did not say so, Anton knew that the five would be arrested upon their return from Afghanistan. He also gave him the names of the three jihadists who were murdered by the Yemenis. Information could also be obtained from their families.

As far as assassinating al-Zawhiri, Anton told him that it was impossible, al-Zawahiri, the same as bin Laden, was always surrounded by many bodyguards.

Anton had resigned his reserve commission and was free of any army obligation.

After having fulfilled his missions, Anton flew to Munich for a few days to be with his mother. From there he went to Israel and visited Amal in Jerusalem and saw his Mossad contact, but there was little of interest he could report from his trip to Afghanistan that pertained to the security of Israel, except the warning he gave Nevot about explosive laden airplanes. He never found out if this information was passed on the United States.

Of interest to the Mossad was the composition of the many volunteers who attended the training camps. Few Europeans he knew of besides the Swede, the German and the two British. He had heard of some Americans attending in the other camps. There were also Chechnians, Iranians, Somalis, some from Asian countries and Indonesia. The others mostly from Arab countries.

Later in October, Natasha Tokareva came to visit. She was now composed about her son's death but wished to know every day, every detail they spent with Sasha. One benefit of her week's stay was that Hanna and Anton received Russian cooking. Anton showed Natasha Cairo and drove her to the pyramids. In November, Anton returned to the academy to teach chemistry and judo.

Hanna and Anton led a good life. They were always together now and deeply in love. In spring, Hanna transferred to the medical school to teach pediatric nursing. Whenever possible, she volunteered in the children's ward as she had a way with sick children and was much appreciated. It helped her overcome her feeling of sadness of not having children of her own. One reason she wanted the teaching job was that the school was closed during the summer and they could spend the long vacation with her mother in Jerusalem. Summer in Jerusalem, winter vacation in Munich. Rosemarie was now old, but healthy and lively and always cheerful.

September 11, 2001: It was during an afternoon class that Anton, or Achmed as he was known at the Academy, heard a commotion outside in the hall. When he looked he saw people running. A teacher yelled to him "The television, watch the television Achmed!"

He called for a recess in the class, rushed to the teacher's lounge and saw many sitting there looking at the set. He stared in disbelief as he saw one of the World Trade Center's tower smoking, a fire high up. Someone said a plane had crashed into the tower.

Then, for a brief moment he saw another large plane hit the other tower. A huge flame engulfed the building around the middle. This was no longer an accident but a deliberate crashing of a plane. TERRORISTS. His first thoughts were, *The poor people in the plane, incinerated alive!* Anton had to return to class. He was devastated by the deed. *How could they do this!*

When he came home, Hanna knew about it. They sat in horrified silence as again they saw the second plane smash into the tower and the explosion. People from the higher floors falling to their death. Just as terrifying when the two towers crumpled, just caked down in a cloud of dust. Another scene of a plane having smashed into the Pentagon in Washington. Report of a fourth plane having crashed in the countryside of Pennsylvania.

By then, it was known that terrorists had crashed these four planes deliberately; reports by cell phones of passengers that planes had been hihjacked. No one knew by whom. Some reports suggested it was bin Laden's doing. Anton understood now why Atta wished to learn about explosive-laden planes. Was he involved? It is one thing to crash a plane like a bomb into a target and another to hihjack a passenger plane with people and crash it into an office building full of innocents. The horrible scenes were repeated many times on Egyptian television that evening and for days to come.

There were also scenes of Palestinian people dancing in the streets full of joy as to so many Americans were killed brutally and celebrating by giving candy to children.

It would be a few days before American authorities pieced together who the perpetrators of this foul crime were. Islamic Fundamentalists, Mohamed Atta was one of their leaders and piloted the first plane into the South Tower. It wasn't explosive laden planes after all but large passenger planes laden with thousands of gallons of high octane fuel. Other facts emerged that Arabs had taken pilot training in America, first with small planes and then in simulators to learn how to fly large passenger planes. The FBI had been negligent, America slept.

Who would ever expect that even terrorists would commit such a vile crime, killing thousands of innocent civilians in such a horrible manner? If not burnt alive, they were smashed into little pieces of humanity by the fall of the towers.

The best comment Anton heard was from one of the Danish teachers who said to him, *"What foul womb vomited these creatures, spermed by the devil, that turned them into these monsters."*

Anton did not discuss it with Hanna. Hanna was deeply saddened and also shocked by the dancing in the streets. "How could they dance in jubilation when thousands died a most horrible death? What kind of people are they? There are no words to describe their inhumanity."

Anton could not help her in her grief and explain how anyone, even fundamentalists could commit such an abomination against Allah or why the Palestinian women could dance and praise Allah in the streets. Yet he understood. Nazis and Islamic terrorists were the same type of people, savages.

He tried to remember Mohamed Atta when he saw him, talked to him. What an aberration of human kind. What made him into a mass murderer, was it religion? He did not believe so. Unless one was a follower of Satan or his god was Kali—the Destroyer, how could anyone believe that God or Allah would wish for him to murder?

No, these crimes had nothing to do with religion. It was hate that drove them into committing these acts. Giving in to the most abominable instincts humans can profess—HATE! Atta and his ilk devoid of any civilized traits that separate mankind from beasts. No, worse; as even the wildest beast has none of those destroying instincts, and then use the mantel of religion, or in the case of Otto, a feeling of superiority, the super-*Mensch*, to justify their inhumanity.

The only justice in all this was that the remains of Atta and his cohorts would be scattered in the landfills around New York and Washington together with the other garbage. No paradise or resurrection for any of them, only hell or everlasting death. This Anton believed, as he believed in a God of Justice.

It was in the year of 2002 that Sidqi married Fatima, a student in medical school. Sidqi Suliman had finally learned what love was and meant.

Sidqi did become a surgeon and Fatima a pediatrician as Hanna had influenced her for a love of needy and sick children. Hanna and Fatima had become good friends and many times the two would spend a couple weeks during the summer in Jerusalem with Sidqi and Anton.

Amal had made many friends in Jerusalem. She had integrated into Israeli society where socializing with neighbors and friends is so important and the main enjoyment of most, if not all Israelis.

Anton was still friends with Tal and her family in Tel Aviv. When in Israel, he would have his meeting with Mordechai Nevot of the Mossad, though by then he was a rather inactive agent. Yet he could bring news from Egypt and Army Intelligence which was battling its own brand of terrorists, and even no news was important if only that it showed that Egypt's was and would remain distant but still on friendly terms and worked with Israeli military along the Gaza to stop weapon and terrorist infiltration.

CHAPTER XIV

GOODBYE CAIRO

It was in the year 2004 that Anton and Hanna, doing their budget, realized that they were no longer affluent and could no longer keep three houses. Neither the Nagil nor the Zapruder families had been savy in managing their finances and never invested their money profitably. While their houses were all paid off, it was property taxes, maintenance, having two cars, house and car insurance and providing support for his mother Rosemarie and Hanna's mother Amal, plus their own lifestyle of traveling to Germany and Israel frequently, that told them that they could not continue in this fashion.

Salaries in Egypt for a teacher and nurse were sufficient to afford them a comfortable living there but not to take care of all the other expenses.

Rosemarie, who was now eighty-one, received a small pension that took care of her personal needs but not the house.

Amal, who was in her mid-fifties, did volunteer work at the Hadassah hospital and used the car going there. She was completely dependent upon Anton and Hanna.

Having two beloved mothers in two different countries, they agreed that to keep their houses and supporting Rosemarie and Amal was the most important matter. It also meant that they had to sell their house in Cairo, give up their jobs there—and do what?

Anton inquired with Mordechai Nevot about the possibility of finding work with the Mossad in Israel. Not being a citizen of Israel it was not possible; it was the same with Shin Bet. What else could he do in Israel? Work at the Egyptian embassy in Tel Aviv? He was certain that Brigadier Amer could help him but it would also mean he had to spy on Israel.

Besides, his mother now being an old lady, he wished to stay with her and Hanna. A job in Germany, in Munich? It was his mother who suggested to Anton to try with the Munich police department.

During the summer vacation, which Anton and Hanna spent in Jerusalem, Anton flew to Munich to spend a few days with his mother and visited police headquarters in the Ettstrasse. He was directed to personnel and at once told that new police recruits must not be older than thirty-four. Anton Nagil was thirty-nine. Anton did not give up but asked to speak to the head of personnel, and was taken to the office of Herr Meier.

"And what can I do for you, Herr Nagil? You were told that we only accept new applicants for the police under the age of thirty-four. Yet my aid tells me that you have special qualifications that would interest us in you. May I ask what these qualifications are? Are you already a police officer?"

"I am a German and Egyptian citizen. I lived in Cairo and speak Arabic and also fluent in English and Russian. I am a chemical engineer and have experience with explosives. I was in the Egyptian army for two years and one year in its special forces, a major in army reserve. I am familiar with every type of small arms. I am also a judo expert in hand combat. As far as police work, I was with Army Intelligence and went on many missions for them to Middle East countries, and also to Afghanistan. Do you think I qualify as a Munich policeman despite my age?"

Herr Meier smiled. "Perhaps. We have a special unit where your qualifications might be needed, especially your knowledge of Arabic. Let me ask you, Herr Nagil, why the sudden desire to live in Germany and seek employment here?"

"My mother was born in Munich as was I, though I grew up in Cairo. My mother inherited the house of her parents in Planegg and moved there permanently in 1995. She is now eighty-one, and even if in good health, I wish to be with her."

"What are you doing now in Egypt, are you still employed there?"

"I am a teacher of chemistry at a prestigious school."

"You have the necessary documents of your degrees and employment?"

"Yes, of course."

"Your army service and membership in Army Intelligence?"

"Yes. However, my work in Intelligence is classified and I cannot give any documents pertaining to my service with them. To get confirmation, your department would have to get in touch with the Chief of the Service and it is up to him to give particulars."

"I understand, Herr Nagil. Please have a seat and I will talk to my superiors." Anton waited and read the newspaper that was lying on the desk. After twenty minutes, Herr Meier returned. He had a number of forms, which he gave to Anton.

"I spoke with Inspector Wagner of the special counter-terrorism unit and he is interested in you and your qualifications. There is use for an Arabic speaking police officer in his unit. Here is the usual application to join the Munich police force, disregard the advice about age limit. Attach to this form your birth certificate. You also have to submit a resume, list your life from birth to present time. In your case, Inspector Wagner wishes to know everything about your life." Herr Meier smiled. "You understand, it is unusual to have an applicant with your qualifications. You need a health certificate. We would prefer if you bring it from a German doctor, we don't read Arabic here," Herr Meier laughed. "I wish you good luck, Herr Nagil, and *auf Wiedersehen.*"

Rosemarie was happy when Anton told her that there was a good possibility he could find a position with the police in Munich.

During the next few days, he visited a physician in Planegg who promised to send the health report to his address there. Some papers he could get in Munich, the rest he would have to get in Cairo. His resume he would write there.

In Cairo, he also visited Brigadier Amer and told him about his leaving Egypt and getting a job with the Munich police department. The brigadier was sorry to lose him but told him that Egypt worked together with Germany combating terrorism and that they should keep in touch through the Egyptian Embassy in Germany. The brigadier asked to let him know of any Egyptian citizen arrested for terrorist activities or suspected in Munich. "We all have to work together to combat the scourge of terrorism, Achmed Nabil. And if I hear of any suspected terrorist coming to Germany, I let you know." And with a friendly handshake the brigadier bade him goodbye.

It took Anton several months to get all the documents together and he then submitted them to Inspector Wagner in October. He realized that it would take a number of weeks, or even months, for them to verify his papers, and make up their minds if they wanted and needed him.

Anton sold the house in Cairo together with furnishings and his car, which again gave him sufficient funds. However, a steady income was needed for the future. He was looking forward to joining the police, and while he would have preferred a position with the police in Israel or Shin Bet, he was quite happy to be in Munich and with his mother for the rest of her years. Hanna also would have liked to live permanently in Israel but she knew and approved of Toni's wish to be with Rosemarie. Now that they were affluent again, they would fly to Israel whenever possible to be with her mother, even during a long weekend they could visit. What would happen later, when Rosemarie was no longer with them, only time will tell.

On the first of November they left for Israel, some of their belongings would follow along, most of their personal possessions to Munich. After a few days in Jerusalem, Anton left for Munich to await a reply from Inspector Wagner. Hanna would follow in December. Hanna found work as a volunteer pediatric nurse in a hospital in Jerusalem, which permitted her to work her own days. While in Munich, he bought a BMW.

CHAPTER XV

ANTON NAGIL IN MUNICH

Munich-Germany. Wednesday, December 1, 2004, a quarter to nine in the morning.

It was a cold, wintry morning with snow flurries driving in his face, when Anton turned into the Ettstrasse and entered the *Polizeipraesidium* (police headquarters). He had an appointment with Inspector Wagner of the Munich counter-terrorism unit. Stating his business and showing his passport at the information desk, which was really a booth with a bulletproof window, a microphone through which he had given his name and showed his identification to the *Beamte* (official), he was let into the building and a directory took him to the proper room of Inspector Wagner. Anton knocked and went in. The man sitting at the desk stood up and greeted him, "I am Inspector Wagner. You are Herr Nagil? Please have a seat. May I see your credentials?"

Anton sat down in front of the large desk and gave the inspector his German passport. The inspector scrutinized the picture, comparing it with the person sitting in front of him. Satisfied, he returned the passport.

Anton saw how the inspector opened a file before him. It contained his application for service with the police department, which he had submitted a month ago, a physician's health certificate, his resume and lists of previous employment and countries he visited.

"I have your application here, your resume is very interesting." The inspector looked up and smiled. "And some other information which was not in your personal file or filled in." Wagner opened a golden cigarette case. "Do you smoke cigarettes, Herr Nagil? Can't stay away from them. Addicted. Well, let us see here . . ."

"I smoke a pipe, may I?"

"Please do." The inspector watched as Herr Nagil pulled out a well-used pipe, filled it from a pouch and lit it.

"You were born in Munich in 1965, son of Rosemarie Nagil, nee Hofer, also born in Munich but resided in Cairo, Egypt. Father is Otto Nagil. Your mother gave birth to you here but returned shortly after your birth to Cairo. Your mother returned some time ago and lives in Planegg, as you do now. You have lived on and off in Munich. Traveled extensively, even to Afghanistan. Member of the Moslem Brotherhood? No? Fine. Report from Cairo says that you were a possible member or sympathizer. Confidential report shows that you visited Afghanistan on a mission for them."

"For t h e m? To whom are you referring, Inspector?"

"Egyptian Military Intelligence of course. Let me ask you, Herr Nagil, to whom do you pledge your loyalty?" He continued without awaiting an answer. "Travels to Syria, Lebanon, Saudi Arabia, in fact throughout the Middle East. May I see your passport again please? Both of them, you have an Egyptian passport as you are a citizen of both countries."

Anton gave him both passports, which the inspector looked over.

"You have never visited Israel?"

Anton looked surprised and answered "What would I have done in Israel? It is not in my interest."

Inspector Wagner chuckled, "No, I guess not. With your credentials of having been sympathetic to the Moslem Brotherhood, or let us say, having friends who belong to the group, you would not have been welcomed there. Or for that matter with Otto Nagil, having been a war criminal and on Germany's list of fugitives. A somewhat complicated affair as Otto Nagil was declared deceased in 1959, but was alive until 1978, as our reports from Cairo show. With Otto Nagil having been a former SS officer, are your sympathies different?"

"They are," replied Nagil, looking very serious.

The inspector looked up from his files, his eyes boring into those of Anton, "And what are your sympathies exactly, Herr Nagil? And you never answered my question to whom you pledge your loyalty?"

"You never gave me a chance."

"No, I did not. So?"

"I guess loyalty and sympathy are the same . . ." he was interrupted by the inspector, "No, they are not. Your loyalty I could believe, your sympathies are yours for me only to guess at."

Anton knew that this was a knowledgeable official and must have so much more in his file than he had thought possible. Inspector Wagner was not just a bureaucrat, but a serious official of the counter-terrorism unit and not to be underestimated.

"My loyalty? I was born in Munich. I feel it to be *meine Heimat* (my ancestral home). My mother loved the city, Bavaria and Germany. I grew up listening to her stories and read many books about the city. And since I was a boy, I have visited the city many times with my mother and traveled in the Alps."

The inspector smiled. "Yes, we are all fond of our city and the beauty of our land, Bavaria and the mountains. So I can understand that your parents imbued you with a fondness for Munich." His smile vanished, and his eyes were again serious and even menacing. "Did your father also give you a liking for Nationalsocialism?"

Anton also looked serious, "I knew my mother's husband to be a confirmed Nazi. However, I also had a mother who was a gentle woman and wished no evil on anyone or hurt any man, woman or child. My inborn feelings came from my mother, plus developing my own *Lebensanschauung* (philosophy of life in her image). No, I do not harbor any feelings of what the Nazis stood for. Perhaps as a boy growing up in the German Colony in Cairo, I was exposed to Third Reich memorabilia, but since I have become an adult I condemn what they did."

The inspector asked, "To the Jews?"

"Jews, gypsies, Poles, whomever they regarded as inferior, sub-humans." He smiled. "Apparently, your file is not complete. I am married to a Jewish Egyptian woman. Her mother was a Muslim but converted when she married Dr. Zapruder."

"Very interesting. There is nothing in your files. Does your wife live here with you?"

"My wife lives at present in Israel with her mother. Her father died some time ago. She will join me here in Munich during the next few days."

"As a German citizen, you won't have any problems visiting Israel. Just don't use your Egyptian passport. Not a *kosher* passport, if you know what I mean." They both laughed. "Why your membership in the Cairo Teutonic Order ? Isn't this organization very anti-Jewish?"

"Yes, I know. I was a member of the Order as most Germans were. My mother and I went to meetings, so I guess even as a child I was considered a member. To me, the Order was just a place to go to and visit and I played with other German boys. As an adult, have a beer and play *Skat*. Very much like the Goethe Society. The Order was welcomed by King Farouk and later by Nasser, after by Anwar Sadat and is now tolerated by President Hosni Mubarak."

The inspector, drummed with his fingers on the folder, "Having lived in Egypt, traveled extensively in Arab countries, with an Egyptian name, did you ever become a Muslim?"

"No. I was and am a Catholic."

"Had your father become a Muslim?"

"I don't believe so. He kept most of what he did a secret from his wife and me."

"I understand."

The inspector shuffled a few papers in the file, "Your letter offering your services; of course, since you were born in Germany, you are German. You also have dual citizenship. You moved recently to Munich to the house of your mother in Planegg, your permanent address? Yes? I tend to believe your loyalty for the New Germany. Do you know that most Germans would prefer to live in Munich?

You are still highly regarded by extremists in Egypt. At least you kept your personal feelings to yourself. You fluently speak Arabic, English, Russian, and your German, even Munich dialect, is perfect. Yes, we could use you in our section. We have many Muslim immigrants here in the city. Your credentials would permit you to be welcomed by those who have sympathies with what the Brotherhood stands for, also with al-Qaeda and other terrorist groups. We cannot infiltrate them or their secret groups; the problem is, would they trust you?"

"Being friends with members of the Brotherhood, and having gone to an Al-Qaeda training camp in Afghanistan, I believe they would."

"Why did you visit Afghanistan?"

"Al-Qaeda badly needed instructors for bomb making. They accepted me and two others from the Brotherhood. However, the reason I went was that my best frend Ali Nasr asked me to come with him. Also the military ingelligence wanted me to report on jihad members and if possible to assassinate al-Zawahiri."

"And you taught bomb making to terrorists?"

Anton gave a chuckle, "Yes and no. Yes, according to the manuals they had on hand in Arabic. Some of the manuals were faulty which I did not correct, and which may result in premature or no explosions. I did not teach them anything valuable. In retrospect, they would have been better off without me." The inspector smiled. "Due to circumstances which caused me to flee, I hardly became an instructor in explosives and bomb making."

"I understand. Most of what you just told me is not in the information we received from Egypt, that you were an instructor in explosives. Or that you met Atta, bin Laden and al-Zawahiri."

"I don't know all that is in your files."

The inspector smiled. "Confidential information that came from Egyptian Secret Service. We cooperate with them and they with us combating terrorism. I believe you could be very valuable to us in the counter-terrorism unit. So do my superiors at the Praesidium here. You stated before you are an expert in explosives?"

"Yes. My major was in chemistry. I did graduate studies in organic chemistry and volatile gases."

"Not only making bombs but also defusing them?"

"Yes. All kinds of explosive devises, from letter bombs to—what the Americans call roadside bombs."

"I have to introduce you to our bomb defusing expert, Sergeant Oettinger. Not that we encounter many bombs but with your combined expertise, we should have a fine bomb squad. Perhaps even help other police departments in Germany. This makes you a welcome addition to the Munich Police Department. A man with many hats, so to speak.

I—we—would like to offer you the position of *Polizeikommissar* (police inspector) in the criminal police department, the CID. Investigating crimes committed by foreigners here, mainly Arabs since you speak Arabic. You would have your office in the criminal investigation division here, but report to me whenever you encounter terrorists or anything of that nature. The chief of your division knows the true nature of your job here. It must be kept confidential. Arabs might trust you being with the police but not if you belong to my unit.

Why we offer this rather high position, which normally takes a policeman ten years to achieve, is because of your education and language skills. You have the necessary training, skill in weaponry. You were in the Egyptian army, Special Forces. I am certain that with your personality and Munich dialect you will make friends easily and fit into our environment."

"This position would be acceptable."

"Yes. It pays a good salary. You have other means of support? Do you still have properties in Egypt? The house paid for in Planegg. Herr Otto Nagil was never well to do while in Germany, only his salary as an SS officer, yet well-to-do in Egypt?"

"Where his wealth came from in Egypt I have no idea. And by the way, we sold our house in Cairo. It should be in your files."

The inspector smiled. "We know. Everything is ready for you in personnel." The inspector stood up and extended his hand, "Welcome to our police force, Inspector Nagil." They shook hands.

Just before Nagil went out the door the inspector called, "We received an anonymous letter from Cairo last year, warning our police here that a plot was underfoot to cause mayhem at the dedication of the new Jewish complex at the Sankt Jakobsplatz. From you, Inspector Nagil?"

"What did you do with the information?"

"We were able to abort the plot and arrest the terrorists. Most of them were neo-Nazis."

"Glad to hear your department is so efficient." Nagil closed the door and didn't hear Wagner say "Thank you, Inspector Nagil."

Nagil went to personnel; they had been informed of his coming. He spent most of the morning filling out papers and having his picture and fingerprints taken.

He then visited Chief Inspector Kirsch, the head of the criminal investigation division, and later was introduced to Inspector Keller, his chief. Both men knew of Nagil's position in the department and were privy to his detached service with the counter-terrorism unit. Inspector Keller informed him that after the holidays he would have to take a course for higher police officers in Fuerstenfeldbruck, near Munich. There he would have to qualify in hand weapons and once qualified issued the weapon commonly carried by inspectors. "You are permitted to have private arms. But you must register them with our department."

Being a police inspector he had his own office, small at it was. It contained a desk, chairs, computer, printer, shelves with various regulations, and a secure filing cabinet; the window looked out over the Ettstrasse. His room number was 202. His detective pass and badge would be ready by Monday.

Anton was pleased that he had been accepted and at a higher rank than expected. When he left, he walked toward the Stachus to catch the S-Bahn, the fast commuter train to Planegg. He felt cold in the icy wind whipping snow through the Neuhauserstrasse and entered a café and ordered coffee and fine bakery. He sipped his hot coffee, not of the flavor of Arabian coffee which he greatly enjoyed, but it was good.

Inspector Wagner had impressed him. A tall, lanky man with a serious elongated face, a mustache, a ready smile, with eyes that one moment were penetrating, even threatening and then again friendly. This Inspector Wagner certainly knew his business.

Anton was told that he should take the next few days off to attend to his private business and report next Monday for work. This suited him just fine as on Friday, Hanna would arrive from Israel.

He picked her up at the airport in his new BMW, and Hanna told him at once of the wonderful news that she had found an orphan boy they could adopt. She told him,

"The mother of Daniel had died in childbirth and the father was unknown. She had not been married and the man known as her boyfriend had denied being the father. The mother, Lena Korznoi, had recently immigrated from Russia and had not any relatives in Israel, so the baby was declared a ward of the State and was born in the hospital where I work. There are problems with the religious authorities as you, the adoptive father, are not Jewish. I am assured that important people were working on the case and while it may take time, perhaps even as long as a year, it looks as if Daniel would be ours. At least I could prove that I was born of a Jewish mother, since my mother had converted before I was born."

"So tell me, Hanna, how does Daniel look? Like us?"

Hanna laughed, "Danny looks more like a German, blond hair and blue eyes, but oh, so sweet when he smiles. He already knows me and cuddles up when I hold him. Amal is doing some of the paperwork and the baby will be given to her shortly for foster care; that is why she did not come with me to Germany. I plan to return to Jerusalem as soon as the baby is given to my mother. But in the meantime, and with snow having already fallen in Munich, I am in the magic Land of White and crystals of ice."

Rosemarie and Hanna got along fine, both being of a gentle and considerate nature. Rosemarie, having lived in Egypt for so many years could speak Arabic though not fluently, and Hanna had picked up some German from Anton. Rosemarie was looking forward to the time when Hanna could come and bring Daniel with her. The third bedroom upstairs was already set aside for the baby's room, Rosemarie and Hanna would go into town for furnishings and baby things.

In the evening, with a warm fire burning in the fireplace, they sat around it with a glass of wine and Hanna at once wished to know all about his new job and his bosses.

"How come they hired you as an inspector, Toni. Isn't that jumping a lot of ranks?"

"It might be. However, with Toni's qualifications, what else could they do?" commented Rosemarie.

"Yes, it is Hanna. And it wasn't that cut and dry. Herr Meier from personnel told me it had never been done before. It was after the Commissioner Kolb read my resume that he wished for me to be hired as an inspector. I never even met the man."

"And how are your bosses, Toni?" asked Hanna.

"What I tell you is confidential. Only you two can know, so don't tell anyone else. I am assigned to the anti-terrorism unit and report to the chief of this small unit, Head Inspector Wagner, who interviewed me. Officially, I work for Head Inspector Keller of the criminal investigation division. I will work on cases of Arabs and Russians who commit crimes."

"How about Englishmen and Americans?" asked Rosemarie, "You speak English."

Anton laughed, "I don't think there are any English speaking criminals in Munich, unless an occasional tourist and I doubt that they came here to commit a crime."

"So, tell me about the people you work for?" asked Hanna.

"Well, there is Inspector Wagner. He seems a very serious person."

"What does he look like?"

"You women always go by looks. He is tall, thin, narrow face with a mustache. Inspector Keller, my boss? A round face, seems to be friendly. Short and stocky built."

"Fat?"

"He has a pouch. I have met them only briefly."

"Can I visit you in police headquarters, Toni?" asked Hanna.

"Of course. Just ask for room 202, my office. By the way, I was told that during New Year's Eve all police officers have a party togther with their wives in one of the hotels. Then you get to meet them."

"Do they know that I am Jewish, Toni?"

"I told Inspector Wagner. He seemed surprised. I, the son of a war criminal married a Jewish woman. He looked at my passports and asked me if I ever visited

Israel. He told me that with my German passport I shouldn't have any trouble visiting there. No one knows, or must know, that I have been to Israel many times. And, of course, my Mossad connection must remain between us, it is a secret."

"When do you start working, Toni?"

"Toni starts on Monday." replied Rosemarie.

"Let's go to bed, Toni. I am tired from the trip." Hanna smiled strangely at Toni, and he understood.

BOOK 3

POLICE INSPECTOR ANTON NAGIL

CONTENTS

ADDITIONAL CHARACTERS

IN MUNICH:
    Police Commissioner Max Kolb.
    Sergeant Franz Oettinger. In charge of the bomb squad.
    Patrolman Hans Maurer. Sergeant Oettinger's assistant.
    Inspector Harteck of homicide.
    Imam Abd al-Rahman Aref at the Munich Islamic Center & Mosque.
    Second Imam Mohammed al-Dulaimi.
    Bomb maker Abdel Karim Hawass from Cairo.
    Karl Seitz. Neo-Nazi.
    Gustav Bachleiter. Neo-Nazi.
    Fred Schultheis. Friend of Gustav.
    Dimitri Djukov. Proprietor of Moscow Nights Club.
    Liesl Kunz. Waitress in Moscow Nights.
    Ludolf Hanfnagel. Serial killer.
    Gerda Leiter. Librarian.
    Ingrid. Receptionist at the Max-Planck Institute.
    Professor Max Klausner. Nuclear scientist.
    Ayat Wahaj & Ahmed Reza Jaafari. Iranian scientists.
    Mahmoud Maliki, Iranian. Visitor from Berlin.
    Raed Zubaida, Palestinian. His driver.

IN RUSSIA:
    General Viktor Alexandrovich Orlov. Russian State Security Directorate.

IN EGYPT:
    Adolf (Gert) Lutz. Son of Gerhard Lutz, former colleague of Otto Nagil.

IN ISRAEL:
    Baby Daniel Nagil. Adopted by Anton and Hanna Nagil.
    Avi Barlev. Deputy Commissioner of the Jerusalem Police.

Esther and David Cohen. Kidnapped Israeli orphans from Kefar Ezion.
Commander Ben Amir, IDF (Israeli Defense Force) commando unit.
Dr. Shimon Herzog. Psychiatric consultant and friend.

Palestinian Territory:
Hassan Abu-Sharif (formerly SS Colonel Streller).
His son Mohammed Sharif. Both of Hebron.
Dr. Mustafa Abu Shanab. Dermatologist in Hebron.
Mukhtar Abu al-Adhami, of the village Bani Na'im. His cruel wife Najiba.

United States:
Agent Burt Johnson of the FBI, Quantico, Virginia.

CHAPTER XVI

ANTON NAGIL, POLICE INSPECTOR

On Monday, Anton appeared punctually at eight at his new job. At a private ceremony attended to by Inspectors Wagner, Kirsch and his own boss, Inspector Keller, the head of personnel administered the oath, and Inspector Nagil received his pass and badge and was now officially a member of the Munich Police Department.

The next few days he was with Inspector Keller, a rather short and heavy built man with a round face which Anton could best describe as roly-poly, with a friendly disposition. However, Anton learned quickly that Inspector Keller was a serious police official who knew his business.

Wednesday morning, he was with Inspector Wagner who gave him an oversight of suspected terrorists in Munich and Bavaria.

For the afternoon, he was scheduled to give a talk to the three inspectors about his knowledge of terrorist, and Islamic fundamentalists, their motivation, and what could be expected of terrorist activities in the near future in Munich and Bavaria within the overall trend of terrorist activities in Europe and Germany.

When they were seated in comfortable chairs in the Chief Inspector Kirsch's office, Kirsch lit a cigarette, as did Inspector Wagner, while Nagil smoked his pipe.

Inspector Wagner began by stating that Inspector Nagil had already briefed him about the Egyptian Brotherhood, the Islamic Jihad and its connection to al-Qaeda. "He has also met, even if only briefly, Osama bin Laden, Ayman al-Zawahiri and Mohammed Atta. I thought we should begin with Inspector Nagil giving us a brief outline of these two men. Atta of lesser importance as he was just a tool in their scheming and has joined Allah in paradise." There were smiles of understanding at this sarcastic remark.

Chief Inspector Kirsch added, "And what can we expect of terrorist attacks in Germany, specifically here in Munich as al-Qaeda has shifted its offices from Hamburg to our city."

Inspector Nagil took a few draws on his pipe. "Bin Laden is a conservative Sunni. Not that the Shiites of Iran and Iraq are any more moderate and indeed, while we see today the Sunnis combat the Shiites in Iraq, they work together and cooperate when it comes to terrorist acts.

Bin Laden, in describing him, I would say he is a tall man and with a flowing beard. He is serious and pious but lacking the charisma of a great leader; this is my personal impression of the man. His followers accept him as a great leader, because of his dedication to Moslem fundamentalism, his wealth which he uses freely to further the cause of the jihad, his declaration of war against all infidel nations and his hatred for the great Satan, the US.

His image was that of the foremost fighter against the Soviets, an image that does not correspond to the truth. He was in Afghanistan fighting the Soviets but rather infrequently and left the fighting to the Afghanis, Arab volunteers and Pakistanis while he sat comfortably in his sumptuous house in Peshawar. Then later, after 9/11, his declaration of jihad against the non-Muslim countries drew the many Mujahedin to his cause. While he lacks the hypnotic charisma of a Hitler, he became the same type of cult-personality. In additon, if I read correctly, followers of Hitler became loyal adherents to Nazism and willingly followed him for the glory of pre-war years, to the conquering of Europe and to destruction and death more so when they personally saw or met Hitler saw his fanatical gaze upon them, were given the Nazi salute or even touched his hand. These became the fanatical Nazis. Likewise, bin Laden influenced in a similar vein those who saw him, listen to his talks—he was not a good speaker—and perhaps were spoken to by him. It is of human nature that personal involvement to a despot has at its most loyal following those who have met the man, the personal touch." He paused and relit his pipe.

"Al-Zawahiri is a physician and an educated man in geo-politics and Islamic religion. He has the title of mullah and can give religious pronouncements or as they are called fatwas. In 1973, as a medical student, he joined the Egyptian Islamic Jihad. In 1981, the jihad and other fundamental groups joined forces and assassinated Anwar Sadat. Al-Zawahiri, not known then to be a leader of the jihad, and thought of playing only a minor role, was sentenced to three years imprisonment. He went to Pakistan in the mid-1980s. From there he sponsored or led terrorist attacks by his jihad in Egypt, which killed 1,200 people there in the early 90s. In 1997, fifthy-eight tourists were killed in Luxor by his order. Egypt finally recognized al-Zawahiri as the leader of these terrorist attacks. He is, as we now know, bin Laden's advisor and mentor, and in videos we see al-Zawahiri sit next to bin Laden. He is a stocky built man in his mid-fifties, wears glasses and of course, has a long beard and always wears a white robe and turban. He is quiet, poised and a good speaker.

My personal impression of both is that they lack the leadership qualities of a Hitler to mesmerize their followers. It is what they represent that gives them their loyal following. Rather in the mold of a Himmler who was uninspiring as a personality, in fact I read where Albert Speer described Himmler as half schoolmaster, half crank."

Inspector Keller interjected, "What made Himmler the all-powerful leader was that he stood at the head of the SS and gestapo and not his personality."

Chief Inspector Kirsch asked, "Inspector Nagil, with all your experiences of having lived in the Middle-East, traveled to Afghanistan, having met bin Laden and al-Zawahiri, what in your opinion turned bin Laden against the US and Western World?"

"Why does he war against mainly the United States? It is not because of American culture, as decadent he believes it is. He understands very well that all of his followers who were in America or are still there, are tasting its culture and most, if not all, break Islamic laws by drinking alcoholic beverages, carousing, gambling as even Mohamed Atta, his most faithful follower had a drink here and there, went on a binge a few days before 9/11; did not grow a beard as is demanded of the faithful. Bin Laden understands human nature and he himself has four wives, so he gets his share of entertainment."

Inspector Keller continued to ask, "How many children does he have by now?"

"I believe thirteen by the latest count. Since Afghanistan was invaded, his private life is hidden and so are his families and his own presence."

Chief Inspector Kirsch asked "To come back to his hatred for the West and foremost America?"

"His hatred for the US, the great Satan, and by now the Western World, is based upon US policies in the Middle East. Its support for Israel; the only democratic country there. Democracies are devilish political entities as they go against strict Islamic laws. Like most Muslims, he hates Israel and the Jews for their successes in defeating the combined armies of the Arabs and did so repeatedly. He really doesn't care for the Palestinians as they are mostly secular and not about to become a Muslim nation under *Sharia*. He blames the Jews for the failures of the Arabs. He uses the Palestinian-Israeli conflict as a rallying cause but to him it is just a sideshow of the conflict between Islam and the West. He rails against the US for having its soldiers in the Arab Peninsula, be it in Saudi Arabia, Yemen, Kuwait or wherever. This is Holy Land and not to be befouled by the presence of infidels. The coalition of US and Western Nations, which defeated his Taliban friends and his al-Qaeda and is now trying to turn Afghanistan into a Muslim-democratic nation. The war of the US against Iraq.

There was no love between bin Laden and Saddam Hussein, but he was at least a Sunni-Arab, and while Hussein was known as a mass-murderer he was an opponent of America.

Then the support of America for nations like Saudi Arabia and Egypt whom he calls apostates of the Islamic faith.

Like Hitler before him, bin Laden became ever more fanatical and murderous. The bombings of the Embassies in Africa made him into a mass-murderer. When he declared war on civilians, women and children, 9/11 followed. Were he to fulfill his dream of becoming the Caliph of a Muslim Empire stretching from Spain to Indonesia, there would be a bloodbath rivaling the genocide of the Nazis. His is not a clash of civilizations, as many believe, but a call to Muslim zealots and other fanatics to rob and kill in the name of Allah under the banner of the Green Flag and the call *Allahu Akbar* (God is Great). The beast in man follows anyone's flag."

Chief Inspector Kirsch said, "So with bin Laden it is power and religion."

"And the low and sordid motive of hate. The same with al-Zawahiri."

Kirsch continued, "Is the problem the Islamic religion? I am not familiar with the Koran."

"Yes and no. I studied the Koran in its classical Egyptian edition. The Koran, according to Muslims, is universal, being the natural continuation of all previous revealed scriptures in Judaism of the Abrahamic tradition as delivered among others, by the Prophets Moses, David, and last, before Prophet Mohammad, by Jesus and the Apostles. Jesus is accepted as a Prophet but not as the Son of God by Muslims.

The Koran is in flowery prose and in continuous praise for Allah the All-Merciful. I quote here what Moslems believe and the Koran bears it out: for a scholar it is knowledge; for a politician in its politics; for a ruler is its justice system. The Koran is all-inclusive. Was the Koran God-given, a revelation to Prophet Muhammad? We Christians don't believe so. There are substantial differences to our Christian scriptures. Ours are for all mankind, the Koran is rather for Arabs, people of the desert. We can see that in how women are treated. Different in its message of how we perceive the relationship between God, man and woman.

Perhaps of more interest are the commentaries; these commentaries are written by scholars. Through the times they bear different interpretations, and supplemented by fatwas—decrees pronounced by clerics. It is with the fatwas that the trouble begins. Let me just quote from the beginning of the Koran. It is in the *fatiha*, or opening chapter of sura 1, section 7, *"The way of those on whom Thou hast bestowed Thy Grace, Those whose is not wrath."* We know very well that for the fundamentalist, it is all wrath, they misinterpret the Koran when it suits them or disregard the Koran altogether. The Koran doesn't make war on civilians. Mohammedans can pick up the sword to defend. There are passages of drawing the sword against the infidels. However, it is not the Koran but the many revelations, interpretations and pronouncements that paint a darker picture of Islam and the Koran, and not one spoken of by moderate Islamists who like for us to think of Islam as a religion of peace that promotes charity, tolerance, and freedom.

Were it not for the fundamentalists, this tolerant picture of Islam would be fine. However, we are all at war with the fundamentalists and their terror and it would be dangerous for us to be blinded and deceived by the enemy that threatens us. Modern Islam betrays a hidden agenda; to discredit Christianity and the West by comparing Islam with a sanitized, idealized religion that bears no resemblance to its fundamentalist teachings or its history.

Chief Inspector Kirsch asked, "Such as?"

"Did Mohammedism bring this benign faith of justice and tolerance to the tribes of Arabia and then spreading it throughout the Middle East, part of Europe and Asia? Or was it through a bloody conquest and accompanying persecution of those he could not convert, Christians, Jews, and other nonbelievers that his new religion succeeded? It is a myth if we speak of the golden age Mohammedism brought. Islam still has at its goal an irreformable commitment of global conquest by any means necessary.

The teaching of Mohammedism is so unlike of what Judaism, Christianity, Buddhism or any other religion is preaching.

The Koran permits Muslims to own slaves by purchasing them or as a bounty in war. Slavery is still practiced by some. Can you imagine Jesus owning slaves?

As Muhammad progressed from visionary and teacher to warlord and ruler, his style and messages became ever more violent and intolerant. It is these later revelations that are considered definite by Islamic authorities when they conflict with earlier ones often cited for Western consumption. I quote the perhaps most important late revelation as it is part of the reason that war can be declared against all infidels and was read to us by al-Zawahiri. It comes from Sura 9:5, from verses called the Sword Verses, *"Fight and slay the pagans wherever ye find them and seize them, beleaguer them and lie in wait for them."*

In Islam, the definition of what is right or just is not empirical but changeable by divine decree—the fatwas—enabling the most heinous sins and crimes to be declared "the Will of Allah."

Remember the paradise promised the martyrs? The joys and glories of the Islamic paradise are tangible and sensual and include the many young virgins. I mean, let us look at that paradise with the eyes of a Christian. The God of the Jews and our same God and his son Jesus, the Savior, regarded man and woman as His creation and not woman as mere pleasure object subject to man. It is just ungodly in its basic tenet. Yet this promised paradise seems such a powerful motive for suicide bombers. To sit in the presence of the Allah and have these virgins cater to his pleasures."

Inspector Keller added, "They speak of seventy-two virgins."

"I believe so."

Chief Inspector Kirsch asked, "In the Koran?"

Inspector Nagil shook his head. "No. One of the later documentaries, perhaps a legend but believed in. Perfect for the desert warrior to fight bravely with his sword and if vanquished enter Allah's paradise.

Inspector Wagner asked, "Propaganda then?"

"More than propaganda. It can't be quoted as a verse from the Koran but when drilled into the believers by a religious leader as a revelation it becomes gospel truth.

"The crusades by the Europeans were a belated response to three centuries of Muslim aggression against Christian land and peoples. Today, the soldiers of America and the Western Alliance are again referred to as crusaders. Again, they came as a response to Islamic terrorism. Muslim persecution of Christians has caused suffering and death for millions over thirteen centuries and continues today. The myth of Islam's tolerance of religious minorities contradicts its teaching, history, and present reality. Islam divides the world into the House of Islam, where Islam rules, and the House of War, where it doesn't. The two are permanently at war. There may be temporary truces, but peace will come only upon completion of global conquest by Islam. In modern times, it was in 1993 that Saudi Arabia's supreme religious authority declared that the world is flat and that anyone who disagrees is an infidel and must be punished. Islam hasn't changed really; it is regressing. Saudi Arabia remains the most intolerant Islamic regime in the world, where the practice of any religion besides Islam is strictly forbidden as in Muhammad's day. The spokesmen of official Islam will not tell us what Islam really is—a return to the sixth century."

Chief Inspector Kirsch said, "The other side of the coin."

Inspector Wagner continued to ask, "What motivates the suicide bombers? I mean it takes desperation or very ill health, like a painful incurable cancer, or a hopeless situation like the Jews were in awaiting the gestapo to ship them to extermination camps. But religious fanaticism? Do they actually believe they go to Allah in paradise and that nonsense of a bunch of virgins awaiting them?"

"A mixture of many motives. Religiously, it may be based upon a verse in the Koran: Sura 3:169, '*Think not of Those who are slain in God's way as dead. Nay, they live. Finding their sustenance in the Presence of their Lord.*' Let us look at this sura more closely and its interpretation by extremist clerics. Suicide is forbidden by the Koran. Fanatical mullahs interpret 'slain in God's way' as a Muslim who was killed serving Allah, if the killing was by the enemy or by his own hand becomes immaterial. Therefore, the injunction against suicide is overruled by the deed of having committed it in the service of Allah. The suicide bomber becomes a martyr. 'Nay, they live.' The martyr sincerely believes that his mutilated form becomes whole again. 'Finding their sustenance,' a man's pleasure of fulfilling his lust with virgins.

'In the Presence of their Lord.' Sitting next to Allah; certainly a gross misinterpretation of the sura.

"First of all, many, if not most of them, are young men, uneducated and failures in everything they did. They are terribly frustrated. They see the world around them, an affluent society. They envy those who have, they begin to hate them and the society that makes it possible but excludes them. Religion at that state of their lives has little influence. If they could become part of that society and its spoils, they would never become bombers. Then they meet someone who is in the inside of a secret society or they attend a mosque were the imam is a firebrand and teaches hatred for the infidels and gives the young men an outlet for their frustration. They become easy recruits. They find Allah and religion, a motivation for their miserable lives. They become attached to a secret society and they are recognized as valuable members. They become important. Now they find a direction for their hatred of society. The leader or mentor of their clandestine group sends them to a Madras, a religious school, usually in Pakistan where they learn the Koran, pronouncements and fatwas of hatred toward the nonbelievers; they turn into fundamentalists, believers in the most extreme form of Islam. Truth, half-truth and outright lies are taught."

Inspector Wagner added, "They are brainwashed."

"Yes, indeed. Once they have become religious fanatics they have to be trained as warriors and are sent to training camps which existed in the Sudan, Albania, then Afghanistan, now perhaps in secret camps in Pakistan also in Chechnya, Indonesia or wherever they have their clandestine camps. They are taught the use of weapons, explosives, how to travel, live within the society they hate without raising suspicion. Again they belong to a cell of like-minded fundamentalists and are indoctrinated by their leader. The trigger of becoming a suicide bomber lies in each individual's personality, fostered by the leader's ability to recognize these traits. The thought of becoming such a self-destructive bomber is not one of an instant decision but rather a spark that ignites all sorts of emotions, even a thrill TO DO IT, to sacrifice his life. The living martyr has become a special person, a hero. Besides, the act will not happen tomorrow or soon. These primitive people live by the hour, by the day.

You know Inspector Wagner, I thought once that this commitment to self-destruction is a most complicated process but as we look to Iraq, the daily occurrence of suicide bombings, many in fact, makes me believe that I am wrong in subscribing a difficult and emotional sequence of events. It must be rather uncomplicated, a quick decision made by a simple mind, corrupted by hate and sadism, at least for many.

Let us look at a real case of such a bomber, a Palestinian. This I read recently in a paper from Egypt. The reporter talked to the bomber's mother. She said that lately her son had become very religious, and had told her that he wished to become a martyr. She said to him that he should get married and have children to give her grandchildren. He said that he did not wish to get married, as he wants to go to paradise to the virgins. She also said that she is very sad that he gave his life but is proud of her son."

Inspector Wagner asked, "A devotion to what? Religion?"

"Partially religious, supplemented by more basic instincts, vengeance, hate, sadism, to kill. They never consider themselves terrorists of course, rather warriors of Allah and to each other heroes. There are exceptions as we saw with Atta, a well-educated young man who was intensely religious since a boy. But we don't see a bin Laden or al-Zawahiri strap on a belt."

Inspector Wagner said, "Today we know more about Mohamed Atta and his cell of four. Very interesting that they were all from different backgrounds and nationalities. Atta grew up in Cairo, a rather normal Egyptian family. Apparently the boy Mohamed was a difficult child, shy, withdrawn and already very religious. He was also very attached to his mother, his mother's *Liebling* (darling). It is reported that as a teenager he sat on his mother's lap and was cuddled by her. He also grew up asexual. When he was teenager and the TV showed a belly dancer, he would avert his eyes and walk out of the room. Yet there is nothing proven that he had homosexual tendencies. It was the continued pampering by his mother that his father wished for him to leave Egypt and study abroad. Atta went to Hamburg and since he had learned drafting in high school, he became a draftsman. A note found by the police of one of his cellmates, Ziad Jarrah, told of the cell's commitment: *The victors will come. We swear to beat you. I came to you with men who love the death just as you love life . . . Oh, the smell of paradise is rising."*

Inspector Nagil said, "This is a good description of Atta, the way I remember him, self-centered, inconsiderate of others, a true fanatic."

Inspector Wagner asked, "Do you think these brainwashed individuals then do believe in the glorious hereafter as they have been taught?"

"Most do, some probably don't. By the time they are sent on a mission they are so indoctrinated with hatred for whoever that they willingly self-destruct to kill. They will be remembered as martyrs. This is why a video is taken of them before. Assured that their families are provided for, again the hero image to their families to whom so far they had only been a disappointment. You said the right word—brainwashed."

"And what do you see in the future of the West's complicated relationship with the Arab Nations? Will fundamentalism wither or succeed?" asked Kirsch.

Inspector Nagil smiled. "I have learned that whatever one predicts for the future, things will always turn out differently. I see three possibilities and I admit that my predictions may not come to pass."

Kirsch said, "Just your opinion would interest me."

"The withering away idea might happen if bin Laden were to be killed. We realize that without Stalin, the Soviet Union might have taken a different turn, and not made an accommodation with Hitler that permitted him to attack the West. Without Hitler, Germany would not have become the outcast nation and the genocide would have never happened. So yes, individuals often determine the future of a country, of a movement, of history. With bin Laden done away with, the fundamentalist movement might wither. There is no one else with his stature. However, this may not happen even with bin Laden dead. There are too many groups with various names and not under al-Qaeda's umbrella leadership. Young, angry Moslems flocking to all sorts of local groups who espouse this violent, irrational terrorism."

Kirsch asked, "But al-Qaeda would disappear then?"

"Al-Qaeda is not as much an organization as a movement. The word itself comes from the Arabic *gafayn-dal,* which only means 'base' as a home or camp. It can also mean a principle, a method, a model or pattern. Al-Qaeda to us is now the all-engulfing terror organization of their leader bin Laden. If bin Laden disappears so would al-Qaeda. But there is the wider movement of the Islamic Jihad, the Egyptian Islamic Jihad, the Pakistani and Afghan Jihad also known as Hizb-I Islam; there is the Palestinian Jihad, Hamas, Hezbollah in Syria and Lebanon, which is supported by Iran. It would be a victory for the civilized world if bin Laden and his al-Qaeda were no longer. Though perhaps only a marginal win.

"Secondly, it is possible with Afghanistan no longer the haven for fundamentalist warriors, for Iraq becoming a more tolerant country like Egypt, or even splitting into three nations of Kurds, Sunnis and Shiites; Iran changing to a modern and moderate nation like they were under the Shah that the necessary bases for fundamentalists no longer exists and it becomes a minor nuisance that can be controlled. Pakistan remaining western-oriented. However, there are many ifs for that to happen. The problem with all Middle East countries is that the majority of the people are poor, ignorant, primitive people and their whole life centers on this fanatical belief in Islam, the rule under *sharia.* If you were to institute democracy and free elections, the moderates would always lose.

"Third, it may happen that fundamentalism spreads more violently and engulfs the whole Middle East. Can you imagine, the fundamentalists in charge of the oil producing nations, the blackmail the West would find itself under, oil deliveries stopped or made so expensive that the economies of the West would be destroyed? If this would happen, I predict and do so confidently, that the West with America would occupy the oil-rich countries. It would become another crusade, but this time for oil. I am realist enough that any of these predictions will not happen and the status quo will continue. I don't see any changes in Iran as long as the army supports the system of the Shura ruling. Iraq will meddle along with its insurgency even when the Americans leave, a religious and ethnic strife between the Sunnis, Shiites and Kurds.

"Syria, under its Baath party dictatorship, is affectively a bulwark against fundamentalism but a one-man rule dictatorship nevertheless, an exporter of terrorism; so it doesn't invade its own house. The same in Egypt.

"Saudi Arabia is playing a dangerous game of supporting the fundamentalists abroad but so far have it controlled at home; though bin Laden would love nothing better that to destroy the Saudi Royalty.

"The Lebanon has its own problem with Christians and Moslems trying to maintain its status quo but there is Hezbollah always stirring things up.

"Can the Palestinian Authority control Hamas, jihad and the other terrorists and become a nation? Not without a civil war and both sides shy away from that happening. So the muddle there will continue. The problem between the Palestinians and Israelis can only be solved politically and from the outside and that only if the Arab countries become more democratic and solved their own problems with the fundamentalists. That brings us back to the second scenario with its many ifs."

Inspector Wagner asked, "Inspector Nagil, what do you see happening terror-wise in Europe, in Germany in the near future?"

Inspector Nagil smiled. "I thought you would ask. With bin Laden still in control of worldwide terrorism, albeit severely restricted, he will seek to punish those nations who are supporting America in Iraq. He has really the mind of a bully, the last kick he received turns his attention to the kicker and not what was before. For some reason he has difficulties punishing America. Either the FBI there is doing a splendid job or he has never built a solid terrorist base there.

"In Europe, he will be going after those countries that have the biggest contingents of troops in Iraq. That is England, Italy and Spain. They can expect terrorist activities, especially in England, as there he has the most support of fundamentalists, mosques with their clergy freely espousing hatred, publications inciting; in fact a good infrastructure for terrorist activities.

"As far as Germany goes, you—I mean WE—don't have any troops there so it is not a problem at the present time. If you say that the Hamburg connection dismantled and re-established itself here in Munich, we have to watch them carefully. Best if you can get someone inside them, someone who can supply you with information."

Inspector Wagner smiled. "That is where you come in Inspector Nagil. We hope that you can penetrate their organization as a trustworthy person."

Chief Inspector Kirsch added, "We will fully cooperate with you. If we arrest someone we suspect is al-Qaeda, we shall turn him over to you. You will do your best to gain his trust. If that person is just a lowly member we can have you release him."

Inspector Wagner continued, "We can try. We don't have any other option."

Inspector Nagil said, "There is the possibility that word from the Brotherhood trickles to jihad members here that I am, well let's say, sympathetic to their work here. If I get approached I shall immediately get in touch with you, Inspector Wagner."

Inspector Kirsch added, "This was a most interesting briefing, Inspector Nagil. I am glad we have you with us. The next time we have a briefing, you need to tell us of your flight from Afghanistan back to Egypt. You went by way of the Central Asian Republics?"

"Uzbekistan." Nagil answered him.

Inspector Wagner said, "One last question commissar Nagil, are you still connected to the Egyptian Army Intelligence?"

"In an informal manner, yes. I am on friendly terms with their chief, Brigadier Amer. He understands that I would never reveal anything pertaining to my work. I can sever any connection to him if you so wish."

Chief Inspector Kirsch assured him, "No, keep your informal contact open to the brigadier, it may benefit us both ways. But I will inform *Bundeswehr* intelligence of your connection and they may be interested in contact with the Egyptian military." This ended the briefing.

Anton, as inspector, worked in civilian clothing. Though issued with the standard pistol, he preferred a Beretta 9 mm, model 92-compact, with which he was familiar and had bought in Munich and registered. It was not a weapon of choice for other police inspectors as it lacked the immediate power to immobilize but Anton Nagil was a sharpshooter with the Beretta and hitting someone between the eyes was immobilizing him. As a higher police officer, he was required to buy a dress uniform, and his epaulettes showed the one star of his grade.

His office was on the second floor of headquarters and looked out over the Ettstrasse. On the door to his office 202, was his name printed:

POLIZEIKOMMISSAR ANTON NAGIL, CID
POLICE INSPECTOR ANTON NAGIL, CRIMINAL INVESTIGATION

Inspector Keller instructed Anton Nagil in the proper method of interrogation. Only one criminal case was pending, an Algerian who had stabbed a neo-Nazi and was in prison. Inspector Keller was handling the case himself but asked Inspector Nagil to attend the interrogations and court appearances of the accused to familiarize himself with proper procedures and of course to interpret. The man the Algerian had stabbed was a Herr Hofmann, a neo-Nazi. He had been released from the hospital and was now also in lock-up.

Inspector Nagil had a meeting with Head Inspector Wagner who advised him of possible terror suspects in Munich and Bavaria. On a CD, he gave him their names, addresses and particulars of how they had come to the attention of the antiterrorist unit.

He also told Inspector Nagil of the large mosque in Freimann, north of the city, which was the center of Islamic activities in Munich and as surveillance indicated, was visited by known terrorists and supposedly under the guidance of the Egyptian Moslem Brotherhood, and financed by them. As Inspector Wagner told him, "This much we know. We have raided the mosque several times and confiscated records, and these documents and computer files indicate a connection to the Brotherhood. But we have yet to establish their cooperation with terrorist cells like the Islamic Jihad, al-Gamaa al-Islamiyya, and al-Qaeda. We hope that your connection to the Brotherhood in Egypt permits you to infiltrate the hierarchy of the Islamic Center. The present leader of the mosque is a Herr Ahmad Denffer who says that the mosque and its Islamic Center are no longer international but purely a local center for religious purposes. We are not clear on the mosque and center's function at this time."

During the second week, he was again invited to Chief Inspector Kirsch's office for a report of his flight from Afghanistan. With the chief were Inspectors Keller and Wagner.

After they had lit their cigarettes and Nagil his pipe and sat back comfortably, the chief began by asking, "Whatever made you go to an al-Qaeda training camp to begin with, Inspector Nagil? I mean, you went as a Christian or did you hide your religion?"

Nagil said, "Yes I did, but not successfully."

Keller asked, "What did it matter, they must have recognized you as a European."

Nagil answered him, "Being suntanned, having grown a respectable beard and wearing clothing like the rest, speaking Egyptian Arabic, I was not seen as a European or infidel. In fact, when I met Europeans they thought of me as an Arab, as did everyone else. I was betrayed."

"I am still interested in what motivated you to go there in the first place," Kirsch said.

"I grew up with an Egyptian boy and we became the best of friends. His name was Ali Nasr," Nagil told them. "Ali was a devout Muslim and like his father, belonged to the Egyptian Brotherhood. He had studied to become a clergy and became an imam at the Great Mosque in Cairo. I already explained the mission of the Brotherhood in the seminar I gave last week, to achieve *sharia* in Egypt by nonviolent means. Let me put a question mark by stating 'nonviolent means', Some, if not many of the Brotherhood, would use any means to achieve their purpose. Ali was a nonviolent person but was under pressure by the mosque to visit one of the al-Qaeda training camps. As Ali told me, the clergy in Cairo operates like a large company; if you wish to advance, you do their bidding. Ali wished to be the imam of his own mosque to teach the young faithful that there were other ways to achieve *sharia*. When he decided to visit a camp, he asked me to accompany him as his conscience, to protect him from becoming a fanatic himself. I was permitted by Egyptian Army Intelligence to go, to report on possible Islamic Jihad members, since the jihad requested me to attend, and sent three of their members along to protect me. Brigadier Amer also wished for me to assassinate al-Zawahiri, as he had become an embarrassment to Egypt. I was known as an expert in explosives and invited by Osama bin Laden to teach bomb making."

Wagner said, "I hope you didn't teach these fanatics?"

Nagil smiled. "What I taught them was the chemistry of explosives for which they had no use, that is, if they even understood what I was teaching them. I let them explode bombs but didn't even let them attach the detonators. I repaired the cannon on a T-55 tank and let them shoot off ammunition. By the time I finished with the first group, they couldn't even put a decent pipe bomb together. Nor did I correct some faulty writings in their manuals, which might lead to premature explosion or failures. They would have been better off without my expertise. They became explosive experts by detonating charges which I connected for them."

Kirsch continued, "Your flight then. Why did you have to flee Afghanistan?"

"That is a long story," Nagil answered.

Kirsch said, "We have all morning, I have coffee sent in." He made a call and his secretary brought in a pitcher of coffee and cups.

Inspector Nagil then related the story of his trip to Afghanistan with Ali and his friend Sidqi Suliman. The rape of Sidqi, the killing of the Swede Mohamed, the missile attack that destroyed the infrastructure of the camp. The subsequent killing of Ali and the flight of Sidqi and him through Afghanistan. The meeting with Sasha, the former Soviet prisoner, and his killing by the bandits and the three-day-and-night flight on the Amu Darya River into Uzbekistan.

With many questions by the inspectors interspersed, it was noon by the time Inspector Nagil had finished telling his story, ending, when they visited Sasha's mother in St. Petersburg.

Kirsch said, "Fascinating. You should get in touch with the film makers in Geiselgasteig."

Keller added, "In any case, write your story and have it published."

Wagner added more, "Name it 'Flight from Afghanistan.' By the way, how many of these people did you kill while in Afghanistan?"

"I don't consider them people; terrorist and bandits, the same sort, human outcasts. The terrorists driven by hate; the bandits by greed. Perhaps the Taliban soldiers we killed at the bridge were people, but this was war."

Kirsch said, "So, there was more to your trip to Afghanistan than to teach Atta and meet bin Laden and al-Zawahiri. We thank you for your report, Inspector Nagil. Well, back to work then. Inspector Keller is right, you should write a book."

Munich was already being decorated for Christmas; snow had fallen since the end of November and both Hanna and Anton were looking forward to the holidays in their fine house in Planegg.

For lunch, the big meal in Germany, they ate at the nearby Heide Inn, which specialized in culinary Bavarian delights. While Anton was fond of pork roast, Hanna did not eat pork, at least not what was offered as pork. As it usually happens in mixed marriages of Jews and Christians, they honored each others religious commitments and celebrated all holidays.

Before Christmas came Hanukkah; Hanna and Anton would light the candles and say the blessings together.

Sometimes Hanna would like to attend the Friday evening services in the synagogue in Munich and Anton would accompany her. As a good Catholic, he found nothing wrong to pray to the same God in accordance with the tradition of the Jewish religion as he understood that Christianity was built upon the Old Testament. Jesus having been the Messiah, and those who believe in him as the Son of God and Savior, becoming Christians, while the Jews are still waiting for the Messiah's coming.

Rosemarie would attend Sunday Mass with Anton but she also enjoyed participating, even if only as silent observer, in the religious rites of Hanna. She was the happy mother of her two children and she knew how deeply the two felt and loved each other.

Hanna described to them how Daniel looked. There always had been the shadow of the marriage unfulfilled, as both Hanna and Anton wished for a child, and so did Rosemarie, and with the adoption of Daniel they would have their child and Rosemarie a grandchild, as did Amal.

Hanna had never learned German in school and at home she and Anton spoke only Arabic but she was learning from Rosemarie and while her German was not fluent, and she spoke with a guttural Arabic accent, she could converse with Rosemarie and others she met or make herself understood when shopping. Her English was not much better than her German.

After the eight days of Hanukkah were over, they could look forward to the joyful season of Christmas and New Year and many days off work.

They had invited their close friends, Sidqi and his wife Fatima from Cairo for Christmas. And in the middle of December, Fatima had called and spoke to Hanna that they were coming. Both had five days off for the holidays, had their visas and would be arriving the noon of twenty-fourth of December. It would be Fatima's first visit to them and really her first trip to Europe. This made the Nagil family very happy and they looked forward to their visit.

Sidqi Suliman, of a prosperous Cairo family, now at age twenty-six, was a handsome man as he had been a delicate boy. Sidqi was now in his last year of medical school and wished to become a surgeon. Sidqi had visited Anton in Munich before but this was the first time Fatima would come with him.

Fatima, the same age as Sidqi, was as beautiful a woman as was Hanna. Both wore their black hair long or in a braid. When they walked together, or for that matter alone, men would stare at them and at once take them for Mediterranean descent, which they were, both Egyptian beauties.

Anton, Hanna and Rosemarie went Christmas tree shopping at the large square before the station, which was in walking distance from their house, and brought home a large tree they decorated together.

They had been in town shopping for presents and visited the Christmas Market where Rosemarie bought a goose. For their guests from Cairo, they decided on a warm scarf in Bavarian colors of white & blue, a matching woolen pull-down cap for both, for Sidqi fur gloves and for Fatima a white fur muff. Also a beautiful big book showing Munich in pictures of winter and summer.

Christmas Eve arrived, Hanna and Anton drove to Franz Josef Strauss International Airport up north and the Lufthansa plane arrived from Cairo punctually at noon. There was Sidqi and Fatima coming out of passport control and they welcomed their dear friends with friendly embraces.

A warm welcome with Rosemarie and their guests were at once made to feel at home. Rosemarie had hot tea ready and then they walked over to the Heide inn for a late lunch. Anton assured Fatima and Sidqi, both devout Muslims, that nothing what of he ordered contained pork.

After, Rosemarie showed them the house, the cozy living room with the Christmas tree all decorated, the hot pool downstairs; Fatima was at once ready to bath. Hanna told her that first they would have to go out for a walk into the cold to appreciate the pool so much more. They let them unpack in their nice room and rest for an hour.

They bundled their guests up in extra warm coats from Hanna and Anton and out they went into the brisk cold wind for a walk in the nearby park and forest until it got dark. Then home, everyone changed into robes and swimming suits and they went into the basement, in the hot jet-pool into which Anton threw pine tablets that bubbled and made the water green and smell of forest. There they sat in the churning hot water and had much to tell each other.

Christmas Eve came, and it was already dark outside when they heard the children's choir and the doorbell ring. It had become traditional that the children's choir from the school came to serenade families of the children and also such distinguished families as the Nagils were and for many years they came to the Nagils to sing Christmas carols. At the beginning, it had been arranged by their loyal taxi driver Sepp Kainz and then they became included in the group of families who were serenaded to. With the cold wind blustering outside, they asked the children to come into the warm living room, Rosemarie lit the tree and turned out the overhead light. It looked beautiful with the many colorful lights on the tree and the lantern each child carried adding a warm shine. Hanna, was made happy by the children and their spirited carols as were Sidqi and Fatima. Rosemarie, who had expected the children, passed out hot cider and baked cookies. With a cheerful "Merry Christmas" by all the children and their adult guides, they departed.

They spent Christmas Eve in joyful togetherness and after opening their presents, watched the Nutcracker ballet, which was a traditional fare on TV. At midnight, Rosemarie and Anton went to Christmas Mass and when they returned their guests were asleep.

It had not snowed lately, but the next morning when they woke up it snowed quite heavily. Anton was detailed for duty Christmas Day at police headquarters.

At least on Christmas day, there was little of any crime reported and traffic accidents were reported to the department of the duty traffic officer. At three o'clock, his shift over, Anton returned home. They awaited him, Hanna having arranged an evening walk in the snowstorm and all dressed warm in coats, their new scarves, caps down over the ears, fur gloves, and Hanna and Fatima warmed their hands in muffs. Out they went into the driving wind of snow and cold to the nearby park where lamps lit up the trees and bushes already coated in white. There, like the children they were from the hot climate of Egypt, they cavorted around throwing snowballs and Hanna showed Fatima what snow tasted like. Then home into the warmth of the house and the smell of a roasting goose. After their dinner, they all sat by the fireplace and ate roasted chestnuts and baked apples. Later, Toni prepared the *Gluehwein* (hot spiced wine), tea for their guests, and they ate cookies and *Stollen*—the special Christmas cake. Hanna played "Silent Night" she had learned especially for this day, happy melodies on the piano and also classical selections.

Life in Munich was good. A beautiful city which had much to offer on cultural activities, elegant stores, the Huggendubel book store on the Marienplatz where they liked to browse and drink good coffee. They saw an operetta at the Gaertner Theater. Anton declined to take them to the opera as most operas shown in Munich during Christmas were those of Richard Wagner and Anton disliked Wagner.

When Hanna insisted, "Let us see at least one Wagnerian opera. Wasn't the wedding march they played on the ship from Wagner? Why don't you like his operas, Toni?"

He smiled, remembering. "That was from his Lohengrin, Wagner's best choral piece. I just don't like his pompous music and the screaming of his heroines or the languorous recitals of his heroes."

"Oh, Toni, the romantic you are. Just once, please?"

How could he refuse any wish from his Hanna. He bought tickets for the four, box-seats and they were very expensive. The production was *Der fliegende Hollaender (The Flying Dutchman)*. They were elegantly dressed when Anton drove to the Prinzregenten Theater.

The stage was darkened when the captain left the ship and to Anton, droned on and on and he promptly went to sleep. When Hanna saw her beloved sleeping, she smiled amused; then she saw Sidqi and Fatima likewise sleeping. This captain wouldn't stop singing in his deep sonorous voice, so Hanna, sitting reclined in her comfortable chair joined them. At intermission, they left and went to the Luitpold Café where they had a fun time and danced to a live band.

"I don't want to see another Wagner Opera," Hanna said emphatically.

Anton smiled. "I take you to Puccini or Verdi's operas, others who wrote good music and fine librettos. You like Mozart, he wrote fun operas, not sleepers." They laughed.

The following Friday, Anton took Sidqi and Fatima to the beautiful Munich mosque in Freimann. Anton had wanted to visit the mosque and had Inspector Wagner's approval to do so.

This was a good and innocent reason to visit there as he was bringing his Muslim guests from Cairo for evening worship.

When they drove to the mosque, they could see the complex in a cove of pine trees, the slender minaret rising up and the blue cupola of the mosque covered almost completely with snow.

There was ample parking room as it was a large lot with many cars already there. Through the tall entrance gate, they came into the elaborate foyer, done in beautiful tile where the men separated from the women, the women going into the separate section of the prayer hall. Fatima wore dark and had put her headscarf on as is proper for Muslim females. Anton took a seat in one of the comfortable upholstered chairs in the foyer to await the return of his friends. On the round table with a lit lamp next to it, he saw magazines in German and Arabic and he chose an Egyptian travel magazine and was browsing in it. Most of the devout had entered the prayer hall and just a few latecomers came by.

"Guten Abend mein Herr (Good evening, sir)." Anton looked up and saw a black-bearded man in a white robe and turban-like cap stand before him. The man's smile was friendly. "Visiting, sir, or are you a Muslim?" He asked in guttural German.

"I am neither," answered Anton, "I brought friends of mine, guests from Cairo, for worship and await their return. You are the imam?"

The man smiled. "You can call me assistant or second imam here at our mosque and my name is Mohammed al-Dulaimi."

Anton stood up, reached out his hand and spoke in Arabic "My name is Anton Nagil, or as I would be called in Cairo, Achmed Nabil."

The imam looked surprised and pleased, and he too spoke in Arabic and with Egyptian accent, "You surprise me, Achmed Nabil. I would have never expected to find a man from Munich speak so perfectly Arabic. I don't understand, you look German, if we can tell a person by the way he looks and dresses. Also your German is, well, let's say it is local dialect. So, please enlighten me Achmed Nabil?"

"It is all very simple Imam al-Dulaimi. My father, shortly after the war, went to Egypt with my mother and I grew up in Cairo."

The imam's eyes looked serious. "Your father, he had to leave suddenly?"

Anton smiled. "Yes, that is correct."

Again the man smiled friendly. "And now? How come you are in Germany?"

"My father died a long time ago. My mother came from Munich and returned to her former home some years ago. Now she is old and I wish to be with her for the time Allah grants her to live."

"You speak like a Muslim but you said you are not. May I invite you for a cup of real Arabic coffee? I am not needed for worship; Imam Aref is conducting the prayer meeting."

"That would be nice." Anton smiled. He followed the imam through a side door into a well-furnished, large office where the imam brewed the coffee, then placed the two cups on a small round table between comfortable chairs. He knew that al-Dulaimi would now try to pick his mind on who he really was.

Anton tasted the coffee and said that it was delightful, "Arabic coffee as I used to enjoy in Cairo."

"I am from Alexandria myself, but I know Cairo well. Where did you live, Achmed Nabil?"

"In the part of Cairo called Gazirat Badra, part of Shubra."

"Yes, I know it well, many Germans live there. And you lived, went to school, and worked in Cairo?"

"Yes. I went to what is now called the International Academy. Earned my degree in chemical engineering at the Cairo University. Spent two years in the army, one year in special forces as a captain and was a major in the army reserve. I taught chemistry at the Academy." "Then you are an Egyptian citizen?"

"I have dual citizenship since I was born here in Munich. My father and I became Egyptian citizens during the reign of Gamal Abdel Nasser. He was friendly disposed to us Germans, as was King Farouq also."

"And may I ask, you are now living in Munich, a businessman, perhaps import-export from Egypt?"

Anton laughed, "No, I am not the businessman type. Recently, when I returned to Germany I found employment with the Munich police department." Anton observed just the slightest tightening of the man's cheeks—in surprise, or did he feel danger? His friendly smile remained. "How come, Achmed Nabil? Could you not find a position at the university?"

"No. I am not a professor; also they have enough teachers in chemistry, a long waiting list. But the police department accepted me, mainly because I speak Arabic."

"Yes, I can imagine. Any particular branch, I understand they have special units. We were even visited by the branch of their antiterrorism unit?"

"No. They needed me in the criminal investigation branch."

"Yes, I am certain they welcomed you. Any problems with our people?"

"Who do you mean by our people, Egyptians?"

"Muslims, Arabs."

"I help with interrogations and in court translating. So far, just minor infractions of German law, nothing of a criminal nature. One Algerian who stabbed someone, that is all."

"No terrorist activities?"

Anton laughed, "Not here in Munich. No, I have heard nothing of the sort."

"Our first Imam Abd al-Rahman Aref would surely be interested in meeting you, Achmed Nabil. He is from Cairo. Would you visit us here? We gladly would show you our beautiful complex of the mosque, our community facilities."

"That would be nice. I would like to see your center."

"May I have your address and phone so we can contact you when Imam Aref is here to receive you?"

"We in the police are not permitted to give our private address and phone number. Just call the *Polizeipraesidium* in the Ettstrasse and ask for Inspector Nagil, I am usually in my office."

"Inspector . . . Nagil?"

"Anton Nagil."

"Yes. And you are Catholic then?"

"As most Bavarians are."

The imam stood up. "We shall contact you then, Inspector Nagil. You liked the coffee?"

"Excellent Arabian coffee, we all enjoy it."

"Oh yes, you are Egyptian. It is so strange to see in you a German police inspector and also an Egyptian. Extraordinary if I may say so. I think I return and assist Imam Aref." The imam guided Anton Nagil back to the foyer, where they shook hands.

"Forsa sa ida (Nice meeting you, Inspector)."

"Ma'as sale'ama Imam Dulaimi—goodbye."

Anton returned to reading his travel magazine and soon the prayer service was over and with the multitude, Sidqi and Fatima came, and they drove back home.

Sidqi remarked how beautiful the mosque is. Then asked, "Terrorists here?"

"I don't know, Sidqi. The Islamic Center is supported by the Brotherhood. Nothing wrong with that, their funds have to come from somewhere, at one time from Libya, also Saudi Arabia. The police know little about the Center. They raided it a few times, but I guess didn't find any connection to terrorists or al-Qaeda."

At noon, on the twenty-ninth of December, Anton and Hanna accompanied Sidqi and Fatima back to the airport for their flight home. For the two from Cairo, it had been a wonderful experience in the magic winter landscape of Munich, the small town of Planegg and participating in the Christian Christmas festivities.

The next morning, Inspector Nagil had a meeting with Inspector Wagner and related to him his visit to the mosque and meeting the second Imam Mohammed al-Dulaimi and his obvious interest in him.

Inspector Nagil told, "I revealed little of my previous life in Cairo, my connection to the Brotherhood through my friends Ali Nasr and Sidqi Suliman, or my visit to the al-Qaeda training camp in Afghanistan. I gave him just enough information to wet his appetite and let him research the life of Achmed Nabil from Cairo."

Inspector Wagner agreed, "Arabs love intrigues and will be more certain of your possible sympathy for their Brotherhood connection if they themselves find out your previous cooperation with them and your trip to Afghanistan to teach jihadists bomb making. Keep me informed."

The Nagils had one more couple coming to play host too. On the thirtieth of December, the MacKenzies came from Edinburgh in Scotland.

Anton and Hanna picked them up at the airport and it was a joyful reunion. Rosemarie was also happy to have them visit.

First, they had lunch at the Heide Inn, and since it snowed, out for a walk in the park. And as is custom after getting frozen in the winter storm, down into the hot jacuzzi.

There the four friends sat and told each other of their lives. Arthur, who worked for the government was now a parliamentarian, having gone into politics and had been elected. Anton told of having joined the Munich police department.

"Going after the baddies," commented Arthur.

"Yes, I was made a police inspector of the criminal investigation division dealing mostly with foreigners since I speak Arabic and Russian."

"Terrorists?"

"Very few here in Munich or perhaps they behave. The terrorists don't consider Germany as their enemy. You, British are, as you have troops in Iraq."

"Yes, I know. They have problems in London with Arab immigrants. Our liberal policies permit them to incite and preach hatred toward us infidels. Not in Scotland though. We keep them under control. Our police keeps a tight tap on them there."

"And when are you two coming to visit us in Edinburgh?" asked Arthur.

"We will friend, Arthur, if only for a long weekend."

When they came from the bath and had dressed, Rosemarie had prepared a cold dinner of delicacies for them and Anton made hot spiced wine.

The next day, the thirty-first, was Sylvester and Anton had been invited to the banquet the police officers held each year at the Bayerische Hotel. Since guests were permitted, though not children, Anton had made reservation for his two friends to accompany them. His mother didn't feel up to spending the night at a party.

Rosemarie had never seen Anton in his full-dress uniform, and she remarked how handsome he looked, "Hanna, you better watch over him. Sylvester is the night when husbands like to flirt with other men's wives."

"He better not or he will sleep downstairs on the sofa tonight!"

"I promise to behave Hanna." And they laughed.

The *Rats Keller* in the hotel was always reserved on Sylvester Night for the police officers; the lower ranks had their night at the Hofbrauehaus. The place, which was in the basement of the hotel, was nicely decorated; on the tables were funny hats, noisemakers and other items for the New Year's festivities and many officers had already discarded their caps and wore the pointed clown hats. Their table was for the inspectors of the CID department. All wore their dress uniforms in dark blue with their epaulettes showing their grades. Anton's had the one star of the inspector. More spectacular Arthur looked in his black-and-white kilt, white jacket with the red sash and knee-high white socks.

Anton could finally introduce his wife to his colleagues and Hanna met Inspector Keller and his wife Hilda, also Inspector Kirsch and his wife and others. Since Anton was a new addition to the police force, he was introducd to officers whom he had not met and he was warmly welcomed by all, and so was Hanna and even more so the Scotsman, Arthur McKenzie, who became the center of attraction.

Inspector Nagil had to interpret as few spoke English and the MacKenzies do not speak German. At once, one of the officers on the table wished to know what was under the "*Rock's* skirt." Inspector Keller's wife Hilda asking, "Man's shorts or panties?" Which caused the table guests to laugh or grin. When Anton translated and he too called it a skirt, Arthur, in good humor at first, stated that a kilt is not a skirt. Then added, "Neither shorts or panties," which Anton properly translated in German, "Weder Unterhose noch Damenhoeschen." This caused an uproar and calls for "Zeigen, herzeigen (show us)!" To which Arthur replied laughing, "Mein Geheimnis (my secret)." When Hilda Keller insisted she needed to know. Gallant Arthur stood up on a chair, the whole place watching and with a flourish raised his kilt which caused the wives on the table to scream and avert their eyes. One officer yelled, "Ein Nacktarsch! (A bare bottom!)" The wives screamed and squealed and all turned their heads to look, only to be disappointed when they saw the Scotsman wear proper men's underclothing. Arthur really in a jolly mood, the main attraction at the table and he danced with all the wives. Anton and Hanna too, rarely going out where they could dance, had a wonderful time dancing the waltz, tango, polka, and foxtrot. The band played only old favorites.

When the band took a pause, Hanna played Egyptian folk music on the piano. Then, when Hilda requested of Hanna to play something fast, like for a belly dancer, she did. Hilda went to the dance floor and did a respectable imitation of a belly dancer, soon joined by other daring wives, shaking and prancing. They all had great fun, as twice year, during Sylvester night and Fasching carnival, the usual reserved Bavarian burghers liked to frolic and have a good time and kiss other wives, some even their own.

The sumptuous food was a buffet, they had to get themselves as were bowls of spiced punch, though many ordered beer, wine and of course *Sekt* (champagne).

Midnight came, the lights flickered, there was the roar of HAPPY NEW YEAR, noisemakers in action, embracing and kissing all around the wives. Hanna commenting later, that she had never been kissed by so many men before.

Soon after, the party broke up as many officers had duty after midnight and the next day. New Year's Day was always a rowdy day in Munich with many drunks still celebrating in the streets.

Another day in Munich and the MacKenzies returned to Scotland. Anton and Hanna promised to visit them soon in Edinburgh.

At the end of January, Inspector Nagil had to take the one-week training course for new inspectors in the training camp for police officers in Fuerstenfeldbruck. This included all new inspectors from Bavaria and not just Munich. While it was mainly classroom work pertaining to arresting suspects and proper interrogation methods, associated paperwork, and courtroom appearances, the police officers also had to qualify in small arms, rifles, machine pistols, the use of tear gas and operating less lethal weapons such as stun guns. They also received instruction by the karate expert in handling resisting suspects, how to immobilize without resorting to a weapon. There, Inspector Nagil showed the instructor a few tricks of his own which resulted in the police school requesting Inspector Nagil's transfer to the school as a hand-combat instructor, which was at once denied by Chief Inspector Kirsch.

When Inspector Nagil returned to his duties in Munich, he began two projects. One was suggested to him by Inspector Wagner, to research the history of the Munich mosque and Islamic Center and the other project he did on his own but he informed his chief Inspector Keller, as it was time consuming and needed the cooperation of the police registrar office, the city address bureau and the Munich Archives. It was a profiling of all persons in Bavaria, both men and women, who had Arabic names. He then cross-indexed the names by the countries they came from. Computers were such a wonderful invention and time saving for such projects. Even though with about five thousand Arabic named persons registered in Munich and Bavaria, this was a large undertaking that consumed many hours each day and took months to complete.

Inspector Keller relieved him of his minor duties and only acquired his help for reading of Arabic written documents, as interrogator and in court as translator.

When he had completed the list, he had the computer separate those of Egyptian nationality and with the approval of Inspector Wagner received a three-day travel permission and took the list to Brigadier Amer in Cairo.

He was cordially welcomed by the brigadier and they chatted about Anton's new life as a police inspector in Munich. When he handed over the list of Egyptian citizen living in Munich/Bavaria and requested from the brigadier to identify those who were members of the Brotherhood or known members of the jihad, Brigadier Amer promised him to have his staff work on the list and send it by diplomatic mail to the Egyptian Embassy in Berlin for transmission to him in Munich.

The brigadier also told him that his agency was now in contact with the Bundeswehr Intelligence Service. When Inspector Nagil suggested that they could keep in touch by e-mail, the brigadier smiled. "And let the CIA in on our communication? No, Achmed Nabil, anything of a confidential or secret nature we work through our embassy in Berlin. They will forward it to you at the police headquarters in Munich and directly to you. No one opens mail addressed to you? A secretary perhaps?"

"No. I receive and open all mail addressed to me."

The brigadier had coffee and sweet cakes served and soon they parted, Anton still an unofficial member of Amer's Intelligence Agency. Anton had told the brigadier that his superiors at the police wished for him to continue his contact with Egyptian Military Intelligence, receive information pertaining to known terrorists or members of banned groups who were Egyptians living in Munich and Bavaria and in turn Anton would provide information to the brigadier pertaining to Egyptian terrorist suspects in Germany.

In due time, Inspector Nagil received the list and it identified those known as members of the Egyptian Brotherhood. Though none of the Islamic Jihad, which did not mean that members were not in Munich. It was a very secret organization. On this list of Brotherhood members, he found the two imams' names.

Since Anton had two extra days, he visited the Suliman family in Cairo.

The last day before his return to Munich, Anton flew to Cyprus and from there, on his Israeli passport to Israel, where he visited his mother-in-law Amal.

Amal took him to the nursery of an orphanage and showed him Daniel, now five months old. Anton held the baby in his arms, he held him dear as he expected to be Daniel's father soon. When Anton kissed the baby's face, it smiled at him, which made Anton's heart pound with joy. "Beni Daniel, ani' ochev otcha (My son Daniel, I love you)," he whispered, and the baby chortled as if Daniel understood.

Amal expected to become Daniel's foster mother in another week and Anton promised her to send Hanna back at once.

The same day he returned to Munich.

A week later, Amal called that Daniel was with her and Hanna at once left for Jerusalem. Hanna would alternate with her mother taking care of the baby and continue with their volunteer work at the Hadassah hospital. Anton would fly to Israel whenever there was a long weekend or holidays. Daniel would recognize him when he came and smile when he held him and look up at him with his trusting blue eyes.

It was during the last week of February that Inspector Nagil received a call from Imam al-Dulaimi of the mosque who invited him for coffee on Sunday afternoon to meet Imam Abd al-Rahman Aref. He at once called Inspector Wagner and told him about the visit. In fact, Anton made it a practice to leave his visits with strange people or visiting dangerous places with someone he trusted at police headquarters. Besides, he had to sign out when he left. He carried his Beretta in a shoulder holster and would do so whenever he visited the mosque, never trusting anyone.

He arrived punctually at three in the afternoon and there was a young man, probably a guard and the caretaker at the door awaiting him. The caretaker took him to the office of the first imam, Abd al-Rahman Aref.

Imam Aref was elderly, perhaps in his late sixties. In his white robe, turban and white beard he looked very much like Ayatollah Khameni, Iran's Supreme Leader. Inspector Nagil bowed. "Es salaem alekum (peace upon you)," and was greeted with a light bow of the imam. "Wa alekum es salaem, tasharrafna (pleased to meet you)." Which was as formal as friendly a greeting. The office was large, and divided in two parts. The section the imam took him to was European furnished with a sofa, a table and upholstered chairs. The other half, as Anton observed, was Arabian style with a low table and cushions placed around. After they were seated, an aide came in with a tray of coffee and small cups, delicate pieces of china.

The imam smiled wryly. "Is it Inspector Nagil?"

"Please, Imam Abd al-Rahman Aref, call me Achmed Nabil." The imam's smile became at once friendly.

"Then you must call me Imam Aref. Your Arabic is perfect, and yes, with the Egyptian pronunciation, as is mine of course, I am also from Cairo. I come from the Mar al-Qadimas and you from the north, the Gazirat Badran section."

"You are well informed about Achmed Nabil, Imam Aref."

"Yes, I have made some inquiries about Achmed Nabil. Greetings from Ali Nasr's father. I am very sorry that your friend Ali was killed in Afghanistan. By a Yemeni? It is always tragic when a Muslim kills another Muslim. It was about a religious disagreement?"

Anton understood at once that the information the imam received was from Zahi Abu Nasr, the father of his former friend Ali.

Anton nodded. "Yes, if I remember, we saw a Taliban poster in the hospital forbidding this and that for women. Ali Nasr thought the manner in which the Taliban treated women was against the Koran. Al-Moqri thought otherwise. That is how the disagreement began and it ended with Saleh al-Moqri shooting Ali."

"Yes, a tragedy. And you avenged the killing of your friend by wounding al-Moqri?"

"Yes, after shooting Ali al-Moqri turned the rifle on me but it misfired. By then my shovel hit his face and he became blinded."

"Was this the reason you then fled the camp? You were there as a teacher in explosives?"

"Yes, I taught the jihadists bomb making including Mohamed Atta. No, this was not the reason. I had killed a Swedish Muslim before when he raped our companion Sidqi Suliman. Though I am not a Muslim, the *jirga* said my killing was justified. It was the American missile attack that infuriated the jihadists against all infidels, against me, and the commander of the camp thought it best if I left. So did Ayman al-Zawahiri when he came visiting with Sheikh bin Laden. The missile attack killed three of the six Yemeni and once it was known in the camp that there was an infidel among them, my being there, even under the protection of the Sheikh—my stay became dangerous. That is why I fled with Sidqi Suliman. Suliman, being my friend became an enemy of the other Arabs in the camp."

"Yes, so much I have heard about the deplorable incident. Later, when you fled, that is not known? How did you manage? I understand that the jihadists blocked all roads?"

"The commander of the camp, though a native Afghan and Taliban, provided Sidqi and I with Kalashnikov rifles. We fought our way through a roadblock before we reached Kabul. Then we were stopped at the Salang Tunnel and were ordered to return to Kabul. We managed to fight our way past Taliban guards into the Panjshir Valley where we were well received by Shah Moussad, who as you know was assassinated in 2001. Commander Amir Khan Haq advised us to take the route north through Alliance territory if we could not use the tunnel. Haq and Moussad were friends despite being from opposite camps."

"But Moussad was the renegade commander, working with the Northern Alliance against the Taliban and Osama bin Laden?"

"While this may have been so Imam Aref, both had the same goal of uniting Afghanistan. I did not mix into Afghani politics. I was there at the request of the Sheikh to teach bomb making as his explosive experts had gone to North Africa to attack the American embassies in Kenya and Tanzania."

"Yes, I remember. They succeeded in their missions. Please continue."

"I had been wounded in the fight with the Taliban crossing the bridge into the Panjshir. I was laid up for many weeks. Then recovered, Moussad gave us a former Soviet prisoner of war to guide us across the Hindu Kush Mountains to reach Tajikistan. However, before we reached the Amu Darya River separating the two countries we were ambushed by bandits and our Russian guide was killed."

"And you and Suliman were able to escape? I heard the bandits there are fierce warriors?"

Anton smiled. "So are Sidqi Suliman and I. We surprised them as they came upon our van, which we had burned. We killed all five bandits."

Imam Aref smiled. "You are a dangerous man, Achmed Nabil."

"Only with my enemies."

"And who are your enemies?"

"I am now a Munich police officer."

"I understand. Are you still sympathetic to the Egyptian Brotherhood as you were while in Egypt?"

"My enemies now are true criminals."

"This I also understand, Achmed Nabil. However, you did not answer my question? By the way, Sidqi Suliman is still one of us."

Anton smiled. "I know, he is a member of the Brotherhood."

"Yes. Achmed Nabil, Let me ask you . . ." The demeanor of the imam became serious, "If one of our Brotherhood members gets into trouble with the German authorities, can we count upon your sympathy, even help?"

"As long as his activities are not directed against Germany and of a purely criminal nature."

"We have no war against the Germans. We wish for Germany to continue to be friendly with our aspirations in the Middle East. It is the Jews we war against and perhaps the Americans who fight our people in Afghanistan and Iraq, also the British who are their allies. Since the Spanish left Iraq, we are on friendly terms with them and ceased our activities there. The Italians are a strange people. Have soldiers in Iraq yet are friendly with us Arabs. We are only trying to have European nations understand, if not support, our rights. The Brotherhood is not on a conquest of the world under Islam."

"As long as the Brotherhood confines its activities to its real enemies, yes you can count on my sympathy for its members. But perhaps, for my help with members who get into trouble, you may advice me of activities of nonmembers of the Brotherhood but Arabs you know of who are planning illegal activities here in Munich, in Germany?"

"Yes. The dagger of friendship cuts both ways Achmed Nabil. Our only enemies here are the Jews, and perhaps some right wingers who hate us Muslims and want us out."

Having established a mutual friendship and trust, the imam then toured with Anton the facilities of the Center. It was a beautiful center for many activities, at least what the imam showed Anton. It even had nicely furnished guest rooms, a large dining room, a small one for intimate guest and a kitchen serving both. Anton noticed certain rooms were not shown to him, none that had communication facilities.

On Monday morning, Inspector Nagil briefed Inspector Wagner about his visit and intimate conversation with Imam Aref. For Inspector Wagner, it was first of all important to learn that Imam Aref was with the Egyptian Brotherhood, something that was suspected but there had been no proof. Secondly, that the Brotherhood in Munich, and by extend in Germany, was not planning any terrorist activities—at least not at this time.

However, there were other elements in Munich not belonging to the Brotherhood but to other cells of terrorists. Jihadists shunned the Brotherhood as too benign.

It was in March, a Friday morning, that Inspector Nagil was visited by Sergeant Franz Oettinger in his office. In fact, Oettinger came storming in, "Inspector Nagil, we have a bomb alert!" As the sergeant told; he was called by the police that a possible bomb was found in a subway car at the Marienplatz. When Inspector Nagil asked the sergeant if it was for real or just suspected, Oettinger replied, "Look at the date inspector." It was the 11th of March, the anniversary of the Madrid bombing.

Polizeihauptmeister, Sergeant Franz Oettinger, was the one-man bomb squad of the Munich police department. His expertise was more in the nature of defusing aerial bombs left over from the war. However, Inspector Anton Nagil was now his colleague on the bomb squad with his expertise in explosives.

Oettinger said that all were evacuated from the subway station, the area was cordoned off and they were awaiting his arrival. He had arranged for the *Bombenrauemung*—bomb disposal truck to wait in front and the protective suits were in it. Inspector Nagil told him to get ready and put on his suit and he would be down shortly. When Oettinger left, Anton called the Munich mosque and asked for Imam Abd al-Rahman Aref. When the imam came to the phone and after their greeting each other in a friendly manner, Anton at once came to the point.

"Imam Aref, I have a report of a possible bomb on a subway train. As the bomb expert, I have to go and see. Any possibility that I might get hurt if it turns out to be a bomb?"

"I have heard nothing of the sort. If there is a bomb it is not put there by any of my Muslims. We are not involved with Germany in our war against enemies of Islam. But let me warn you Achmed Nabil, it may be the work of the Zionist Mossad. Put there to discredit our mosque, our Islamic Center, our people."

"*Shukran*, I thank you for your honesty and advice, Imam Aref."

"Ma'as salelama (go in peace)." Anton hung up and picked up his coat, rushed down to the truck where Sergeant Oettinger was just putting his protective suit on. He climbed into the back of the truck with the sergeant but declined to put on his suit.

"I am not certain it is a bomb, Franz."

Sergeant Oettinger replied, "The latest report I received is that they heard a ticking inside the backpack."

"Nevertheless, unless a deranged person put a bomb there it is unlikely that anyone else did it."

"But the date, Inspector Nagil?"

"Coincidence, that is all."

"How can you be so sure?"

"Ah Franz, politics. If it were a bomb, placed there by whom? Arabs or Muslims? No, they are not at war with Germany, we are friendly with all of them. No troops in Iraq. Who else would do it? The neo-Nazis? No, they have never before placed a bomb into a public place. But we will be careful and check it out."

It was only a short distance from the Ettstrasse to Marienplatz and they drove with sirens howling along the Kaufingerstrasse, which is a pedestrian mall and otherwise closed to vehicular traffic. The entrance to Marienplatz was blocked, but their truck passed at once and they stopped at the stairs leading down into the subway. Inspector Wagner was waiting, as were other police officers. Inspector Nagil and Sergeant Oettinger went down the broad steps leading into the large station where almost all Munich subway lines passed through. Now the place deserted and all shops closed. There, a policeman pointed out the train. He had been the first one to be alerted to the possible explosive device by commuters who rushed in panic from the train. Alone, he had found the backpack and when he examined it briefly had heard the ticking. He told security who evacuated the station, stopped all trains, and had called police headquarters.

Anton was impressed with the policeman for his efficiency, took his name and told sergeant Oettinger to see if the man is interested in joining his bomb squad. "He seems like a most cautious and reliable man."

Before they entered the car Anton turned to his colleague Franz Oettinger,

"Perhaps you wish to wait outside?" He smiled.

"I trust your knowledge of such things, Inspector. If you enter without even the suit on, I can too." He followed in his heavy attire, though he had not put his protective helmet on.

In the back of the car and well lit, they saw the dark-blue backpack in a corner. It had the logo of the Luitpold Gymnasium on the flap. Anton bent over it and he too heard the ticking of a clock. To him obviously not a bomb as any terrorist would use a softer ticking clock or rather a watch. He gently touched different parts of the pack and felt hard rectangular blocks inside—what? Blocks of dynamite? It could be but he didn't think so. Slowly he moved one hand underneath to see if it was connected with a wire—nothing. Just as carefully he opened the pack and shone his flashlight into it, books! He took them out one by one; there were also folders with writing. And last, he extracted a large alarm clock. The books all marked as belonging to the Luitpold Gymnasium.

"This school pack belongs to a student who left it here. Why—the police can find out, only strange that there is a clock in it." He put everything back and carried the pack with him as he and Sergeant Oettinger went back upstairs. He handed the pack to Inspector Wagner, "Either a prank by a school boy or forgotten. His name is on one of the folders. Might be interesting to find out what happened."

"Thank you for a fine job, Inspector," said Inspector Wagner and smiling added, "You had some inside information that it was not a bomb?"

"I did," replied Anton, "But then we never know. It was handled properly by Patrolman Maurer, he deserves a commendation."

"Yes, he does. Perhaps you care to take Maurer and Oettinger out to lunch? Put it on police expense account."

"Thank you, Inspector Wagner, good idea." He told Oettinger to get Maurer who had already informed security that all was well. Upstairs a police car with a loudspeaker informed the public that it was not a bomb and the trains can be boarded again. People already began to fill the square and rush down into the subway, all was well.

Inspector Nagil took his two fellow police officers to a *Bratwurst* luncheonette across City Hall; it too was cleared before and now lunch guests entering. They ordered the place's specialties and a glass of beer. The proprietor came by, asked if they were the ones from the bomb squad, and then when assured so, told them they were his guests.

"Tell me Inspector Nagil, how did you know it was not a bomb?" asked Oettinger.

Anton laughed, "I did not know. But I had inside information that if a bomb, it was not placed by locals, by terrorists."

"And how did you get that information so quick?"

Anton smiled. "That is none of your business, Franz." He looked at Patrolman Maurer,

"Interested to join Sergeant Oettinger in his bomb squad?"

"What do I have to do?"

Sergeant Oettinger explained, "Most of what we do, or I do, is defusing bombs left over from the war. Few left now. Plenty when Munich built the subway and we found them unexploded. My father was also a bomb diffuser. There were many when Munich was rebuilt. I learned the business from him. Now it is mostly ordinance from the *Bundeswehr* that did not explode. Terrorist bombs we have had rarely so far. You would work with me and learn from my expertise. Inspector Nagil is the expert of bombs placed by terrorists. Right, Inspector?" Anton nodded.

Maurer said to Oettinger, "I am interested. Can you get me transferred to you?"

"I arrange it with my chief, Inspector Keller," proposed Anton. He raised his glass, "Let us drink to the best bomb squad in Germany. And as we are called upon to do really dangerous work, when we work together, I am Anton, this is Franz and you . . . ?"

"I am Hans!"

"Then let us drink to success and per DU as is fitting for men who face danger together." They banged their glasses together and drank of good comradeship.

It was a few days later that Inspector Wagner came to Anton's office and told him about the found backpack. "This boy who owned the school pack had been late getting up, so his mother had put this very loud ticking alarm clock next to his bed. It jarred him out of sleep; she had set it much earlier than he usually got up. He had put the clock in his pack, very angry at his mother, and when in the subway decided to skip school, left the pack in the subway. He had not meant to scare anyone, just hoped that someone would take the clock out so he could tell his mother that it was stolen, and return the pack to his school. He was not suspended from school for three days as he also hoped for. Instead, he was ordered by the youth authority to spend three weekends picking up trash in the *Englisher Garten*."

CHAPTER XVII

LETTER BOMBS

However, a few weeks later there was a real bomb threat.

When Sergeant Oettinger came into Anton's office, this time not in a rush, he announced, "We have received a call from the main post office in the Residenzstrasse, that they suspect a letter to contain a bomb. I have the bomb disposal truck outside with Patrolman Hans Maurer, newly assigned to our bomb squad." Oettinger smiled. "It used to be a bomb squad of one, now it is of three. I got Hans a license to drive the truck and he is with me now when I take care of unexploded ordinance."

"How is he doing?" asked Anton.

"Fearless. I have to teach Hans to have more respect for explosives."

Anton told Oettinger to go ahead and he will be down in a minute. When Anton called the mosque, neither Imam Aref nor al-Dulaimi were available.

This time all three donned their protective clothing. At the post office, they were met by the supervisor who told them that this rather thick brown envelope had looked suspicious when handled by a clerk, the room was at once cleared and the police called. He also wanted to know if the building should be evacuated.

Anton told him that as long as the handling room was evacuated there was no danger to other rooms or the building.

With their protective clothing on the two went into the large handling room. On a long conveyer belt was the mail and laying by itself the brown envelope. Anton checked the envelope and felt a protuberance, like a detonator? Anton read the address; it was handwritten in block letters and addressed to:

PRAESIDENTIN DER ISREALITISCHEN
KULTUSGEMEINDE
REICHENBACHSTRASSE 27, 80469 MUNCHEN.
President of the Jewish Community Center, Munich.

The return address was also in block letters, and Anton did not even read it as he was certain that is was a bogus address.

That bastard Imam Aref! He had assured him that there would be no terrorist attacks against Germans or German facilities. He had made no such promise of attacks against their enemies. Jews were their enemies and the president of the Jewish community their main target. The president, a woman who was a survivor of the Holocaust, had recently been designated as *Ehrenbuergerin*—honored citizen of Munich, only the second woman ever to be honored with this title. They knew her as it was addressed to the *Praesidentin*—that is, the female president of the community. They wanted to honor her in their dastardly way.

Anton took his heavy gloves off. If it was a letter bomb it was not fragile to touching as it had been dropped into a letterbox, transported, handled carelessly until some smart clerk became suspicious.

"Any ticking?" asked Franz.

"If it is a letter bomb it is not fused with a timing device. They want it opened by the addressee."

"I have no experience whatsoever with letter bombs," admitted Franz.

"We have to X-ray it first to see if it is an explosive device."

"I don't have an X-ray machine in the truck and as far as I know we don't have one at headquarters," answered Franz.

"We have to use the facilities of a clinic or hospital. Which one is the nearest from here Franz?"

"I guess the *Frauenblinik in der Lindwurmstrasse* (woman's clinic), Inspector."

Anton smiled. "Remember Franz, when we are alone doing our dangerous work, it is per *Du*, and you call me Anton."

"All right, Anton then. Wouldn't it be best to just dump the letter into the tank and explode it?"

"We aren't certain that it is a bomb. Also I wish to know how it is triggered. Perhaps we can find fingerprints inside, I doubt if we find any on the envelope. Please tell the supervisor that most likely it is not a letter bomb but we wish to check it out to be certain, have him call the clinic to prepare them for the X-ray. I have my reasons why I don't want anyone to know if it is a bomb. Please take the gloves off." Anton carried the letter in his bare hand to the truck, waved it at the spectators. "Not a bomb!" He smiled at them and put it into the truck.

Outside, police had kept spectators far away and most left. A nosy reporter asked who he was, "Inspector Nagil and Sergeant Oettinger of the bomb squad." He wanted the paper to write about this minor incident and use his name.

"We should paint out the sign BOMB DISPOSAL TRUCK, just frightens people. We know what it is for," Anton said to Franz. The sergeant said he would do so.

They sat with Hans Maurer in front and drove to the clinic. The director of the clinic awaited them, nervously asked if there was any danger.

Anton told him, "No. There is not. We don't even know if it is a letter bomb and if it is it can't be set off by a timing device, only if the letter is opened."

"Won't X-rays explode it?" asked the director.

Anton assured him that it couldn't.

Anton got the envelope and together with his colleagues went into the X-ray Department. A woman technician waited for them. "Any danger?"

"No, Frauelein, no danger whatsoever."

Anton had Franz place the envelope on the exam table. The technician adjusted the apparatus over the envelope, stepped behind the barrier and they heard the machine hum and click. It only took a short while to get the film. When Anton hung it on the illuminated case, he told the technician that is was not a letter bomb. "You can leave and tell the others that all is well." When she left they looked at the film again. "Yes, it is a letter bomb, Franz. Here at the end you can see the spring and on the other side the friction-detonating device. Very sophisticated in fact. When someone pulls the contents out it can be detonated by the friction-detonator, and if that shouldn't work, then the spring would work. A very intricate job; must be by a professional."

"What do we do now, Anton? Put it back into the tank, I can set it off with a small charge."

"No, Franz. I want to examine it. How it is built is the trademark of a bomber. Also I want to look for fingerprints. I doubt that he worked on the inside with gloved hands. But we also check it outside for prints first. We need a secure room. Perhaps in the basement of headquarters?"

"I check with the housekeeper." He called in on the cell phone and was promised the downstairs.

Anton had Hans Maurer accompany them to teach them both; he took the envelope downstairs into a sort of cleaning room. Anton ordered a bright lamp, other equipment he needed and a small beaker. When everything was in place, Anton held the film against the bright light, examined the contents more carefully and pointed out the intricate mechanism to his colleagues. He adjusted the lamp over the envelope and put on plastic gloves. He dusted the outside and brushed it but there were no discernable fingerprints.

Anton advised, "The clerk who handled the envelope must have been at once suspicious and touched it only by the edges." Next he affixed two large clamps around the envelope, one on each side and explained to Franz and Hans what and why he did certain things.

"As long as the two cardboards are kept together, the triggering devices can't go off. Now I extract the explosive material, probably smokeless powder." With the scissors, he cut both edges off the envelope, turned the envelop sideways over the beaker and shook the powder out in the form of tiny granules, he gently flung his finger against it, then turned the envelope around and repeated the task, a little more powder came out. "It is smokeless powder, enough to kill someone. What we have now is the two detonating devices probably each one containing just a small amount of lead azide or mercury fulminate, both very sensitive stuff and set off quite easily. The friction-device strikes like a match, causes a flame and sets off the detonator charge but it only works if the extraction is done with a swift movement. Another is the spring device. If the spring is released and jumps up, it sets off the detonator either by a similar friction device or by a stab detonator. What we do now, Franz, is carefully extract the two detonators."

Anton put his protective gloves on, as did Franz. Franz asked, "Anton, what happens if either detonators go off now?"

"Just a hot flash, would burn our fingers if not protected."

While Franz held the envelope, Nagil extracted the two detonators.

"It is a stab detonator, very professionally done."

He disconnected the spring and the inside shaft from the cup which held the detonating charge. "All delicate in workmanship. A professional bomb maker worked on this." They took their gloves off. Anton dusted the two cardboards and was able to get decent fingerprints. "For later use." He smiled. "The powder is yours, Franz. I might need some later. Can you secure it safely?"

"I can store it inside the tank. I am the only one who has access to the inside of it." "Put the smokeless powder in a plastic envelope, it is quite safe to handle. You two come up to my office and I order coffee, we deserve some."

While Franz left with the beaker and powder, Anton took all the parts of the defused letter bomb to his office and locked it up in the bottom of his filing cabinet, as he did with the fingerprint sheet.

Before Franz came, he called Inspector Wagner to give him the report. "And please, Inspector, make it known that this was not a letter bomb. Perhaps you can inform the newspapers so."

"Want to come to my office to tell me all about it, Inspector Nagil?"

"I have Oettinger and Maurer here for some coffee."

"Good, later then. Where was the envelope posted?"

"According to the post office it most likely came from a letter box nearby. It was dropped in last evening or during the night."

"And where from do you think it was sent, by whom?"

"Probably by our friends from Freimann. A very professional job, but I shall find out. I doubt if anyone in Freimann has the know-how. Could we check if anyone from the Middle East has applied for a visa to Germany recently, perhaps to study at the mosque here in Munich?"

Inspector Wagner said, "I shall inquire. How far back?"

"I suspect this was their answer to the President of the Jewish Community Center having been made an honorary citizen of Munich. Whenever that was in the papers, any time thereafter."

"That would be less than a month ago. I will work on it. Again, good job."

Next morning, the Sueddeutsche Zeitung and Merkur, the two Munich papers, carried a small notice that a suspected envelope was examined by the bomb squad and it was not a letter bomb. When opened it contained advertisements and coupons meant for the Jewish Cultural Center in the Reichenbachstrasse.

Three days later, on Friday, Inspector Wagner gave Anton a list of ten people who had applied for visas recently, the dates of arrival listed during this time period. One man had come from Egypt to study at the Munich mosque. His name was Abdel Karim Hawass, from Cairo, age forty-five. Profession, a cleric, visa for three months, residence while in Munich was listed at the Islamic Center.

Anton visited Inspector Wagner, had coffee with him and smoked his pipe; Wagner lit his cigarette. "So Inspector Nagil, tell me all about it." Anton told him.

"Why did you want me to post this phony story in the paper, and by the way I did, in both papers."

"When I had my talk with Imam Aref, he assured me that no one planned any action against German and Munich interests. He also said their only enemies were the Jews and some right-wing people who wanted all Muslims out of Germany. The recent honoring of the president of the Jewish community by Munich must have embittered them and they wished to honor her by sending this lethal letter bomb. If we had suppressed any mentioning of the letter they might have surmised that it didn't work when opened. Oh, it would have worked, believe me Inspector Wagner, it was a very sophisticated letter bomb. By planting this bogus story that it was opened and found to contain just coupons it will make our friends wonder who was professional enough to defuse it. They know that I was, or am, an explosive expert. The man who made the bomb will wish to know how it was defused. As intricate as the two devices were, and almost impossible to open safely, he will be most interested to learn how it was done. They realize that the story in the papers was false; there were coupons inside but also the explosive devices—yet apparently it was opened. They would rather have expected that the envelope, if suspected, was detonated in the tank of the bomb disposal truck. I am certain they know of the truck's existence. The imam will guess it was I who defused the letter bomb. The professional wants to know how it was done. I would not be surprised if the imam now invites me for a chat."

"A real cat-and-mouse game." Inspector Wagner smiled.

"And perhaps I can meet this Herr Hawass from Cairo."

"Which is no proof that he is the bomb expert."

"No. But if I meet him, let us see if the talk will turn to letter bombs. In addition, I have the fingerprints of the bomber. Somehow I need to get those of Herr Hawass."

"Please be careful Inspector Nagil. Let me know if you visit Freimann."

"I will. I make it a practice to let someone in the office know whenever I go to dangerous places. Also, I take certain other precautions for my safety."

"You are always armed?"

"Yes. I never use my car going to do police work or coming here. I watch my back before I take line 6 to Planegg. If I cannot be sure that I am not followed, I go on to Stanberg, then change platforms and if I do not see anyone changing with me I return and get off in Planegg. My phone is unlisted as you know. I don't want these people ever to learn of where I live. Knowing how they work, they would retaliate against my family if they consider me their enemy."

"Let me know as soon as you hear from Freimann," replied Inspector Wagner.

It was the following week that a message came to Inspector Nagil's office that Imam Aref invited him for Sunday afternoon coffee. The invitation did not come directly to his office, but was given to the operator, who in turn sent a written message. The name of the caller was the only indication from where the call came.

After informing the duty officer in headquarters by phone, Anton had his taxi friend Sepp Kainz take him to the mosque and told him to wait and if he doesn't return within two hours to notify police in the Ettstrasse and gave him the phone number. "Be sure to ask for the duty officer."

"You expect any danger here, at the mosque, Toni?" The two had been friends for many years.

Anton smiled. "Not really, but it is alien territory here. Undertand?" Sepp did.

The caretaker awaited him, at once asked, if he should send the taxi away. "No, the taxi will wait for me." The caretaker took Anton to Imam Aref's sumptuous office. Imam Aref, in his long white robe and turban, welcomed Anton.

"Right on time, Achmed Nabil," he greeted him after the usual salutations. With him, by the desk, sat a man, tall, haggard in face, a well trimmed dark beard, and also dressed in robe and turban.

"I want you to meet Mullah Abdel Karim Hawass, also from Cairo. Mullah Hawass is here to study." Anton and Hawass greeted each other. The man smiled friendly enough. His handshake was soft which already made Anton dislike him.

"Let's sit by the table, Achmed Nabil and I have coffee and sweet cakes brought in." He clapped his hands and the caretaker took his orders, and returned almost at once with a tray of refreshments. Hospitable, as the imam was, he poured the coffee from a large carafe under which was a candle. They sipped; Anton commented that there was no better coffee than from Arabia.

"Yes, I have it sent from Cairo. One of the little favors I indulge in." They sipped in silence, enjoying the rich flavor.

Anton began, "I bought a cute toy yesterday at Hertie department store. Perhaps you wish to sell it at your gift shop?" Anton extracted two small, oval glass toys from his pocket and gave one to the imam and the other to the mullah. Each one held a miniature mosque in a liquid. "A replica of your mosque imam, please shake it." When both did it snowed over the mosque. Anton had given the mullah the toy holding it by the base and the mullah held the glass in his fingers as he shook it.

"Very nice, for children, yes, it would make a nice gift. Winter over our mosque. How much do they sell it for?" asked the imam.

"For 4.50. I am certain the manufacturer will sell it half price to the mosque for its gift shop. Permit me." And he took the toy back from Mullah Hawass, taking it by the base and turned it around. "On the bottom here is the name and address of the manufacturer." Anton put the toy back in his jacket pocket. The imam also looked at the back of the base and then shook the toy again to make it snow. Then wanted to return it but Anton told him to keep it.

Again silence as they sipped the coffee and the imam refilled their small delicate cups. Anton was amused, he knew what they wanted of him but did not know how to broach the subject.

"Imam Aref, you invited me to visit with you. I live far away."

"Ah, where do you live, Achmed Nabil?"

"Near the—*Stanberger See*—the lake by Stanberg. Is there any special reason you wanted to see me? Perhaps to meet Mullah Hawass from Cairo?"

The imam seemed flustered for moment, then smiled. "Yes, of course. Mullah Hawass is a good friend of Zahi Abu Nasr."

The mullah looked at Anton, "Yes, this was a terrible tragedy when your friend Ali was killed. Zahi Abu Nasr cannot overcome the horror of losing his only son." They spoke about Cairo, where the mullah came from. "I also studied at the university of Al-Hazar which Ali Nasr attended."

"Did you know Ali?" asked Anton.

"No. He was there in the early nineties, I studied earlier."

Again silently they sipped coffee.

"Achmed Nabil," the imam addressed him and looked serious, "There was a small news item in the paper last week, about a possible bomb threat against the Jew building?" *Here it comes,* thought Anton, *at last.* "Yes, we had a call from the main post office about a possible letter bomb."

"And?"

"When we opened, it contained only gift coupons."

Anton detected a momentary look of annoyance in the imam's face. "Achmed Nabil, you are their expert, you dismantled it?"

"Dismantled what, Imam Aref?" Again the look of annoyance.

"The . . ." Mullah Hawass did not finish as the imam raised his finger, cautioning him.

"Achmed Nabil, Inspector Nagil if you wish. Am I right in seeing in you a friend of our cause?"

"Of the Brotherhood?"

"*Na'am*—yes!"

"Let us say, I am in sympathy."

"Then let me be frank, Achmed Nabil. You know very well that it was a letter bomb."

Anton smiled. "We all know that."

Mullah Hawass asked, "And you defused it?"

"Yes."

Imam Aref asked, "Why? It was not directed against Germans, only against our enemies?"

"Yes, I know who it was for and sent to. Why then? Let's call it professional curiosity."

He turned to the mullah. "Let me congratulate you, it was an excellent job. Very intricate mechanism, especially the spring device." The mullah wanted to say something but the imam cut him off, "Mullah Hawass has nothing to do with it. I only heard about it later, else we would have warned you. Achmed Nabil, it was sent to the Jews. Why not let it be sent to them? I thought we have an understanding about our common enemies?"

"We do have the same enemy, Imam Aref."

"Your father, a high ranking SS officer who eliminated many Jews."

"You are well informed about my family."

"We are. SS Officer Otto Nagil considered the Jews as enemies of Germany as we do. Why then your generous dismantling the device instead of sending it to the Jew woman?"

Anton smiled. "For two reasons. First of all, since I was called by the post office as they suspected it to be a letter bomb, I could not say it was not and let it pass. I would have lost my reputation as an explosive expert and perhaps even be dismissed from the police department for negligence. It was also my curiosity to see how it was constructed, as a professional."

"Yes, I understand."

"In the future, if you wish to harm your enemies, don't use an explosive device. It sets me up as your adversary. If you wish to eliminate, shoot or kidnap."

"Well advised, Achmed Nabil." The imam smiled.

"Now if this was the purpose of our meeting I must leave, it is a long way back to Stanberg."

"You came in your car?"

"I don't have a car, Imam Aref. I came by taxi from headquarters. And I shall return there."

After the usual parting ceremonies Anton left and had Sepp take him to the Ettstrasse headquarters. When he checked, he saw that he was not followed. He had Sepp wait while he went to his office. He put on a pair of plastic gloves and took the toy out, put it into a paper bag and locked it up in his cabinet. Monday morning, he took the toy to the finger printing office and had them check for prints. There were good prints on the glass and of all five fingers. When he compared them with those he took from the letter bomb, they matched. Mullah Hawass was the bomb maker. He took both sheets to Inspector Wagner and showed him.

"We can arrest Hawass and charge him in court with attempted murder."

"And my usefulness as a trusted police officer would end with the Brotherhood. I would have to testify against him in court."

"What do you suggest, Inspector Nagil?"

"Let it go. We were able to abort their plot. We know where it came from, that Imam Aref is a terrorist or supports them. Prevention of terrorist attacks here in Munich is more important than convicting one bomber. I don't believe they will try it again, at least not with explosives."

"I agree. However, I shall have communications, in the form of an advisory letter, sent to the pertinent police departments in Germany. They in turn can alert main post offices to the possibility of letter bombs. If they have brought a bomb maker, especially one as skilled as Hawass is to Germany, he might try his expertise in other cities."

Two weeks later, Inspector Wagner received a call from the Cologne police department that a suspicious letter had been received addressed to the Jewish Community Center. He at once advised Inspector Nagil and had him fly to Cologne. It was the same type of letter and had been posted from Munich. After he had the small package X-rayed, he found the same two detonating devices within. Knowing the mechanism he defused the bomb safely after first extracting the smokeless powder, put all parts into his briefcase. Hawass was still doing his mischief and needed to be stopped.

Anton briefed Inspector Wagner about his successful mission.

"What do we do, Inspector Nagil? We cannot let this terrorist continue to send letter bombs to Jews or their facilities here in Germany. I also realize that if we expose him, you would have to testify in court and . . . you understand what I mean."

Anton gave a wry smile. "Let me handle it in my own way. I will try to stop Hawass from sending any more letters. He is a rare expert in making letter bombs. Few explosive experts are as skilled."

"May I know how you will accomplish this?"

"I have an idea. Let me work on it. I wish to stop this man from using his expertise permanently."

"Kill him?"

Anton remained silent.

"Then I do not wish to know. Can it be done without involving the Munich police department?"

"Yes."

Anton set his plan in motion. He needed some Deta Flex explosive material and knew there was some at the Fuerstenfeldbruck Police Academy. He drove there and known as the head of the Munich bomb squad, he procured a sheet of 3 mm Deta Flex RDX high explosive.

Using again the downstairs room in headquarters where the janitors kept their equipment, rigging his light, having his tools ready and the parts he had kept from the two letter bombs, he constructed his own letter bomb. He used the undamaged envelope from the Cologne letter and cut a piece off the Deta Flex sheet, half the size of the envelope. To this 3 mm thin sheet he affixed a detonating device made of tiny flat computer batteries which he had procured; hair-thin wires leading to a strip coated with mercury fulminate, a tiny resister imbedded with the wires only making contact with the batteries if the contraption was pulled from the envelope. This would initiate another strip coated with ground up Deta Flex, pure RDC explosive material. The small explosion would in turn set off the sheet. The explosion would be large enough to kill any person standing close. It was a much more powerful letter bomb than the one with smokeless powder. In between the cardboards, he loosely placed the two devices minus the detonator caps. Anton hoped that while the envelope and cardboards were not needed by Hawass, the friction device and spring might be useful to him and he wished to reuse them.

Anton drove out to the mosque in a police car. In the foyer, he found the caretaker and told him he wished to see Mullah Abdel Karim Hawass. When the mullah came and they greeted each other friendly, the mullah eyed the brown envelope Achmed Nabil held.

"Greetings from Cologne friend Mullah Hawass. Please do not send any more envelopes to your enemies in Germany. All post offices have been alerted to look for suspicious brown envelopes. Why don't you send them to Paris or London? They are not expecting any greetings or gifts of coupons. I thought you might need these delicate devices and put them back in the envelope, they are not attached and the powder poured out. And here the detonating caps I extracted." From his coat pocket he took a plastic bag with the small detonators.

Mullah Hawass took the envelope and bag, "I thank you, Achmed Nabil. I shall make good use of these toys, and appreciate your warning. Yes, there are many enemies in Paris and London. Won't you come in for coffee?"

"I have to return to work Mullah Hawass. *Ma'as saleama* (Go in peace)."

Shukran, thank you and peace be with you."

The next day, around ten o'clock in the morning, the intercom rang in Anton's office.

"Good morning, Inspector Nagil, Wagner here. I just received a call from the North Fire Department in Freimann. Their automatic alarm indicated a fire at the Islamic Center. Since there was no follow up phone call they responded with just one piece of equipment. They were met at the Center by the caretaker who announced that they had a small fire in the basement but extinguished it themselves. There was no need for them to come in. However, procedure is that fire department officials must investigate any fire reported, and the chief insisted that he must inspect to assure himself that there was no danger of the fire igniting again. After the caretaker went in to speak to people from the Center, he finally permitted the chief to inspect. The fire was apparently in a room in the basement. In the hall, fire damaged furnishing. In the room, the floor was wet as if scrubbed, so were the walls. Whatever had burnt, the fire was completely extinguished, the smoke ventilated. The only reason the chief called me was that when he inspected the furnishings in the hall he found part of a finger on the bottom shelf of a book cabinet. He put it into a plastic bag, and did not mention it to anyone. The caretaker said, someone had been cleaning car parts with gasoline and carelessly smoked. The person had not been hurt. This was obviously a lie, as the chief realized, and this was the reason that he called me. He asked if his report should state the finding of a finger part. I told him to state so in his report, send a copy to us and also the evidence found. However, not mention it to anyone and not to communicate with any newspaper. The police will take it from there. It is suppose to be the first digit of a finger. Anything you can add to this strange happening, Inspector Nagil?"

"Only that if we can get a print we could compare it with the others. Nothing else."

"I didn't think you would know anything about the matter. When the finger arrives, and it will be brought to me personally, I have it examined for a possible printing. I will let you know."

It was after lunch that Inspector Wagner came to visit Anton in his office. He brought a sheet of the fingerprint with him. They compared the print with those on hand of Herr Hawass. It was a perfect match.

"Herr Hawass has been playing with envelopes again," said Anton.

"A fingertip off a person, that would indicate that it came from a body?" suggested Inspector Wagner.

"The body, meaning a mutilated corpse? Most likely, Inspector Wagner. Perhaps we can monitor the air freight department at the airport and find out if a corpse is being shipped back to Egypt."

"It can only be done with a doctor's certificate that the person has died under normal circumstances."

"Heart attack surely. There must be a Muslim physician here in Munich who can testify to normal circumstances as cause of death."

Inspector Wagner smiled. "Yes, I am certain there is. This should be the end of letter bombs being dispatched from Munich. Any possibility that you become involved, suspected?"

"I should not think so. Yes, I saw Herr Hawass yesterday and as a friendly gesture returned the Cologne envelope to him, but it was minus the powder and detonators. He must have been careless refilling the envelope. Even the best can make mistakes."

"Yes, that must be the case. By the way, I received a purely informative notice from the explosive department of our academy in Fuerstenfeldbruck that you checked out a sheet of plastic explosive?"

"I conducted a small experiment with part of the sheet, the rest I shall return to them."

"The experiment was then successful, Inspector Nagil?"

"Yes, I believe so."

(At about the same time, Imams Aref and al-Dulaimi sat together and questioned the caretaker. He told the imams that Inspector Nagil had come the day before and requested to see Mullah Hawass. He had seen how the inspector had handed him a brown envelope. They only talked for a brief time and Mullah Hawass had passed him going into the center and waved the envelope at him, "Empty, not dangerous" he had said. He also showed me a plastic bag with little cups inside and said "All my things are in here." This morning, Mullah Hawass had gone down into his workroom and when he had heard the explosion he had rushed into the room. Mullah Hawass was dead, mutilated by the explosion and there was a fire, which he extinguished. Fearing that the fire department would come he had dragged the body next door and also body parts he had collected, and washed the blood off the floor and wall. He had taken all bomb-making equipment away before the fire truck came and had removed the damaged furniture.

When they were alone, the two imams realized that Hawass had been careless and must have caused the explosion and his own death. He must have made a very powerful letter bomb.)

Two days later Inspector Nagil received a call from Wagner.

"I have confirmation from air freight that the body shipped back to Cairo was that of Mullah Abdel Karim Hawass. You were right; he suddenly had a fatal heart attack. The death certificate was signed by a Dr. Salah Mahmud. I put him on our list of suspects."

"Thank you for the interesting news."

"You are a dangerous man, Inspector Nagil."

"It is all part of the dangerous work of the bomb disposal squad."

Anton heard a soft chuckle. "Natuerlich (sure)." The phone disconnected. Head Inspector Wagner neglected to write a report.

CHAPTER XVIII

POLICE WORK

Police work for an inspector is drudgery unless he is a detective investigating. As inspector, Anton read files, statements, detective reports, attending interrogations or interpreting for Inspector Keller. Perhaps the only interesting part of his work was to meet the accused, the interviews and questioning and court appearances.

Since Anton spoke English and Russian, he also investigated those who came from European countries where Russian was spoken. Rarely did he meet an Arab who was charged with a crime. Not so with Russian speaking people. There were occasional robbers and even muggers. He really disliked those who used violent methods to commit a criminal act and treated them ungentlemanly, though he had learned to control his anger. There was a Russian Mafia in Munich but they dealt in organized crime, drugs, prostitution, identity theft and forgeries of ID cards, licenses, passports. They were a close-knit bunch of criminals and when one was arrested, they adhered to their code of silence.

On the first of April, Chief Inspector Kirsch held a meeting in his office with the chief of the CID, Inspector Keller and his people, a foreign liaison officer and an official from the immigration department. Inspector Wagner set in as chief of the special or antiterrorist unit. The agenda was the Russian Mafia. There was little Inspector Wagner could contribute. "Unless," as he stated, "the police department classified the mafia as a terror threat."

Inspector Kirsch said, "We might as well as it is a criminal conspiracy, directed against the populace of Munich with its foreign connection to mobsters in Russia."

Inspector Wagner added, "But not the conventional terrorist organizations such as the Brotherhood and al-Qaeda, or the neo-Nazis. With my small staff, we can't handle this too."

"Just an idea, my good inspector," interrupted Kirsch. "We have to marshal all our resources to combat this scourge. And it has foreign connections."

The chief turned to Herr Lotringer from the immigration department. "Is it not possible to be more selective whom we let into the country?"

Herr Lotringer answered him, "The problem is that we do not know if an emigrant is part of the Russian mafia. The emigrant will lie on his entry application and without checking, the Russian authorities we will never know."

The chief asked, "Well, don't we do that?"

Lotringer answered, "We cannot check with each emigrant, for example a child."

"We are not interested in children," the chief added.

Lotringer explained, "No, of course not, yet they come in as family members. Families are less scrutinized. We seem to accept families as more legit."

The chief agreed, "We should not. In America, the Italian mafia consists of large families."

Lotringer continued, "Still, if we suspect anyone, the head of a family, and write back to the Russian authorities, it takes months for them to reply if at all."

"In today's computer age, it is ridiculous to write letters," the chief quipped.

Lotringer said, "Letters, e-mail, if they don't answer our inquiry, what difference does it make? If I may suggest, Berlin should take that up with our foreign office and connect to the Foreign Ministry in Moscow."

The chief inspector said, "I shall take it up with the commissioner. It couldn't be only Munich that has a problem with the Russian Mafia. I am certain they are also well established in Berlin, Hamburg and other cities."

He turned to Inspector Keller, "Do we know of any mafia members besides the couple little fish we catch occasionally, try and send to prison? Can't we ever get to their top people?"

Inspector Keller answered, "It is like an octopus. We cut off one tentacle and it grows a new one. With their code of silence, we never get to the body or head."

"Do we know of at least suspects with whom they associate? You know, widen our investigation and catch many octopuses in the net. With our witness protection program, we might find someone who talks. But we need names, bodies to interrogate," the chief said.

"There is a restaurant in Schwabing where I am told the Mafia hangs out," Inspector Keller said.

The chief said, "Well, you have a good man who speaks Russian?" He looked at Inspector Nagil.

Keller said, "I have a talk with the inspector. A possibility."

The chief continued, "I understand their underground network produces just about any bogus document, even passports. How about counterfeiting the euro?"

Keller replied, "Counterfeiters have had little success in Germany. They have tried and had some success with new member nations of the European Union where businesspeople are not familiar with the currency. We had some problems here years ago but not lately."

The chief further told the group, "I speak with the commissioner and see that we get Moscow involved with our inquiries. Herr Lotringer, your department must become more aggressive in requesting information. Inspector Keller, you work with Inspector Nagil on infiltrating the mafia. Little fish might lead us to the sharks. Inspector Wagner, if not busy with foreign or native terrorists, you might give CID a hand with your expertise. This concludes our meeting. Inspector Keller, keep me informed of any progress."

When they left, Keller asked Inspector Nagil to come with him to his office. From his file cabinet, he took an envelope and shook two matchbox covers on the desk.

"From the last four criminals who were Russians, two of them we believe to be mafia members, from these we found these same matchbox covers. Perhaps a lead?" Anton looked at them. On the front was the advertisement:

MOSKAU NAECHTE
KLUB UND RESTAURANT

The address was Leopoldstrasse, in Schwabing. Inspector Keller advised, "It is on the eastside and just before you get to the Herzogstrasse. The proprietor is a Dimitri Djukov. The club is registered as belonging to the FRARUS Company, an export-import company of Russian and French goods. We have nothing in our files of any criminal nature against either the club or the company. Well, there were a few misdemeanor charges against the club of loud noises, drunks misbehaving, urinating in public. I sent a detective there and he visited a few times at night. Just visited by Russians and tourists. They have a show but again, all legitimate and following our restrictions on night clubs."

"What were the two Russians arrested for?" asked Anton.

"It was about a year ago. Extortion of other clubs in the area, offered protection and threats of consequences. Then when there was a fire at one club, we stepped in. We had detectives at all clubs who were solicited for protection. When these two came in, they were arrested. We could not prove that they started the fire, but we convicted them for extortion. They are sitting for four years. This was the end of this extortion racket. These two claimed they were working alone, wanted to make some easy money. Even when we promised them probation, they insisted that there was no mafia support. We knew better but could do nothing. I thought with your fluent Russian you might make connection or at least pick up some loose talking, Inspector Nagil."

"Let me investigate."

"Keep a book of matches."

Inspector Nagil smiled. "I intend to get my own."

"Be careful. Let us know when you visit there. If you don't return we know where to look for you."

Anton took the U-6 to Muenchner Freiheit, the nearest subway stop and walked back a few blocks. He saw the neon sign of the club in both German and Russian. The club was a few steps down from the pavement. He just strolled by and looked at nearby businesses. On the corner of Herzogstrasse, he saw a sign *ALLIANZ VERSICHERUNG*, Alliance Insurance.

CHAPTER XIX

MOSCOW NIGHTS

Anton walked into the office, which was at the ground floor and told the receptionist he wished to speak to the director.

"About what?"

"Private business."

She called on the phone. Then asked his name. "Inspector Nagil." He had to wait for a few minutes. Then a short, heavy built man came out. "I am Director Mueller. What can I do for you?"

"May I speak to you privately?"

Director Mueller led him into his elegant office. Anton then showed him his identification as a police officer of the CID.

"And what can I do for you, Inspector Nagil?"

Anton explained to him in confidence that he wished to investigate the Club Russian Nights. He needed a cover of working nearby so he could frequent the club at lunchtime and when asked, state that he worked nearby at the insurance company. Director Mueller was most helpful. He even offered Inspector Nagil an empty office for his use as a cover. "I let the staff know that you are a new underwriter, which means that you are absent most of the time. I have a nameplate put on your desk, also your name on the door. Do you wish to use your own name?"

"Perhaps I am Herr Hagen, *ja*—Julius Hagen."

"Always ready to cooperate with the police." Director Mueller smiled. "Mafia, yes? We heard of the fire in the club and the papers wrote about an extortion attempt. It was a year ago, I believe. It would help if you come every so often and spend an hour or so in the office. I have your name added to the directory. My receptionist, Frau Mittermeier must know in case she gets calls for Herr Julius Hagen."

"Frau Mittermeier can be trusted?"

"Oh yes, I trust all my people, but in this case it is best if no one else knows. Perhaps you wish to put a picture of your wife on the desk?"

"Herr Hagen is not married." Anton smiled.

"And the ring?" Mueller looked at his hand.

Anton laughed, "We need you in our detective department. I have to remember to take it off before I enter here."

"Or have lunch at the club."

"Yes, and I wish to thank you for your cooperation Director Mueller. The police will appreciate it. My chief, Inspector Keller will get in touch with you." When Anton left he was the new insurance underwriter of the Alliance Insurance Company, Herr Julius Hagen.

The next day, at eleven in the morning, Herr Hagen appeared at the office, dressed in a suit and coat as is proper for an insurance agent. He was greeted with a friendly smile by Frau Mittermeier, and when he entered his office he saw his name on the door and a plastic plate with his name on the desk. There were even files on his desk. He stayed an hour undisturbed and read the paper. Half past noon he put on his light coat and went to the Club Moscow Nights for lunch. Before he entered, he slipped off his ring. He rarely wore it anyhow, his life very private, and usually only when he was with Hanna.

With the large basement windows and proper lighting, it was bright in the club. The club was not very big. A small stage at the back and before it a long bar; in front the dance floor, tables and chairs to either side. Off to the left it was open and leading into the dining room, half filled as he saw. Only one side of the bar seemed open now and a burly man in a white shirt was busy there. He sat on the bar and ordered a beer.

"What kind of a beer, Herr?"

"Loewenbrau, dark. Can I eat here too?"

"If you wish." He called loud, "Liesl, a customer for you."

The beer came from a bottle. A minute later the waitress came in her dark, short dress and white apron, a pretty woman, perhaps in her midforties. She handed him the menu. Nice legs in heels, he noticed when she walked back. The bartender who observed his looking at her smiled.

She returned after a few minutes and he ordered steak and *pome frites* (french fries). She asked how he wanted his steak. He told her, "Well done, with plenty of onions." No one else was at the bar and the bartender poured a vodka for himself and came to Anton, "New here? I have never seen you before in my club." He spoke good German but with a heavy Slavic accent.

"I just started to work at the Alliance Insurance Company next door. Hate to cook for myself, and dislike sandwiches."

"You are always welcome here, Herr?"

"Julius Hagen." He extended his hand, which the bartender took, "I am Dimitri. I run the club. Live in the neighborhood too?"

"No, I live out in Stanberg."

"Far away."

"No, not really. Takes just forty-five minutes on the *S-Bahn*. Not any longer than other people need to get home."

"U-6 from here and then S-6 from Marienplatz. Yes, good connection."

Dimitri took his glass of vodka, lifted it. "Na zdorovia."

"I guess this means *prost*," They banged glasses. Dimitri drank his drink in one gulp and wiped his lips and mustache with the back of his hand. Anton took a sip of his beer.

"Then you don't speak Russian. Any languages?"

"I can speak High German."

"You are speaking it now. I can't understand the Munich dialect. What did you do before you began this job selling insurance?"

"I worked for a chemical company making paint."

"Then you are a chemist?"

"No. I just learned chemistry on the job. Making paint is mixing chemicals."

He took anther sip of beer. "Need insurance, Dimitri?"

Dimitri laughed, "That is what I call a good insurance agent. Comes in for a beer and meal and wants to sell his insurance. No, I am self-insured."

Anton smiled. "Just trying to drum up business. I am an underwriter. I sell, I make good money. I don't sell, I eat carrots."

"You work on commission then?"

"Only. That is how the business works."

"You are not married; I saw how you looked at Liesl. Pretty lady, no?"

Anton laughed, "You don't need to be single to appreciate a pair of shapely legs, and she is pretty. No, I am not married, still looking."

"So is Liesl."

Just then she brought Anton his steak. Dimitri left him alone to eat.

When Anton paid, he gave Liesl a generous tip.

"Thank you . . . what is your name?"

"Julius."

"I am Liesl." She smiled at him.

When Anton returned to headquarters he saw in on Keller. He told him what he had accomplished and that he met Dimitri Djukov.

"I have to call Director Mueller and thank him in the name of the department. Have your own office; that is remarkable. Excellent cover I must say. Keep me informed."

Herr Hagen made it a practice to eat his lunch at the Moscow Nights and became friendly with both the bartender and the waitress. He no longer ordered steak, which was expensive but the daily special which was always a different Russian dish. He was disappointed that at lunch none of the Russians came in. Mainly people who worked in offices nearby and tourists.

"You should come in the evening, Julius," Dimitri invited him. He was now called by his first name. "And see the show. Many pretty legs."

"I might just do that, come in after work. What time does the show start?"

"At eight. If I know you come I reserve a table. Maybe I find you even company."

"How late does Liesl stay?" Dimitri raised his eyebrows and broke into a grin, "Like the woman, ha? Well, I think she has an eye for you too. I could tell her to stay late. She normally leaves before the show starts. She likes to dance. You two would make a nice couple."

"Yes, that would be nice. Ask her, and if she has time, I stay late too, always paperwork to be completed."

The next day, it was Liesl who, when she brought him his special, smiled at Anton and whispered, "Tonight, I stay late. Will you come?"

"I'll be here."

He saw Inspector Keller in the afternoon and told him about his rendezvous with the waitress.

Keller said, "Liesl Kunz has worked there for many years. She must know something even if she is not part of the gang."

"It is hard to believe that she isn't part of them. They wouldn't let her work there."

"Yet, she is a good cover for them as she is a native of Munich. I checked on her. Divorced, no children."

"Just a feeling I have. I want to take her out."

"I am not quite sure I follow you. She is obviously, what you tell me, enamored in you. I have met your Hanna. How can you . . . I don't understand?"

"Oh, I just like her. Like to talk, dance, just friends."

"She expects more?"

"I guess I have to confess that I am really gay."

Inspector Keller laughed, "I hate to have you as my adversary. Just be careful in the mafia den. Are you always armed?"

"Yes, nice to wear a jacket."

"Just be sure to report in with the duty officer first."

Anton came already at seven and sat on the bar with others. Liesl was still serving in the dining room. His neighbors at the bar were obviously Russians. They had stopped talking when he sat down. Now there were two more bar tenders but Dimitri came to him,

"Julius, the usual, a dark Loewenbrau? Sorry, Liesl is still serving."

When Dimitri poured the beer from a bottle and brought it and also had a glass of vodka, he said, "*Prost* Julius." Anton smiled. "*Prost* to you, Dimitri." They clinked glasses, and Dimitri drank his down. To the Russians sitting next to Anton, he said, "You can talk freely. This dummy here doesn't speak a word of Russian; well, he knows one—vodka. An insurance agent, wanted to sell me a policy." They all laughed. Dimitri smiled at Anton. "Vodka, *ja?*" And poured him a glass. Anton downed it, shook himself. "Brrrr, awful-tasting stuff." They laughed again,

Dimitri added in Russian, "The fool, he is after Liesl, and she likes him."

One Russian asked, "Are we safe with Liesl?"

"Yes, I am sure of her. She is still one of us," Dimitri replied.

The Russian continued to ask, "But you ditched her, not jealous?"

"Who me or her?" asked Dimitri.

"She, of course," the Russian answered.

"No, she gets a good salary besides her tips to keep her trap shut," Dimitri informed them.

"If you say so, boss," the Russian said.

Dimitri moved on to other customers. Anton sipped on his beer. He felt the Russian nudge him on the elbow, "Panymayu poruski?" Anton looked at the man. "*Was*-what?" The two laughed. "He is a dummy," said the second Russian. Anton was indignant; they didn't even have the courtesy to talk to him decently, instead addressed him like one would a kid or family member, the familiar form. Their faces impregnated in his mind. They had addressed Dimitri as boss.

Anton turned around with the beer in his hand and looked toward the dining room, waiting for Liesl, listening intently to the Russians. Their conversation was about the dancers who were to appear and they liked.

The first Russian asked, "Is Sonja still in the business?"

The other replied, "*Da*—yes, she hasn't paid her coming off yet. And she never will."

"Still free for us?" the other asked.

"Courtesy of our boss." Anton pitied Sonja, what an ugly brute the Russian was who asked for a freebee. Nothing else of interest until a half hour later, a third Russian appeared, a young man. This time with Slavic features and in a workman's outfit. Anton would remember his face too. He didn't turn around when the newcomer was greeted with *ztravstvuyte Ivan*, and he greeted the two Russians in turn with their names, Vladimir and Serge. Though who was who?

The first Russian said, "Working tonight, Ivan?"

"Psst, we can't talk here, Serge," asked Ivan.

Serge replied, "Don't worry. This man doesn't speak a word of Russian."

Vladamir added, "Yes, he does. He knows how to say vodka." They roared with laughter.

Anton turned around. "Was komisches, ja (something funny)?"

Serge said, "Ein Witz (a joke)."

Anton said, "Tell me too, I love good jokes."

Serge started to say, "An American joke. There is this Jewish woman. Her son takes up with a Shikse, know what a Shikse is? No? A non-Jewish woman, in fact he married an Indian Shikse. So, mama is mad at him. Tells him she will disown him. Nine months later she gets a call from him. 'Mama, the wife had a baby, a boy, and we gave the baby a Jewish name.' Mama is pleased about that. 'So what did you name him?' He tells her, 'Smoked whitefish.'" They all roared and Anton laughed with them. Anton turned around again and sipped his beer, looking in the dining room. The Russians continued with their conversation.

Serge asked, "So, what is happening tonight, Ivan?"

Ivan answered, "A shipment is coming in from Slovakia on Easter Sunday."

"Hashish?" asked Serge.

Ivan answered, "No, the white stuff, snow. We bring it to the warehouse."

Vladimir said "Then we have work again."

Anton got up. "Auf Wiedersehen."

"Ja, auf Wiedersehen," replied Serge. Anton rushed to Liesl who had her coat on and came to him.

"Auf Wiedershen," called Dimitri from the bar and added, "You two have fun, hear!"

"Let's go somewhere else," said Liesl, and they left hand in hand.

Anton suggested a place to dance. A block to the Herzogstrasse, then another block to a club where dance music could be heard in the street. It was only half full and they found a nice table in the back. Anton ordered a bottle of champagne. They had a great time dancing and talking about each other's life.

Once when sitting together Anton asked her, "Liesl, who were these three Russians sitting by me?"

Liesl asked, "Why do you want to know?"

"When Dimitri told them I was waiting for Liesl, they laughed and I think they made derogatory remarks about you. I don't like that."

"Oh, that was Serge Andropov and Vladimir Cherkovski. The young one, Ivan Ivanovich Karpov. They are dangerous people, don't mess with them," replied Liesl.

When it was late Anton said he had to return, "A long way to Stanberg."

Liesl smiled lasciviously, the way only women can smile. "You don't have to go so far, my place is just around the corner."

Anton bit his lip, even managed to blush, softly he whispered to her ear, "So sorry, Liesl, but . . . I am . . . gay."

He saw the surprise in her face, shock, and then she broke out in laughter, though to him it looked forced. "My luck! Hell, a friend is better than a lover. Last longer. But I can't believe it, you look so normal, very handsome too."

Anton smiled. "Perhaps that is the cause. I was always a pretty boy and attracted the wrong kind of gender. So it happened."

"Can you at least kiss a woman?" He kissed her mouth gently with his lips. She brushed his wavy hair back, smiled, and said, "Can I call you Julie? I hate Julius."

He nodded, chuckled, "Though I usually don't take the female part."

Liesl asked, "So there are female parts? And you are the man then. Well, my friend Julie, glad to meet you!" They shook hands and laughed. He walked her home.

The next morning, he visited Inspector Keller.

"Dimitri Djukov, the boss. Serge Andropov and Vladimir Cherkovski are the pushers, Ivan Ivanovich Karpov is the supplier. A shipment of cocaine is coming in from Slovakia on Sunday. I don't know where. They said to a warehouse." Inspector Keller wrote it all down. "Dimitri Djukov might be their boss but there are people above him. Did anyone mention the name of Andre? No? No last name for him. One of the top echelons here. Something else, Inspector Nagil. The chief has been in contact with Berlin. They are sending an immigration official from Berlin and want us to send a qualified police officer along. That is you; you speak the language. Get your travel authority from me, I have it prepared and your tickets from our travel office. You fly to Moscow in two days and check in at our embassy. They make the arrangements for you and Herr Stoecher from Berlin, to see their people from the emigration department. Also check these names you gave me with their police headquarters. The embassy can arrange that too. You leave Thursday morning. Good luck."

At lunch Anton dined at the Moscow Night and told Dimitri that he had to leave for a week and sell insurance in small towns. "At least they provide a car and pay expenses."

"Like a vacation."

"Some vacation talking to peasants." They laughed.

Anton also told Liesl. She looked flustered, "Will I see you again, Julie or is this goodbye?"

Anton smiled. "You will see me again in a week."

"And go dancing again, whisper surprises in my ear and kiss with lips?" They laughed.

In the evening, he called Hanna. He told her he had to go to Moscow, police business. How long would he stay? Just a few days. She told him about Daniel, how sweet he was, "And he says goo-goo."

"In what language?"

Hanna laughed, "Baby language." They had a nice conversation, Hanna of course asking when he would come to Israel. Easter was several days off, but because of his trip he couldn't come. "I am certain that I get a few days off when I come back."

"I miss you, Toni. Shalom, dearest."

"Shalom, Hanna. We'll be soon together."

On Thursday morning, Anton flew to Moscow arriving just before lunch at the Sheremetyevo International airport. The last time he had been here was in 1998, after his escape from Afghanistan. As he saw, very little had changed, it was still a crummy place.

He changed euros into rubles and by taxi went to the German Embassy. There he met the official from immigration, Herr Stoecher. They saw the third secretary who was in charge of Russian visitors and emigrants to Germany. The trouble was, as he explained, typical Russian bureaucracy. His inquiries rarely answered; if at all, late and incomplete. He had made an appointment for them to see the head of the emigration office, which was part of the Interior Ministry, and for tomorrow morning at Police Headquarters in the same building. He had booked two rooms for them at the Russiya Hotel.

They checked in at the hotel, a modern building along the Moscow River and near the Kremlin. They had a quick lunch and by three o'clock were at the Interior Ministry and saw the head of emigration, Wanda Petrovska, an elderly woman with her long gray hair in a bun.

Herr Stoecher, who also spoke fluent Russian, explained their problem of not getting the necessary information on potential immigrants. It was often incomplete and many times unanswered.

"The reason for that was," as she explained, "that the inquiries came by mail. Had to be translated, sent here and there, to the State Police, many offices were involved, and some inquiries might end up in our dead file."

"And what is the dead file?" asked Stoecher.

"The waste basket," answered Wanda Petrovska without even cracking a smile. This gave Anton a bellylaugh, "Russian bureaucracy."

However, she was helpful in suggesting that inquiries should come by e-mail and if at all possible in the Russian language. "We have young people working on the computers. They enjoy their work and can get most information directly from the various departments, also from the State Police, by computer."

Anton and Stoecher dined together at the hotel. Stoecher then left to see some of the nightlife in town. Anton had a beer at the bar and smoked his pipe. He decided to take a stroll along the river. It was a clear night, still chilly in April in

Moscow. He watched a large tour boat pass by brightly lit, music drifted over the water to him, saw people dancing through the large windows; then it was gone. He walked along the path behind the hotel, which was well lit, then he was past and there were few lanterns. A young man came out of the shadow of a tree and approached him, Anton tensed.

The man flashed a knife, "Money! *Geld!*" And when Nagil did not reply, in Russian, "Dy mne dengi (Give me your money)."

Anton disarmed the robber, probably broke his wrist, and threw him into the icy water of the river, flung the knife after him, then saw him swim to the other shore. He returned to the hotel.

The next morning, after a breakfast of *Bleenee*—pre-Lenten pancakes with a side dish of caviar and terrible coffee, he went alone by taxi to the Police Ministry and saw an official of the State Police. He was told that all inquiries by the emigration department were promptly answered, "or in due time." Anton could imagine what due time was, if ever. The official also said that if inquiries came by e-mail it was more certain to get a prompt answer. "We cooperate with Interpol."

Anton then showed him the list of names: Dimitri Djukov, Serge Andropov, Vladimir Cherkovski, and Ivan Ivanovich Karpov. The official typed the names into his computer but there was no record of any of them. However, when he brought their names up in the Department of Emigration, they were listed. Even relatives and character references were listed. Next, he entered the names of the men, relatives and references into the Department of Moscow Archive. None appeared. "Forgeries then. These names do not exist in our archive, nonpersons."

Anton then asked if he ever heard the name of Andre mentioned. The elderly official remembered, "Andre de Phillip-Roussak. Such a person existed many years ago. A well-known entrepreneur, also a crook or what Americans call a gangster. Disappeared around *Glasnost* time."

"Why the French name?"

"If I remember, the man Roussak, and we must go back to Tsar's times, married a French woman and she kept her name de Phillipe. Their descendants kept the name de Phillipe-Roussak and always had a French first name. Of course, your Andre could be another Russian. No last name?"

"No. Do you have anything in your files on de Phillipe-Roussak?"

"So long ago? It would be in our end-file."

"And what is your end file?"

"Shredded. We keep criminal files open for five years."

"We for ten years in Munich. How old would this Andre de Phillipe-Roussak be now?"

"Let me see. He was in his early fifties then. Midsixties."

"And no picture exists?"

"Shredded."

Anton took the noon flight back to Munich. He arrived at the Ettstrasse before five on Friday afternoon. Inspector Keller was still in his office and stayed late to hear Inspector Nagil's report.

"It is too late but Monday morning we search for an Andre de Phillipe-Roussak. If he is fond of French names he might have kept his, perhaps without the Roussak." When Inspector Nagil asked him for a few days off, with Sunday being Easter Sunday, he was granted leave till Tuesday.

He went home and packed a few things; said goodbye to Rosemarie and promised her to take pictures of Daniel. Anton rushed out, Sepp was waiting for him and he made it for the evening flight to Frankfurt and the night flight to Tel Aviv. He took a taxi to Jerusalem and arrived at his house before six.

Hanna, still in her night cloth, flew into his arms. She made good Arabian coffee and they were joined by Amal. Baby Daniel still sleeping and Anton kissed his blond, curly head softly. Then they sat together as a happy family.

"How was Moscow, what did you see?" asked Hanna.

Anton had to admit that he saw nothing. "I was in a rush to get in and out. Someday, I will visit the sights with you." After coffee they entered the baby's room, Daniel lay there with his eyes open and stretched out his little chubby arms to the man who was to be his father.

"Danny remembers you," said Amal. Anton doubted this. He had to let Hanna first diaper and clean the baby, feed him before he could take Danny into his arms and hold him dear. The baby, with a pacifier, held still and seemed contented.

Saturday, Shabbat, is quiet time in Jerusalem. He walked with Hanna, with the baby in the stroller, and was happy when Danny smiled at him. Hanna would play with Danny. When Anton held the baby in his arms, Danny remained still as if he felt secure in the arms of this man.

Three happy nights with Hanna and wonderful days with his family; he took many pictures. While these were sunny days, it was still cool at night. Hanna stayed home from her volunteer work at the hospital but Amal went to work. Like Hanna, she was a volunteer.

When alone with Hanna, he told her about the Moscow Nights Club and that he was undercover there. The episode with amorous Liesl and how he warded her off by pretending to be gay which made Hanna laugh heartily. However, then she became serious, "You are in danger again, Toni!" He assured her he was not. Only getting information on some Russian crooks. He didn't tell her about the robbery attempt in Moscow.

There was nothing Anton could bring for his Mossad contact but he called Nevot and briefly spoke to him. He told Nevot that he liked police work and was involved with the Russian Mafia in Munich. Nevot told him they function in Israel too; they had their share of trouble. That the mafia was handled by the police, and also Shin Bet was involved as the Russian Mafia was a threat to Israel's internal security.

Early Tuesday morning, he said goodbye to Hanna, Amal, and kissed the sleeping baby. At three in the morning, his taxi was waiting and took him to the airport and before noon he was back in his office. After lunch, he saw Inspector Keller who had interesting news for him.

"Andre de Phillip. Supposedly French citizen, owner of the FRARUS import-export company. Age sixty-four. I received a copy of his passport from Koblenz; we have his picture. Distinguished looking, permanent resident permit, owns a house in the Moehlstrasse. The business and warehouse is out in Milbertshofen in the Knorrstrasse. I get more particulars of his company from the Trade Commission. He is our man. We are all set to raid the warehouse, his residence, the club tonight and simultaneously. They couldn't have disposed of the shipment so fast. We have the addresses of all the men you mentioned and I have search warrants for their places. We should find something incriminating. All officers participating in the raids will assemble here this afternoon. This will be a *Grossfahndung*—a major police action, our first since I came to work here. We hit them at 19:00 hours sharp. I don't want you in on the raids but remain here and when we bring Liesl Kunz in, I want you to talk to her. We need her as a witness."

"Fast work, Inspector."

"Yes. The chief thought we should act fast with the shipment having come in on Easter Sunday. We had men hidden near the warehouse on Sunday and a van came in during the afternoon. The chief will arrest Andre de Phillip himself. I lead the contingent to the warehouse."

Anton suggested, "You might want to round up this Sonja also. She is probably indebted to them and has to work as a prostitute; a dancer or stripper at the club. I don't know her last name. She might not be there at seven as the show starts at eight."

"Well, we find her. We raid the club at the same time. She would be a good witness too, testify about their prostitution racket. At four this afternoon, we meet all inspectors and policemen who participate in the raids for a briefing. At six we roll. You have been up all night?"

"Since two this morning."

"Rest. Get something to eat. We should be back by nine, or shortly after. Then we want to interrogate them while they are still in shock of being arrested. We plan that once we arrest them to keep them separate and bring them in in different cars. We must not let them talk to each other and have them reminded of their code of silence."

There were rooms in headquarters that had sleeping arrangements but Anton could not sleep now. Nor was he hungry. He went to his office, called home and told his mother that he will not come home and stay at headquarters. And no, he could not tell her what it was about, but that he was needed for interrogation. To reassure her, he told her that he was not going out on a police raid and she could call him any time at his office. Anton relaxed with his pipe and thought about meeting Liesl, this time as Inspector Nagil. He liked Liesl, she seemed a decent woman who just got involved with the wrong people. That, after a bad marriage and divorce—poor thing. He would have to offer her witness protection. He called Inspector Keller and was assured that Liesl would be afforded this protection. After a cup of coffee in the cafeteria, he retuned to his office. A few pipes, and reading the paper he dozed off in the chair . . . .

The phone rang. My God, it was already half past nine! It was Inspector Keller, "We have Liesl Kunz in interrogation room four. Be sure to record it all."

He washed his face in the bathroom and went downstairs where all the arrested were being questioned. His room was just a large cubicle with a table and two chairs, not one of the mirrored rooms. He had the guard unlock the door and he entered.

Liesl sat there and stood up, "Julie! What are you doing here?"

"Inspector Anton Nagil of the CID. Sorry, it had to come to this, but it may be your lucky day. Please sit down again. Like some coffee or tea?"

"How about some champagne." She smiled. "You sure fooled me. Do I really have to call you inspector—what was it, Nagel?"

"Nagil. No, for you I am Julie. Nothing changed, I am still you friend."

"Gay friend." She smiled.

"I am married, Liesl."

"Oh . . . that is beastly," and she began to cry. He let her. Then when she wiped her tears, he let her compose herself.

"So ask, Julie." She tried to smile.

"It will be all right Liesl, you don't need to cry."

"I am crying more about you fooling me, that being gay bit. That hurts, and then telling me you are a married man."

He smiled. "Women! More hurt by being fooled than being arrested and in a jam."

Anton took her hand, she let him. "Liesl, I am truly fond of you. We were friends and we shall remain friends; that you must understand. Now I want you to know that we rolled up that bunch of crooks, our Munich Mafia and we need your cooperation to put them away."

She looked terrified, pulled her hand out of his, "They will kill me, I know too much about them. I am sure you didn't get all of them. There is Andre."

"Andre de Phillip is arrested. We know he is their kingpin." He told her of what had happened. Most, if not all, had been arrested. All their places are being searched at this moment. He explained the witness protection program. She would get a new name, a family history, could move wherever she wished to live. Help in finding a suitable job. However, they needed her knowledge of what they did, what she knew; other members she knew of besides those arrested this night. People like her who got sucked into their criminal behavior, "Like Sonja. We want to help her get free of them. She won't even get deported back to Russia if she cooperates."

"Can I smoke? I am a little nervous." He gave her a light, and smoked his pipe.

She smiled. "Aren't you going to write everything down?"

"There is a microphone here. It is all being recorded."

"Our private conversation too? You being gay?"

He laughed, "It is all down on tape. They know about me being gay."

"Bastard, Julie." She smiled.

Then she talked.

Sometimes, Nagil would ask for clarification but most of the time he just let her tell all. Give names. When he was satisfied that he had most on tape, it was past midnight.

"Can I go home now?"

"No. We will take you to a hotel. Tomorrow, a policewoman will accompany you home and you will pack. Your place will be sealed off. Return to the hotel, and stay there. Eat in their dining room. Call no one."

"My mother lives here. She would wonder if I don't call her."

"You call her every day?"

"Just about."

"Call her from the hotel. She wouldn't know from where you are calling. Say nothing. You will stay at the hotel until all the trials are over and you are no longer needed as a witness. Then you will be taken cared of by the protection program."

"Can I stay in Munich?"

"They prefer other cities. But I don't see why not. New name, maybe you dye your hair a different color, wear a pair of plain glasses. Glasses make you look like a different person. Buy new clothing. A different job, other friends. If anyone is left from that bunch, they wouldn't know where to look for you. Probably believe you left the city."

"Will you kiss me goodbye . . . Julie?" He laughed—*the mind of a woman*. He would never understand the female gender.

He took her to the lobby where several policewomen waited, embraced Liesl and kissed her and introduced her to Detective Lehmann. They left.

Inspector Keller was still in his office when Anton came by and was told, "Only Sonja is still being questioned by a detective, all others are in cells below. Ivan Ivanovich Karpov had also talked. He is young and doesn't want to spend twenty years in jail. He wants to get back to Russia. Detectives are still searching the warehouse and the apartments, houses and de Phillip's house. Tomorrow, I want to listen to Liesl Kunz's tape."

"She added a few names we might not have arrested."

"Good night, Inspector Nagil. I don't want to see you until after lunch tomorrow." Inspector Nagil went home.

A few days later he was invited for a cup of coffee with the Police Commissioner. Anton had met the commissioner before and of course, was introduced to him at the New Year's Party. Commissioner Kolb was a short, heavy built man with a handlebar mustache, the very image of a Munich burgher. However, he was known as a chief who demanded fulfillment of their duties by his officers and could be very pushy with his inspectors and detectives to solve a criminal case. In fact, he was feared by many.

After first congratulating Inspector Nagil for his part in solving the case of the Russian Mafia, he told him, "I have familiarized myself with your background. Your resume very interesting. I heard about your part in solving the letter bomb scare here in Munich and Cologne. Fine work. Now tell me about your wife, I heard she lives with her mother in Israel?" Inspector Nagil explained why his wife went back to Israel—because of the adoption. It was only a brief visit with the commissioner, but he had found favor with the chief and was highly regarded by him.

This wrapped up the Russian Mafia in Munich—though for how long? Liesl Kunz, wearing glasses and her hair done differently, worked now at the police cafeteria. She had a different apartment. She was safe. Before long, she married a policeman and Anton was their best man. The reception was at the *Rats Keller*, and when he kissed the bride, Liesl kissed him more purposeful and hissed "Gay Julie," which made them laugh.

Anton and Liesl remained good friends. She would call him Toni when with others or her husband but always Julie when alone. It was a joke just between them.

The cocaine was recovered at the warehouse of de Phillip. The police found a trapdoor, which led down into an underground level with many rooms. One room contained a complete set up for forgeries and boxes of new, unused passports, drivers licenses, and to falsify just about any official document. A Leica to take pictures and developing and printing equipment. In a computer, the names of associates and their addresses, names of the prostitutes working for them. Also a list of contacts to whom *Rauschgift*—illegal drugs were sold.

(At city hall the lord-mayor congratulated the Commissioner of the Munich police, also Head Inspector Kirsch and Inspector Keller for rounding up the Munich Mafia. Both received a promotion.) Inspector Nagil received a Certificate of Commendation from his boss Keller; it was also signed by Commissioner Kolb. In it he was commented for his undercover work which led to the arrest of the mafia. He framed it and put it in his mother's room "Sorry, Inspector Nagil, but we cannot promote you as you haven't even been here for one year," Inspector Keller told him privately.

The Antiterror Unit of the Munich Police Department was actually a small section and consisted only of Inspector Wagner, two detectives, several sergeants and one secretary-typist. However, the unit had a backup force of the *Ueberfallkommando*—swat team at its disposal.

The Antiterror Unit was established after the Olympic incident in 1972, as this terror attack had shown that the department was not prepared to deal with this type of terrorist activity and that it was important to get intelligence of Islamic Fundamentalists and at the same time keep tabs on the neo-Nazis, which so far was handled by the regular police department.

Since Inspector Nagil had become part of the unit, made contact with the Islamic Center and was able to provide information about their activities or lack thereof, the unit was mainly concerned with the neo-Nazis. Intelligence about their doings came mainly from Chief Inspector Kirsch, who unknown to even Inspector Wagner, had an informant with the neo-Nazis. One morning when Anton came to work, he received a call from Inspector Wagner to come to this office. With the inspector was a pretty woman, who though modern dressed, showed the black hair and features of a Mediterranean female. The inspector introduced the woman as Frauelein Zayna and said that she was from Egypt. Anton greeted her with *sabah el kher* (good morning). She looked at him, then smiled and said in Arabic, "I am so glad to meet you. My German is the Yiddish-German. I learned it from my father, but people here hardly understand me."

Anton replied, "Inspector Wagner does not speak Arabic, so I have to translate." Then she told her story. But first she explained that her father was Jewish, her mother is a Muslim as she is. "This is important for you to know so you understand why I am suspicious about the whole thing. I live in Alexandria and attend the university. There I met a student, his name is Ahmed al-Hamed, he is of Nubian descent." She smiled. "He is rather dark in complexion but very handsome, and I fell in love with him. We became close and at least, it is my belief that when you are in love you should not have any secrets from each other. I told him that while my mother and I are Muslims, my father is a Jew. He said that he has nothing against Jews but he is glad that I am a Muslim as he wishes to marry me. He also told me that since Egypt is now friendly with Israel, he wishes to visit Israel with me. It was then that I told him that my father has a brother in Tel Aviv and he has visited with him and his family. And that they have a big house there and we would be welcomed. He wanted to know more about my uncle Noam and I told him that he is an antiquarian and has a bookstore. It was a few months later that Ahmed invited me to come and visit Munich with him. There he has a friend who is also an antiquarian and he has a valuable manuscript in Hebrew which he will give to me to send to my uncle. Then later he told me that the manuscript is so old and precious that I must take it myself to my uncle and he asked me to get a visa for Israel. When we came here a few days ago, I thought we will go to his friend who has this manuscript but Ahmed was kind of secretive about it and said he will get it alone.

Also for the past couple of mornings, he left alone to see his friend like again today. A few days ago we went to the El Al office and he bought me a ticket to fly to Israel. You see, Inspector Nagil, it is all so strange. Why doesn't Ahmed come with me, he was also invited? Why do I have a different airline ticket coming back, but to Israel I have to fly on El Al? Why doesn't he take me along to see his friend, the antiquarian? And two days ago, when he brought the manuscript it was already packed up in a box. I would have loved to see it."

Inspector Wagner asked, "When are you supposed to fly to Israel?"

"Tomorrow," Zayna answered.

Inspector Wagner looked at Anton. "Zayna can fly but minus the manuscript?"

"Or the manuscript must be checked thoroughly first," answered Anton.

"A book-bomb hidden in the manuscript perhaps?" asked Inspector Wagner.

"Looks like it may be."

Inspector Wagner then asked Zayna, "In which hotel is Ahmed al-Hamed staying?"

"The Regina Hotel, we have two rooms together. I don't understand; the little German I know, what do you mean, a bomb in the manuscript?"

Anton explained, "We are also suspicious of how the matter is arranged. There is a possibility that the manuscript is a bomb, meant to blow up the El Al plane. I have to talk it over with my colleague but first of all, you will have to go through inspection. By then, you are alone and Ahmed will have left. We shall inform El Al that you are coming and you can be certain that they will inspect the manuscript thoroughly. If it is a manuscript everything will be fine. You fly on with it and return to Ahmed and I wish you both happiness. If it is a bomb, then you will fly to Israel but not come back here or to Egypt."

Inspector Wagner added, "We will have you sign a disposition which we need for the court in case it turns out to be a bomb."

Zayna shook her head, "I just can't believe that Ahmed would do that to me. I mean, we are both in love with each other."

Anton looked serious when he explained to her, "Love and hate are very close to each other in human relations. Please act natural with your friend, he must not think that you suspect anything. And it may very well be that we are all wrong."

Inspector Wagner asked, "Did you notice any difference in his behavior toward you lately or the past few days?"

She smiled. "No, he is just as loving and passionate as he has always been." Anton chuckled and when Zayna looked at him he explained, "Even if Ahmed wishes to kill you, that doesn't mean that he can't be passionate. It has happened before."

Inspector Wagner wished to know on what flight she will be and what time the plane left. She provided that information.

"And what will happen to Ahmed, if it turns out to be a bomb?" she asked.

Inspector Wagner replied, "Ahmed will be arrested and tried for attempted murder." They saw a hesitation in her face and she whispered, "Maybe I shouldn't have told you." Inspector Wagner said firmly, "How can you think otherwise? This man tries to kill you and perhaps three hundred people with you. It is a terrible terrorist act he may commit, with you as his unwilling accomplice."

A vague smiled appeared, and almost whispering she said, "I am sorry, you are right. We women, I . . . we often think with our hearts instead of our heads."

They said goodbye to Zayna, and she left.

El Al Flight 47 was to depart from Munich at noon. Passengers had to arrive three hours earlier for check-in. Inspector Wagner had informed El Al the day before, and they had all their security people on hand, though at the check-in all looked very normal. Before passengers arrived at the security check-in, they had to leave those who bade them goodbye. A last embrace by Ahmed and a passionate kiss and Zanya walked alone into the restricted area. Once out of sight she was at once taken by security personnel to an adjoining room, the package opened and the manuscript placed under the X-ray scanner. Inspectors Wagner and Nagil were with the security personnel and Zayna. She told Inspector Nagil that Ahmed had repacked the manuscript before they left and did so alone. And he had admonished her that it was very fragile and she must not drop it or bump it against something, which caused Anton to look at Inspector Nagil with his brows raised. When the manuscript was X-rayed, it showed nothing unusual, not metal components of any sort. It was a large manuscript of parchment and in Hebrew writing and it looked old. Anton thought that since it was in print and not handwritten it could not be that antique and it was not fragile. The El Al security man let the pages glide through his fingers. They seemed to be loose pages with nothing hidden within. Anton wanted to see the X-ray again. He pointed out what he had noticed before, just a different shading along the edge of the manuscript. "This looks a little opaque."

The El Al security man voiced, "The binding is always thicker because of the glue."

Anton replied, "Nevertheless we must puncture the binding. The man's suggestion to Zayna that the manuscript is very fragile, that she must not drop it, sounds very suspicious. It does not look that fragile. I need something sharp to drill a small hole." The security man produced a Suisse pocketknife that had an instrument like a narrow metal shaft with a sharp point. "It is for puncturing a can, it should do," the man said. Anton pushed the point into the back of the binding, did it a few times and then his fingers became moist, wet almost, with a thick, colorless oily liquid.

Anton tasted. "Nitroglycerin!"

"I don't understand," the security man said. "Even if there is nitroglycerin within the binding, how is it to explode without a triggering mechanism?"

Anton explained, "Let us assume that there is a thin glass or plastic tube imbedded into the binding filled with the nitro. The triggering device can be a capsule inserted into the tube that contains two acids separated by another component of plastic. When the acid burns through and the two liquids come in contact, they will explode and set off the nitro."

While the man looked interested, he smiled. "I never heard of such a thing. Are you an expert in explosives?"

Inspector Wagner said, "Inspector Nagil is from our bombsquad and highly knowledgeable in all types of explosives. If he believes it is a bomb, it is!" He turned to Anton. "I have Sergeant Oettinger standing by at headquarters, please call him to come at once with the truck. The manuscript is all yours. After you extract the explosive we need it for evidence. As a precaution, I had my detectives follow this man Ahmed and I call them to arrest him. Inspector Nagil, please get enough of that liquid out to have it analyzed and be careful, even I understand that it is dangerous stuff. If it is nitroglycerin, we go to court and charge Ahmed with attempted murder of a terrorist attack on a plane. I don't want you any further involved in this case Inspector Nagil, and you understand why not. Please tell Frauelein Zayna that she may board the plane after she signs this disposition I have prepared."

To the El Al security people, he said, "Gentleman, it is now a matter for the Munich Police Department to pursue this case."

Before Zayna left, she spoke to Anton and asked him if he really thought that she must not return to Alexandria. Anton advised that there must be other people involved, both here in Munich who rigged the manuscripts and in Egypt who were Ahmed's cohorts.

"I don't believe that they will come after you Zayna, but we will never know or understand these terrorist. For your own safety, it is best that you stay in Israel, perhaps come for short visits to your parents. "Besides"—he smiled—"Israel is a beautiful country, and you will like it there. When you get to your uncle have him get in touch with the Shin Bet and tell them your story. El Al will also inform them. I am certain they will take good care of you."

The analysis of the liquid showed that it was nitroglycerin. When Anton extracted all the nitroglycerin and dismantled the binding he found the plastic tube with a screw-on lid. A glass capsule was inserted and as he had suspected, a barrier within contained acids. It would have taken about six hours for the acid to eat thru the barrier and permit the two volatile liquids to mix and explode which in turn would have set off the nitro. If Ahmed had added the capsule before Zayna left for the airport, it was perfectly timed. Three hours before departure; three hours later the plane would have had been over the Mediterranean Sea. The manuscript, tube, components, and the disposition of Zayna became evidence when Ahmed al-Hamed was tried.

Ahmed was sentenced to thirty years in prison. However, he did not give any information about his Munich connection or his cohorts in Egypt, or even if he belonged to any terrorist organization. The newspaper accounts spoke of the bombing attempt foiled by the efficient Munich Police and its antiterror unit under the leadership of Head Inspector Wagner, who was a witness at the trial. The name of the woman who was to carry the bomb on the El Al plane was kept secret and Inspector Nagil's name was not mentioned at the trial.

When Anton visited the mosque after the trial, Imam Aref asked him about the bombing plot and if he, as the explosive expert, was involved. Anton assured the imam that it was discovered by the El Al security people and the antiterror unit of the police.

He smiled at Imam Aref. "El Al have their own explosive experts at the airport. They in turn let the Munich anti-terror unit handle it, I was never involved.

There must be a real expert here in Munich who devised this bomb. Using liquid explosives is new to me. I don't believe it has ever been tried before."

Imam Aref smiled. "And you wish to meet such an expert. But Achmed Nabil, I have no idea who that may be. I have heard nothing of an expert coming to Munich. It definitely was not a member of the Brotherhood but another affiliation. You know that there are other groups here who don't like the Zionists."

Anton could never discover who that other group was or who their bomb making expert was. He believed Imam Aref that the Brotherhood was not involved.

(Zayna stayed in Israel and was taken cared of by the authorities who appreciated that she reported her suspicion to the Munich Police. Zayna met an Israeli Arab, married him and had many children. She would visit her parents in Alexandria, or they came to Israel where she lived in Nazareth.)

CHAPTER XX

IN THE MOUNTAINS

Beginning of May, Sidqi Suliman wrote to Anton and asked him if he and Fatima could come for a week later in May and do some mountain climbing with him.

Anton would have rather spent a week with his wife Hanna in Jerusalem but if Sidqi requested, any wish of him he wanted to oblige. Anton remembered as a youth the wonderful tours he made climbing the peaks around the Koenigsee. All, except the mighty Watzmann. He also remembered fondly his onetime girlfriend Betty with whom he had climbed most of the peaks. She had married Josef who, as she wrote to him in Cairo (they remained in distant contact by sending each other Christmas cards), was a mountain guide in summer and a ski instructor in winter. She and Josef lived in House Tanneck, which belonged to her parents.

If Anton wished to show his friends from Cairo the mountains from the top, he needed a reliable guide. Perhaps it was possible to engage Josef without having to visit the family.

Anton called the Schoenauers and was lucky that Betty answered the telephone. After the usual greetings, Anton asked about Josef and politely how her parents are. He told her he wished to come with his good friends from Cairo and engage Josef as a guide. He had written her in Christmas and told her that he was living in Munich and had applied for a position with the police. Therefore, her interest was if he got the job. He told her he did and was an inspector with the criminal police in Munich.

"And Hanna, your wife?"

Anton had never told her that he had married a Jewish women or about Israel, so he had to continue his lie and told Betty that Hanna was still in Cairo, winding up things and she would soon come to Munich.

"You know, Toni, you can stay with your friends with us. Josef and I have the whole downstairs with plenty of room for guests."

Anton declined and asked her to make reservation at the Edelweiss inn in the village. Betty knew why, she knew of his dislike for her father and the reason for it. As a young person, born in the sixties, she had no feelings or admiration for the Nazis or what they had stood for.

She only wished to know what dates he would come with his friends and who they were, how many. Anton told her, and she promised to have Josef available as a guide and she would come along. "Like old times, Toni."

Betty mentioned to her father that Toni would come and bring friends from Cairo, that Toni was now living in Munich and was with the Munich CID as a police inspector

Herr Schoenauer did not care for Anton Nagil. He felt sorry for him. He expected him to appreciate his heritage and what the Nazis had stood for, what his father had accomplished. The two had always been cool toward each other for that reason. That Anton Nagil was now with the police in Munich and even a high-ranking inspector pricked his ears. He told his daughter that when Anton comes, he wished to see him privately.

Anton picked his friends up at the airport and they stayed one day in Munich. Anton took them to a sports store where they bought good climbing boots. Everything else he could loan them.

They drove to the Koenigsee and stayed at the Edelweiss inn. In the evening, Betty and Josef came to see them. Anton had to interpret everything that was said.

Early the next morning, Betty and Josef came and they climbed up to the Stahlhaus and spent the night in the loft. For two wonderful days, they toured the same peaks Betty and Anton had climbed as teenagers. On the fourth day they returned.

On the way down the Jaennermountain, Anton walked with Betty and they talked about olden times.

Anton asked, "Did your father ever rebuild the cabin?"

"Oh yes. He had it rebuilt in stone and with two rooms. One is now the bedroom."

"Did he ever get electricity up there and indoor plumbing?"

"No. It is still rather primitive but cozy. The outhouse has to do and a barrel for washing. Josef and I spend some weekends at the cabin when he doesn't take tourists up the mountains."

By early afternoon, they got back to the hotel.

They parted from Betty and Josef. Sidqi and Fatima invited the two to visit them in Cairo and they accepted which caused Anton to chuckle—thinking how they would communicate not knowing each other's languages. They packed their things and were ready to leave when the office boy came and told Herr Nagil that he had a phone call at the desk.

It was Herr Schoenauer who asked Anton in a friendly manner to please come by his house for a short visit. For Betty's sake, he accepted and walked over to House Tanneck where he was received by a very delighted Frau Schoenauer—Inge, as he called her, who wished to know how his mother Rosemarie was.

"Theo wants to see you. I know, but please see him. He is in his office. I bring you coffee or you wish a beer, wine?'

"Coffee would be fine."

He went into the familiar office, was greeted friendly yet reserved. That suited Anton just fine. They sat by the small table; at least Schoenauer had the courtesy not to sit behind his desk as if he were a stranger.

"Anton, I understand, we have never been seeing eye to eye as I did with your father. Did you ever have any sympathies for the Third Reich and what it stood for?"

"For some of the things Hitler did, yes."

"Like . . . ?"

"He took Germany out of the recession, provided jobs, a Volksempfaenger (cheap radio)." They both laughed.

"And the negative side?"

"He lost the war and led Germany into misery."

"You were glad that we lost the war?"

"Yes, I admit. After what Germany had done, yes."

"To the Jews?"

"Yes. Over a million children were killed."

"They were our enemy!"

"They didn't bother anyone."

"They poisoned our blood."

"Herr Schoenauer, is that all you wish from me? I have friends waiting." For a moment, the man's eyes showed anger. Just then Inge came in with a tray of coffee and cakes, poured some for both. "You two are having a nice talk?" She left them alone.

"Look, Anton, we wished to live alone, without THEM. We gave the Jews every opportunity to emigrate. With their intermarriage, they soiled our German blood. Some of us feel very strong about our pure Aryan heritage and we still do. Now, we have become polluted by other races, the Turks, North Africans, Arabs. We wish to be left alone, that is all. Not too much to ask, right?"

Since Schoenauer mentioned Arabs, Anton decided to stay even though this was all hateful garbage talk to him.

"Yes, I can understand your point. But Arabs, Muslims, what do you have against them? There was even a Muslim SS division fighting alongside our SS."

"Yes, I know about this Muslim SS Division. A bunch of cowards, left our troops in the lurch when fighting the commies got tough, threw their weapons away and ran, ran right back into Germany to surrender to the *Amies*. All right, I understood that they couldn't return to wherever they came from as Stalin would have killed them all. So they nested here. Fine. But you know, those Arabs are good-looking men, and our stupid women prostitute themselves to them. Arabs also have Semitic blood, like Jews. Foul blood. Thousands of them in Munich, plus the Turks who came. They even built this temple out in Freimann and a big cultural center. We don't want their primitive culture here, we are a civilized nation. Like Jews, they don't eat pork, have the same Sabbath."

"Yes, I can see your point. Maybe, I even agree with you."

"All right, we then have a common base if not goal." They sipped their coffee. "Inge makes excellent coffee," Anton said.

"You drink good coffee in Cairo. I understand that you moved to Munich recently and even joined the police department, Anton?"

"Yes, I was accepted as a criminal inspector."

Schoenauer smiled. "Inspector Nagil. Your father would be proud of you. Then, if I understand you Anton, you feel like I do, Germany for the Germans, yes?"

"Perhaps, yes."

"We wish for all these foreign elements to leave Germany."

"Who are WE?"

"Well, it is no secret that I belong to the *Blut und Erde Bund* (Blood and Earth society). In fact, I am their leader here in Berchtedgaden. It is just a small organization to honor what has been and to promote Germanhood. There is a bigger organization in Munich, several hundred members. Last November, one of our members was assaulted by an Algerian Arab and stabbed repeatedly. He was unarmed but the Arab planted a pistol on him. The Arab said in court that it was in self-defense that Hofmann threatened him with the pistol. The judge, can you imagine a German judge, believed this Arab and his German girlfriend and only sentenced him to six months in jail, and that only for carrying a switch-blade. Our man got nine months for carrying a pistol. Next month, that Arab will get out of jail and as you can understand we are very bitter, we want to teach that Arab bastard a lesson. He is one of those religious fanatics; all they can do is strap on a belt and kill a lot of innocent women and children."

Anton thought, *Nazi Schoenauer suddenly becoming concerned about women and children.*

"So? There is nothing I can do for your man. He has to serve his time."

"I am not asking you to help him. We want to know where this Arab lives."

"Don't you have his name, Herr Schoenauer?"

"Yes, but they kept his residence a secret."

"And you want me to find him for you?" Schoenauer nodded.

"Look, Herr Schoenauer, I can't do that. I would lose my job. Well, perhaps there is a way. Let me search in the computer and see if somewhere, for some reason his address was listed. Have one of your men come by my office in the Ettstrasse, make it three days from today."

"We would appreciate it, Anton. Your father would have liked for you to help us." They parted with a reserved handshake and smile, a friendlier goodbye with Inge. Anton returned to his people and had a leisurely drive back to Munich.

Two more days with his friends and they returned to Cairo. Then Anton had to return to work.

Anton had been surprised by the enmity between the neo-Nazis and the Muslims, or specifically the Arabs. While Hitler, or his purity leader Rosenberg, had not thought of the Arabs as Semites, or rather they were acceptable Semites, the neo-Nazis disliked them. He realized it was because many of them were the handsome Mediterranean type and the new generation of women, not bothered by racial ideas, catered to them. Mixed-blood marriages always the bane of the Nazis. He also knew that the Muslim living in Germany, in fact most of them if not all, were anti-Jewish and anti-Israel. If this Algerian Ibrahim Makhous was a fanatic, and he must be! Walking around with a switch blade knife and a pistol and had gotten into a fight with a neo-Nazi, let them fight each other.

He had taken part in the trial as interpreter for Inspector Keller and knew about the case. The German Alfred Hofmann had made some sarcastic remark about the pretty blond that was with Makhous. Makhous had gotten into a fight with Hofmann. According to the blond and Makhous, Hofmann had pulled a pistol and Makhous had stabbed him several times, a case of self-defense. There were no fingerprints on the pistol. If it was planted or not, had never been established, it was the testimony of two against one. First thing when he came to work, he researched in his computer the newspaper reports. There was a detailed description about the incident and with the names of those involved but no addresses given. It was easy for him to look into the criminal file and find Ibrahim Makhous' home address. This he typed to the story at the proper place.

About ten o'clock he had a visitor, a young man well dressed. He introduced himself without giving his name as a friend of Theo.

"I need to see some identification, anybody can come in here and tell me he is sent by Theo," demanded Anton.

"I am not supposed to give you my name. I was told to just come here and get this address."

"*Auf Wiedersehen*—goodbye then."

The man hesitated and then gave Anton his driver license.

Anton went to his computer and brought up the newspaper story. "You could have found the story yourself if you had bothered to do a little research." He gave the man paper and pen who then copied the address, while Anton wrote his name and address down. He returned the license to him.

"We thank you, Inspector." The man left.

The man's name was Karl Seitz. Just a courier or someone of importance in the *Bund?* Anton erased the address of the Algerian from the computer.

A few days later, Anton was told by Inspector Keller, that this Algerian they had tried had been released from prison and was killed by an unknown assailant. "He had his throat cut. We cannot blame it on Hofmann as he is still in jail. Surely an act of revenge by the neo-Nazis."

CHAPTER XXI

SUMMER 2005

In July, came the reports of the horrendous bombings in the London subways and the bus. The Muslim Fundamentalists were active in England to punish them for having their troops with the Americans in Iraq. Shortly after, more bombings, but this time the bombers had failed to have the fuses set properly and many were arrested. The British finally cracked down on imams inciting hatred against the infidels and closing down or warning Muslim publications to stop their diatribe of hate. When Inspector Wagner asked Nagil if he thought that Germany was next, Anton thought it was time to have another chat with his "friends" at the mosque.

He made an appointment to see either Imam Aref or al-Dulaimi for Sunday afternoon. He had Sepp drive him, cautioned him again never to tell where he lived.

Sepp then asked, "Where are you suppose to live, Toni?"

"Stanberg. This is where I live."

Anton got there at three and was received by the waiting caretaker and led into Imam Aref's office. Both imams were there. Al-Dulaimi dressed in a suit, Imam Aref in his white robe. At once, coffee was served with little cakes. Imam Aref asked if there was a special reason that Achmed Nabil came visiting.

"Nothing special, Imam Aref. After the bombings in London, some of my superiors wondered if Germany was next?"

Imam Aref smiled. "No reason why. We have good relations with the Germans. Well, most of them, not the Jews, and there are again many in Munich. They are even building this complex in town."

"A future target?" Anton smiled. Imam Aref shrugged his shoulders in answer.

"Perhaps you can explain the hostility shown to us Muslims by—what you call—the neo-Nazis? I thought we have the same enemies, the Jews and Israel? So why?"

Instead of answering the imam's question, Anton said, "I heard of course, that Ibrahim Makhous was assassinated. One of your people?"

"A brother."

"You believe the neo-Nazis killed Makhous?"

"Certainly. A matter of revenge."

"Then why? It is typical of Nazi mentality. Yes, you are right to ask why the hostility between Muslims and neo-Nazis. We all do have the same enemies. It is particular to the old credo of keeping the Aryan bloodline pure. You, most Muslims in Germany, are Arabs, Semites. The Nazis, and now the neo-Nazis are still influenced by what the Third Reich was teaching about purity of blood of the Aryan race. Under Hitler and his expert on racial matter, *Reichsleiter* Alfred Rosenberg, only the Jews and Slavs were thought of racially inferior, *Untermenschen* (subhumans). Muslims generally were not thought of as Semites, of impure blood. However, the Jews by intermarrying with Germans, were poisoning German blood."

"I understand, but why the change? Under your fuehrer, Arabs were thought of as equals."

Anton smiled. "It is . . . it has to do with sexuality. Most Arabs who are of the Mediterranean type are handsome men, virile men. German women, no longer influenced by the racial purity philosophy of Hitler times, like Arabs as lovers, marry them. Every time the neo-Nazis see an Arab with a German woman, their gender gets up like a cockerel seeing one of his hens inseminated by a stranger. To each other, and when they have their meetings, they complain about Arabs taking their women and poisoning the pure German bloodline."

"This is nonsense," remarked Imam al-Dulaimi.

"You and I understand that it is so, but these men are fanatics. Many of them young, immature, full of half-baked Nazi ideas. It is your success as good lovers, while their young men have no longer their pickings that is the cause of their enmity."

"Stupid. Sexual jealousy," offered al-Dulaimi.

Imam Aref said, "But Achmed Nabil is probably right. I understand their animosity. While it isn't our men's fault that they represent virile manhood to the German women and attract them, we must find an understanding with the neo-Nazis."

Al-Dulaimi added, "We can't just tell our men to disregard their favorite pastime. They have little else to pursue here in this foreign land. The Bavarians are a closely knit people and dislike foreigners."

"They even dislike non-Bavarian Germans," Anton said.

"Bohemians!"

Al-Dulaimi asked, "What are Bohemians, Imam Aref?"

"Someone who disregards social conventionalities. Not including you Achmed, but then you are Egyptian. So I do believe that a dialogue is in order with these neo-Nazis. Are you in touch with them, Achmed?" That the imam was now addressing him by his first name showed Anton that Aref regarded him as a friend.

Anton answered him, "I have a friend who is the leader of the group in Berchtesgaden and of course, is connected with the larger cult here in Munich."

Aref asked, "You call it a cult?"

Anton smiled. "Well, they call themselves Blood and Earth. The name alone will tell you of their fanaticism for purity of blood."

Aref exhaled deeply, showing his disgust. "Yet, a dialog is in order. Can you connect us?"

Anton replied, "Give me time. I try. I talk to my friend."

"By the way, how is your wife? Her name is Anna, yes?" Aref asked.

Anton was surprised that he knew his wife's name, or close to it. "Amal? She changed her name to Anna here in Germany; she is enjoying Stanberg. She rarely goes into town."

Aref continued, "You had a wonderful time New Year at the Bayerische Hotel?"

Anton showed his surprise. "How do you know?"

Aref smiled. "One of our Brothers is a waiter at the hotel. He said that Anna played Egyptian songs. Some of the policeman's wives did a belly dance. There was also an Englishman in a skirt?"

Anton laughed, "A Scotsman, Arthur. Don't call it a skirt, it is a kilt, traditional wear for soldiers."

Al-Dulaimi said, "Ridiculous."

"Not anymore than wearing robes like long dresses, at least to Germans," Anton said.

Aref said, "Achmed is right. Different cultures. Scotsmen are brave soldiers. We don't bother them."

Anton smiled. "But you bother the English."

Aref replied, "Not we of the Brotherhood. This was the jihad. They deserved the bombings; they have many soldiers in Iraq. Please pour us some more coffee, Mohammed."

Al-Dulaimi did.

Aref continued to ask, "And how is police business, Achmed?"

"Drudgery. Paperwork. I rarely go out like detectives do; I do interpreting in court."

Aref said. "We feel here that the Munich police has become more friendly toward us. At one time, it was nasty business; they even raided our center. But the way they treated Ibrahim Makhous, our Brother, very respectful and rather lenient." Anton thought, *How wrong Aref was. The police in general distrust the Arabs and don't like them. It was a lenient judge.*

Anton answered, "Yes, I hear nothing unfriendly about the Arabs or Muslims in the department."

Aref asked, "Were you involved in the mafia business? I read in the newspaper; your name was mentioned."

"Yes. Bad people; into drugs, prostitution, forgeries. We cleaned them up, though for how long?" replied Anton.

Aref said, "Yes, scum from the godless society. The Russians are not much better than the Soviets."

"Same people, same corruption."

Aref asked, "You haven't been back to Egypt for a long while?"

"No, I have been kept busy."

Aref asked again, "Anna has family in Cairo?"

"She was the only child, and her parents died." The conversation became too familiar for Anton's taste. He felt that Aref was investigating him. "I am afraid I have to leave, I still have work to do at the office. I must return there. I thank you for your hospitality and I shall get in touch with Herr Schoenauer in Berchtesgaden." After their salutations, he left.

When he drove off in the taxi, he had Sepp watch his back. Soon Sepp said that a black Mercedes seemed to be following them. "Want me to shake him off, Toni?"

"No. Just take me to police headquarters, and I take the train home." After a while, Sepp commented that the Mercedes was still following. "Dangerous people, these Arabs. Or is it all the Muslims are dangerous?"

"No. Not all, but many. Those who work at the Center are not very well disposed to the Germans. We are all infidels, nonbelievers."

At HQ, he got out and paid Sepp. He went to his office, read some papers and then went home by train. Changed cars a few times. No one followed him.

Monday morning, he saw Inspector Wagner and told him about his visit to the center. The conversation he had with the two imams and the waiter who spied on them.

Wagner said, "Easy enough to find out who he is. Should we have him released? The hotel will gladly cooperate with us."

"No. That would send the wrong message to the center. As long as we know who he is. I am certain he is a member of the Brotherhood and takes his orders from the Center. We can add him to our list of terrorist suspects. And by the way, Germany is still safe from their activities."

Wagner added, "Even though, we will continue to keep tabs on them. You never know with these fanatics."

"And please remember, Inspector, when at the Bayerische Hotel, Hanna's name is Anna."

"And how is your wife? Have you visited her in Israel yet?"

Since his German passport, or for that matter his Egyptian, had never had an entry visa to Israel he could not admit having visited. "No. I wanted to, but then friends showed up from Egypt and I had to entertain them for a week. I hope that soon I can visit. My wife has adopted a baby; she can't have children, so she is busy and can't come here."

Wagner said, "I am certain that anytime you wish to take another week off, Inspector Keller will approve. Nothing important is pending."

When Anton went to his office, he found a note from the secretary that Inspector Keller wished to see him. He at once went there.

"Ah, come in Inspector Nagil, please have a seat." While Keller lit a cigarette, Nagil lit his pipe.

Keller said, "Well, now, I have an interesting communiqué from our foreign office in Berlin, that the Russian Security Directorate in Moscow would like for you to visit them to give them particulars about dismantling the Russian mafia here. They also requested that we extradite their kingpin Andre de Phillip to face murder charges."

Anton smiled. "Andre is safer here in Stadelheim prison."

Keller laughed, "Yes, I agree. If you go, and it is only a request and you may not wish to do so, but if you do, you can advice them that after de Phillip has served his twenty years, ten years and then probation, then they can have him. And by the way, our foreign office wishes for you to travel there, as a goodwill gesture. They would pay all expenses, first class on Aeroflot and your stay there paid for by the embassy. I am certain spending money is provided."

Anton said, "I don't believe I told you of my little adventure meeting up with a hoodlum while there the last time?"

"No. Please tell me. There was nothing in your brief report?" Keller insisted. Nagil related the incident.

"Did you report it to the police? You were at their headquarters," asked Keller.

"No, it wasn't worth to report it and then become involved with their ponderous bureaucracy. I wanted in and out. Besides, the robber was sufficiently punished. A broken wrist and a bath in the ice cold river," replied Anton

"You can request a different hotel?" Keller told him.

"No. The Russya hotel is just as safe or unsafe as any of the others. How does the Russian Security Directorate know of the roundup and that I personally was involved?"

"Our foreign office read or heard about it and requested a full report. I guess they send a copy to them in Moscow," answered Keller.

"Well, I might as well pack."

"Fine, shows Berlin that we are doing good police work here. Might help when we submit a supplemental budget, they are always interested in good relations with Russia. I have your travel voucher ready later. You wish to leave tomorrow morning?"

Anton laughed, "You are eager to get rid of me, Inspector Keller."

Anton called Hanna in the evening and told her of his trip to Moscow. "And how is Danny Boy?" Hanna told him how cute and smart little Danny was, now ten months old.

"A joy to Amal and me, and could be to you if you would only come." Toni promised her that he would take a week or even longer in August, as soon as he came back from Moscow and took care of some unfinished business.

The next morning, Inspector Nagil left for Berlin and was well received by the foreign office. He had his passport taken by an official to the Russian embassy for a visa. The foreign office also gave him the name of the official to see at the State Security, a General Viktor Alexandrovich Orlov. They would advice the embassy in Moscow of his arrival the next day and arrange for an appointment. He also went to the Israeli embassy and applied for a visa, which would take several weeks. When Anton then asked to see an official for expediting the visa, the secretary to the ambassador saw him. He asked the official to place a call to Mordechai Nevot of the Mossad and to advice him that "*Sav*" was coming. Soon he came back and asked Inspector Nagil for his passport and entered the visa. This time, Anton had used his German passport. Anton spent the night at a Berlin hotel, courtesy of the foreign office and left the next morning for Moscow. He checked in at the embassy, received his spending money in rubles, and his reservation at the Russya hotel, a familiar place to him. His appointment to the State Security was for the next morning at nine o'clock.

He took his leisurely walk along the Moscow River. Now with the evenings warm he met many others taking a promenade.

The next morning, after a delicious breakfast of caviar on little roasted breads and so-so coffee, all paid for by the embassy, he took a taxi to the imposing building that was the Directorate of the State Security. He was taken to the office of General Orlov.

The general, a tall imposing figure in his uniform and with a bushy mustache, the image of what a Cossack might look like, greeted him friendly and was delighted to speak to him in Russian, "My German is poor. Please have a seat, coffee or tea? Coffee, fine." He made a call and soon a tray with a can of coffee, cups, milk and sugar was served. The general lit his *papyrosa*, Anton his pipe.

Anton related the whole affair, his undercover work, which delighted the general. The report he had received from the German foreign office only gave the outline of the operation. General Orlov wanted to know every detail. He invited Inspector Nagil for a sumptuous lunch at the restaurant in the building, then left him there for a while as he had some important matter to take care of.

When he returned, he gave Anton a tour of the building that was formerly the KGB headquarters. Then took him to the museum, which was of great interest as it contained many of the memorabilia of the KGB. Anton was especially fascinated with the spy cameras in vogue then, listening devices—all outdated now. The arms employed by the agents. The general also showed him the deadly cyanide weapons used then. "Marvelous contraptions for eliminating enemies of the USSR."

He showed him an umbrella, which contained a single charge of a cyanide pellet in the handle. Similarly, a fountain pen an agent could carry inconspicuously in his breast pocket. This item interested Anton and he asked how it operated. The general took it out from the glass case and showed him. The body and cap were made of stainless steel. He separated the top and showed him how the pellet was introduced. Then holding the pen, he operated the clasp and pulled it up, "This activates a spring. Pushing the lever down would release the spring and the pellet is expelled at great force, but limited in distance. It has to be within a few inches. First, the tip of the pen has to be unscrewed. It looks like one could write with it, and can, there is a tiny inkpod in it." Anton asked if it was deadly.

"When shot at, for example at the face or better neck, it is fatal within a minute, at most a few minutes. At the hand for example, it would take an hour to work its way into the bloodstream and become fatal. The nice thing about it is that there was no noise of discharge and the recipient would only feel a sting, like an insect bite, raises a little red swelling. The recipient would never know he had been shot by a deadly projectile."

"Is it still in use, General?"

General Orlov laughed boisterously, "We are no longer the KGB. However, they are still in our arsenal. We have many left in case we . . . well, I cannot give away our workings."

"General, what is the possibility of acquiring one of these marvelous pens?"

The general looked serious. "You are not becoming an assassin, Inspector?"

"No. I think more in the nature of a self-defense weapon. Like the last time I was here . . ." And he told the general the story of the robber.

Again the general laughed with a roar, "So you broke his wrist and sent him to a cold bath. Did you report it to the city police? No? Well, I still could check with hospitals or clinics and see if someone came in with a broken wrist during April, and"—he laughed again—"and having a bad cold or even pneumonia. So what for the pen? You seem to be able to take care of yourself?"

Anton explained that he deals with religious fanatics, terrorists and also with the neo-Nazis. "When I have to visit them in their lairs I get frisked, they are armed. It would give me a last resort capability."

"Yes, I can understand. Then you are dealing also with neo-Nazis. Evil people the Germans were under Hitler. Now a new generation; we get along with you and your people. As to the Muslim terrorists, we have our problems with them even here in Moscow."

The general called the attendant who was nearby. "Leonid, get me a cyanide pen and a box of pellets. I sign for it."

The man left and soon brought the items. The general checked the spring and discharged it. Then he checked the date of the box of pellets. "Recently filled, good till 2010." He signed the sheet.

"Here, in appreciation for having nabbed Andre. He had a friend of mine, also a police officer, assassinated. How long will he serve?"

"He received a twenty year sentence. This makes him eligible for parole in ten years. I have been assured that he will then be extradited to Russia."

"We will wait for him. About the pen, best to immediately put it into the tray at security checks as it is metal and would trigger the buzzer. Might be a good idea to place it with another pen into your breast pocket. And now Inspector Nagil, I have to attend to some more business. Please be in my office at three. You can browse here some more, Leonid will show you anything you wish to examine." General Viktor Alexandrovich Orlov left.

Anton spent another hour in the museum then went into the restaurant for another cup of terrible coffee, flavored with his pipe. At three o'clock, he appeared at the general's office. To his surprise there were a number of people and he was introduced to the German ambassador.

They all stood around General Viktor Alexandrovich Orlov, who read from a letter of appreciation, "In honor of Inspector Nagil for his work in rounding up Andre de Phillip and his gang." Then the general pinned the Medal of Friendship on Inspector Nagil's jacket. The burly man then hugged Anton, a bear hug it was and kissed him on each cheek. *Sloppy kisses,* Anton thought. *Liesl would have enjoyed watching.* Pictures were taken. All congratulated him. With his visit to the State Security Directorate over, he returned to his hotel and the next morning flew back to Munich.

He visited Inspector Keller, gave him a report and showed him the medal, omitting the gift of the poison pen.

"I can't read the writing. Is it in Russian?"

"It says, PEACE AND FRIENDSHIP."

Keller was pleased, "We made Berlin, and I guess the Russians happy. Wear the order for our next official gathering. So, what did you enjoy most in Moscow, Nagil?"

"The caviar breakfast." They had a good laugh.

Anton contacted Herr Schoenauer by phone and told him of Imam Aref's suggestion to meet with members of the *Bund* here in Munich. Schoenauer was pleased and thought that the active Muslims and the Bund members should get along. He would send a letter to Imam Aref at the Islamic Center, outlining possible cooperation and contact the leaders of the *Bund* in Munich to arrange a meeting. He also wants to assure the imam that the *Bund* had nothing to do with the killing of the Algerian. "It would be futile to start a war between them and us. And Anton, I appreciate your involvement in our affairs. Never too late to join our nationalistic movement."

"I doubt that, Herr Schoenauer. I can't as a police officer. Goodbye, give my regards to your wife and Betty."

At his next visit to the mosque in August, and before he left for Israel, Imam Aref told him of the nice letter he received from Herr Schoenauer. However, then he was advised that the *Bund* in Munich did not wish to meet or cooperate with the Islamic Center.

"It is your Semitic blood they object to, Imam Aref."

"Their sexual insufficiency is a more plausible excuse." Of course Aref was right.

A few days later, Keller informed Nagil that Hofmann had been released from jail and was killed, "He had his throat cut as the Algerian was killed in the same manner. I guess that means war between the Brotherhood and the neo-Nazis. There are no suspects. Well, there are many but we cannot arrest five thousand Muslims. Any ideas, Inspector Nagil?"

"None at this time. It is even useless for me to question the two imams. I thought this might happen after the Algerian was assassinated. There was really no way for us to prevent this killing. Hofmann should have left the city."

A few days later, Anton had a call from the reception booth that a visitor was here for him, a Herr Karl Seitz. "Please let him come in. He has been here before and knows where my office is." It was the same young man, well dressed and not of the skinheads who are either Nazis or associate with them. Anton was pleasant enough and offered him to sit and if he wished coffee.

"No, thank you. I come here representing the *Bund*. You have heard of our man Hofmann assassinated?"

"Yes, someone cut his throat. A most unpleasant way to die."

"You have any idea who might have committed this dastardly crime, Inspector?"

Anton smiled. "I have five thousand names I could blame it on."

Seitz said, "We know names. We need addresses."

"Check your computer, Herr Seitz."

"You know very well that they are not listed."

"Whose addresses are you interested in if I may ask?"

"First of all Imam Aref and al-Dulaimi."

"Simple enough, the Islamic Center."

Herr Seitz's eyes were like daggers, "Don't joke with me, Inspector. You know very well that they are guarded at the center. We don't want to start a shooting war with them. We have to avoid open confrontations."

"Just peaceful assassinations? I am afraid I can't help you. I don't know where they live. When I visit them it is always at the center."

"But you could find out."

"We can find anyone's address. I know where you live for example."

"So do we."

"Which I doubt very much, Herr Seitz."

Karl Seitz smiled, or rather he smirked. "Planegg, Bergstrasse 7."

Well, he was off a number but close enough. Anton stood up, "I am afraid I cannot help you. And I would suggest you forget my address. People who know my place are always in danger."

"Is that a threat, Inspector?"

"Take it any way you wish, Herr Seitz."

"One more suggestion Inspector, your friend Theo Schoenauer knows I came."

"I doubt this. Herr Schoenauer tried to find an accommodation with Imam Aref."

"Yes, we know about this. He acted without our approval and regrets he ever made an attempt to find this accommodation. Is this your last word, Inspector?"

"Goodbye, Herr Seitz."

Anton looked out the window and saw Seitz leave. *That insolent bastard!* It perturbed him that the *Bund* knew his home address. He had tried so hard not to let anyone know. He doubted that the chiefs knew except for Inspector Wagner. His phone number was known of course here, but it was unlisted in any public records.

There was one man who knew his address. Herr Schoenauer. His wife Inge had visited Rosemarie years ago. He would have to take other security precautions at his home, foremost a noise making alarm system. Perhaps a camera to show Rosemarie who was at the door and warn her not to let anyone come in who is a stranger. His doors were of heavy wood, he doubted that anything but a high caliber rifle bullet could get through, the same with the window shutters. He must tell Rosemarie to lock up at night. She would ask why and wouldn't like to be like a prisoner in her own house. She was a gentle woman but a feisty old lady if needed.

This was sweet, the Islamic terrorist and the neo-Nazis fighting each other. He certainly didn't want to get in the middle of their turf war. Both were a danger to Germany, less so the Islamists, at least at the present time. On the other hand, they presented a much greater danger to Germany as they employed tactics of unconventional warfare if they had it in mind; witness what they had done in Madrid and London. The neo-Nazis were a much smaller group and seemed to be satisfied with occasional protest marches, usually directed against foreigners and for that found sympathy among the populace. Of course, they held their secret meetings, planning mischief yet doing very little to disturb the peace.

The Islamists in comparison presented a lurking danger of great magnitude. Therefore, he could disregard the neo-Nazis and let Inspector Wagner and his crew handle them. His job was the surveillance of the Islamic Center, which he knew was the power of the many Arabs in Munich. Five thousand Islamists incited by preachers of hatred against all infidels and especially the Jews here in Munich.

Before leaving on his vacation, he decided to see Imam Aref. In his police car he took a quick trip there. Besides the caretaker, who came at once to see what he wanted, there were some other men around which he took for security personnel. The caretaker took him to the imam's office and Aref welcomed him friendly.

Anton declined the offer of refreshments, "I have come to warn you Imam Aref that the neo-Nazis are planning to revenge the death of Hofmann. They have contacted me and wanted addresses of you and Imam al-Dulaimi and others."

"And?" Imam Aref looked serious. "They had the audacity to come to you for that purpose? How did they contact you, if I may ask?"

"One of their men came to my office."

"And?"

"I was very short with him. That I would never help them and told the man to leave."

"I thank you, Achmed. I am glad we have you as a friend. Who was the man, if I may ask?"

"His name is Karl Seitz."

"May I write his name down? Yes, please spell it for me." He wrote the name down.

"Then we may hear from you if anything else develops untoward to us here? Yes? Thank you, Achmed. How does your friend Herr Schoenauer fit into it all? I thought he wished to have an accommodation with us? Isn't he a leader of their group?"

"Not here in Munich. He is their leader in Berchtesgaden, apparently he was overruled by the much larger and powerful group in Munich. As a loyal follower, he had to comply. So please beware. If I hear of anything else I will contact you." After their friendly salutations, he left. Anton was pleased with his mission.

Anton got ready for his visit to Jerusalem. He had booked his evening flight to Tel Aviv, and had promised his mother Rosemarie to take many pictures and call often.

Sepp had assured Anton that he would make himself available to Rosemarie if she needed him. He would stop by every day to see to her welfare. Just in case, Anton gave Sepp his phone number in Jerusalem.

On Tuesday, the sixteenth of August, he flew to Frankfurt and took the night flight to Tel Aviv. He did, as the general had suggested, bought a ballpoint with four colors, had them both in his shirt pocket and placed them into the tray when passing through security.

He arrived at Ben Gurion airport early in the morning on Wednesday. This time with his German passport and he filled out the required form for non-Israeli citizen, had his passport stamped and after changing euros for shekels, walked out of the terminal. It was five in the morning. There, a smiling Hanna flew into his arms.

The two were in love just as they had been for so long now, perhaps even more as separation made them long for each other. With his handbag, they walked to the parking lot where his old Ford was, still in good shape as Hanna and Amal maintained it properly, or rather their caretaker friend, Eliahu, who took it to the service department.

It got light by the time they drove along the broad highway leading to Jerusalem. They listened to the army station and Hanna talked about nothing but Danny who was now almost one year old and walking. After a good hour's drive, they reached their house. And Anton was home.

Amal was waiting for them with breakfast and Arabian coffee, though it was Israeli coffee made strong. First he had a peak into Danny's room; the little blond boy still sleeping and Anton bent over his son and kissed him gently on his forehead. Then breakfast, with salad—what else, Amal having learned to cook the Israeli way.

They were a happy family—was it their talking? They spoke softly, maybe Hanna laughing? The door to the kitchen opened a little and a blond-headed face appeared. And then the little toddler ran, fell, got up, and rushed into the arms of the man he seemed to remember, and Anton held him dear, his son Daniel. Danny cuddled up to the man he did not know as *avi'* (my daddy). With his thumb in his mouth, he rested still and satisfied in Anton's arms.

(Unknown to Inspector Nagil, the day after he left he had a phone call to his office. His secretary who took it inquired who is calling. When the man said he did not wish to give his name, it would be a nice surprise for the inspector. The secretary told the man that in this case, she cannot connect him. "Then please tell the inspector that Theo is calling."

"I am sorry, Herr Theo but Inspector Nagil *is auf Reisen* (he is traveling)."

"Oh, what a shame that I do not catch him. Will he return shortly? Where to if I may ask?"

"I believe he is visiting with his wife in Cairo. He should be back in a week."

"Thank you, please do not tell my friend Anton that I called. I wish to surprise him when he returns." Every call to the police department is recorded on tape. However, Inspector Nagil could not listen in on calls he received while he was gone until the incident was over. Anton had arrived in Israel the morning of the seventeenth; the same day Theo had called his office.)

Amal had stayed home from work at the hospital and they spent the day together as a happy family. Anton had to learn how to handle and play with a little toddler, but it came naturally to him, as he was a gentle and loving father. Later in the morning, they took Danny in his stroller, Anton pushing the stroller for a walk to a nearby park and playground where Danny could meet other little children and learn to play in the sandbox, babble with the other youngsters, smile and laugh with them, and then wait in turn for using the little swing. Anton pushed him and Danny screamed when either Hanna or Amal tried to push him swinging. It was the same in the stroller, Anton had to guide the stroller. Hanna was very happy that Danny accepted his daddy so readily, though Danny at his young age did not know what a father meant. He just felt good and safe with the "man." Then home for a light lunch and Danny took his after dinner nap.

Since the days in August were hot in Jerusalem, Hanna, Danny and Anton spent a good part of the afternoon in their pool. Danny could swim, a little anyhow. When Hanna released him and Anton stood a few feet away, he would swim to the man under water.

Amal had prepared a genuine Arabian dinner. Danny sat in his high chair and Hanna fed him his baby food. Then they went into the garden where Anton and Danny played together. They took many pictures as they had also done at the park. Hanna let Danny stay up a little longer than usual but when she put him to bed in his crib, Anton stood by and Danny seamed happy and pleased, stuck his thumb in his mouth and was contented when Hanna then sang the Lullaby, in German.

When Danny was asleep, they went into their big living room and Hanna played softly on the piano. When it was cooler they sat on their balcony and Hanna wished to know everything her Toni had done with the police. He told them of his undercover work and his visit to Moscow, the general who awarded him a medal. Hanna laughed when he told about the sloppy kisses he had been given. Then it was time to go to bed and to enjoy their passions for each other.

CHAPTER XXII

THE INCIDENT

The next morning just past nine, as they were getting ready to take Danny to the park before it got hot, the phone rang.

Amal looked at Anton, "I think it is for you. I don't understand a word, he speaks German but I heard him say Toni." Anton felt a shiver running down his spine.

He took the phone. "Ja, hier is Toni."

"Sepp Kainz here. Did I wake you people up? It is just after eight here."

"No, we are an hour ahead in Israel. What's up, Sepp?" Anton's heart racing with foreboding.

"Look, Toni, I just came by your house to bring Rosemarie some fresh milk. The door was open and Rosemarie is nowhere to be found. I searched the whole house. I am calling from your place. She wouldn't leave the house so early with the door left open."

Anton was now calm as he would be when alerted to action. "Sepp, I need your help. My car is in for servicing. I need you to drive for me. There is a plane to Frankfurt before noon. I should be in Munich by late afternoon. Make yourself available to me all afternoon and evening and if needed, all night. I call you by cell phone from Frankfurt and tell you when I arrive in Munich."

"You want me to call the police?" asked Sepp.

"No, they can't help me."

Sepp asked, "Look, Toni, we are friends. I do whatever you want me for. I stay here in your house in case Rosemarie comes back. I call you immediately if she does."

"No need to. I am coming. I call you from Frankfurt. It will be around four o'clock." He hung up the phone. Hanna, who understood some of what he had said, looked shocked.

She didn't ask any questions and only told Amal that Toni had to return urgently to Munich. She ran down to the garage after Anton who only grabbed his passports, wallet and rushed off. They drove in silence to the airport. Hanna hoped and prayed that all would be well.

At the terminal, he kissed Hanna goodbye. "Please, Toni, call me when it is all over, I wait for your call." He watched her drive off and rushed into the terminal. He used his Israeli passport to get through control.

He caught the eleven in the morning flight and was in Frankfurt shortly after three.

Anton called Sepp. Rosemarie had never returned. He told Anton that he found a note at the inside of the door and read it to him:

> R IS WITH US. WE NEED ADDRESSES.
> CALL KS AND GIVE THEM TO HIM. DO
> NOT VISIT HIM, CALL! THEN R WILL
> RETURN. B&E

Anton told Sepp when he would arrive in Munich at 6:10 p.m. Sepp's taxi was waiting when Anton came rushing out. They drove first in silence. "Look, Toni, something is very wrong, this I understand. The note. R is Rosemarie, that I also understand. I want you to know that if you need me, count on me. I am with you through fire and hell."

"Yes, I need you, Sepp. I need your help to drive me to wherever I need to go. First home so I can change. I need to read the note, also to get my pistol. This is dangerous."

"I am with you, Toni. Now can you tell me what this is all about?"

"They have kidnapped Rosemarie. They want something from me I can't give them. So I cannot make a deal. Not with these people."

"Who are THEY?"

"You deserve to know who they are. Neo-Nazis."

Sepp whistled through his lips. "The bastards. Why don't you let the police handle it?"

"They would just bang their heads against the wall. They could round up some Nazis and only be met with silence. I have to do it my way. Are you still with me?"

"I was from the beginning and I will stay to the end."

"Thank you, Sepp." Anton grasped the man's hand. "Thank you."

At the house, Anton read the note. It was printed in block letters. "KS stands for Karl Seitz. I write his address down on the back of the note. If anything should happen to me take the note and give it to Inspector Wagner at police headquarters. Tell him that this B&E on the note means *Blut und Erde* (Blood and Earth). That is the name of the Nazi party. Karl Seitz is their spokesman so he would know. When I changed, we drive to his place, Prinzregentenstrasse 12. I just put on my dark clothing and get my pistol."

"Do you have one for me, Toni?"

"Do you know how to handle a weapon? No? I want you to stay out of it, Sepp. These are dangerous people."

"I told you I am with you. Just tell me what to do."

Anton changed into a dark tracksuit and put on his special boots, his Beretta in his holster under his jacket, loaded, an extra clip in his pocket. He also took a dozen plastic handcuffs and a powerful flashlight. He gave Sepp a warmer jacket to wear. Sepp then called home and said that he would be late or even stay overnight with Anton. They drove through the city and east to the Prinzregentenstrasse.

Anton explained, "I want you to see this Karl Seitz and tell him that you are a taxi driver and wish to take him to the Ettstrasse police where you will be handed an envelope at the booth which has the information he wants, that you called me when you didn't find Rosemarie and I arranged it all. He won't have to go into police HQ, in fact he can wait nearby. I just want him to get into your taxi. I will be waiting at the next corner; I show you where when we get to his house. You drive him where I am waiting and I jump in with him."

"What next then?"

"We shall see. I have to talk to this Seitz. He should know were Rosemarie is."

"And if he won't tell you?"

Anton gave a bitter laugh, "He will talk."

Sepp gave a short laugh, "I would hate to be in his shoes."

When they came to the Prinzregentenstrasse they passed house number 12, a large and elegant apartment house. Just past, Sepp stopped the taxi. "What if he isn't home?"

"He should be, it is dinner time." It was eight in the evening and getting dark.

"What if he doesn't wish to come? And where are you supposed to be? Where from did you call me?"

"From Cairo. Never tell anyone that I visit Israel. All right, I will be across the street from number 12. When he gets in, and make certain he sits in the back, rules, go up the street until you can make a U-turn, then stop for me. I jump in and off we go. I tell you then where to."

Anton went across the street and watched as Sepp turned around and stopped in front of number 12. With so many cars he doubleparked his taxi, and left his lights on. Anton saw him go to the entrance and push a button. He saw him talk into a receiver for a short time and then wait by the door.

A few minutes later Karl Seitz came out, spoke with Sepp, who pointed at his taxi. They walked to the car and Seitz got into the back. Anton saw the taxi drive a short distance and then make a U-turn, come back and stopped before him. He ran to the car and opened the back door and entered—to see a surprised Karl Seitz look at him, "Where do you come from? I thought you are in Cairo?"

"I was. But I need to take care of this matter myself."

Seitz asked, "You are not arresting me, Inspector Nagil?"

Anton laughed, "Why would I do that. I just want to talk to you."

"And give me the addresses."

"That is right."

They were driving across the Prinzregenten Bridge. "Driver, past the bridge turn right and stop by the river." Sepp did so. "Turn the lights off else someone might want a taxi."

"All right, Karl Seitz, now we can have our little talk. Where is Rosemarie?"

"Where are the addresses?"

Anton gave him a forceful backhand across his face. His nose began to bleed, run down his chin and wet his suit jacket. Seitz tilted his head back and held his nose closed to stop the bleeding. Anton let him absorb the shock. Seitz sniffed a few times. "So it is a double-cross. You have no intention to give me the addresses. You want to beat it out of me. But let me assure you, Inspector, I have no idea where Rosemarie is."

"Karl Seitz, you seem to be an educated man and not one of the skinheads or rowdies. What do you do for a living?"

"I am an accountant."

"As one intelligent man to another, Rosemarie is my mother as you know?"

"No, I did not know she is your mother. I know nothing of the affair, only that you are supposed to give me some information."

"You have a mother? Yes? What would you do if she were kidnapped?"

"Report it to the police."

"I am the police. So I reported it to myself. Now I ask you, where is she?"

"You have the wrong man, Inspector. I am just a courier."

"You still don't seem to understand, Karl Seitz. I urgently need to know where Rosemarie is!" And softly he added, "Please understand that she is my mother. How would you act if blackmailers took YOUR mother away?"

"I would comply with their demands to get her safely back."

"Turn around and put your hands behind your back."

"Are you arresting me, Inspector Nagil?"

"Yes. So please do as I tell you."

"This is very foolish of you and it will not help you to get your mother back. In fact, let me warn you, if you arrest me or do anything to me, you will never see her again."

Anton took Seitz's arm and pulled it back sharply. "Now both hands back or I wrench your arm off you shoulder."

"You are making a big mistake!" But he turned around and put both arms back. Anton put a plastic handcuff around his wrists. "Taxi driver, open the door for us please."

Sepp got out of the taxi and opened the back door. Anton got out and pulled Seitz after him, made him stand facing away from the taxi so he couldn't read the license plate.

"Driver, do you have a rag?"

"I have one to check the oil, but it is soiled."

"Good. Get it. You stay up here, driver."

Anton grabbed Seitz by the arm and led him down the embankment to the river. He then pushed Seitz down in front of a tree. It was dark by the river, only the lights of the bridge faintly illuminating the area.
Seitz was sitting by the tree and leaning against it.

"Seitz, now we are alone. This is no longer a game. I am asking you one last time, where is the old woman!" Only silence.

"Open your mouth, Seitz." Another sharp backhand across his face made him comply. Anton stuffed the oily rag in his mouth. Then with one hand, he held Seitz's head against the tree, with the other he pushed his thumb into the side of his left eye and with a swift movement wrenched out his eye, and threw it into the river. He then held the man against the tree. Seitz was groaning like an animal and convulsing in the strong hands of Anton. He held him tight until his violent movements stopped, though still making unearthly noises.

"Listen, Seitz. Are you listening?" The man seemed to nod though still groaning in agony.

"Good. Now you are blinded in one eye. You still have one eye to see. It is horrible to be blind. I will give you this last chance to tell me what I need to know. Tell me or I tear the other eye out!" He felt more than saw the man nod.

"All right. I will remove the rag. You must not scream. You tell me, then I will dress your wound and the taxi will take you to a hospital. Understand?"

Anton removed the rag, Seitz took a deep breath, whimpering now, "Inspector Nagil, all I know is that they took her somewhere to Berchtesgaden."

"To Theo Schoenauer's place?"

"Maybe. I just don't know. Please don't hurt me anymore, that is all I know." He began to whimper again. Anton stuffed the rag back in his mouth. Then went up to the taxi.

"Do you have a first aid kit, Sepp? Yes? Get it please."

Anton went back down to Seitz and inserted cotton into his empty eye socket, blood still running out. Over it, he fastened a wound bandage and taped it. He took the rag out and taped his mouth shut. He could breath but not scream. He pulled Seitz up and led him up to the taxi.

"What happened?" asked Sepp.

"You don't need to know driver. Open the trunk." He helped Seitz get into the trunk and closed it, then got into the front.

"I think I know where Rosemarie is Sepp. We have to drive to Berchtesgaden and then to the Koenigsee."

"Race?"

"Drive fast. It is nine now, we should get there at midnight. Are you still with me?"

"Of course, Toni!"

"We have a good two hours march up to the cabin. I wished we wouldn't have to take Seitz along but we can't leave him here. He whimpers, if someone found him, he might alarm them." Sepp raced along the Autobahn. They drove in silence.

After a while Sepp asked, "What did you do to him that he talked?"

Toni took a deep breath, "I didn't like to hurt him, but he gave me no choice. I blinded him in one eye, told him I take the other eye out too if he doesn't tell me."

"I understand, Toni. If it were my mother I would have done the same thing. Well, I might not have thought of blinding him, just beat the shit out of him until he talked."

They got to Berchtesgaden past midnight; another fifteen-minute drive and they were in Schoenau. The village was quiet and dark, few lights to be seen. Anton had Sepp drive closer to the lake and to the houses at the end of the Koenigsee. There was a small parking lot that said PRIVATE. They stopped. "What do we do with him?" asked Sepp.

"I hate to take him along, but we can't leave him here."

"Are there people in the cabin?"

"I am certain. If they keep Rosemarie up there, they would remain with her."

"Well, we can have him knock on the door and say who he is. They might not open up for us."

"You should become a detective, Sepp. Great idea. Do you have a flashlight? Yes? Then we have two and can see better in the forest. And take a tire iron along."

They got out of the taxi and helped Seitz get out of the trunk. By the shine of a few streetlamps, they walked past the houses up the dirt road into the forest. Here they used their flashlights to see. Anton walked ahead holding Seitz by his arm, his wrists still tied, his mouth taped. He was whimpering softly.

After a good two hours hike, they saw the dark shape of the cabin in the meadow. With a half-moon high up and the cabin built of light stone and rock they could see it more clearly when they got closer. They shut off their lights.

"Wait here, driver as I look around. Hold on to Seitz and hit him with the iron if he makes any loud noises."

Anton moved swiftly to the cabin. The shutters were closed. No lights, all was quiet, he tried the door; it was locked. He went back to Sepp. "I don't know who is in there. Do you know how many are up here, Seitz?" The man shook his head. Anton took his Beretta out. "Listen, Seitz, first of all stop your whimpering. Here is what I want you to do. I knock on the door, someone will ask who it is. You give him your name and tell him you come from Theo Schoenauer with an urgent message. You see this pistol here? You do anything wrong, give the alarm, the first shot will hit you right between your eyes, or as it custom with you Nazis right in your neck, either way you are dead. You behave, hear?" The man nodded. Anton removed the tape from his mouth; Seitz had stopped whimpering.

"Sepp, when the door opens, we turn our lights on and I cover anybody who is in there with the pistol."

Anton held Seitz by the arm and led him to the door and knocked, knocked more strongly when nothing was heard. At last a voice came from inside. "Was is—loss (who is it)?" Anton pushed Seitz to the door and held the pistol to his neck. "It is me, Karl Seitz. Theo Schoenauer sent me up with a message for you." They heard voices inside, then the door swung open. It was light inside the cabin, a man in just this trouser had opened the door, he held a kerosene lamp in his hand.

Anton pushed Seitz into the cabin. "Polizei, alle Haende hoch (Police, raise your hands)!" One man stood in the middle of the cabin, raised his hands, another man had his head out from the door of a side room, he disappeared. Anton fired a shot after him and the man came out with his hands up. Anton shouted, "Hinlegen (Lay down)!" The three men lay on the wooden floor. "Put your hands behind your backs!" They complied. Anton pushed Seitz on the floor.

"Driver, if one moves, hit him with the iron and hit him hard!"

Anton used his flashlights and checked the other room. It was empty. He returned. "Is this all of you, just three?" Silence. He kicked the man nearest to him in the side; he kicked him hard with his steel-pointed boot. The man yelled then said, "We are just three." Then he just groaned in pain.

"Where is the old woman?"

"There is no woman here," the same man answered.

Anton took plastic cuffs and cuffed them. He did the same with each man's ankles, including Seitz. They were now helpless. Sepp whispered at Anton's ear, "Maybe we were wrong, and Rosemarie isn't here?"

"Why would three of them be up here in the cabin? I check if there is a trapdoor. You, go outside and look around." Using his flashlight, Anton checked the floor in each room. He couldn't see a trapdoor.

Sepp had come to the door and motioned to Anton and whispered, "I think I found her, come with me." Anton followed Sepp who lead him past a vegetable garden to an outhouse. In the shine of their lights they saw a pit behind the outhouse with a ladder leading down. A heavy steel plate on hinges closed the space under the outhouse.

"Rosemarie," Sepp called softly.

"Oh Holy Mother of God, who is it?" They heard a voice from inside the pit.

"It is me, Sepp, Toni is here with me."

"Mom! I came to get you!"

"My son Toni came to get his old mother." Then there was only crying.

It took them both to lift the heavy plate and lock it, and there, on a burlap sack, laid Rosemarie. Right behind her, the large wooden vat of the human dung—a foul smell came from it. Anton took his mother in his arms and lifted her up to Sepp, not before kissing her cold lips; she was shivering in her light summer coat.

"Toni, Toni . . . I knew you would come and get me." Her wrinkled lips tried to smile. "At least, I didn't have to go far to relieve myself," she joked.

"They kept you in this stinking hole?"

"Yes, Toni. They were not very nice to me. I could lie down, sit up but not even stand. And I couldn't lift the plate. I tried. Toni, I don't think I can walk."

"Don't worry, Mom, we carry you down." He lifted his mother up and carried her to the edge of the forest. Sepp took his warm jacket and put it around Rosemarie, she laid down on the soft ground.

"We will be soon back Mom. We have to take care of your guardians."

"Oh, please don't leave me, Toni."

"You are safe here, Mom. The men are no longer dangerous." In his light, he could see her smile at him.

"Let's get the bastards and shove them down in the hole," said Anton.

"I have an idea. Toni, come with me." They went back down into the pit and moved the barrel out. Then went to the cabin, untied their ankles and made the men get up and follow Sepp lighting the way. Anton followed with the iron and pistol. At the edge of the pit, Anton refastened the cuffs to their ankles. Sepp climbed down. "Now Inspector, let me have them, one after another."

"We can't climb with our ankles tied," the first man said. Anton gave him a push and he fell into the pit, about six feet deep. Sepp had him crawl into the hole and shoved him along by his feet. One after the other, they were deposited in the same manner. Like four long packages they lay next to each other.

"Now help me," Sepp said. Together they pushed the barrel at the feet of the four and turned it over, the oval pouring over them. Then they let the plate back down.

They went back into the cabin and Anton found what he was looking for, bottles of Schnapps which he smashed on the floor; to that he added a can of kerosene. From the open door he threw a match and the inside of the cabin went up in flames. They returned to Rosemarie, and Sepp lifted her on Anton's back. It was past three when they went down the path, behind them the inferno of the burning cabin.

Though Sepp wanted to help, Anton carried his mother all the way down to the taxi. It was getting light. Anton put his mother in the back seat and sat next to her, gently padded her face. "You will be all right now, Mom." He held her hand.

She smiled. "I need something to drink, I am dying of thirst."

"Didn't they bring you something to drink, eat?"

"Nothing. For the two days and nights I was in that hellhole, Toni."

"Sepp, we want to get out of here but stop at the first restaurant you see in Berchtesgaden."

Berchtesgaden was just waking up. It was six in the morning, a gray morning, and it rained.

They found a breakfast place open and stopped. With Anton's help, Rosemarie walked into the place and went to the ladies room. She smiled. "I can take it from here Toni, wait outside, please. Better, order me a glass of water."

"How about a good breakfast and coffee."

"And water." She smiled at her son.

Anton ordered a big breakfast of bacon and eggs, home fried potatoes, buttered black bread, coffee, and a pitcher of water. It took a while for Rosemarie to return, but when the door to the rest room opened the little old lady was walking out, unsteadily but on her own. Anton rushed to her, "I can manage, Toni." Rosemarie sat down and Anton poured her a glass of water. She downed three glasses and then said, "Now I am full, I am not hungry anymore." But she ate her breakfast, all of it. Then sipped her coffee.

"How did you find me Toni, and so fast? And you were in Israel."

"Sepp called me and told me the door to the house was open and you nowhere to be found. I rushed to Munich and asked someone."

"Yes, I can imagine how you ask someone. Is he still alive? How about the men up there, I hope you didn't kill them?"

"They are all alive. All together in your hellhole and tied up."

Sepp added, "And we poured the barrel of you-know-what over them." The feisty old lady laughed. It was good to see her get her spirits back. Sepp then called home to tell his wife Inge that he was all right and would be back by noon.

Anton got up. "I have to make a call too." He went to the phone and called Theo Schoenauer. It took a while before there was an answer.

"Ja . . ."

"Theo Schoenauer, Anton Nagil here."

"Ah, Inspector Nagil. So early?"

"Did I wake you up?"

"Ja, it doesn't matter. What can I do for you?"

"I came by your place and picked up Rosemarie."

There was only silence at the other end.

"Did you hear me, Theo?"

"Yes, I understand."

"Now listen carefully, Theo. I don't know how much you were involved. It doesn't matter much but of course, you knew. They used your place."

"Believe me . . ."

"Shut up and listen! I don't want a war between you and your people and myself. What you wanted I couldn't get for you, so forget it. I have this incident all written down and it is with the police in Munich. If anything happens to me they will get it. From now on, you and your men stay away from my family, my house, never call me—in fact, I suggest you just forget my address."

"What happened to my men?"

"They are all right. Karl Seitz is with them. He lost an eye before he told me. He is not very strong; better take him to a hospital. I hope you realize that I mean business!"

"Yes, I do."

"One more thing. I burned your cabin down again. I suggest you don't rebuild it. And know this, if anything happens again to my family, my house, I torch House Tannek. No, I blow it up with you in it. Do you understand what I am talking about Theo?"

"Yes, no war. I agree. Let me ask you Anton Nagil, did you kill Hamann when you burned the cabin down?"

There was only a click when the connection was broken.

Rosemarie slept all the way to Planegg in the arms of her son.

(When Theo Schoenauer made his way up to the cabin, he could see just a little smoke high up. No one had seen the fire during the night. The cabin was just a burned out shell of rock walls. He didn't find any bodies inside nor anywhere near the cabin. When he called loud for Gustav, Max, Bernhard, Karl—he heard voices. They came from the outhouse.

He climbed down into the pit and heard them talk. He couldn't lift the plate all the way up, had to find a stout timber to get it partway up and then brace it. He had to crawl into the hole. The stink awful. With his pocketknife, he cut their cuffs; and they climbed out, washed themselves at the pump though they couldn't get their clothing clean. All their things burned in the cabin. They told him what had happened. Gustav yelled, "That fool Karl, he knocked on the door and called that he was sent by you with an important message. So I opened and was threatened with a revolver."

"I had too!" Karl complained, "He already tore one eye out of me and held his pistol to my neck."

Theo said, "Don't blame Karl. You men are lucky that he didn't kill you, burn you with the cabin. He already did it once before and burned the cabin with a man inside." He lectured them that they must leave Anton Nagil, his family and house alone. The war was over. Neither side had won.

Karl Seitz whimpered again, said that his eye was hurting badly and complained about the loss of his eye. Theo told him again that he was lucky to be alive. He took Karl later to the hospital in Berchtesgaden. Gustav said that he was hurting so badly where Nagil had kicked him into his ribs, "He must have busted a few of my ribs and I can't walk. Every movement hurts." Theo told him to walk slowly down the mountain. The others ran, more than walked, to Schoenauer's house. Theo made them take off all their soiled clothing before he let them in, take a shower and after getting new clothing and waiting for Gustav, they returned to Munich.)

When they arrived in Planegg, Rosemarie at once had Anton fill the tub and she took a long hot bath. She was now steady again on her feet, the water and breakfast had done wonders for the old lady, and so had the long nap in the car feeling free and secure.

Anton wanted to know how much he owed Sepp. He had to gas up twice besides.

"How much do you charge extra for a two hours climb up the mountain, your helping me, hell there is so much you did for me, you could just itemize it and send me a bill, Sepp."

"What one does for a friend can't be paid for in money, Toni." They shook hands, looking deeply into each other's eyes. Sepp walked to his taxi. He heard Toni call after him, "Thanks, friend." He waved back.

That evening, and after Anton called Sepp, he came to take both to the airport and this time he took payment for the fare. Sepp said that he slept all afternoon until Toni called. When Anton asked him what he told his wife Inge? Sepp answered, "To tell her a fairy tale? What could I tell her? I told her I drove you into the mountains on police business."

From Frankfurt, they took the night flight to Tel Aviv. There, Anton asked for the local Shin Bet agent and explained to him why his mother did not have a visa for Israel in her passport. After a call to the agency headquarters, they were passed through customs. However, Anton used his Israeli passport as he had done when he left.

A taxi took them to their house in Jerusalem. When they stood before the gate and Anton looked up, he saw Hanna looking down from the window. She hadn't slept all night and stayed up waiting for Toni to call. Anton was spared a royal chewing out because when Hanna came running out of the house the two women were in each other's arms crying. For Anton, it was a good sign that he saw his mother cry—she was a *Mensch* again.

Then they all sat together for breakfast and Rosemarie told how early in the morning a man had come to the door. She had been careful and only opened it partway, still secured by the chain. The man had told her that he had a message from her son; he had a piece of paper in the hand. She let him in and then two other men followed. They said that Inspector Nagil had come back, was in an accident and they would take her to him. She dressed quickly, put on a light coat and got in the car. They drove her to the Koenigsee. When she asked why into the mountains, she was told that Inspector Nagil had come back from Cairo to go on a hunting trip, and that he was injured as he accidentally shot himself and was laying up in the cabin.

By then she knew it was all a lie. Toni was in Israel and not Cairo. She refused to walk and they beat her and then carried her, stuck her into the stinking hole. "What is it all about, Toni?" Anton explained that they wanted certain information from him, which he had but could not give them. "They thought by kidnapping you they would force me." Just then a little blond boy in his pajamas appeared and smiling ran over to the man, and Anton took his son into his arms. Finally, Rosemarie met her grandson, Daniel.

They spent four happy days together as a family. Privately, Anton told his wife Hanna all of what had happened. She was worried. "Will you be safe with all these Nazis after you?" Anton assured her that all was well; that he and Theo Schoenauer had agreed to leave each other alone. "Schoenauer had understood that else his house would be blown up with him in it. I am certain that he will persuade their leader in Munich to leave me and my family alone."

"But if they kill you, Toni?"

"Then there is a brief in my office with all the details of what has happened. Kidnapping is a serious offense and I have all their names listed. Gustav, the one I kicked a little, is the son of their leader Horst Bachleiter, so he would be implicated as his father would be. They know about the brief."

When it was time for Anton to return, he was surprised to see his mother packing. He had wanted her to stay in Israel.

"What would I do here, Toni. An old horse you don't transplant into another barn."

"But everyone loves you here. Danny-boy needs you. He gets along fine with you!"

"I love the little tyke, you know that. I am very fond of your Hanna and Amal. But Toni, I don't know the language, people are friendly but I can't talk to them. Let me just return to my own stables, to the other old horses. I couldn't be happy here without you." Anton understood. Rosemarie was a spunky old lady; and when she promised him to be more careful and let him install some safety devices and not let anybody into the house unless she knows the person, he gave up. Besides, he didn't expect any more troubles from that side.

Little Danny was crying when he saw the man leave, the man he had come to like so much and felt so happy to be with him. He just didn't understand why the man had to leave, and telling him he would soon come again didn't mean anything to a one year old.

He bade goodbye to Danny and Amal, who stood by the gate with the boy in her arms, and waved to them when Anton drove with Hanna and Rosemarie away. Danny crying bitterly as he did not understand that his *imi'* (mommy) would return soon. He only knew that when the man left he would not return for a long time and now his mommy went with him.

At the airport. Rosemarie and Anton said goodbye to Hanna, a last embrace. When Hanna drove away, she let the tears flow. Why did her man always have to be in danger! But like Rosemarie, she was a brave woman, and there was her mother Amal and her son Danny to return to.

A few weeks after Anton's return, he received a call from Chief Inspector Kirsch who asked him to come by his office. "And please bring your German passport along." Since he kept his German passport in his office, but his Egyptian and Israeli at home, he brought it along. He suspected that Inspector Kirsch learned of the incident, but how? The Nazis couldn't have been so stupid of reporting it to the police?

"Have a seat please, Inspector Nagil. How was your trip to Israel?"

"Wonderful, nothing like Jerusalem. You should visit me someday. I love to show you the city and the country."

"I might just do that. Can I bring my wife?"

"Yes of course, we can accommodate you. We have a guest room in the downstairs for just such distinguished visitors," they laughed. Anton handed the inspector his passport,

"You wished to see it?"

"Yes, thank you." Inspector Kirsch thumbed in the passport. "Let's see. You arrived in Israel on the eighteenth of August and left on the twenty-fifth. Strange, very strange."

"What is strange, Inspector Kirsch?"

"I was told of a certain affair that occurred while you were in Israel. An elderly woman by the name of Rosemarie was kidnapped by some Nazi thugs; taken to the Watzmann Mountain. Then rescued by her son, who has the same name as you do, Inspector, Anton. Some of these thugs got hurt, I understand. One man even lost his eye."

"And this strange incident was reported to you, to the police?"

"No. We have a man with the *Bund* who reports to me, an informer if you will. He told me of this affair. It was just a personal talk I had with this man, nothing in the form of an official report. Of course the familiar names, Rosemarie and Anton rang a bell. But then you were in Israel on these dates."

"Yes, strange indeed, as you said Inspector Kirsch."

The inspector handed the passport back, he looked very serious at Anton, "Are you taking certain precautions that your mother Rosemarie is safe?"

"Yes, Inspector Kirsch, I do. In fact I did."

"That is all. I am glad to have you back safely. I read where terrorists in Israel are active? I hope that our local terrorist behave, the Islamic ones, Inspector Nagil."

Anton smiled. "I have their assurance that they have no interests in harming Germany. As far as the neo-Nazis, there won't be anymore such affairs."

"Good."

Anton was of course, surprised. He had not known that Inspector Kirsch had a spy in the *Bund*. He realized that Inspector Kirsch knew very well who this old woman and her son Anton were. Probably the name of Nagil was also known to the spy and must have been told to the inspector. Kirsch used the subterfuge of mentioning only first names not to implicate him as his passport had shown him to be in Israel during the affair.

Though there was this informal agreement to leave each other alone, "no more war," Anton did not trust the Nazis. Hate and vengeance was their creed.

He had several cameras installed: one pointing at the entrance door, one at the gate, and one with an overall view of the back, also a speaker at the door. A button by the inside door which would set off a shrieking howl. He was extra careful watching his back.

One late afternoon, when Anton returned home with the commuter train, he entered the first car as was his habit, and walked into the next compartment. He at once spied an unsavory character, a big young man, blond, with his hair down to his shoulders. After a quick glance at him, and disregarding him as a Nazi, his eyes were riveted at a man sitting next to him who obviously was hiding his face behind the newspaper. He walked by the two, then looked again—seeing him from the side—he saw Gustav Bachleiter, the son of the leader of the Munich neo-Nazis.

He took a seat farther back and watched the two; they were talking. Once, the blond man turned around, his eyes searching for him. When he found Nagil, he saw him sleeping.

Anton passed his station and went on to Stanberg. He exited in the back and did not turn around but knew he was followed. In front of the station were a number of taxis. The sky was black, heavy drops were falling; Anton ran to a taxi and told the driver to take him to King Ludwig's Memorial. The driver looked surprised, "In this weather, Herr?"

"My darling is waiting for me, what can I do?"

The driver laughed, "Yes. Love, what can you do."

It was not far to the memorial, a fifteen-minute drive. There was hardly any traffic in the thunderstorm, a downpour now, and lightning—thunder booming and cracking loud when a strike came close. They passed through the last village and were in the forest.

The driver commented, "There must be another person looking for his darling."

"What makes you think so, driver?"

"I see a taxi following us. Perhaps, your *Liebchen* (darling)?"

Anton looked back and saw the lights a good ways behind, "Maybe."

The driver stopped by the memorial, a huge edifice, which was off the road and halfway down to the lake. Anton paid, gave a generous tip and the driver turned around and headed back. Anton rushed to the opposite side of the road into the uphill forest and doubled back near the road. He was already soaked by the downpour. He could see the taxi stop and the two men get out. Like he had done, they ran into the forest but not as high up, and advanced cautiously parallel to the road, running from tree to tree.

Hiding and crouching behind a large tree, Anton saw them pass him and he followed them, he needed them out in the open. They paid no attention to their backs and only looked toward the memorial. When the two were close to it, they crossed the road—Anton right behind them yelled at them, "NOT A STEP FARTHER! RAISE YOUR HANDS!" They stood in the middle of the road, turned, and when they saw the pistol pointing at them raised their hands.

"Hello, Gustav, came to visit me?" Just then a lightning strike hit a nearby tree and split it in half. The two jumped, lowered their hands and wanted to run. Anton fired a shot at their feet, "No, no my friends, just stand still and keep your hands up!"

The tall blond said, "The lightning, it is dangerous to stand here in the open."

"Then I suggest you lay down, makes you less of a target. MOVE!" He yelled when they did not get down. They lay down in a large puddle in the road. "HANDS BEHIND YOUR BACK, NOW!" And he fired a shot in front of them, the dirt sprayed into Gustav's face. They complied and Anton cuffed their wrists. He searched them; Gustav had a pistol; the blond, a switchblade and a piece of lead pipe. He had them get up, walked them down into the memorial and had them sit against an inside wall.

"Who is your friend, Gustav?"

When Gustav didn't answer, Anton spoke softly, "Your ribs Gustav, think of your ribs."

The young man looked up in fright. "I am still hurting and bandaged."

"So? You don't want to get kicked again." Was it the threat or the piercing eyes of Anton, but his answer came fast. "His name is Manfred, Fred."

"Freddy-boy; I can't imagine you being a member of the *Bund*, not with your long, shaggy hair."

"I am not with the Nazis."

"Who are you with then?"

"I am just a friend of Gustav."

"And you came with Gustav to kill me?"

"No, not kill you, just work you over like you did with Gustav."

"Did Gustav tell you why I was angry with him? No? They kidnapped my mother and were ready to murder her if I did not do what they wished. You didn't know?"

The blond shook his head.

"You know Gustav, you were lucky that I didn't just leave you four in the cabin when I burned it down."

"Yes, I know, Theo told me."

"Then why didn't you leave me alone?"

"I hate you, Nagil. What you did to me, you broke three ribs; I was hurting so bad when I had to walk down the mountain. I swore to get even with you."

"Tsk, tsk . . . hating. What for did you bring the pistol, Gustav?"

"To kill you!"

"At least you are honest. What am I going to do with you two? This is the second time, Gustav. It would be foolish for me to let you live, and leave a witness." He glared at Fred. At once the blond begged, "Herr Nagil, believe me, I did not mean to kill you. Please don't kill me, I want to live."

"Well, that is debatable. I have to make a phone call, then we shall see. You are not going anyplace, or are you? Let me tie your ankles together." Anton took two more plastic cuffs and approached Fred. When he saw Fred bring his legs up, he laughed, "Still spunky, Freddy Boy. Just be a good boy and stretch out your legs . . . long!" He tied their feet. He then asked Gustav for his phone number.

Anton went outside. It was still raining, but the storm had moved on, and the lightning and thunder came from farther away. He dialed.

"Ja?"

"Is this Horst Bachleiter?"

"Yes."

"This is Anton Nagil. You remember me."

"Yes. What do you want?"

"I have Gustav with me." For a moment there was only silence.

"Did you hear me, Bachleiter?"

"Yes. Where are you?"

"Gustav wanted to kill me."

"The stupid fool. I told him to stay away from you. Is he alone?"

"Fred is with him. Both are shackled on their hands and feet."

"I see. But where are you?"

"In a safe place. Out in the woods, far away from anyone. I am just debating what to do with them. Kill them both? I mean, it is only fair. They came after me to kill me." Anton detected urgency in the man's voice, "Herr Nagil, don't we have a truce? The war is over. Theo told me so. I promised Theo we wouldn't come after you."

"But you didn't teach your son."

"Yes, I told him. I told all my people to leave Anton Nagil alone. That damned kid; I should have suspected him to try something stupid when he kept going out with his friend. Fred is a bully. But look, Herr Nagil, I am certain that my boy would not wish to kill you. He only wanted to get even with you for kicking him. He was suffering with broken ribs."

"He told me he hates me and wants to kill me, brought a pistol along."

"Oh God, how stupid of him. Herr Nagil, Gustav is our only son, please. I beg you don't kill him. You might think he deserves to die . . . please, don't do it. You are a good Catholic like I am. We Catholics believe to forgive our enemies," Anton laughed.

"Do you think you can teach your stupid son to leave me and my family alone?"

"Yes . . . YES! I swear to you Herr Nagil, no one will ever bother you or your family again. The war is really over!"

"You can pick both up at the memorial of King Ludwig in Stanberg."

Anton then called for a taxi on his cell phone. It was only drizzling when the taxi came.

A few days later, Inspector Nagil had a call from the booth. "A Fred Schultheis wishes to see you, Inspector."

"Please check him for weapons. Then send him up."

Fred looked different than the last time Nagil had seen him. The blond young man had his hair cut short and was wearing a decent suit.

Anton did not get up to greet him nor offer him a seat. But he smiled. "Freddy, I almost didn't recognize you."

"Inspector Nagil, I wish to thank you personally that you didn't . . . . that you let us go. I want to be your man. Work with you, even against the Nazis." (In due time, Fred Schultheis became a policeman, joined the Neo-Nazis, who were glad to have one of their men with the police; and became Inspector Nagil's informant.)

CHAPTER XXIII

THE CASE OF LUDZIFER

One afternoon in September, Inspector Keller called Nagil and said that he wished to see him in his office.

Inspector Keller was with Inspector Harteck from homicide. Harteck was the very opposite of Keller, tall and slender built, youthful and athletic looking. Anton would think of him later as all brawn and little brain. Harteck and Nagil knew each other of course, but Inspector Nagil had nothing to do with homicide.

"Have a seat, Inspector Nagil. Where is your pipe?" Anton filled it and puffed. The other two smoked cigarettes.

Inspector Keller continued, "While you were on vacation, Inspector Nagil, we had a strange homicide. A young couple was murdered sitting in their car. No robbery, no one was touched except both the young woman and man were shot in the head. They were parked at the end of the Veterinaerstrasse by the entrance to the Englischer Garten. It is forbidden to park there but they must have parked in the evening, it is somewhat secluded at this time of the day. A squad car, which came by around midnight, found the couple. The coroner stated that they must have been shot between nine and ten. Inspector Harteck, continue please."

Harteck turned to Nagil. "No robbery, no fingerprints. Shot with a 7.6 mm caliber pistol. Could be any make. They were fully dressed. Well, the young man had some lipstick on his face, so they were close friends. Both were students. The young man from a well-to-do family, he had over three hundred euros in his wallet. There is a fast-food place at the corner of Veterinary and Kaulbach streets, and the saleswoman heard two shots. She rushed out and saw a person cycling into the garden, it was dark there and all she could say was that it was a man. She never saw the car. This was shortly after nine and she had just closed up. The bicyclist didn't use his light on the cycle and he is of course someone we are interested in, though he could have been there innocently. This is all we have, no motive of course."

"A jilted suitor perhaps?" offered Nagil.

Harteck said, "We worked on that angle. I had my detectives question friends, families, and we are still working on this but nothing so far. They had been friends for a long time, actually since high school. Neither one having other close boy or girlfriends which of course doesn't mean that she didn't have a close admirer, or someone stalking her. But this was the only direction we could pursue really, and as I said, we still do."

Nagil asked, "So, how can I help?"

"Last evening we found another couple murdered with the same M.O, two students from the university, obviously lovers. The young lady half undressed, at least her blouse and bra were off. Again shot in the head from close range, this time through the window. The young lady was shot twice," Keller said.

Harteck continued, "This couple was found near the Jewish cemetery, near the main entrance, a rather secluded area, at least in the evening when the cemetery is closed. The administrator heard the shots and came out but saw nothing except the car parked nearby. He then went back to get his flashlight and approached the car and found these two young people shot. He at once called the police. This happened approximately twenty minutes after eight."

Keller added, "Since it was by the Jewish cemetery, any connection to the Islamic Center? It is not far away. What do you think, Inspector Nagil? We must not overlook any possible connection."

"Was the couple or one of them Jewish?" Nagil asked.

"We checked on that at once. No, and no Jewish connection. Yet, why in front of the Jewish cemetery?" replied Keller.

Nagil said, "A secluded place. Our killer apparently has cased both places and found that couples used it for romantic rendezvous. I still don't know why you want me, Inspector Keller? I know little about homicides, and not much more about discoveries at the crime scene."

Keller said, "We apparently have a serial killer at work. Here in Munich, even in Germany, we rarely encounter a serial killer. The police commissioner spoke to me this morning and suggested we send someone to the FBI in Washington as they have experience with that type of criminals, someone who speaks English well. I have your travel documents prepared; you leave tomorrow morning. We called them at Quantico and they are expecting our man. You, Inspector Nagil!"

Harteck said, "One more strange thing. We found in both cars all mirrors broken, just smashed. The killer must have used a club as there were no fingerprints."

"Where are the cars? I like to look at them. Mirrors broken, that is indeed strange," Nagil said.

Harteck replied, "They are both impounded and downstairs in our garage."

Nagil added, "Well, I might as well start packing."

Keller said, "My secretary has your travel vouchers. Business class, you go in style. Reservations made with Lufthansa. Submit your expense account when you get back."

Inspector Nagil got his voucher then went down in the garage. A policeman took him to the two cars. Apparently, the one from the night before was the Volkswagen Jetta as the trunk was still open. The other car was a BMW. There were black powder stains all over, they had checked for fingerprints. He saw the side-view mirrors of the VW smashed in. Anton sat in the driver's seat, the rearview mirror broken. He wondered if the vanity mirror had been broken also and pulled down the sun visor. The vanity mirror was busted in, a small piece of paper fluttered down. He picked the paper up with his handkerchief; it was a drawing of Lucifer. Under the picture was written in block print: LUDZIFER WAR HIER (LUDCIFER WAS HERE). He thought how odd the word *Lucifer* was misspelled. He wrapped the paper into his handkerchief. He found nothing else of interest in the car; it had been searched throughout otherwise. He then checked the BMW. It was an older model and didn't have a vanity mirror; all the other mirrors had been smashed. The broken shards in both cars taken away and probably checked for prints. He drove in his police car out to the cemetery. There showed his badge and identification to the administrator. "I already told the police what I know, Herr Inspector."

"Did you see any traffic, a car driving away, a bicyclist, someone walking nearby?"

"Come to think of it, I saw a bicyclist turn into the Leonardstrasse."

"Did you tell the police?"

"No. They only asked me if I saw anyone near the cemetery. It is dark around here at night. Lovers like to come in their cars and park here. No harm done. They don't disturb the silent ones."

"You saw someone turn into the street? That is pretty far away from the gate."

"But the street has lighting."

There was nothing else the man remembered seeing or hearing.

Anton returned to the police headquarters. First, he made a copy of the picture on his scanner. Then he visited Inspector Harteck and gave him the drawing he had found and also told him about the bicyclist seen by the administrator.

"I talked to the man myself and he said nothing about the man on a bicycle."

Anton smiled. "You asked him if he saw anything near the cemetery, Leonardstrasse is pretty far away."

"The nincompoop, of course I meant if he saw anything. How could my investigators have missed the piece of paper? You said it was by the vanity mirror?"

"Yes, when I looked at it the note fell out."

"This killer obviously wanted us to find it. Someone belonging to a cult, devil worshippers, or what. Well, the police in America have more experiences with cults. Make a copy and take it along."

"I already did."

"What do you think? Is it Lucifer or the devil?"

"Take your pick, Satan in any case. Of course Lucifer also refers to Venus, the morning star."

"So we know now that the killer uses a bicycle. Not affluent then, like his victims. He seems to know where to find lovers, probably also a university student. He knows the victims perhaps. That brings us back to jealousy, he must know the ladies, and they knew him, so he possibly could approach the car without the couple getting alarmed. But now the cult angle, I am really baffled. Do you think he will strike again, Inspector Nagil?"

"I depends; if it was jealousy, I hope there aren't any more young ladies he had his eyes on. If it is a cult thing, he may strike again."

Inspector Harteck took a deep breath and exhaled, "The commissioner is on my back. He also feels that we have a serial killer on hand. He wants a quick solution. How can we find this killer? No real leads. I hope you can bring us some help or ideas from the FBI. Good luck."

Rosemarie didn't like for Toni to leave for this long trip. But she had these new security devices and Sepp would stop by in the morning and evening. Anton assured her that it was all over with the Nazi thugs. They would leave her alone. Rosemarie believed her son.

At ten o'clock the next morning, Inspector Nagil was on his flight to the United States and arrived at Dulles airport nine hours later early in the afternoon. After customs and changing some euros into dollars, he looked for a taxi and told the driver to take him to Quantico in Virginia, headquarters of the FBI. He had to show his passport at the gate, and state the purpose of his visit. Since he did not know the person he was to visit, there was a considerable delay and a number of phone calls. He was finally told to see special agent Burt Johnson. It was now close to five and he hoped that the man was still there.

He was expecting his visitor. Agent Burt Johnson was an elderly man, with a small gray beard.

"Inspector Nagil, from Munich homicide?"

Anton explained that he was with the CID, not homicide, but asked to come here for expert consultation. He was familiar with the case and spoke English.

"Well, good that they sent me someone who speaks English. I don't speak German and it makes it awkward if we have to go through an interpreter. Please tell me what you know. By the way, I am a psychologist and study the behavior of serial killers. So what do we have in Munich?"

Anton told the agent what he knew. Then showed him the picture he had found.

Agent Johsnon looked briefly at the picture. "Lucifer all right. More interesting the handwriting. This is the German way to write Lucifer with a Z?"

"Yes. But why the D in it? If he is a student, he knows how to spell."

"He is giving you a hint. These types of psychos like to do that. Take the first three letters, L-U-D, could be your German Ludwig. I am not an expert in graphology. I have to make a copy and give it to our handwriting experts. The little I understand, the un-unevenness of the letters calls for an unstable person to begin with. I doubt that he is trying to disguise his writing, again a hint for you. There was nothing like this in the first car? No? Well, his first killing went so well that he is becoming daring."

"Is he trying to be found out, a case of remorse, feeling guilt?"

"No, I doubt it. Serial killers avoid being captured. They like what they are doing for whatever twisted purpose. Some like playing games with the police; gives them a sense of power. Let me ask you, any of the females were molested? The one with bare upper torso, did the coroner mention that she had been touched, perhaps the breast molested?"

"Nothing. I read the report. His first shot graced her face; the second into the head by the ear which killed her, of course. The young man was close enough to have powder burns."

Johnson continued, "Most likely he shot first at her through the window. Then killed the man, then the third shot killed her."

"Why this sequence?"

"He shot at the girl first, the man was going nowhere sitting close to him. I also agree with you that the Islamic Center nearby has nothing to do with it. If he is a religious fanatic, he would not go into town to shoot a couple young people. You said the first shooting was far from the cemetery? Yes. While there is a quasi-religious motive involved, Lucifer or Satan, it has nothing to do with terrorism. Not the common terrorism of a Muslim fanatic. It is random killing. He, as you so rightly suggested, caged the places first."

"So what is the motive? What is his compulsion to kill unknowns to him?"

"Compulsion is the right terminology for it, Inspector Nagil. Let me think. This case is more along the killings of Sam. Ever heard in Germany of the Son of Sam? It happened a long time ago."

"I was in Egypt then. I just returned to Germany ten months ago. No."

"You lived in Egypt? Policeman then?"

"No. I taught chemistry. I was with Egyptian Army Intelligence, but that has nothing to do with police work."

"Then you speak Arabic? Can we offer you a job with the FBI?"

Anton laughed, "No, I am quite happy in Munich. My elderly mother lives there. I wish to be with her."

"I see you are married. Your wife lives with you or in Egypt?"

"She lives in Israel."

Agent Johnson shook his head, "Quite a combination. German policeman who lived in Egypt and his wife lives in Israel. Well, to come back to the Son of Sam. His name was really David Berkowitz. In different locations in New York City, he would kill at random, couples sitting in a car, just walk up to them and shoot."

"The why then?"

"When he was finally captured, he claimed that he heard voices that told him to kill. His insanity plea misfired. He sits for a lifetime."

"So what do you believe? Why did this Sam kill, Agent Johnson? You are the psychology expert."

"You know, Inspector, I really believe he heard voices. When he began to kill, he told himself that he heard these voices, a kind of reason for him to shoot. Like self-hypnosis, he came to accept his own excuses, which does not make for a legal insanity plea. As to why he killed? He was not a sadist, simply put—he enjoyed killing. He had power. In his own lonely lunatic world, he was somebody. Yet the picture of Lucifer, it becomes a different ball game. Are you familiar with American idioms?"

"Yes. I studied in San Diego for two years. Perhaps a cult connection?"

"He is a loner, possibly a student. The couples he killed were students, you told me. Perhaps he knew them, though I doubt it. It all sounds like random killings.

By the way, my experience with serial killers tells me, or suggests that his first killing took place near where he lived. To be safely home after, fantasize about it in his lonely place. I realize that Munich has many students, a big university?"

"Yes, it is. All in one area, from music to engineering schools, tens of thousands of students."

"And where do they live, in large dormitories?"

"No. They must look for their own apartments or rooms. The university has contracts for dwellings, but no, not dormitories."

"That he uses a bicycle, you mentioned that twice a person was seen leaving the area on one, means that he is not affluent. I doubt that he lives with family. So what do we have so far?" Agent Johnson went to a blackboard and began to write. "These are all now just suppositions, but we must start with what we have." He printed in capital letters.

FIRST NAME: LUDWIG. A STUDENT. A LONER.
SHUNNED BY OTHERS.
LIVES NEAR THE FIRST KILLING, SMALL ROOM
SOMEWHERE.
USES A BICYCLE. NOT RICH. PROBABLY FROM OUT OF
TOWN.
KILLS RANDOMLY. SON OF SAM M. O.
ENJOYS KILLING FOR ITS OWN SAKE. HAS POWER
OVER LIFE AND DEATH.
LUCIFER?

He returned to his seat. "A cult person belongs to a group, like Satanists. Almost all of these cultists, Satanists, devil worshippers have as their real deity sex. An excuse for free and abnormal sex; pedophiles, and so forth, but they don't kill, or rarely. There is a fictional book by a writer, Thomas Harris, the *Red Dragon*. This was his God. The Red Dragon gave him power. It doesn't make much difference if the deity is a dragon or Lucifer. Even though it is fiction, well, let me suggest that you read both books. The *Red Dragon* by Thomas Harris and the *Biography—David Berkowitz: Son of Sam* by Dr. David Abrahamsen. Perhaps your man has read them. You never heard of either? Check if these books have been translated and are available in Germany. Some serial killers are copycats. Your man fits Berkowitz's random killings, the symbol of Lucifer suggests that he seeks ultimate power. If you find this man, most likely you find more symbols of Lucifer in his room, which of course, doesn't help you find him. He will kill again. Either he already has cased suitable places where young couples congregate or he is casing them now. Might help for the police to look for such isolated spots."

"There are too many such places in Munich."

"I realize that. I am just trying to help. I tell you what I do, Inspector Nagil. Tomorrow I get together with other forensic experts of serial killers and we discuss this case. Perhaps someone else comes up with ideas. I also make a copy and give it to our handwriting expert in our graphology section. I personally don't believe we can get much from so short a message or from the style of printing. However, these people are good. Detective work, as you know, is building up a wall brick by brick and every piece helps. You can sit in on our meeting if you wish or I send you a full report?"

"Well, I don't think I can contribute anything else. But I appreciate if you send me this report and also what your handwriting experts have to say."

"Good." The agent gave Inspector Nagil a pad to write his address down. On another sheet, Anton copied what was written on the blackboard. He also wrote down the names of the two books agent Johnson had suggested.

"Mr. Johnson, one question. How was this David Berkowitz captured? Did he also leave clues?"

"As a matter of fact he did, or perhaps he became careless. Of course, the police in the various boroughs of New York were looking for him. They had many task forces established; if I remember, about 120 detectives were assigned. It was the randomness of where he killed which made it so difficult to find him. The newspapers wrote almost daily about the Son of Sam. After they arrested him, they found the many clippings he had cut out and saved. Thousands of calls were received by the various police departments; after the fact they found one woman who had reported that she believed Berkowitz was the Son of Sam. I am certain many other suspects were so reported.

During the last killings he had parked his car near a fire hydrant. When he returned to it he saw a police car near it and a patrolman writing down his license number and his car ticketed. To him it didn't matter much, so he would pay his fine and that is it. However, his name was checked out, his address was known, though he was not suspected, of course. Other clues were received by the police pointing to a David Berkowitz as a person of interest. He set a fire at the door of a neighbor he didn't like. As it happened this neighbor was a security man and suspected Berkowitz of setting the fire. He reported it to the police. Clues were falling into place and he became a suspect. They staked out his apartment. When Berkowitz went to his car, they arrested him. He immediately admitted that he was the Son of Sam. However, it was never established if he left the car in a restricted zone to give a clue or if he was just careless. Perhaps your man thought it was a clue to tantalize the police, and he did so by leaving this note. Interesting, as I said before, Berkowitz admitted at once that he was the Son of Sam. But again, it was his need to be somebody. It fed his desire to be someone of importance. The high point of his arrest must have been when the lord-mayor of New York came within a couple hours to see him in jail."

"He didn't resist arrest? Wasn't he armed?"

"He had his pistol with him and rifles in his trunk. However, the security man and other police officers had their weapons pointed at him. He could have reached for his weapon and thereby commit suicide. For him, it was a new beginning of life as a person of infamy, a man of great importance." Johnson put on his coat.

"Can I give you a lift into town? We have good hotels in Washington near the government buildings. You might wish to look around tomorrow morning, perhaps take in a museum? The monuments, they are all in the same area. Have you been to Washington before? No? There is much to see."

"I think I have a taxi called and return to the airport."

"I live in Falls Church, not so far from Dulles. I gladly drop you off and you won't have to wait for a cab." They parted with a friendly handshake at the airport.

There was a late flight to London and many flights from there to Munich during the day. Without a reservation he had to pay for first class—quite expensive. Luxurious accommodations and a fine dinner, he would put it on his expense account.

Anton slept on the plane until breakfast. Washed up, shaved first, and after breakfast took out his notes. He liked the way Agent Johnson had used the blackboard to write down known facts, no, not facts just suppositions. Then it came to him! He should have stayed another day in Washington and bought these two books. He would have to order them through the internet. Possibly they were available in Munich? He doubted in bookstores. This MO of Berkowitz sounded just like the Munich killer. The dragon book, which was only fictional, could give a possible explanation of a person seeking the ultimate power over life and death by becoming like a dragon? Or like Lucifer?

Anton arrived at noon in London and took a two o'clock flight to Munich. He took the fast train connection home to Planegg. He had been gone only two days.

The first thing the next morning, Thursday, he visited Inspector Keller who was surprised to see him back already. "You were only gone for two days, but I am glad you are back already. Every morning I have to report to the commissioner about any progress we have made. City Hall and the lord mayor are on his back, yet there is never anything new to report. What have you got?"

Inspector Nagil told him of his visit with Agent Johnson of the FBI.

"Nothing much. But then I didn't expect for them over there to solve our problem. Let me call a meeting with Inspector Harteck and his team and we sit together and discuss what you brought back. How about ten o'clock this morning?"

"Fine. Could we have a blackboard? The American system of enumerating what is known or supposed."

"We can use our classroom," suggested Inspector Keller.

At ten they were all assembled in the classroom. Inspector Nagil had already written the points on the blackboard as he had seen Agent Johnson do it. There were Inspectors Keller and Harteck with his team of six detectives. Before they started, Commissioner Kolb walked in and sat behind the detectives, "Go on gentlemen, I am just listening in." Inspector Keller invited Nagil to come up to the lectern and enumerate. Anton went up front. He pointed at the first writing on the board, which read: FIRST NAME LUDWIG.

Inspector Keller asked, "How did the FBI agent come up with this first name?"

Nagil answered, "These are all suggestions by Agent Johnson, nothing is a known fact, he supposed. If we look how LUDZIFER is written, the D after the U. Johnson thinks that the killer is playing games with the police. Throws them little hints; serial killers do that sometimes. If we take the first three letters, LUD, it suggests the first name of Ludwig."

A detective spoke up, "How about a last name?"

Nagil answered, "I asked Johnson. He thought that the killer would not give that much away. Even if we realize that LUD may stand for Ludwig, there are many Ludwigs."

Keller continue to ask, "Then it is not a matter of the killer wishing to be discovered?"

"No. Serial killers like what they do. The hints they give are meant to tantalize the police; not to be discovered." Anton pointed at the second line. "Agent Johnson thought that the killer lives near his first murder. He said that with their experience, they found that serial killers chose a place near where they live for their first murder. They are unsure, even scared, and need to hide. Then in the safety of their lair, they like to fantasize about the crime they committed."

Harteck asked, "And the small room?"

Nagil replied, "He thinks that the killer is not rich; therefore, the bicycle. When I explained to Agent Johnson that there are no dormitories for the many students, only contracted dwellings, or they have to find their own places, he thought of a room."

Harteck continued, "All right, we agreed that he uses a bicycle. Why out of town?"

Nagil explained, "If he is not rich or from a well-to-do family, he would live in Munich with his family but . . ."

Harteck interupted, "If his family is poor, wouldn't this suggest that he lives at home in the city?"

"This is where the Lucifer phenomena comes in. Agent Johnson suggests that the killer needs to worship his deity, have images of Lucifer in his place. He couldn't do that with his family," Nagil explained.

Harteck said, "Kills randomly. This much we have realized. How about this son of Sam MO?"

Nagil explained, "Some years ago, they had a serial killer in New York City. His name was David Berkowitz. Why he was duped as the Son of Sam, I don't know, but that is what he was called by the press. He also killed randomly, young women and often couples who sat in a car. When he was apprehended he claimed that he heard voices that told him to kill."

Harteck said, "I wonder if our killer will use some excuse like that."

Keller asked, "For an insanity plea?"

Nagil continued, "Berkowitz was convicted and sentenced to life." He pointed at the next line, "He likes to kill. It gives him the power over life and death. Agent Johnson compared it with a fictional book where the killer was seeking this power through his deity, a dragon. Johnson believes that in our case, the dragon could be Lucifer."

"Well, our case is reality and not fiction. I rather think that Lucifer is his deity he seeks to please. How else can you please the devil but by killing people?" Harteck said.

Nagil said further, "Agent Johnson told me that he would call a meeting of his forensic experts on serial killers and send us a report of their conclusion. Also, his handwriting will be analyzed by their graphology experts and their report sent to us."

Keller said, "This is it then? Let us get back to work. Thank you, Inspector Nagil." When Nagil left, the commissioner motioned him to stay behind.

Commissioner Kolb asked him, "And what are your plans, Inspector Nagil? Which direction will you pursue? We are desperate to have this case solved. The press already duped him the 'Car Killer' and talk about police incompetence. They have no idea how difficult it is to find the killer. Nothing to go by except a bicycle."

Nagil said, "I am trying to get hold of this book on the Son of Sam. It is a biography and might give us an insight into the background of this man. An assessment of his personality."

"Good. After lunch?" Kolb asked.

"I don't have time for lunch." They parted.

It was now eleven o'clock. Where would he find this book? Which library would have American literature? He went to his office and got out his map of Munich and the university complex. Of course, with the university was the Bavarian State Library. He checked out a police car.

At the state library, he was advised that their foreign language library consists mainly of books for higher learning and political, historical, geographical literature but not novels or police accounts. He also checked with their computer on foreign books of every type translated in German but the two he was looking were not available in German. However, the librarian suggested that the State Foreign Language Institute in the Amalienstrasse had such books as novels in many foreign languages.

He went there and was directed to the basement and there met Frau Leiter who spoke a number of languages and was the guardian of books. After he identified himself as Police Inspector Nagil and told Frau Leiter what he was looking for she asked, "Do you speak English, Inspector Nagil? Yes? Please let us speak the language; I don't have many opportunities to use English here. What novels are you looking for?" He told her American. "Oh, we have many American novels. Down the street is the *Akademie der Bildenden Kuenste*. How would you translate that, Inspector?"

Anton said, "I guess the Academy of Arts?"

"Yes. Well, they have many students from America. We also get many books from American publisher for free, not all but many. We have a rich collection, especially older novels. Lately we have received less. So, which books are you looking for?"

Anton said, "First a biography by a David Abrahamsen, *Son of Sam*." She wrote it on a piece of paper. "And by Thomas Harris, the *Red Dragon*."

"Oh, I have read this one. Fascinating. There is a sequel, The Silence of the Lambs. Gruesome. There is also a sequel to that; it is really a trilogy, Hannibal. I never got a copy of it, I might buy it myself." She went to the computer and began to type in.

"Let me ask you, Frau Leiter, do students check out these books? Or for that matter anyone?"

"Mostly students. Ah, here we are, the *Red Dragon*. Oh, I am sorry the book is no longer available. Lost, the student never returned it. Now let's see the other one. I can't believe it, also lost."

"Let me ask you, Frau Leiter, when a student checks out a book, do they need to show identification, you keep a record?"

"Of course. We put his name, affiliation to his learning institute and address into the computer. We ask for a nominal loaning charge."

"And when the book is returned?"

"It is deleted. I see your face drop. You are looking for someone who might have read these books, by any chance the Car Killer? Yes? Well, Inspector, you can lift your face again. If a student reports a book lost, first of all we make him pay for it. Of course, we loose. Many of these books are irreplaceable, some no longer in print. However"—and she smiled up at the inspector, her face radiating her happiness to be able to help—"we keep a record of the student. If he loses a book again we do no longer permit him to check one out."

"So it is possible that you kept this information in your computer, Frau Leiter?"

"It is not only possible, it is recorded. I have to go to a different program, lost books." Anton felt a shiver surging down his spine. *Oh God, let it happen!*

She switched the program. "Let's see. The *Red Dragon* . . . reported lost on twentieth of August of this year. The culprit is a Ludolf Hanfnagel, student at the Academy of Arts. His address is Kaulbachstrasse 42, second floor, by Pension Gaertner. Now let me check the other book . . . tra-la-la," she hummed. "The *Son of Sam*. Here we go, also reported lost on twentieth of August by the same person. By the way, I remember this man. He checked out the *Red Dragon* once before, beginning of the year but then returned it. We discussed this book. He spoke English well, like you do, with British pronunciation. Mine is American."

Frau Leiter, an elderly matron with her gray hair, tied into a pigtail was as surprised as tickled when the handsome inspector bent down and kissed her! She giggled. "Och, Herr Inspector!"

"What is your first name, Frau Leiter?"

"Gerda, Gert for short."

"Silence of Gert, please!"

"Silent like a lamb." She stood up and the inspector embraced her. "THANK YOU!"

"You seem nervous, excited, Inspector."

"I have every reason to shake in my shoes."

"Is this the man . . . the killer?"

"Perhaps. We have to check him out. Again PLEASE, Gert, do not tell anyone. We will be in touch with you." He was ready to leave.

"Don't you want me to write his name and address down, Inspector?"

"It is burnt into my memory. But please do." She wrote the name and address down on a three-by-five card.

"I remember him. The first name Ludolf is rather unusual. He enjoyed speaking English with me, also knows French. A little red-haired man with what you call a harelip, kind of twisted when he smiled, which was rare."

"Where is he from, do you know?"

"From a little town or rather a village up north, Krumbach. His family has a big farm, he told me. He had it rough as a kid because of his lip; children can be cruel. He is studying music, piano. According to him, if I remember, he gives solo performances, so he must be gifted. I see that you are itching to get back. Will they give you a medal for this, Inspector?"

Anton laughed, "More likely a pat on the back." The laughing did him well; he was composed again.

When he was in his car, he regretted not to have a siren on top. Yes, he was itching to get back, yet he drove careful and relaxed, returned the car and made his way to Inspector Harteck's office. He would have loved to just rush into the commissioner's office; however, going to the inspector who was in charge of the case was the proper thing to do. His secretary informed him that Inspector Harteck was with Keller. He knocked.

"Herein (come in)." Anton walked in, both sitting together, Keller behind his desk. Without saying anything Anton handed Inspector Harteck the card. He read it and looked up at Nagil. "Is that him?" Anton nodded. Harteck handed it to Inspector Keller. Inspector Keller's face flushed. He shot up from his chair, his chair crashed to the floor, and the man rushed out of the office, shouting, "You two stay frozen!"

Harteck asked, "Is that really him?"

"I hope so."

"How did you find him?"

"Wait for Keller to come back, I hate to have to tell it twice."

"Why don't you sit down, Nagil?"

"He told us to stay frozen." They laughed and Anton sat down.

A few minutes later Commissioner Kolb and Inspector Keller came in. Harteck and Anton stood up. The commissioner flashed the card to Nagil. "Is that him?"

"I am pretty certain."

"How certain are you, Inspector Nagil?"

"It is him!"

Kolb said, "Prove! How did you find him so fast?"

Inspector Nagil told about the books; Frau Leiter who was so helpful.

Kolb asked, "Do we nail him now?"

Keller said, "If I may suggest." He turned to Inspector Nagil, "A student? Yes? Which school?" Anton told him. Keller turned to the commissioner; "I suggest we have a team at his place of residence. Mainly that when he comes home he does not go out again on his bicycle. We let him go to school tomorrow, Friday. In the meantime, I get a search warrant and we take a look at his place. If we find any evidence, we arrest him either at the school or when he comes home." He turned to Harteck, "Inspector, have your team inconspicuous, perhaps across in an apartment overlooking the place. No one must be seen near the house number 42. An all-night watch. Who knows how edgy he might feel suddenly. I don't trust these lunatics; they seem to have a sixth sense, smelling danger. If he should leave on his bicycle arrest him. Also have people at the Academy of Arts tomorrow, maybe disguised as workman doing something. We can arrest him at any time then. Does that agree with you, Commissioner Kolb?"

Kolb said, "Yes, I think you have everything covered. Most important that he doesn't go on a bicycle trip again."

Keller added, "And Inspector Harteck, if he leaves his premises, maybe to go shopping or get something to eat, have some of our female detectives follow him, incognito, of course."

Harteck said, "I arrange it properly. I myself will be there and supervise my men. May I leave to get organized?" He left.

Keller said, "Harteck is good. A man of action, less so of brain, but he has good detectives. This man will not escape him."

Kolb added, "Inspector Keller, I want to be with the team that enters his apartment. Let's say at ten o'clock in the morning? He will then be at the Academy even if he leaves late. You, Inspector Nagil come with me. Be in my office at 9:30. Has anyone told Kirsch yet? No? Well, I inform him. I am certain he wants to accompany us." The commissioner left.

Inspector Nagil returned to his office. He was still excited. What a break with those books. Agent Johnson was right with the name also. Not Ludwig but Ludolf. He would have to write him a thank-you note.

His mother saw the excitement her son was in when he came home. "Had a good day, arresting some baddie?"

Anton smiled. "I don't arrest anyone. I sit in my office doing paperwork. But I believe we found this Car Killer."

Rosemarie smiled. "WE? You mean you did. I knew you would make a good cop."

"Mom, I am not a cop, I am an inspector."

The next morning, Anton was waiting impatiently in his office. Not being able to concentrate on any files, he read the *Sueddeutsche Zeitung*. Suicide bombings in Iraq. Terror in the Middle East. Just accidents and small crimes reported in Munich. He could already see the headline tomorrow CAR KILLER CAUGHT. Our able police force, etc.

It was barely nine o'clock that the phone rang. "Commissioner Kolb here. Our man has left on his bicycle; he is followed by unmarked cars. Meet me in the garage." Together with Chief Inspector Kirsch, the commissioner, his driver, Anton was driven to the address in the Kaulbachstrasse. When their staff car stopped at number 42, Inspector Harteck and several detectives came seemingly from nowhere and joined them. They had been here all night and reported that Hanfnagel had come home at five in the afternoon. Left at six for a bite at the corner fast-food place, always under the observation of several female detectives. Had returned shortly after and remained in his room until close to nine this morning; when he left on his bicycle he was followed by detectives.

Keller also joined them having driven in his own car. Preceded by Kolb and Kirsch, they went to the first floor office of the Pension. A Frau Gaertner, the owner of the place, opened and Inspector Kirsch showed her the search warrant.

Frau Gaertner explained, "Herr Hanfnagel is a quiet resident, causes no problems. Why the warrant? What has he done?"

Inspector Kirsch said, "Just open the apartment for us, please."

She opened the main entrance, "There are several students living here in my rooms. Only Herr Hanfnagel has two rooms." She pointed at one door. "He had his own lock put there. He is my only boarder who never lets my cleaning woman into this room. Here is his main room. Sometimes he plays his organ music too loud and I have to knock on the ceiling with a broom. But the other students play their modern music also too loud. I live downstairs, it disturbs me; they all do."

Kirsch smiled. "Lots of knocking then."

She unlocked the door.

Kirsch said, "You can go now, Frau Gaertner. We let you know when we are finished." She left. Kirsch, the commissioner, Keller, Harteck, Anton and two detectives entered the room. It was none descript. Orderly, but obviously the room of a student with school books, sheet music lying on the desk.

Keller said, "Start searching this room," he told the detectives, "Find his pistol." They put on plastic gloves. They went to the door leading into the connecting room; there was a strong padlock on the door. "Detective Schuler?" The man had to go to his car to bring his bolt-cutter; he then cut the lock off.

Keller opened the door; it was dark. He turned the light switch and the room blazed in red light. They entered; at once they saw what looked like an altar illuminated by two red spotlights, behind it on the wall a large poster of Lucifer. Anton saw that it was the same image as on the small picture, only hugely enlarged. On the altar lay a 7.65 mm Sauer pistol, like an offering. As the others looked around, Anton went to a small bookcase in the corner and found what he was looking for, the two lost books. He did not have plastic gloves on as the detectives so he left them alone. He studied the other books, literature on satanism, devil worship. In a folder were paper clippings of the murders.

Commissioner Kolb said, "We have the evidence to arrest the man. Inspector Harteck, please drive to the Academy and arrest Hanfnagel. Inspector Nagil, go with him." Harteck and Anton rushed out. All left except for the two detectives who continued to search the room, but first took pictures before anything was removed, and then packed all the evidence.

When Harteck and Anton left the house, they were joined by the other four detectives and three female detectives.

Harteck was now the man of action. He gathered his detectives around. "We are going to the Academy of Art to arrest Hanfnagel. He is our man. Is anyone familiar with the Academy? No? I have to call Detective Schall, he is in charge of the detail we posted there. We need to cover all exits including windows that are low enough for him to jump out. You three detectives come with me in my car, you men follow me; we stop in the Amalienstrasse a block away and walk to the Academy. By the time we get there I have particulars from Schall. Nagil, you drive my car so I can talk freely to my man." The female detectives got in the back, Anton in the drivers seat; Harteck took the phone.

"Schall, Harteck here . . ."

"Yes, Hanfnagel is our man. How many detectives are with you?"

"Good, all six men. I can give you four more. We need to cover all exits to the building and along the sides where windows are low . . ."

"You can do it, ten men are enough?"

"Yes, you can shoot if he tries to escape, but just wound him, tell the men to shoot at his legs. I, Inspector Nagil and my three detectives will go into the building. We should be there in a few minutes; we will be coming from the Amalienstrasse. Out." They stopped a half block from the Academy. When they got out of their cars, they were joined by the six detectives from Schall's group. All in civies, two wore painter's outfits, one looked like a janitor. The detectives followed Schall who distributed them around the building. Harteck, Anton and the three detectives went up the broad flight of stone steps and entered the building. There was an office to the left; Harteck motioned to Anton to come with him. Harteck identified himself as a police officer and told the surprised secretary that they came to arrest a Ludolf Hanfnagel.

The secretary, a Frl. Schneider asked, "What for? What has he done?"

Harteck said to her, "Just tell me where we can find Hanfagel. He is a student here."

Frl. Schneider said, "Yes, I know he is a student. I know him, our fine pianist. Let me see . . ." She looked at the schedule on a board. "Hanfnagel is now with the music appreciation class, in the theater. The stairs down and to your left, the double door."

Harteck asked, "Are there other exits from the theater?"

She replied, "Well, like any theater, there are exit doors on both sides."

"How many students are in the class, in the theater now?" asked Harteck.

Frl. Schneider answered, "I don't know. Usually for a music appreciation in the theater there are several classes listening. Maybe around a hundred student and several teachers."

Harteck told her, "Then please come with me and point Hanfnagel out to me. You said you know him."

Frl. Schneider said, "You are all with the police? My God, what has he done? Five of you? Is he that dangerous? That meek person?"

Harteck finally told her, "He is the Car Killer."

Frl. Schneider surprisingly said, "Oh God. There must be a mistake. Please follow me." They followed the secretary down into the basement. By the double doors, Harteck stopped and assigned two female detectives to either side. "You detective Rossmann, guard the entrance, let no one come out. Nagil come with me. Please, Fraulein."

The secretary opened the theater, it was in subdued light. Only the exit lights and small lamps along the rows of seats illuminated the place, and at once they were received by the beginning haunting concert of the Valkyre blaring from several loudspeakers.

Harteck said, "Lights. Can you turn the theater lighting on Frauelein, please?" At once nearby couples disturbed by the light from the open door hushed them, "Quiet . . . silence, close the door."

The lights came on. The students, many as couples and close together, some in embrace looked back at them. The music, the "Rites of the Valkyre," played on and loudly. The detectives followed the secretary down the middle aisle; she was looking right and left.

Some elderly, probably teachers, shouted at them, "What are you doing here . . . get out." On they walked until close to the front when the secretary pointed at a man with red hair who seemed the only one who did not turn around. "That is Herr Hanfnagel!"

Inspector Harteck rushed at him, but already the red-haired man jumped up, in his hand a switchblade. He ran to the front and grabbed a girl in the first row, dragged her to the podium and held the knife to her throat. Inspector Harteck had drawn his pistol but stopped short of Hanfnagel when he saw him bring the knife close to her throat and actually drew blood. It was when the students saw the inspector draw his pistol that pandemonium broke out and many rushed back to the exit.

Harteck shouted over the loud blaring of the Valkyre, "Nagil, tell Detective Rossmann to let them leave. We got Hanfnagel." Anton did so and then returned to the front. Many had rushed back and left but others remained; standing and watching.

To Anton it was a surrealistic scene. Wagner's Valkyre blaring through the theater and on the podium this serial killer holding a student hostage. Then suddenly the concert stopped—an eerie silence in the theater. Anton was glad, as he would state later, "That is not what that lunatic needed, to be excited by Wagner's rousing music."

He walked slowly to Inspector Harteck who stood a few meters from Hanfnagel, his pistol pointed at him. Hanfnagel held the frightened girl around her chest and pressed to him, his knife poised to slash her throat.

"Let the girl go!" Harteck shouted in the silence of the theater. Hanfnagel tightened his grip, his upper hairlip distorted in a macabre grin.

Anton spoke softly to Inspector Harteck, "It is a stand-off. May I try? Please lower your pistol and walk back a little ways." Harteck did so and walked back to the middle. Anton, who was very calm, took out his pistol and laid it on a seat. He faced Hanfnagel, took a few steps toward him. "Stop! Or I cut her throat!"

Anton stopped. "Let me talk to you, Ludolf. You see I am unarmed now. I am not going to hurt you, just talk."

Ludolf said, "I am not going to let the girl go."

"I am not asking you to let her go. I just want to talk with you."

Ludolf seemed calmer now, "Talk."

"I know what you want and you can never get it killing the girl. You slash her throat and Inspector Hartek back there will shoot you, kill you. Then it would be all over and your needs unfulfilled," Anton explained to him.

Ludolf asked him, "How would you know what I need?"

Anton answered him, "The same as what the Son of Sam needed." Ludolf at once seemed relaxed and even lowered the knife from the girl's throat. "You know about the Son of Sam?"

Anton smiled. "David? Yes. You are very much like him. He had the same needs as you have."

"To kill?"

"Yes, to kill. To kill young women because he was unhappy. Like him you had a difficult childhood.

"So?"

"So he killed. He had power. He was important. They paid attention to him. He heard and obeyed voices that told him to kill. Like you, obeying Lucifer."

"He tells me now to kill this woman!" Ludolf said.

"Yes, he does, I know. Lucifer compelled you to kill. But you don't need to obey him any longer. You are free of him now. He can no longer protect you. You kill the woman and you will be killed. Your dreams unfulfilled, you don't want to end it like this."

"What do you know about my dreams?"

Anton smiled knowingly. "To be famous, a person who has become recognized by all. Just like David Berkowitz. David is now a famous person, literary men seek him out to write his biography; psychologists study him to find out what made him kill. It is not all over now, not for him, not for you. A new beginning for you, Ludolf."

Then there was only silence in the theater; Anton observed a calmness in Ludolf's features. He reached out his arm to Ludolf. Ludolf offered the knife. Anton slowly walked to him and took the knife.

Ludolf gently pushed the girl away, held out his hands together. Already Inspector Harteck was there and put the cuffs on him, took him away. All the detectives left in a rush to get their prisoner back to headquarters and somehow Inspector Nagil was overlooked and had to make his way in a taxi.

When Anton returned to police headquarters, Commissioner Kolb called Inspector Nagil to come to his office. He shook Nagil's hand; "I want to thank you for the fine job you did. I wished I could show my gratitude by promoting you, but we have our rules. When did you begin working here?"

"I was accepted on the first of December but sworn in on the sixth?"

"Well, on the sixth then, I personally will give you your promotion to *Polizeioberkommissar* (head inspector). And of course a letter of commendation. I like to do something else for you. I understand your wife lives in Jerusalem as you are adopting a child? Take the month of October and visit with her. I cannot grant you a month leave but we can put you on detached service, consultation with the Israeli Police. Start packing, Inspector Nagil."

It was still a week to October. There was work to do, some unfinished files. Hanfnagel was now in the care of Harteck and his team and was questioned by them. There were examinations by psychiatrists and psychologists awaiting him.

The librarian Frau Gerda Leiter was invited to the *Praesidium* by Commissioner Kolb and honored in a small ceremony attended to by the inspectors involved in the case. She was presented with a Letter of Appreciation and a bouquet of roses. After all, it was she who supplied the name and address of the serial killer. Afterward, the commissioner gave Inspector Nagil his credit card and told him to take Frau Leiter out for lunch.

Anton and librarian Gert Leiter became good friends and Anton would use her library to check out books in English, Russian and Arabic, usually mystery novels. He became a firm believer that even fictional novels of crime educated in police work.

The next morning, in all Munich and even national papers, were the headlines of the Car Killer having been caught by the efficient Munich police. Inspector Nagil's name was mentioned in having helped to solve the case. As always, most credit was prominently given to the police commissioner and his splendid *Mord Kommission*—forensic murder detail, under the brilliant leadership of Head Inspector Harteck, who arrested Ludolf Hanfnagel.

Anton wrote a letter to Agent Burt Johnson in care of FBI Headquarters, detailing the discovery and arrest of the car killer. Thanking him especially for the help in suggesting these two books to him which ultimately led to discovering the murderer. Also, the suggestion of LU(D)ZIFER as part of his Christian name was correct, though his first name was Ludolf. When Anton received the psychological profile of the killer from the FBI, he marveled at the suggestion that the killer, probably in young age, mutilated himself either in the face or genitals, that he developed a hate-love relationship with himself, and hated happy young couples; therefore, he went on a killing spree and would continue to do so until caught. As Inspector Nagil was informed, Ludolf Hanfnagel injured his upper lip, a self—inflicted wound, as a teenager when a girl repeatedly teased him about his twisted mouth when he smiled. It was not a harelip. Ludolf Hanfnagel was declared psychotic and incarcerated in an institution for the criminally insane—his case never came to trial.

However, when Inspector Nagil requested the two books, the *Red Dragon* and the *Biography of the Son of Sam*, they were given to him and read them with great interest. Rosemarie wanted to read the books but didn't know English. Anton related each story as best as he could without going into details. Her comments then, "Evil people. It doesn't matter if they are criminals, neo-Nazis or terrorists. They all belong in that barrel of you-know-what because that is what they are, rotten, foul, trash."

"Exactly my sentiments, Mom."

Anton told Commissioner Kolb that he wished that the German psychiatrists who examined Ludolf Hanfnagel, had consulted with the American psychiatrist David Abrahamsen who examined Berkowitz. He was one of the few who had found him sane and not psychotic and upon his expertise he was brought to trial. Interesting, as he told the commissioner, was that Berkowitz was adopted by loving parents, too loving perhaps? His birth name was Richard Falco. The commissioner made an interesting observation to Inspector Nagil. "Yes, I also wished that Hanfnagel would have been tried, sentenced to life and locked into a *Zuchthaus* (prison). Politics, my dear Inspector. America can afford to have, and to try serial killers. It is part of their open society. We in Germany wish to show the world that we are again a civilized nation and we just can't have such killers. Psychotic killers, yes. Every nation has people who are insane."

When Anton packed for his month-long trip to Israel, he took his Egyptian passport along as he wished to visit his good friends Sidqi and Fatima in Cairo. Since he kept his old press card for the al-Ahram newspaper in his passport, he took it along.

CHAPTER XXIV

THE SECOND INCIDENT

The Munich police department had arranged for him to visit the Jerusalem police Deputy Commissioner Avi Barlev for consultation on police matters, "Just a polite visit," as Commissioner Kolb put it. "He expects you to drop by sometimes in October. Give him a call first for an appointment. We told him you were the expert on the Russian mafia, as they are also active in Israel." So with the blessing of the Munich police and an invitation by the Jerusalem police, he had an official mission to pursue on own his time, whenever.

Hanna and Amal were expecting him and delighted that he could stay for the whole month of October, with a side trip to Cairo as he told them to visit Sidqi. Danny was now thirteen months old and could utter a few words and seemed to remember him, though he spoke of *ishi* (my man), instead of *avi'* (my daddy). This was Amal's fault. She always referred to Toni as "ishi."

And then, on the second of October, early Sunday morning after an hour's drive from the airport, the taxi dropped him off in front of his house. There on the balcony, bathed in the golden light of the rising sun, stood his Hanna and she waved down to him; and then rushed into his arms, her loving kisses were all over his face. Amal already up and in the kitchen preparing breakfast and he embraced his mother-in-law who was more like a second mother to him. Danny still sleeping. They conversed in Arabic but always switched to Hebrew when Danny was around. There was much to tell, Amal volunteering at the hospital during the week and Hanna only on Sabbath. Hanna told the wonderful news that Daniel was to be adopted and all papers are ready.

"We were just waiting for you, Toni to be here and I made a court date for Friday."

Hanna told Toni, "Nahik Rubin is now with the Jerusalem Police Department. He had called me a couple days ago, and had asked where you are. I told him that you are coming today. He wants to you see you, kind of urgent he had said." Anton told her that he was supposed to visit the police as part of his coming for a month to Jerusalem, "Kind of liaison work with them. I look forward to meet Nahik Rubin who has been my welcoming committee many years ago and more like a friend."

Anton was on his second cup of Israeli coffee made the Arabian way when they heard quick footsteps, and Daniel rushed in, pointed at Anton, "man" and ran to Anton who took him on his lap and there Danny sat with his thumb in his mouth and just sat quietly and smiling. Hanna laughed, "Danny, this is not the man, this is your daddy. Can you say 'my daddy'?" Danny repeated, "my man," and that was it. Anton kissed his son's blond curls and then just held him.

It was only after a while, and the boy listening to the big people talking that he let Amal put him in his high chair to have breakfast, eating while his eyes were fixed on the man who smiled at him bemused. It was seven o'clock that the phone rang, and Amal told Toni that is was for him; Nahik Rubin was calling.

After greeting each other briefly, Nahik Rubin asked him to come by at police headquarters as soon as he can.

"What is up, Rubin?" Anton had made it his practice to call the Shin Bet agent by his last name.

"I can't tell you over the phone, but please come by. I'll wait for you." Sunday was a regular workday in Israel.

While Danny was being dressed by Amal, Anton got into his old Ford and drove to National Police HQ, skirting the old city, then out to Clermont Ganneau, the seat of police headquarters. He was checked at the entrance, and then in the lobby asked for Nahik Rubin. The policeman at the desk did not know this man, but when Anton said, "If not Rubin then I wish to see Deputy Avi Barlev." The policeman made a call, then advised him to go to the second floor, room 24. "And there, *Adon* Rubin is with the deputy."

Anton knocked and then walked into the big office and there met Rubin. They welcomed each other with a firm handshake. Rubin no longer the young man; it had been more than twenty years that they saw each other. Rubin introduced Anton to the Deputy Avi Barlev; an imposing man in his khaki police uniform, tall and lanky in build, narrow stern face, who addressed him as Inspector Nagil. The three men sat in a corner of the office, a low table before them and from a pot of hot water the deputy made three glasses of tea. Anton took a sugar cube between his teeth and sipped the tea.

Barlev commented, "The Russian way of drinking tea?"

"Also the Afghan's," replied Anton.

Barlev asked, "Where did you encounter Afghanis?"

Anton chuckled, "In Afghanistan, of course."

"You were there with the Americans or British?"

"No, I was there at bin Laden's invitation," replied Anton.

Barlev didn't pursue this line of conversation any further of what he took for a sarcastic remark.

Rubin lit a cigarette. "Do you smoke, Anton?"

Anton looked at the deputy who smiled pleasantly. "I don't smoke, but go ahead and poison the atmosphere, I don't mind." The windows were open.

The two men watched as Anton filled his pipe and puffed.

The deputy began, "How is police work, Inspector Nagil, I understand you are newly employed by the Munich police?"

"Since last December."

"And what is your specialty?"

"I am with the antiterror unit but attached to the CID."

The deputy continued to ask, "Anything interesting going on in Munich?"

"We had a letter bomb scare. Then we were able to round up the Russian mafia. A little incident with the neo-Nazis in Munich. A serial killer who shot two young couples whom we were able to apprehend before he killed more. This was an interesting case as I was sent to the FBI in Washington, who gave me information that led us to the murderer."

Rubin commented, "At least we don't have serial killers in Israel, unless they are terrorists who murder many."

Anton turned to Rubin, "I detected some urgency in your call this morning Rubin, I just came in from Germany and have a family waiting; you are no longer with the agency?"

He replied "I am still with the Shin Bet; however, no longer concerned with agents who come visiting. As a chief in the agency, I am involved with internal security matters pertaining to terrorist activities." He turned to the deputy. "Perhaps you wish to explain, Deputy Barlev?"

Deputy Barlev took a deep breath. "What I tell you, Inspector Nagil must remain confidential." Anton nodded. "Five days ago, we had terrorists break through the security fence of Kefar Ezion at night. They entered one house near the fence and killed a man and his wife and kidnapped their two young children; Esther who is three and David six. They left a note in Arabic which only stated, 'do not publicize the kidnapping or killing. We will be in touch with you.' The note was signed with—*al-Nakbab brigade*. Which means—you speak Arabic? *Al-Nakbab* is the term the Palestinians use for what they refer to as the disaster. To us, the War of Liberation. This is to us a new name for a terrorist unit, but we are certain it is part of either Hamas, Islamic Jihad or the al-Aqsa Martyrs Brigade. We complied so far that we had the people of Kefar Ezion remain silent about the murders and kidnappings, and did not publicize it in the newspapers, radio, or TV. Immediately, we sent search squads of the IDF to the nearest towns of Bethlehem and Hevron. One company even searched the tunnels of Solomon's Pools. No luck and we didn't expect any results. It is like searching a needle in the proverbial haystack. Three days ago, a Palestinian came to the gate of Ezion, the IDF unit arrested him. He had a letter with a demand for the release of numerous terrorists we hold. The IDF commander called his superiors and read the demand. The Arab emissary was released with a note that we are studying the demand and we need at least a week to reply. The Arab was then released. He had no identification on him and just called himself Abdul, an alias name for anyone of course. This Abdul returned two days later with a note that the release of the prisoners should take place in six days at the gates of Kefar Ezion. After they are safely taken away, they would release the children. The commander, who speaks Arabic, asked for Abdul to prove that the children are still alive. Abdul then used his cell phone; spoke into it saying that the Jewish commander wished to hear the children speak. He gave the commander the phone. He heard someone say in Hebrew, 'Say your name.' Then a child's voice, 'I am David.' A moment later, 'I am Esther.' Then the commander heard the shrieking of the children, and the phone disconnect. The commander lost his cool and punched Abdul, which did not help the situation but also did not hurt it, we hope. The Arab was let go after his broken nose was bandaged. This was yesterday. This gives us five days to comply one way or the other."

"Will you exchange?"

Barlev said, "We can't. We never did. Well, we did with soldiers and agents but on a one-to-one basis so to speak. The list is too large and most of those on the list are terrorists who murdered innocent people. Perhaps one we could release they want badly, their Tanzim leader Marwan Barghouti. He directed suicide operations and we could connect him to five killings. He was tried and received a life sentence. But not the worst of them."

"Well, why don't you give them a list of these people and tell them if the children are murdered those on the list will be executed."

Barlev smiled for a moment, then again looked serious. "We can't. We are a democratic and civilized country. Our laws will not permit it."

Anton Nagil showed his anger and shouted, "When will you people realize that you cannot deal with terrorists! You have to fight fire with a fire storm!" He relaxed after this emotional outburst, "I understand." He turned to Rubin, "And what can I do to help?" Rubin looked at the deputy.

"You don't approve of me, Inspector Nagil?" asked Barlev.

Anton shook his head, "No! I have nothing personal against you, I just don't like the way you do business with them."

Barlev said, "We cannot do otherwise. Oh God, how we wished we could rescue the children. Two little children in the hands of these evil people; a sweet girl only three years old. They must be in terror, and who knows where they keep them and under what conditions. This morning when Rubin told me that you are in Jerusalem. He said that you are an agent of Mossad and that you have Egyptian citizenship, that you are now with the German police and are therefore familiar with police work. There is a remote possibility that you can help us. We must try anything before we sacrifice the innocent lives of two Israeli children. Our surveillance unit traced the call to a Hassan Abu-Sharif in Hevron. We immediately sent a unit to his house and searched it. Nothing. We were certain that the children had been there, but they must have realized that we traced their call and hid the children somewhere else. We did not arrest Abu-Sharif. We knew he would not talk, but we knew he is involved and knows the whereabouts of the children. We can always arrest him if we need to. Now this man Hassan Abu-Sharif is a Palestinian but he originally came from Germany. His name is Hans Stettner. He came after the war and while we cannot pin anything on him, we are certain that he has been involved in every war against us, and in terrorist attacks. Survivors of Kibbutz Ezion told of a German being with the irregulars that subdued the kibbutz in 1948 and saw him shoot down captured men and women in cold blood. These survivors never saw him, his face, and only knew him to be a German by his heavy accented Arabic. We are certain it was he; there were no other Germans in that vicinity. We checked his German name with the BND (*Bundesnachrichtendienst* [German Intelligence Service]), but they do not have a Hans Stettner in their listing. It is obviously a false name but his German passport looks authentic. One collaborator gave us the information that Stettner was an SS officer with the *Einsatzgruppe 3,* in Lithuania. He is the owner of a hotel in Hevron but lives in his own villa."

"Did you search the hotel?"

Barlev replied, "Of course. Nothing, not even weapons."

"And what can I do?"

Rubin then said, "Anton, we know, Tal told us, that you eliminated SS officers from that group, or that she supplied you with their names and addresses? Also that you executed your father who was with them."

Anton interrupted, "Not my father, he was Otto Nagil."

Rubin continued, "We thought that if you visit this German Palestinian talk to him about your fa—, about Otto Nagil having been part of this group. Perhaps you can gain his confidence. Maybe he will brag about things he does now along terrorist activities, know what I mean?"

"Yes, I know what you mean. It is unlikely but possible, if I could gain his trust. Of course, he will wonder why I would show up now after so many years, at this critical time when he is involved in this terrorist activity with the children. I must try to get introduced to him by someone he knows, a like-spirited person of his ilk."

Barlev said, "Time is short. We have five days. Possibly we could drag it out. Negotiations are taking place, we can offer them Barghouti, but we need another week or a few extra days."

Anton said, "There is a colleague of Otto in Cairo, actually his son. Gerhard Lutz died during a robbery in 1982."

Rubin asked, "By your hand, Anton?"

"The execution? Yes, but not the robbery. He has a son by the name of Adolf, or Gert as we called him, who was three years younger, so we were never close playmates. Nor did we visit after his father died. His father started an import-export business that his wife Elke continued and then was taken over by Gert. When I left Cairo last year, he was still in business. I could visit him. Perhaps over time he doesn't remember how his and my family became estranged. When Otto died, he was ten. We saw each other at the Teutonic Order and spoke together but we were not really on friendly terms. When his father was killed, he was fourteen."

Rubin asked, "And how does that connect to our man here in Hevron?"

"German expatriates, especially those who had to flee and settled in Middle Eastern countries kept in touch with each other; visited, loved to talk about olden times, the good old times under Hitler. I knew many in Lebanon, Syria, Iraq; they accepted me readily as the son of a well-known SS officer. That is how I received information for the Mossad. It is very likely that Gert Lutz knows this Stettner."

Barlev said, "His passport shows that he traveled frequently to Cairo and Alexandria. Well, it is a possibility. I also realize that an introduction by someone else, at this critical time for him when he is engaged in the kidnapping, might be received as just a coincidence. When can you leave for Cairo?"

Anton smiled. "Later on today. Now what do you know about this Hans Stettner?"

Barlev said, "According to his passport he was born in Dresden on July 4, 1921, which gives his age as 84. He is short, slender, has a white beard and carries himself as a Muslim. He changed his name to Hassan Abu-Sharif in 1947. Of course his Arabic is faultless and Palestinian. He married a local Palestinian woman, who passed away in childbirth. He has one son, Mohammed Sharif. Mohammed is married to a Palestinian woman and has many children. He lives in his father's villa on El Malek number ten, it is across the mosque. Of course, we searched the mosque also. It is the son who now manages the Hotel Palestine, which is on Shaddad Street, number 37, not far from the villa. We have one Palestinian collaborator in Hevron, a physician by the name of Mustafa Abu Shanab. He is Egyptian but married a beautiful Palestinian. Shanab is a womanizer and therefore needs money, lots of money. Once a month or so he travels to Amman in Jordan for consultations or training, besides having a mistress or several in Amman. That is when we can get information from him as we have one person in the hospital he visits who questions and pays him. He is pretty regular in his visits and not due for two more weeks, so we cannot question him. Too dangerous for one of us to visit his practice in Hevron, but he might know something. His specialty is dermatology. While you are in Hevron, you need to see a dermatologist because you have a skin rash on your arm. He lives on Shaddad Street 53, close to the hotel, in his house is his practice. When you see him privately, the code word to use is *al-Asifa*—which means "storm." The counter sign he will give you, if he trusts you, is *al-Ard*, "the land." Work it into your conversation. It is a possibility. Now, Inspector Nagil, at the remote chance that you are discovered, I don't know what to advise you, but it might become very unpleasant. Some of our agents carry a certain pill?"

"You mean a suicide pill? If it comes to that I have this here." And he pointed to his steel pen. "It shoots a cyanide charge."

Deputy Barlev smiled. "I have heard of them. Where did you get if from?"

"A long story."

Rubin asked, "Do you need anything? How will you travel?"

"I can't come through Israel. I will take a flight from Cairo to Amman, and then see how best to get to Hevron. I shall use my Egyptian passport of course which I never used to come to Israel. And no, I don't need any money; I have dollars or euros to change in Egypt."

Rubin added, "Use euros, you come from Germany. As far as a personal weapon, you could never get it through security checks in either Cairo or Amman. The doctor might supply you with a pistol; yes deputy?"

"Yes, he has weapons as many Palestinians do. One more item, we have the IDF, in fact a commando unit outside Hevron. If you need them and can get hold of a cell phone, dial this number, 343-4444. Someone will always be listening for this signal and if needed, the commando will be with you in a very short time. One more thing, don't call the city Hevron as we Israelis do, the Palestinians call it Hebron."

Rubin said, "Let's use your old code word of *sav* to identify you."

"Well, if this is all, let me pack and get going to Cairo. I hate to do this; it always ends up with me playing the anti-Semite and anti-Zionist."

"I am sorry I got you into this Anton. It is dangerous," Rubin added.

"There are two little orphan children waiting for me."

Barlev said, "One more thing." He took a jar from his desk, "This salve will give you a good rash, even blisters. Are you ready?" Anton who wore a short-sleeved shirt held his left arm up. The commander put on plastic gloves and rubbed the salve over his forearm.

"It will begin to itch in a few hours, even burn. By tomorrow you have a good case of eczema. It is not debilitating, just don't open the blisters, it will heal and go away in weeks time. Please don't let anyone touch your arm until the salve dries, best to put on a long-sleeved shirt. Good luck, Inspector Nagil." They shook hands and Anton left.

When he got home, at once Hanna asked, "What did Rubin want, Toni?"

"I tell you in a minute Hanna, I have to do something quick." He rushed to the bedroom and put on a white, long sleeved shirt, by then Hanna stood behind him.

"And?"

"Hanna, something important has come up and I have to fly to Cairo."

"Dangerous something?"

"Of course not!"

"Anton Nagil, you are lying to me!"

He smiled. "So formal. What makes you think what I have to do in Cairo is dangerous, dear Hanna Nagil?"

"Because your face is expressionless, I can't read it. That spells danger."

"Hanna, there is little danger involved in what I have to do in Cairo. It is true; I have to visit an old nemesis. Remember the Lutz family? Gerhard Lutz was killed in a robbery. Before that he was nasty to us, we became if not enemies, at least estranged. Now I need to get some information from his son who is in the export-import business. There is smuggling involved, so that is always a little dangerous. It depends how he will receive me and if I can get the help I need."

"Anton Nagil, you are lying to me!"

"God, what a wife I have, she sees right through me. So it has nothing to do with smuggling. But it is true that I need some information from him!"

"Important enough that you need to gauge his eye out?"

"Oh Hanna, that was necessary to get Rosemarie back. No mother involved this time. Hanna, I have to pack. Please call me a taxi."

"And when will you be back, Toni?" He saw that she was placated, even if she didn't believe what he told her.

"In three days, at most in five days Hanna.

"I have to cancel the adoption."

"Not cancel, I should be back by Friday morning."

"Toni, when will you give up these dangerous assignments? You are not only a husband now but a father."

"Remember, I am a policeman."

"Then do police work and not go on some spy mission."

"It has nothing to do with spying, Hanna. It is . . . well, let's say I do something for your country."

"It is your country too, Toni."

"That is why I must do this." He saw that she drove herself into a corner. He threw a few things on the bed and she packed it into his handbag. He took the Egyptian passport with him.

"Where is Danny?"

"With Amal in the garden. She took the week off. Yes, you better not say goodbye."

He looked down into the garden. There he was riding his little plastic tricycle, pushing it with his feet and Amal sitting on the bench, knitting.

He embraced his wife with a gentle loving kiss. There was the impatient tooting of the taxi and he grabbed his bag and rushed down.

When Hanna came to the gate he had disappeared.

DAY ONE

It was nine in the morning when Anton left. Before noon he was in Nicosia, Cyprus and a noon flight took him to Cairo where he arrived at three in the afternoon. He changed euros into Egyptian currency and took a bus into the city. In a clothing store, he bought himself a cheap white cotton suit, a dark blue open collar shirt, made in Egypt. He smiled when he saw the sticker Made in China. He also bought a pair of shoes made in Egypt. In the dressing cabin, he changed into what he hoped made him look like a reporter. His forearm by then red, a little swollen and it itched more than it burned. His notebook with nothing written in, he stuck in his shirt pocket along with his two pens. His special pen would be a one-shot deal; he couldn't afford to have extra capsules with him. His own clothing and shoes he threw into a trashcan. For his briar, he bought local tobacco.

He was now Achmed Nabil, a reporter for the prominent al-Ahram paper.

It was five when he took a taxi to his familiar neighborhood in the Gazirat Badran section of Shubra. Just carrying his handbag, which contained only extra underwear and a pair of sandals, all bought and made in Germany, he rung the bell of the house he had not visited since 1982. The man who opened the door was Gert Lutz, a blond man, strong in build, the image of his father Gerhard. Gert looked at him in surprise then smiled. "Anton Nagil, is it you? Come in, come in, long time no see." Anton breathed a sigh of relief, he was accepted, and in a friendly manner.

They shook hands and Gert took him into the house and introduced him to his wife, Josepha who wore the cross of the Coptic on a necklace.

"Jose, please bring us a couple beers, or you want coffee, Anton?"

"Beer is fine." His wife brought a couple bottles and Gert poured for them. "Prost Anton." He smiled.

"Prost Gert. Yes, it is a long time that we didn't see each other." They drank the cold beer.

"Look Anton, I don't know what happened a long time ago when your father died suddenly. I was only ten then. But what happened that our families split apart?"

"Ah, it is a long story. Your father came to our house and threatened my mother with dire consequences if she didn't give him all the documents pertaining to their working together during the war. It involved documents that labeled them as war criminals. She didn't want to give them to your father as she wanted to keep them for my education and he told her she better give them to him, all of it, or,"—and he made a slash mark at his throat—"he would kill her. She gave him everything but also avoided your father and his family. And of course, so did I."

"My father could be cruel at times. You know, Anton, it is strange that he threatened your mother in this manner because that is what happened to him. My father had his throat cut by robbers." Anton knew how Gerhard Lutz died.

"We were of course, shocked by the robbery and killing," Anton said.

"Remember the good times we had as boys, playing in your downstairs? You had that large table we put the SA and SS troopers in parade with the fuehrer in front?"

"And we played with the tin soldiers, us against the Russians."

"Your mother was never a real Nazi, Anton. How about you? As a boy you were proud to wear the HJ uniform, sing the songs and raise your hand in Hitler salute. Are you still with it?"

"Yes and no. I am still with it in spirit. But how can you be with the new Nazi Party in Germany? Most of the men from our father's times have died. The young ones, many are just rabble, skinheads. I am friendly with their leader in Berchtesgaden, Theo Schoenauer. He has just a small group, but they are good men."

"What do they call themselves now, Anton? I don't think Nationalsocialist Party?"

"No. Their new organization is called *Blut und Erde Bund.*"

"Did you return to Munich? People said you sold your house, got married, and went back to Germany?"

"Yes, I sold the house. My mother went back to Munich, and we bought a house in Stanberg. I married an Egyptian woman, Anna, an orphan. However, I am still based here in Cairo. Anna is with my mother now."

"So what do you do?" Anton took his press card from his wallet and gave it to Gert.

"I see, you are a reporter for the al-Ahram paper. Achmed Nabil, you changed your name to Egyptian?"

"Otto changed his name a long time ago under the King and my name too. Your father changed his name, but not you?"

"My mother didn't want to. She died a long time ago. My sister Erika lives back in Munich, married and has two kids. Erika should remember your mother, give me your address and Erika will visit with her."

"Yes, I write it down later. What is nice about my reporter's job is that the al-Ahram has me reporting in Germany. I give the German papers' news and articles about Egypt; every night I get an e-mail from Cairo and in turn, I send German news to the al-Ahram. Germany is very Egyptian-friendly. I give articles to German travel agencies; good for tourism. I am also accredited to Reuters and freelance for German newspapers like the *Sueddeutsche Zeitung*, the *Berliner Abendblatt,* the *Frankfurter Allgemeine.* In fact, their news center, a pool for news from Middle Eastern countries, sends me to Amman to report on Palestine, how it suffers under Zionist occupation. I have an appointment for tomorrow afternoon with Prime Minister Abbas in Ramallah. Then, I travel to Bethlehem and get the religious angle under the occupation and visit Hebron. They all suffer terribly. Someday they will get their country back. And you? You are doing fine with your import-export business?"

"Yes, I am doing all right. Rich enough to give it all up and move to Munich. I should get a lot of money selling my business and house. Then just retire in Munich, buy a nice villa, maybe a mountain cabin. Who is the leader of the *Bund* in Munich? I might just join the *Bund*."

"His name is Horst Bachleiter. But I tell you something Gert, you are better off with the branch of the *Bund* in Berchtesgaden. Theo Schoenauer is a personal friend of mine. His members are a better group of people."

"Let me write it down. I am serious about selling my business and moving to Germany. I would love to live in Berchtesgaden."

"Theo Schoenauer . . . Schoenau am Koenigsse, House Tanneck. That is all you need. I don't know his phone number at the moment."

"I find it when I get there. Oh, I have an idea Anton. One of my father's, and also your father's, fellow SS officer lives in Hebron. His name used to be Streller, SS Colonel Streller. He was the commander that took care of the Vilna ghetto, gave the Jews hell there, what was left of them. He came to visit here a few times and talked about my father. He knew your father also; he had only good things to say about Otto Nagil. He changed his name to a Palestinian one. Let me get it and write it down." He returned a moment later with his address book.

"All right, well, he changed his German name to Stettner, Hans Stettner. His Arabic name is Hassan Abu-Sharif, and he lives in Hebron, El Malek ten. When I visited him, I stayed in his house, but he also has a hotel in Hebron. When you have someone drive you there, ask in Arabic for Al Khalil or Hebron."

"I love to visit Hassan . . . what?"

"Hassan Abu-Sharif."

"Yes, you wrote it down. I would love to meet someone who knew Otto. Could you introduce me? I mean, he doesn't know me personally. He has to be careful whom he receives."

"I call him right now." He dialed on his cell phone. Anton heard him speak German.

"Hans? Gert Lutz here . . ."

"Thank you I am fine, and you?"

"Oh, don't give me that getting old stuff. You were in terrific shape when you were here a few years ago. Look, the reason I call, I have a rare visitor here . . ."

"Who? You remember your old comrade, Otto Nagil?"

"Yes, he died in the late seventies. His son Anton is with me. An old comrade of mine . . ."

"I know you never met him. You didn't come and visit us, until when?"

"Yes, it was after my father was murdered. You were busy giving the Jews the business. Are things quiet now?"

"Yes, I read of fighting the Zionists. Look, Anton works for the al-Ahram newspaper and is stationed in Germany. He also freelances for Reuters and a combination of German papers, and they are sending him to Palestine to do a write up of life under the occupation. He has an appointment with Premier Abbas tomorrow in Ramallah. He has to do a religious story in Bethlehem. Then he thought to have a look at Hebron . . ."

"I know what it is called, but I am German and not Egyptian. When I told him about you, an old friend of his father . . ."

"Yes, he would like to visit with you and hear about you and his father and my father working together to get rid of the Jews . . ."

"What? I ask Anton." He turned to Anton, "When can you visit him?"

"Tomorrow morning, I have to go first to Ramallah. I guess I could visit Bethlehem after I visit Hebron. In Bethlehem I would spend a few days; lots to write about religious wise. How far is it to travel from Ramallah to Hebron?"

"I ask Hans."

"Hans, Anton wants to know how long it takes to drive from Ramallah to Hebron?"

"Anton, do you have your German passport?"

"No. I am an Egyptian citizen and have only an Egyptian passport."

"Then you served in the Egyptian Army?"

"For three years. It was just easier to travel around. I went even to Afghanistan."

"What did you do there?"

"I graduated from Cairo University in chemistry. I became an explosive expert and went to an al-Qaeda training camp teaching the Mujahedin bomb making in '98."

"Guess what, Hans, Anton is only an Egyptian citizen, was in the army, became an explosive expert and went to Afghanistan to teach the Mujahedin bomb making . . ."

"Yes, I tell him. All right, I explain that to him too. Four to five hours then from Ramallah. *Auf Wiedersehen,* Hans. Visit me again soon."

Gert laughed, "What Hans was saying, he could use your expertise of bomb making. Hans also said that with your Egyptian passport and without a visa to Israel, you have to skirt Jerusalem. Just tell the driver to take you to Hebron from Ramallah, that is to al-Khalil, without going into Israel. About four to five hours. If you leave at noon, you should be in Hebron by five. He expects you then. I wrote his address down. Now, let's go out and eat. Then you stay here tonight, we have extra guest rooms."

Together with his wife Josepha, who spoke German very well, they went to a fine restaurant in the city and later sat together with a couple more beers, reminiscing about olden times as boys together. Anton stayed in their house the night.

DAY TWO

Gert Lutz drove Anton to the airport early in the morning, they said goodbye. Gert said that Anton should visit him when he gets back to Cairo.

A couple hours flight and he was in Amman. He found a taxi that was willing to drive him to Ramallah for good money which he had to pay in advance, Egyptian currency accepted.

Most of the way they traveled on a good four-lane highway, then it became two-lane to the King Abdullah Bridge, across the Jordan River. Here was the checkpoint, manned by both Palestinian security and Israeli custom. Also, there were many Israeli soldiers with their M-16 slung over the shoulders. The Palestinian and Israeli custom inspectors checked him. The Israeli scrutinized his Egyptian passport and the press card, asked in Arabic what his business was visiting the Jericho Palestinian Autonomy District. He stated that he has an appointment for a press conference with Prime Minister Abbas in Ramallah. The Palestinian official stamped his passport with an entry permit. He was then frisked with a metal rod for weapons, as was the Jordanian driver, and soldiers searched the taxi. They were permitted to proceed and after another hour's drive over both good and bad roads, they came to Ramallah where the driver took him to the partially destroyed compound of the prime minister.

In an office with many security personnel, he stated his business that he wished to see Prime Minister Mahmoud Abbas for a brief interview for his Cairo al-Ahram paper and showed his credentials. He was frisked for weapons again and told to have a seat. After a short while, a secretary took him to the prime minister's office and Achmed Nabil was advised that the prime minister could only spare a few minutes. The secretary and a guard remained with him when he entered the office.

Mahmoud Abbas got up from behind his desk and greeted Anton friendly, "I am always glad to give an interview for the al-Ahram paper, but without an appointment I can only spare a few minutes. Also it is lunch time." He smiled pleasantly. "What in particular is your newspaper interested in?"

Anton stated that his paper was mainly interested in the upcoming elections and if the prime minister will permit Hamas to participate. The prime minister gave a short explanation why the Palestinian Authority will permit Hamas to participate. Anton wrote into his notebook. The interview over, Abbas asked where else he wished to travel.

"To Bethlehem for religious interviews. You would do me a great honor by signing my notebook, it is for my son."

"What is his name?"

"Mohammed Nabil." The prime minister signed, *"Regards to Mohammed Nabil, Abu Mazen."* He then turned to his secretary and told him to make out a passage pass for travel to Bethlehem for Achmed Nabil. "You will have to travel through Israeli checkpoints around Jerusalem to get to the main road to Bethlehem." Abbas shook hands with Achmed Nabil and he was guided out of the compound.

Outside were many taxis and he took one that accepted euros to take him to Al Khalil. He had to pass through several checkpoints around Jerusalem manned by Israeli soldiers, each time he had to show his passport, press card and passage pass. At every checkpoint, he was frisked with a metal rod, and his small handbag searched. By the time they were on the road to Bethlehem, it was past three.

The main highway south bypassed Bethlehem; then he saw a tourist sign in Arabic and English SOLOMON'S POOLS. Shortly after, he saw a detachment of the IDF by a dirt road leading to a settlement. The sign was in Hebrew and said Kefar Ezion.

Another twenty kilometers or so and the large road sign read, AL KHALIL and smaller in English HEBRON. He had the driver take him to El Malik number ten, a nice villa with palm trees and surrounded by a six-foot high wall. He paid the driver and dismissed him. With his handbag, he stood before the gate and rang the bell. A man, a servant came out and asked him if he was Anton Nagil; he was expected. They walked through a flower garden in front of the house and by the entrance door stood an old man in a white robe, a white but trimmed beard. He held out his hand, "Anton Nagil?" *Ein froehliches Willkommen in meinem Haus* (A happy welcome in my house)." They shook hands. Their conversation was now only in German.

"Do I call you Hans Stettner or Hassan Abu-Sharif?"

"Anton, for you I am Hans, and per *du.* I was an old comrade of your father." He led Anton into the house; from the foyer into a large living room which was divided into a comfortable European furnished part and the other half Arabian style with low tables, cushions, and expensive rugs.

"On this side you drink coffee, on the other side a cool beer or wine. What shall it be, Anton?"

"A cool beer please, as long as it isn't from the other side."

"I understand, Anton. It is imported from Jordan. What I can't get locally, I import from Jordan. I also distain anything that is sold by the occupiers." They sat around the large table on upholstered chairs, and the servant brought them the Jordanian beer in bottles and glasses.

"For dinner, we go to my son's hotel. He has a restaurant with it and since we were expecting you, his cook prepared a German meal. Now tell me about you. You are a correspondent now?" Anton showed him his press card from the al-Ahram paper then told him about his work as a reporter for the paper in Germany, that he freelanced for Reuters news agency and for various German papers and was sent to Palestine to report on the life of the Palestinians under the occupation.

Hans asked Anton how his interview went with Mahmoud Abbas. He told him briefly that he asked him about the upcoming elections. Then showed him his notebook with his greetings to his son, Mohammed.

"He signed with his favored name, Abu Mazen. My son's name is also Mohammed. Your son and wife are in Egypt or Germany?"

"They are in Munich."

"You make a good income Anton, as a correspondent?"

"Together with my freelancing, I am doing all right. For that I get paid in euros."

"Funny looking money they have now in Europe. I haven't been back to Germany for a long time. It is a different generation now. I am myself from Dresden. You still speak your Munich dialect."

"I can speak High German."

"No, I understand your Bavarian."

Anton then talked about his visit to Gert Lutz and told Hans of the new movement of nationalsocialists.

"These young people who claim themselves to be Nazis, most are rabble. Nothing like it must have been when you, Otto and Gerhard were in Germany."

"I agree. What I have seen and heard, it is nothing of what we presented, the movement, the comradeship."

"As an Egyptian, I am in with the Brotherhood in Cairo. They oppose the Zionists as I do."

"Then you support the Muslims? Good, I fully agree with you. I am with the Muslims also; I became a Muslim a long time ago, though my son is still a Christian. I fully support the Palestinians in their fight against the Zionists."

It was already evening when they went to the hotel. Though Anton saw children, he was never introduced to them or to the women he saw who must be Mohammed's wife.

In a white Nissan pickup, Hans drove to the nearby hotel. Anton had brought along his bag as he was to stay at the hotel. There, Anton was introduced to his son Mohammed. Mohammed was like his father, small in stature but without a beard.

As the owner of the hotel, he wore a suit, his shirt without a tie. They had dinner together, a fine German meal of a roast leg of lamb with salad and potatoes.

After they had eaten, they sat together with glasses of Jordanian beer. Once Hans said to his son, "Might be good time to take care of your personal business, Mohammed." While Anton did not pay particular attention to this, he later realized what it meant. His handbag had been searched. When Mohammed returned, he said to his father, "My business turned out fine. No problem."

While he was gone, Anton complained about his arm, "It itches and burns terrible. I was on a picnic before I went to Cairo and I must have touched some poisonous plants."

"I have some soothing ointment at home," Hans offered.

"Do you mind if I take my jacket off, Hans?"

"Please do. The other guests don't wear jackets. It is out of season right now and most of my guests are traders from up north or Jordan." Anton took his jacket off and then rolled the blue shirtsleeve up. His forearm now all red and small blisters showed.

"This looks terrible, Anton. My ointment won't help for that. You should see a doctor."

"Do you have a good doctor here in Hebron?"

"Yes, we do." Just then Mohammed came back.

"Look at that arm, Mohammed, doesn't that look awful?"

"He should see doctor Abu Shanab, his specialty is dermatology," Mohammed said.

Hans told Anton, "Yes, first thing tomorrow morning, Anton. It is just a few blocks down the road. Mohammed will take you."

Mohammed commented, "I won't be in the hotel until ten."

Anton said, "If it is not far, I can walk. It is nice and cool in the morning."

Hans then asked, "So tell me about your teaching the Mujahedin bomb making. You were in an al-Qaeda camp, when?" Anton told his story, omitting most. That it was in August 1998 at the invitation of the Egyptian Islamic Jihad.

Hans asked, "You are a member of the Islamic Jihad, Anton?"

Anton smiled. "I can't be, I am a Christian. Only Muslims can be members. I was invited by Emir bin Laden as his bomb making experts had gone to North Africa; remember the embassy bombings? The Islamic Jihad in Cairo arranged my visit and they sent a group of jihadists along to protect me." He continued telling his story how each week he schooled a dozen freedom fighters the art of bomb making, including Mohamed Atta, who wished to crash a plane laden with exposives into a target.

When Mohammed interjected that Atta used large passenger planes, Anton explained that first bin Laden and his military advisor, Atef wanted to use explosive laden small planes. He had taught Atta and made the fuses for just such small planes, "Of course, they never used them as they realized that a large plane full of fuel can do more damage. And as we now know, Atef was right." He told of the American bombardment with missiles of his camp, al-Badr. He also told how bin Laden and al-Zawahiri came to visit the camp after the missile strike and how he met al-Zawahiri.

"I see that you are devoted to the jihad cause?" Hans said.

"I am in the image of Otto Nagil. His enemies are my enemies."

"The Americans, British, Russians and Jews?"

"Foremost the Jews. Remember, *die Juden sind unser Unglueck* (the Jews are our misfortune)? It still is."

"You should live here," Hans suggested. "Many opportunities to kill Jews. I was in charge of the Vilna ghetto, killed thousands of them but not enough. The military always prevented us from cleaning up completely. I knew your father well. We sent him many to get rid of them in Fort IX. However, that is all past, new work to be done here and now. Let me ask you Anton, you are an explosive expert?"

"I learned it in the Egyptian army, special forces. I served for three years, left as a captain and was for many years in the reserve as a major. Here, let me show you my ID card as a major in the reserve." He took it out of his wallet and showed it do Hans, who scrutinized it closely, then showed it to his son.

"I went to the University of Cairo and became a chemical engineer, so I knew already about explosives. It was my specialty in the army. Why, can I help you with something along this line?"

Mohammed said, "We have an explosive belt which a martyr put on and went into Jerusalem, but it didn't work. He had to bring it back."

"Probably a loose wire somewhere or old batteries?"

"The batteries were new, I put new ones in," explained Mohammed.

"How could he get into Jerusalem? I thought, with their damned wall they are building, that it is impossible to get in?"

Hans said, "Through the Negev, if needed to. But that would be a long way and the martyrs might be discovered. We bring them in through Jerusalem in a car. Someone who lives in Jerusalem and has a passage pass, and one made out for our man, forgeries of course, but genuine looking, really a residence permit. The belt is easily enough hidden in the car, separate from the explosive sticks; they can't take a car apart."

"Don't they use dogs to sniff out explosives?"

Mohammed said, "We pack the sticks into plastic, and we add a smell dogs don't like."

"As you can see, my son has taken over my work. My eyes, even with glasses, are not as good anymore and my hands tremble," Hans said.

"I don't think I am able tonight. I had too many beers. It is delicate work."

Hans told him, "No, not tonight, tomorrow after you come back from the doctor."

"You don't keep your things here in the hotel, I hope?"

Mohammed laughed, "No, in case of a mishap it would be terrible, what with many guests in the hotel. We have a secure place."

It was past midnight before they finished telling their stories. However, there was nothing about their present involvement in this terrorist attack and the kidnapping of children. Mohammed gave Anton the key to his room and told him that the restaurant opens up for breakfast at seven. "Just tell the waiter what you like; he knows that you are our guest here. Dr. Abu Shanab opens his clinic at nine. I already called him before that you are coming and introduced you as a good friend of ours and told him your name. His clinic is on the same Shaddad Street, number 53. Just two blocks away, walk east from here." He looked at Anton's arm. "It looks nasty." They told each other *Gute Nacht* (good night) and shook hands. In his room, Anton saw that his handbag had been searched. They were cautious, but so was he.

DAY THREE

Anton showered in cold water—some hotel that can't even provide hot water for its guests.

He had a light breakfast, the Arabian coffee was excellent and he had several cups. Anton was dressed in his white cotton suit, which was fine this morning as it was cloudy and rather cool. He walked east from the hotel; Shaddad Street must be one of the better neighborhoods of Hebron as all the houses were villas. Two blocks and he came to a compound. The house number was 53, and there was a sign in Arabic at the gated entrance:

Dr. MUSTAFA ABU SHANAB
DERMATOLOGY & MINOR SURGERY

He rang the bell by the gate and a servant in traditional Arab dress came and asked if he was Anton Nagil. He followed the man through a rose garden into the smaller addition to the villa.

There he met the doctor, a middle aged and handsome man with a mustache, looking very much like the actor Omar Sharif. He was dressed in a doctor's coat. With him, his assistant whom he introduced as his wife Sadia; she was a truly beautiful woman. She would be the joy of any man, but as Anton understood, he was a womanizer and even the most beautiful woman was not enough for him. After the usual salutations and introductions, it was business.

"My friend Mohammed al-Sharif called me last evening and said his guest, Anton Nagil has a bad eczema, may I see?"

Anton took his jacket off which the assistant Sadia hung on a coat hanger. He rolled his shirt sleeve up and Anton was surprised how nasty his arm looked. From his wrist up to his elbow, it was red, swollen and with many small blisters and it had begun to burn, not only itch.

The doctor examined his arm; Sadia looked at it and shuddered, the doctor even looked at the blisters with a magnifying glass.

"A classic case of poison ivy or oak. When did it begin to itch and redden? Where have you been the past couple of days? You didn't get it from here; we don't have such poisonous plants."

"I come from Germany. Saturday we were on a picnic and I remember that we played ball and I tripped and fell into some nettles. Could nettles have such an effect? It started to itch yesterday and today it burns."

"Yes, if you are allergic to the poison in nettles. I clean it with hydrogen peroxide and put some soothing cream over it, then a light bandage around your arm to keep the blisters from opening and prevent any infection. Do you have to wear that jacket?"

"Yes, I am a reporter for the al-Ahram paper in Cairo, and when interviewing I need to be dressed properly. I saw Abbas yesterday. Tomorrow I will have an interview with the Archbishop in Bethlehem, again I need to be dressed properly."

"You are Egyptian then? So am I, from Cairo."

"I am from Cairo, also. When I left there yesterday it looked like an *al-Asifa*—a storm was coming."

Without even looking surprised the doctor asked, "Over Cairo or *al-Ard*—the land?"

"The land." Anton smiled. The doctor turned to his assistant. "Sadia, please leave us alone, I have to check Anton Nagil completely." Turning to Anton, "You can undress behind the curtain here."

Sadia left them alone.

After she had left, the doctor told Anton not to undress but come with him to his office next door. He closed the door, "Here we can talk freely. I am amazed the Shin Bet sent me a genuine patient."

"You didn't seem to be surprised when I said the code word?"

"I expected it. You see, I am really an experienced dermatologist. In examining the little blisters, I saw that they were not active pustules, but caused by some irritation material, a fake rash but looking genuine to the untrained eye. Did you show it to Mohammed and Hassan? Yes? Well, a legitamite reason for you to visit me. So you are a Shin Bet agent and came to seek the children?"

"No, I am not a Shin Bet agent. Who I am is not important but as a reporter I am free to travel wherever I wish to go. I was asked to get information about two kidnapped children; I don't approve kidnapping children and using them as hostages. How the Shin Bet involved me is not important."

"But you knew the code words, so there must be a connection with them. Again, as you said, it is not important. Here is what I know and why I know about the children. First, I must tell you that Mohammed and I are good friends. We both enjoy certain activities and Mohammed accompanies me on my monthly trips to Amman." Anton remained silent though he knew what activities the good doctor was talking about. "Otherwise, we lead our own lives. His father, Hassan, is a member of the Palestinian Islamic Jihad but Mohammed is not. Both are very anti-Zionist, though Mohammed really doesn't hate Jews as his father does. My own beliefs . . ."

"I understand your liberal philosophy, Doctor. The children?"

"Two days ago, Mohammed called me on the phone and asked me to accompany him in the evening to a patient, a little girl who was injured. A minor surgery I was supposed to do.

"He came at nine in the evening when it was dark and I took my surgical kit along. In his Nissan, he made me swear that what I see I must never tell anyone. I did, though I had no idea what it was all about, except that he needed a doctor. He then told me that for my own safety, he would have to blindfold me. He did. I sat next to him in front. He drove for about an hour, maybe a little less. I understood it was to hide the destination. I knew where we were going. I make house calls often, and I am familiar with all the roads leading from Hebron in every direction. Also I knew it was going uphill first, and then again and again. He was really driving me in a circle. When we stopped, he led me blindfolded into a structure. Then he and someone else assisted me climbing down the ladder. There was light as I could distinguish under my blindfold and then it was taken off. At once, I heard the whimpering of a child. "I found myself in a small room, the walls and ceiling made of concrete, a plain light bulb illuminated the room. There in a corner huddled two little children under blankets. He took the blanket off one and I saw it was a little nude girl. Her legs were bloodstained and she began to cry.

"I asked, 'Who is she?'

"Mohammed said, and by the way we were now alone, whoever had been with him had left, 'You don't need to know, Mustafa. The children are trade objects to get many of our men back incarcerated by the Zionists.'

"'A Jewish girl?' I asked. He just shrugged his shoulders. I saw at once what had happened to the little girl; she had been raped repeatedly and she kept her legs parted. She was still bleeding.

"'Mohammed, I told him, 'that is stupid what someone did to her. Even if she is a Jew girl, to rape a child so young is criminal. Also, if she is Jewish, why would a Muslim wish to touch her?'

"He again shrugged his shoulders, 'I agree, it is stupid and unworthy of a Muslim, but we could only hide them here and there is a man living here who is rather cruel. He assured me he would not touch her again. So please, Mustafa, fix her up so the bleeding stops.'

"I tried to be gentle with her. She did not understand Arabic, she spoke in what I realized was Hebrew, and she cried bitterly. Of course, injecting a local anesthetic hurts and she screamed. But then when it became numb, I had no trouble stitching up her torn membrane tissues, though the poor thing was still crying. I then bandaged up her wounds. I also gave her an injection of an antibiotic.'"

"What else did you see in the room?"

"The other child huddled under a blanket, I never saw. There was a bucket, foul smelling, where the children must relieve themselves in. The whole room stank, some torn newspapers, a can with water, and two plastic dishes like you feed dogs with, in one still some rice. Yes, there was a door leading to another room.

"When I was finished Mohammed put the blindfold on me again. I climbed up the ladder. He came behind me and then he spoke angrily to someone; told him to have the bucket emptied and to leave the trap door open to air the room out.

"I was then driven straight back, took about ten minutes, and when he took the blindfold off, I was in front of my house. Mohammed then said to me, 'Mustafa, forget what you have seen or heard. It is all necessary for our cause.'

"I said to him, 'I have seen or heard nothing,' and he seemed satisfied."

"And where is this place, Doctor Shanab?"

"I am almost certain that we were in the village of Bani Na'im. Oh, about ten kilometers from Hebron, up in the hills, the only road leading out to the east."

"And where do you think the children are hidden in that village?"

"I don't know for certain. However, I believe in the compound of the mukhtar. Mukhtar Abu al-Adhami."

"Why do you believe it is him?"

"First, it is well known that the mukhtar is a member of the jihad. Also, I heard chickens all over the place, and more so when we entered the structure. I have been to his house and his chicken coop is a small concrete structure. There must be a trapdoor inside that leads down."

"Do you have a cell phone I can use, doctor?"

"Yes, I do. But you cannot use it. Your call can be traced to me."

"I just need to say two words. If it gets intercepted it has to be a large communication center which I doubt is available anywhere except in Amman or Cairo."

"It is dangerous for me. You are certain about limited interception? Two words only?"

"Yes."

He gave Anton his cell phone, who dialed, listened, and when he heard a man's voice, "Ken?" said quickly, "Sav, Bani Na'im." He pushed the End button and gave the doctor the phone back.

"You have weapons for sale?"

"What do you need?"

"A small pistol I can hide easily on me."

"I have one which is small. I hate to part with it as I use it myself on some trips. We have bandits around here."

"I see to it that you get it back, perhaps by another patient with a rash on his arm."

The doctor unlocked a cabinet and took out a very small pistol. Anton read *Bauer Automatic* on the outside as the manufacturer; he was not familiar with it.

"It is a BAUER STAINLESS, 6.35 mm, only four inches long, weighs less than a half pound and I have only one clip with six bullets. But let me advice you Anton, with the short barrel, it doesn't have much power, better shoot twice if you have to use it." Anton worked the chamber back and forth, it moved smoothly. He put the magazine in and chambered a round.

"I doesn't have a safety device, you are ready to shoot now."

"How much?"

"Two hundred dollars. The money I will give back when someone returns the pistol. You in your flat suit, even the small bulge of the pistol would show. I have an idea."

"What else do you have I could use?"

"Look yourself."

Anton checked inside, there were two more pistols, more powerful but much larger, an Uzi, and boxes with ammunition. Then he also saw half a dozen long metal tubes.

"What are these?"

"Flares. They work like fireworks. You pull the end of the tube back which expands a spring inside, release the little knob and it springs back and ignites a small charge which shoots the burning flare out." Anton counted out two hundred dollars. "And for these flares, for two?"

"A gift."

"You said before you have an idea how I can hide the pistol on me?"

"Yes. But let me first clean you and put some soothing cream on your arm and wrap a bandage around so they see that I did something for you, you my patient." He cleaned with saline and applied a cream from a jar, then wrapped a bandage around the forearm and taped it. He then took a white cloth and made a sling, braced Anton's arm up, and into the fold of the sling inserted the pistol. While his arm was now kind of immobilized, Anton knew that when needed, he would just pull his arm out of the sling. The two metal tubes of flares he stuck inside his pants into his socks, the wide trouser legs hiding them nicely. "Well hidden," the doctor commented. He also gave him a prescription for some antihistamines against the itching.

"We are appreciating what you do for us, Doctor Shanab."

"Let's say I wish to do something for the poor girl."

Anton walked back to the hotel; it was almost noon. In the lobby, he met Mohammed and Hans. Since Anton carried his jacket and had his left shirtsleeve rolled up, they saw the bandaged arm.

Hans asked, "So what did the doctor say?"

"That I must be allergic to the nettles I fell in. He cleaned my arm, put a cream on it and gave me a prescription for the itching. He said I should keep my arm in a rest."

Mohammed asked, "Do you wish to get the medicine first? Have lunch before we go?"

"No. Let's take a look at the belt, I have all afternoon. The cream did wonders."

They got into the Nissan pickup and Mohammed drove. He followed the dirt road east when they came out of town; a bumpy road going steadily uphill and around many curves. Then they came to the whitewashed village of Bani Na'im before them, there was a wooden sign, and to the right, in the distance the minaret of a mosque. To his great disappointment, Anton did not see the commando unit he expected, not a single Israeli soldier to be seen. A foul up somewhere, even the efficient Israeli army can make mistakes. He knew he had to get those two terror stricken children to safety and the girl to a hospital. He was on his own and he was very angry! Mohammed stopped before one of the better looking houses in the middle of the village and honked the horn. The gate was opened and they drove into the large courtyard.

The one who had opened the gate was a younger man in a dirty robe, a servant? The other elderly, looked clean and with a white beard, barefoot in sandals, white robe and turban. Hans, speaking Arabic, introduced the man as Mukhtar Abu al-Adhami, "And this is my friend, Anton Nagil with whose father I cleaned up Lithuania of Jews." They did their salutations, al-Adhami cursed all Jews; his eyes flashed menacing.

Hans said, "Anton Nagil is an expert of explosives and bombs, he wishes to look at the belt."

"It is not dangerous?" the mukhtar asked.

Mohammed replied, "I removed the dynamite sticks, I told you."

They followed the mukhtar to a small structure in the garden where the servant already chased the chickens out. Inside, the trapdoor was opened.

Hans asked, "The goods have been removed?"

"Yes," answered the mukhtar. To his servant he said, "Salim, turn the bulb to give us light, then you can leave." Salim climbed down the ladder, the light came on and he returned and went outside. The mukhtar went down first, then Hans, followed by Anton and Mohammed came last. The room they were in was made of concrete, while it was empty now, there was still a bad odor. Anton knew he was at the right place; the children had been here.

Mukhtar commented, "Underground it always smells bad." He unlocked the door and they came into another concrete room where he reached up and turned the bare bulb for light. Anton saw wooden shelves. There were the sticks of explosives, the empty belt, and boxes with ammunition. On the wall hung several Kalashnikov rifles and one American M-16 rifle. To his delight, he also saw several metal handcuffs on the bottom shelf. Anton wished he knew if the rifles were loaded. He had to rely on his little pistol. As he looked around, he found a small door about three feet high—leading to what? He heard nothing from inside.

Mohammed took the belt and gave it to Anton who examined the detonator. "There is nothing wrong with it," he laughed. "Your martyr became anxious to spare his life, he never pushed the button."

"The miserable coward," shouted Hans, "all the trouble we went through to get him into Jerusalem and then they saw him go into the market filled with Jews."

Anton laughed, "No virgins for him."

Hans screamed, "Who gives a damned about the virgins, to kill Jews is what I want!"

Anton suggested, "I can rig the detonator so it goes off by dialing a preset number, or even just pushing a button on the cell phone."

Hans commanded him, "Do it."

"I need a cell phone," Anton said.

Hans gave him his. Of course, without proper equipment he could not do it. He fussed around with the detonator, added a little wire. Then told Hans, "All you need to do is to push the End button on the cell phone and the belt will detonate."

Anton had come to seek information about the children and that was all Deputy Barlev had asked him to do. However, what he had learned from Doctor Shanab changed his mission and he would have to try to find and rescue the children and get the girl to a hospital. He would have to act alone as the commando unit was not outside the village. Either the children were behind the small door or he would have to make them talk, that is most likely the mukhtar knew where they are, or even the servant. He knew that even if his pistol did not work, he could handle these three men. He was angry, in fact in a silent fury. It had been hard for him to keep his friendly composure, but now this was no longer necessary. His heart ws pounding madly as he went into action.

With one quick shrug he threw off his jacket which hung over his shoulders, he reached into the sling, grabbed his pistol and pulled his arm free. He yelled at them, his voice was cutting and his eyes dangerous, "All of you raise your hands or you get shot." He pointed the pistol at the stomach of Hans, "And you are the first one to get shot." The three looked in shocked surprise at Anton.

Hans was the first to speak, "What is this? I don't understand Anton?"

Anton stared at Hans, his eyes like daggers, "What is there to understand? I am not Anton. We captured him today in Jerusalem. We made him talk and we found out that he was visiting you. You, Hassan Abu-Sharif, the kidnapper of little children, the murderer of their parents. I came in his place, I came to get the children!"

Hans was grim, "You are a goddamn Jew then? A Shin Bet agent?"

Anton slapped the old man with a sharp backhand that his glasses flew off, "That for the goddamn Jew! Now raise your hands or you get it right into you old belly!"

Mohammed said, "Do as he says, father. The Jew children aren't worth for you to suffer."

He turned to Anton, "Whoever you are, you can have the children. Just don't hurt my father." He raised his arms, so did the mukhtar, who uttered in rage, "Infidel, may Allah destroy you!" The mukhtar never saw the fist that smashed his nose and squirted blood all over his robe. Hans raised his arms, deep hatred in his eyes.

"Turn around, put your hands behind your back and don't move!" They complied. Anton cuffed each man; then told them to lay down on their stomachs. When the muktar didn't get down Anton kicked his legs away and he crashed to the floor.

"Who moves gets a bullet right up his ass. Tears your inside, so lay still! You behave. I get the children, you live."

Anton then took his steel pen, unscrewed the head, held it against the hand of Hans, worked the lever back, released and he could feel the charge escaping. There was no sound, only Hans said "Ouch, what was that?"

"Just shut up, Streller!"

Hans said, "That damned Jew even knows my old name."

Mohammed told him, "Father, why don't you just lay still, all he wants is the children."

"I want to see him try to get through the village with the Jew kids, they massacre him," Hans said.

"Father, please."

Anton bent down and pushed the bolt back on the small door and opened it. There was enough light that he could see the outline of small figures laying there covered with a blanket. He pulled the blanket off. In the semi-darkness he could see their nude bodies, they were tied up and when he pulled them out by their feet he saw their mouths taped. Their horror filled eyes looking at him. They did not understand what was happening to them, did not know that they were in the hands of the most evil and savage people in the world, a former SS officer and an Islamic fundamentalist.

Anton was angry enough that his first impulse was to kill the three. But he needed Mohammed. Hans Streller would die anyhow. And for the mukhtar, the rapist, he had something special in mind.

He spoke softly in Hebrew, "I am the man who came to take you home, Esther and David. Don't be afraid anymore. You understand me?" David nodded, Esther still in shock, her eyes wide open in terror. Anton first removed the tape from their mouths. The boy asked, still fearful, "Can I cry now?" Anton nodded and smiled; both began to cry bitterly.

On the shelf he had seen a knife and with it cut the ropes that held their arms to their bodies and around their legs. Esther at once parted her legs; she was hurting. She sat up and stretched out her little bare arms to Anton. She looked so fragile, pitiful; he picked her up and cuddled her, her tears wetting his face. She was whimpering softly. David stood up and put his arms around his legs, pressed himself against him. For a short while, Anton just stood still and let the children be.

He kissed the tearstained face of Esther, "Now we go home." She nodded. He put her down and draped his jacket around her; he saw she had burn marks. Cigarette burns! He buttoned the jacket in front, the poor child was standing there spread-legged; again a deep anger possessed Anton. The mukhtar, THE BEAST! He draped the blanket around David; he too had burn marks all over his small body.

"Just stand still here for a moment, Esther and David, I have to look upstairs." He had whispered to them and just as quietly and urgently, David whispered back, "Don't leave us," and Esther whispered "Don't leave ish—man." Anton had to smile for a moment, would he ever be anything to his children than "the man"? He put Esther's hand in that of David. "David, now for just a minute you must guard your little sister. These bad men won't hurt you anymore. See how they are tied up? I just need to look up to see where Salim is."

"A bad woman is here," said David. "Bad woman, bad men," the children had no comprehension in their limited minds and words in what hellish place they had been in and why bad things had been done to them.

"Come with me to the ladder," said Anton. He had them stand by the ladder holding on to each other and climbed up. He saw the servant by the house. He called to him,

"Salim, mukhtar Al-Adhami wants you to come down." When the servant climbed down the ladder, he hit his neck forcefully and Salim fell paralyzed. Again he climbed up and looked around, no one to be seen. He couldn't see past the wall. The village seemed quiet.

"Mohammed, stand up!" It wasn't easy to get up with hands cuffed behind, but he managed. "Mohammed, I understand you love your father, right? You don't want him to get hurt?" The man nodded. "Then you do exactly as I tell you. Understand?" He nodded again and said, "Just don't hurt him. You can go safely with the children."

Anton yanked Hans up, the old man spit in his face, he gave him a sharp backhand. His nose and lips gushed blood; then fastened the belt around Hans and inserted the dynamite sticks.

"Mohammed, you go with us, you drive us to Hebron, to Kefar Etzion. Any treachery and I activate the cell phone and explode your father."

"They will arrest me."

"I promise you, if you get us there safely, we get out before and you can turn around and go back and free your father."

"All right, I do as you say."

"Who burned the children?"

"It must have been Najiba, the mukhtar's wife. He said she played with them."

"You call torturing little children playing?" Mohammed shrugged his shoulders.

"Now get up the ladder, I help you that you won't fall. Crawl a man's length away and lay there. Don't get up or I kill all of you. Where are the keys to the handcuffs?"

"There are on the bottom of the shelf."

Anton found them. He took Mohammed by the arm and walked him to the ladder, helped him get up. Right behind him he watched Mohammed crawl a short distance and lay down again. He took David's hand off Esther's, "Now David, get up the ladder and sit right behind the bad man. Then when Esther comes up you have her sit by you and hold her hand again." He was right behind David as the little boy climbed the ladder and sat down. Poor Esther couldn't climb, she was hurting too much. Anton took her into his arms and carried her up, sat her next to her brother who at once held her hand. The children had stopped crying but Esther was whimpering.

Anton went back down, he now acted quickly. He took the M-16, he preferred it to the AK-47, more accurate. He worked it and it was well kept. He inserted a magazine of fifteen bullets and stuck two other clips into his belt.

He grabbed the mukhtar by his beard and yanked him up, pulled him to the corner and slammed him into the wall. He looked fearful now as Anton's eyes were staring at him in fury. Anton hissed, "You will never again rape a little girl!"

He reached down, drew the flare from his sock, charged it, held it toward the lower belly of the mukhtar and fired. There was the explosion of the charge, a flame shot out from the tube. He never saw the flare but the bright fire on the lower torso of the hand-cuffed man as the magnesium flare burnt into him. Then his robe was in flames. The mukthar's unearthly shrieks followed him up the ladder. Anton went to the gate and unbolted it, opened it, looked outside; a few men and women had gathered as even up here the shrieks could be heard.

He heard the shrill screams of David and Esther. He turned, saw an old woman drag the little boy by his hair toward the house. She saw him running to her, in her hand a dagger poised to cut David's throat. She was yelling in high-pitched screams. For a moment the picture of dancing women with lifted arms and trilling in joy after the towers fell flashed in his mind. A lightning fast and hard jab with the edge of his flat hand against her throat which severed both her trachea and esophagus and the old woman was trashing on the ground, convulsing, unable to breath, her fruitless gasping for air mixing with the shrieks from below. He put her dagger into his belt.

Anton picked up David and returned to Esther, uncuffed Mohammed; then had them follow him to the pickup. He put both children into the back and told them to lie down and not even raise their heads. He put David's blanket over both of them. Then he got into the passenger side of the pickup, and told Mohammed to drive. When they passed out of the gate, Anton saw many people who had gathered in front, some of the men were carrying rifles. He fired a burst from his M-16 at their feet and they scattered in panic, some fell, hit by the ricocheting bullets.

When Mohammed raced down the street, Anton told him to drive slower. "The girl is hurting, try to avoid bumps." He drove slower.

Mohammed spoke, "Look, whoever you are. I admit, we were involved with the kidnapping, but we never meant to hurt the children. This was all the mukhtar's and his wife's doing. He is an animal. What did you do to him? He screamed terrible."

"You don't want to know." They left the village.

"Mohammed, I see some humanity in you, you didn't want the children hurt. Why don't you pack up and move to Germany. Forget all about the fanatical Palestinians and their way of terror. You have a nice wife and children. Live like decent people."

"I would, it is because of my father; we have always been close. I am a Christian, not a Muslim with their fanatical religion, their Prophet Mohammad who in one hand offer's them their Koran and in the other the bomb. My father was never an observant Muslim. It disgusted him to see a bunch of men with their heads on the floor like slaves and their rumps up in the air. It was this Jew hatred business that he became a Muslim. Once he is gone, I sell everything and get out. You didn't hurt him back there?"

"Mohammed, I swear to you, I didn't touch him again."

"You swear by your Jehowa?"

"I am not Jewish."

"Who are you, then?"

"I am not a Jew or Muslim but Christian. Who I am is not important."

Mohammed looked briefly at Anton, "But you must be a German. You speak the language fluently. You didn't learn it, you were born with it."

Anton replied, "Perhaps."

"Then you understand. We Germans are superior to both the Jews and the Muslims; that my father taught me since I was a boy. They are both Semites. I am German and want to live among my own kind. Get away from these primitive people."

"Why then did you marry a Muslim?'

Mohammed laughed, "Who else was there? No German women around. What I don't understand is that your Arabic is also perfect, you speak it like a native."

Anton did not answer.

"Look, cars are following us. Should I drive faster? Some in the village have rifles."

"No, keep driving slow," Anton told him.

There were three cars following and still pretty far back. Anton used the butt of the rifle to knock the back window out then crawled through it, laid down by kids.

"Esther, David, I am back here with you. When you hear my rifle shoot, don't be afraid. I am just shooting at some cars with bad men following us." He crawled to the end of the pickup, a quick glance over the tailgate; they were closing in fast, raising a cloud of dust behind. He put the rifle on automatic, flipped the safety off. When he heard the car behind, it was an old diesel, he raised his rifle and head, fired a burst at the driver. The glass splintered and the man slumped over, another burst at the two men sitting next to him. The car went off the road and overturned several times. Now he saw the other car behind. A quick reloading of a new magazine, he shot. The rifle misfired. Anton yelled at Mohammed, "Race!" The pickup lurched forward; now they were raising a cloud of dust. He drew his pistol and the other flare. The car came alongside, trying to cut them off. Anton quickly looked over the side, the man looking out the window aimed his Kalashnikov at the back of the cab where he had been before. Anton fired twice with his pistol, the man slumped down; his rifle fell on the road. Then he fired the flare through the open window. There was an immediate fire inside and the car dropped back. The third car kept coming—fanatics. Then he heard Mohammed yell.

"LOOK ANTON!" Mohammed still called him by his name.

Around the curve going downhill, Anton saw the most beautiful sight!

A column of Israeli military vehicles racing toward them in a cloud of dust.

"Stop, Mohammed." The pickup came to a screeching halt.

"The car following us has turned back!" Mohammed yelled. The car had turned around and was speeding away; farther back, Anton saw the two burning wrecks.

"Mohammed, when I have the children out you can go back too."

Anton first threw the useless M-16 on the road, then climbed down and lifted the two children out and held them in his arms—the Nissan raced away.

There, Anton stood in the middle of the road with the two children in his arms, their little arms around his neck, their faces pressed to his, still in fear.

The first car, a jeep, came to a halt before him. A uniformed man approached him, "I am Commander Amir; these are the children?"

"Yes, David and Esther. I see an ambulance in your column, the girl needs attention."

"We have a doctor and a nurse with us. Please follow me; may I take one of the children?" They clung tightly to him; he carried them both. A soldier came up with a camera. "Please, no pictures, Commander Amir. I cannot afford to be known and no mention of me."

"But we need your name, you saved the children."

"No picture, no name. Check with Deputy Barlev from the Jerusalem police, he understands." The commander waved the soldier with the camera away, "No pictures!"

They came to the ambulance, the female nurse in uniform took Esther from his arm and this time she let herself be taken. The uniformed man who identified himself as the doctor took David. The commander told Anton, "I take the kids back to Kefar Ezion; then I will arrange to have you taken wherever you wish to go . . . *sav*, I don't know what else to call you?"

"*Sav* is fine. But you better take Esther to a hospital, she needs immediate care." Just then the doctor came back, returned his jacket. "I have to take the girl to the hospital in Jerusalem, commander; she has been raped and injured. The boy can return to Kefar Ezion."

"David needs attention also, he has painful burns. These aren't dirt marks over his body but cigarette burns. You better let the kids stay together; they have been through terrible times, they need each other now without their parents," suggested Anton.

"The girl is calling for her mother," responded the doctor. "Might be a good idea to keep them together."

The commander replied, "Then we all go together. I have only orders to bring you back. And now of course, also the children."

Anton walked back to the jeep with the commander. He sat in the back; then the driver turned around and went along the column of the many jeeps, each one cheering as they drove by. All vehicles turned and the column headed to Jerusalem.

The commander spoke on his cell phone, reported that the mission is completed, "Yes, the children are safe and with me . . . and yes, Inspector Nagil, also." He handed the phone to Anton,

"Deputy Barlev of the Jerusalem police wishes to speak to you."

"Yes, deputy?"

"I thank you in the name of Israel, shalom." The connection went click.

"At least I know your name now, Inspector Nagil."

"And what kept you? I called in at noon, now it is three in the afternoon?" Anton did not sound angry, rather amused.

"Lack of proper communication, all my fault. I was called to a staff meeting at noon and did not return until a short time ago when I received your message. I was told to expect your call any time after today. While we manned the phone, my man did not know your code name. You wish to tell me, Inspector Nagil."

"Not really. I am sorry but I am tired."

"May I ask one question please, what happened to the rapist?"

"He burned in hell!"

A couple hours later, they were at the Hadassah hospital in Jerusalem where white clad medical personnel received the children.

"May I take you home, Inspector Nagil?"

Anton gave him the address.

It was almost six o'clock when Hanna and Amal heard the sound of a convoy approach and when they looked down from the balcony, Danny in Hanna's arms, they saw the many military vehicles stop by their house. From the first car, their man emerged with a uniformed soldier who shook his hand and saluted him.

Then they saw the soldiers come out of their vehicles and stand by them and when Toni walked to the gate they cheered him, saluted him and some shook his hand as if he was some kind of personality—or hero? Hanna, with Danny in her arms rushed down to the gate. The convoy drove off, the soldiers were waving to her now and Danny waved to them.

Hanna fixed her dark eyes on Toni and demanded in a determined voice, "And now Anton Nagil, you tell me, and all of it!" But already Danny stretched his arms out to Anton and he took his boy into his arms.

"Later Hanna, later."

In the evening, Deputy Barlev called and asked Inspector Nagil to come by, at his convenience. Anton promised and also requested that his name not be mentioned in any public statement. "But then we don't have a story? By the way Nahik Rubin is still with me."

"That suits me just fine," replied Anton, "Give my best to Rubin."

"Then please come by for a police report." Anton promised.

(Deputy Barlev looked at Nahik Rubin, "Who is this man really? He left Sunday for Cairo to get information and now, three days later he comes back with the children." Nahik Rubin told him what he knew about Anton Nagil. It wasn't much, and added, "By the way Deputy, when he told you that he went to an al-Qaeda training camp at the invitation of Osama bin Laden, that was true."

The mukhtar, Abu al-Adhami died a horrible death. His wife Najib died within a few minutes. Within the hour, Hassan al-Sharif passed unexpectedly away. When Mohammed returned, his father was already dead. The servant Salim recovered from his blow, but was paralyzed. Mohammed Sharif would in due time sell his hotel, the house and with his family move to Dresden where he had relatives.)

As had become the habit of Hanna, after they had supper, they went into the living room and Hanna played on the piano. Before Danny was put to bed, she would play light music, melodies for children, "I have a new lullaby for Danny. I play it on the piano and later I sing it to him and he turns around and before I finish he is asleep. Want to hear it, Toni?"

"Of course I do. What is it called?"

"It is a song for Danny and it is called 'Danny Boy,' right, Danny? It is your song?" Danny who sat on Anton's lap nodded smiling.

"I have it on a tape of Harry Belafonte; I mean, he sings all these songs. I don't know all the words to it yet, then I just hum along. I learned to play from listening to the tape; I should try to get the sheet music. Of course, I can never sing it as beautiful as that Belafonte guy does."

"You have a beautiful voice, Hanna. Let's hear it."

When she played and sang "Danny Boy." Anton knew it was one of the old-time folksongs, which make one immediately catch the melody and remember it. Then of course, it was also special as it was Danny's song. Soon Danny was put to bed and after he was kissed good night by all, he checked that his man was standing by the crib, stuck his thumb in his mouth, turned over and Hanna sang softly and before she finished, he was asleep.

Anton took a long hot shower, and as he enjoyed doing it, he sang. What old folksong could he sing? Then it came to him how he, Sidqi and Sasha had sung Evening Bells together. He would have to teach Hanna, maybe find a CD of it. Later he had Hanna put on some cold cream and bandage around his terrible looking forearm and had to explain to her that it was a gift of Deputy Barlev.

Then they sat together, with good wine late into the night and this time Anton told it all.

Hanna was happy that the children were at the Hadassah hospital where she volunteered and said that she would go in tomorrow to see the kids. When she asked Toni what he did with the pistol, he remembered it was still in his coat pocket. She wanted to see it and Anton got it after first removing the round in the chamber and taking the clip out.

When he gave it to Hanna she cried out, "That is a toy pistol! And with it you subdued these three men?"

"No, I had two more weapons." He showed her his hands, which really did not impress Hanna. He also showed her the beautiful dagger he had taken from the woman.

"Toni, can't you do something ordinary men do, like a businessman, have a store?"

"And sell what?"

For a moment Hanna could not think of what he should sell; then she blurted out, "Like milk, butter, cheese?"

"Can you really imagine me standing behind a counter? 'Yes, Mrs. Levy, a liter of milk, and a half pound of butter, some cheese perhaps?'"

She laughed, "No, I can't."

Amal pitched in, "Toni is a good policeman, be glad that he is doing something worthwhile for all people."

When they went to bed, Hanna left her husband alone though consumed with passion. She had seen him touch his bandaged arm repeatedly and understood that he couldn't concentrate. Silently, she cried herself to sleep; her Toni had been in danger again.

When in the morning Anton read the *Davar* paper they received, he saw the short article that "the Cohen children from Kefar Ezion had been found by a commando unit of the IDF, on a street near Hevron. The children, Esther and David are at the Hadassah hospital and well taken cared of."

When he showed it to Hanna, she was disappointed. "And not a word about their rescuer?" Anton explained that he could not afford to have his name printed. Not if he wished to stay on "friendly" terms with the Munich Islamic Center. "Who knows who reads the paper."

The next afternoon, Hanna went to the hospital. Anton stayed home to play with his son and took him for a walk in his stroller. He also called Deputy Barlev and made an appointment to see him after lunch.

After they ate and Danny was put to bed by Amal for his nap, Anton drove to police headquarters and went to Deputy Barlev's office. With a strong handshake and sincere words of appreciation for what he had accomplished, they sat together with glasses of tea. The deputy put a tape recorder on the table, adjusted the microphone, "Now, please Inspector Nagil, your report."

Anton told his story from the time he crossed the King Abdullah Bridge into Palestinian territory. After he had finished, the deputy apologized for the foul up, "My fault entirely. I had no idea that you find and rescue the children and in just three days. And the mukhtar is dead?"

"When I left him, he burned like a torch. His wife was breathless when I left her. So is Hans Stettner by now. I was assured that the cyanide, when shot into the extremities, would be fatal within the hour."

"His son, Mohammed?"

"I let him live. He is punished enough by the death of his beloved father. He is not the fanatic." He smiled. "And he doesn't care much for Muslims, nor did his father."

"We have to send an extra five hundred dollars to Dr. Shanab. His help led you to the village of Bani Na'im."

"Well, they would have taken me there anyhow. However, I would not have had knowledge that the children are in the chicken coop, or rather underneath. This brings up the point that I still have the small pistol. I paid for it and like to keep it."

"Will you let us reimburse you? No? Of course you can keep it, just register it with us. By the way, the commander of the unit brought us the M-16. You may keep it also, a sort of protection in your house."

"It misfired. But yes, I'd wish to have it."

"The cartridge was defective; otherwise it is in good order. We will register it for you. I give you a permit that you can buy ammunition for both weapons. Might be a good idea to teach your wife how to use it, one never knows. Now let me ask you something else, we would love to write the true story of what happened, you are averse to it, why?"

Anton laughed, "That is all I need, big headline in the *Davar* 'Inspector Anton Nagil from the Munich police helps free kidnapped children.' No thank you."

"You didn't help, you did it all."

"Well, it helped when your commando unit came charging like lancers. I was down to my toy pistol and four bullets."

"So why? Everyone likes to be a hero sometimes and you deserved it, it is human nature. Commander Amir told me he was so sorry that you didn't let the soldier take your picture with the two rescued children in your arms."

"Well, first of all I am not a glory seeker. What you said on the phone to me was my medal, so to speak. The award was the moment I held the two kids in my arms and your unit came up to me. Esther and David were safe. The why? I belong to the Munich antiterror unit. I am on bad terms with the neo-Nazis, but they present no problem. I am on good terms with the Muslim people, a friend of the clergy of the mosque and the Islamic Center. They trust me even though I killed their bomb maker which they don't know; they think it was an accident on his part."

"What was a bomb expert doing in Munich?"

"Sent letter-bombs to Jews. Now things are quiet, but who knows for how long? What the paper wrote this morning is just perfect. Only your department and the hospital know how the children were abused and tortured. All three who were guilty are no more."

"I understand and agree, Inspector. I told the hospital to hold back any news on the condition of the children. I make it permanent. Well, what else can I say than tell of my and Israel's gratitude."

They shook hands. At the door, the deputy turned, "Inspector Nagil, come by at my office any time you are in Jerusalem. May I consider you a friend?" Anton nodded. Back home, he wrapped the M-16 in a blanket and stashed it in the small attic.

When Hanna came home, she told about the children. Though Esther was in recovery, they had to change the stitches, "I saw her briefly; she was sleeping. Such a lovely girl with her black curls. But I talked with David; he is with the other children on a ward.
Being with other kids is the best medicine for him now. I told him I am the wife of the man who rescued him. He wants to see you, Toni. I told David that your name is Toni. He told me," she stopped, tears were rolling down her face, "that his mommy and daddy are in heaven with God and someday he will see them."

"Oh, Hanna, you are such an emotional woman." He took his wife into his arms and let her cry.

This was relaxing time for Anton. No police work, no problems, just taking care of his women and Danny. Hanna went again to the hospital in the afternoon. There were visitors from Ezion who saw David. They want to take the boy back as soon as the hospital releases him. While the Cohens, who came from South Africa, did not have any relatives in Israel, there were many couples that would love to take and raise the two children. Everybody thought that would be the best for David and Esther to be on home grounds and with the people they knew. Well, not everybody. Hanna related her visit to the hospital. "When I visited Esther, she was together with another little girl who had been in an accident, and a doctor who was a psychologist was with her. The doctor introduced himself as Dr. Shimon Herzog. When I smiled at Esther, the child smiled back at me.

I was told not to speak about what happened, but I had brought Esther a little stuffed monkey and gave it to her.

"'What is his name?' asked Esther as she cradled it.

"For want of a name I said, 'It is a Man-Monkey.'

"Esther shook her head, 'No. Just monkey. Man is he who took me away from the bad people.' I sighed and said, 'Not again.'

"'What is it?' the doctor asked.

"'Oh nothing,' I answered him.

"'So, why the sigh, the not again?'

"'The man she is talking about is my husband.'

"'Oh really? I only heard that the children were found on the street near Hevron.'

"'No. There is more to it. My husband, who rescued them, well, he is a German police inspector, but he wishes to remain anonymous because of his position there. I already told too much; please don't ask me any more questions. No, what I meant was, we have a little boy we are adopting, Danny is just a little over a year old and loves his to-be daddy. Because my mother, who lives with us, always refers to my husband as "the man." Danny picked that up and calls him "my man." And now Esther too referred to him the same way."

"The doctor smiled 'Nothing wrong with that. Esther needs people around her whom she trusts. You seem to get along fine with her.'

"I told him, 'I get along fine with all children. I am a volunteer nurse here in the hospital. You don't work here, Dr. Herzog? I have never seen you before.'

He explained, 'I work at the Mental Health Center in the city. They called me in for consultation. It isn't just that her body has been violated but also her mind, a real trauma, physical and mental.' He turned to the girl, 'Esther, do you wish to see the man, the one who took you away from the bad people?'

The little girl's eyes slit up. 'Yes' and despite her suffering, she smiled.

"'His name is Toni.' I smiled at her.

Esther shook her head, 'He is *ha ish* (the man).'

"'Oh god,' I said, and tears ran down my cheeks. I wiped them away, embarrassed.

"Dr. Herzog said, 'Nothing to be ashamed to cry, Hanna. We all could cry seeing her and knowing what happened. Have your husband come by tomorrow afternoon. I will be here with Esther every afternoon between two and four. It is then that she can have visitors while I am here. Her brother David is doing fine.'

"'Yes, I saw him yesterday. He too wants to see Toni. The poor guy told me that his mommy and daddy are in heaven, and he will see them some day.'

"Dr. Herzog then said, 'I had David in before to see his sister, and he just held her hand, and they talked. Well, we don't believe in a heaven and hell, but whoever told him, that did the right thing. The children must have something to believe in to overcome their grief.'

I told him, 'I might not talk about heaven, but there must be a hell, and those two child tormentors must be in it!'

Dr. Herzog agreed, 'They will be.'

"'THEY ARE! My husband made sure of that!' I said that loud enough that the other child in the next bed woke up. I went to her and spoke comforting to the child. When I left to visit David, I apologized to Dr. Herzog.

He smiled. 'You have a way with kids, Hanna.'

"'I guess the best thing is for the children to get back to Kefar Ezion as soon as Esther is healed?'

Dr. Herzog looked serious. 'I am not certain of that.'"

I then went to the ward where I found David kicking the ball along the hall with other boys. He asked where you are. He wants to see you, Toni. I told him that you would come for sure tomorrow.

Anton shook his head. "That I wished I would not have to do. I love them both. The more often I see them, the more attached I get to them. I am really sorry that they remember me."

"The doctor said that they should be with people they trust. Well, Anton Nagil, they trust you so you better visit them tomorrow." When Hanna addressed him by his full name, he knew he better do as she said.

Visiting time for children was between two and four in the afternoon. Visits to Esther were restricted to whomever Dr. Herzog permitted.

When Hanna and Anton came to the desk, the nurse went first into the room of the two children and then waved at them to come in. Before Hanna could even introduce Anton to Dr. Herzog, Esther cried out "the man" and stretched out her little arms to him.

"You can't lift her up, *Adon* Nagil," Dr. Herzog advised him. "She is in a contraption to keep her legs separated until the stitches come out."

Anton took her small hands and kissed them both. "How is my sweet Esther?"

"Fine," she said bravely.

Anton had brought her a box of chocolates, and while Hanna opened them and gave her a few to eat, Dr. Herzog introduced himself to Anton.

"In two days, her stitches should come out. Then another week, and she can leave the hospital. After her stitches are out, she can join David in the ward. Look at her eating and beaming at you." Anton sat at her bed. Hanna had taken the candy box to the other girl who was in traction and fed her chocolates.

"So my little Queen Esther is fine?"

She nodded, smiled. "I don't like tied."

"Soon you will be freed."

"Look the monkey Hanna gave me." The monkey was lying next to her, and when she pulled it from the cover, its legs were tied separate to small sticks. "Nurse Sara did it. The monkey hurt like me."

They only stayed a short time as other visitors from Ezion were waiting to see Esther. Hanna and Anton both kissed Esther when they said goodbye and promised her to come again the next day.

They then went to the ward to visit David, and for him, Anton had brought a yellow ball. David greeted him with "Hi. Toni" and at once wanted to be taken in his arms. In his arms, he told the other children, "Toni shot at the bad men."

Friday morning, Anton, Hanna, Danny, and Amal went to court; and the adoption of Danny, who was in Anton's arms, went smoothly. There had been some opposition by the religious people because it was a mixed marriage, but in the end, the religious court gave their blessing. When they left court, Daniel had become their legal son. "Now you can say *Avi'* to your daddy," said Hanna, which made Danny only smile and say "Ishi."

Every afternoon, Anton and Hanna visited the children. If they liked it or not, Esther and David became attached to them. As Dr. Herzog told them, "They are only waiting for your visit. There is going to be a problem when they return to Kefar Ezion and miss their parents." Two weeks later, when they came to the hospital they were told that the children had been returned to Kefar Ezion. It was the last week of October and the last week of Anton's leave.

Sunday morning, Anton took Hanna to the police rifle range; he had brought his M-16. An instructor spent a good while teaching Hanna how to shoot the rifle. The M-16, when fired semi-automatic has less kick than most other rifles. While she could never hit the bullseye, she did fine. She learned to load, operate and change magazines, and fire automatic. Anton knew that if need be, she would defend the house and family.

Early Monday morning, the telephone rang and Dr. Herzog was on the line; when he talked to Hanna he told her he wished to come by and talk to her and Anton. She invited him for lunch. After lunch, they sat together in the living room with a glass of wine.

Hanna asked, "How are the children doing?"

Dr. Herzog took a deep breath and exhaled sharply, "We are having problems. I was called by the hospital yesterday and asked to go to Kefar Ezion. I went there in the afternoon and found David and Esther sitting in front of their old house,

David holding his sister's hand and both crying. They had been back three days, and every day after school and kindergarten, the two go to their house and sit there, like I found them. The trauma is too deep for Esther, and David feels himself as her protector. I feel that even though they are with their people, it is not like being with their parents. A lack of trust for anyone." He looked at Hanna and then Anton, "Except for you two. I don't know your situation. I understand that Anton is a police inspector in Munich and has to return, probably only infrequently be able to come and visit here. The children need you both, desperately. They trust you, you are like . . . I did not know their mother and father, but they seem to accept you two like substitute parents. My recommendation is, for the sake of both, but especially Esther, that at least temporarily they should live with you. Would that be possible?"

When Anton looked at his wife, he saw her happiness. She looked at him, and he knew and understood. When she said, "Anton Nagil, what do you say?" His heart too was filled with joy! "Can you be a mother to three children, Hanna?"

"And don't forget me!" said Amal, "As a Jewish grandmother, I love to have a brood of grandchildren." Hanna couldn't say anything but nod emphatically.

Dr. Herzog smiled, relieved. "Then I can take that as a YES? Now just a few questions as I have to recommend the foster care. Anton, are you financially secure? In foster care, you would get a monthly allowance for the children. I am not certain but it must be around three or four hundred shekels a month per child."

"We are financillay independent. No problem there."

Dr. Herzog said, "Fine. Now may I see the house? It seems big enough for a family with three children."

They walked from the large living room to the hall and showed the doctor their three bedrooms, the master bedroom, then Danny's room, and last Amal's bedroom. At once, Amal announced that she would move down in the basement and sleep in the guest room.

"Oh mama, you are so good!" Hanna cried out and embraced her mother.

They took the doctor downstairs and showed him the large kitchen, dining room, the study and small library and the basement with the guest room and a bathroom. "We have to have another guest room built down here," Hanna said, "There is enough empty space." They went out into the garden; Anton explained that the swimming pool is heated thermally. "And as long as the sun shines, we have a heated pool."

"The swimming pool is fenced in, good. And I see there is enough garden for the children to play in. Perfect."

Hanna at once said to Toni that they must go into the city and buy furnishings for the bedroom. "I have to call Eliahu Zamir to help us move mother's things downstairs and store the guest room furnishing in the empty space."

Dr. Herzog asked, "Then by Wednesday?"

"It will all be ready for David and Esther."

Dr. Herzog said, "I start the paperwork and give you the authority to pick up the children on Wednesday. I call Kefar Ezion. I already told the administration that there is a possibility you might agree. The foster care will be partially under my control, though there will be authorities who will visit."

Even before the doctor had left, Hanna had called Eliahu and he promised to have the movers come and bring Amal's things downstairs. Later, Hanna and Anton drove into the city and in a furniture store bought two children's beds, dressers, a small table and chairs, all in cheerful white. In a linen goods-store, bedding; all to be delivered Wednesday morning.

Wednesday morning, the store brought the children's bedroom. The bedding came before noon, Hanna and Amal made the children's beds up. Danny watched with a puzzled smile on his face, not understanding what they said about siblings coming to live with him.

By Wednesday noon, all was ready. Punctually at one o'clock, a convoy of three jeeps arrived with Commander Amir in charge to take them to Kefar Ezion, which meant driving into the Westbank. Anton, in his Ford, with Hanna sitting next to him and on the floor between them his loaded M-16, they drove behind the first jeep.

The convoy arrived at the administration building of Kefar Ezion a little past three in the afternoon. Inside the administrator, his secretary, and a couple who had taken care of the children. Esther rushed at once into the arms of Anton and David to Hanna. Helpers put their things into the trunk of the car. This time, Hanna sat in the back with them when they left the compound with many of the residents by the gate and waving at them. The convoy made it safely back to Jerusalem. By six o'clock, they were back and drove through the gate where Amal awaited them. Anton said goodbye to Commander Amir. When he came into the dining room, the children were already having their supper and a happy Danny sat in his highchair looking and smiling at his siblings.

Amal cancelled her volunteer work at the hospital. Hanna would still go in on Saturdays. Arrangements had been made for David to go to school; a bus picked him up and returned him in the afternoon. Hanna drove Esther to the nearby kindergarten. During the next few days, Anton showed David and Ester how to use a computer and he bought them games for their age group, both for learning and playing. Hanna and Anton also decided to e-mail daily, if not calling, as Anton might be on duty or late in his office. Amal didn't wish to have anything to do with the computer, nor did Rosemarie.

The two children were kept busy with school, homework, on the computer and playing with Danny. As Dr. Herzog explained, "Keep them busy and love them, that is the best medicine."

Some of their male friends promised to come often when Anton was away.

Dr. Herzog would be a frequent visitor; Eliahu Shamir would come by almost every morning to see if the women needed any help. Commander Amir came once during the week, he had become a friend of the family. Barlev included their street in the nightly patrol of police cars. There was manpower available, if needed.

Then on Sunday morning at three o'clock, the taxi came to take Anton to the airport. Hanna was sad that he had to leave but she was a happy woman being the mother of three lovely children, busy and looking forward to Toni's next visit. He promised her that he would arrange his vacation time so he could leave once a month on Wednesday evening and spend the next four days at home. This would take only twenty-four days from his thirty days a year vacation. Then he had still a week to come during the year and long holidays. Hanna came to the gate in her nightgown, a last embrace and lingering kiss and Anton was gone.

Anton was home Sunday noon and had much to tell Rosemarie, well not all. He told her that they took little Esther and David as foster children as their parents had been killed.

"Yes, it was a terror attack on their kibbutz," Anton explained.

"And how did you meet the children?" Rosemarie wished to know.

"Well, Hanna of course, as she was their nurse in the hospital."

"And why were the children in the hospital?"

"For psychiatric care as they witnessed the killing."

Then Rosemarie wanted to know if he killed the murderers? "But mother, I wasn't there when it happened. Nobody knows who the killers were." He told her of the adoption of Daniel. "Are you going to adopt Esther and David also?"

"Maybe," Anton responded, "They already call me papa and Hanna mommy." Which wasn't quite true but he didn't know how to explain Esther calling him something else. Then they sat together and Anton showed Rosemarie the many pictures they took of Danny, Esther and David.

Everything had been quiet in Planegg while he was gone. Sepp had come by every evening and morning.

Later on in the evening, Sepp Kainz came and they sat together with a light supper and glasses of good beer. When Sepp asked if everything was fine in Jerusalem, Anton told him it was. Though with Sepp being a close friend and having helped him rescue Rosemarie, he wished he could tell him all of what had happened but not with his mother sitting with them.

CHAPTER XXV

THE THIRD INCIDENT

MONDAY, 31 OCTOBER 2005

Monday morning, Inspector Nagil was back at work in his office. He first reported in to Inspector Keller. Later Commissioner Kolb came by and inquired how his liaison with the Jerusalem police went. Inspector Nagil told him of several visits he had with Deputy Barlev. "They could use some help with their mafia but it has to be an inside man, they are on top of it." Later when he went to the cafeteria for some coffee, he saw Inspector Wagner sitting alone. He joined him.

"How was Jerusalem, Inspector Nagil? Your liaison works with the police there?"

"I met several times with Deputy Barlev, they run a very efficient department. He works close together with the Shin Bet, their security service and the army."

Inspector Wagner smiled. "Any close encounters with the terrorists while there? I read that a suicide bomber blew himself up on a bus in Jerusalem and killed many people, even children were among the dead and injured."

"Well, ... no, I had nothing to do with that incident."

"I noticed a certain hesitation, Inspector Nagil. Want to tell me about it?"

"Officially?"

"Yes."

"I have nothing to report officially, Inspector Wagner."

"Then let us go to my office. I have some more coffee brought up and you can puff your pipe. New rule here in the cafeteria, no smoking."

"Yes, I heard about it when I came to work; as of today, the circular read. Let me get my pipe and I'll be with you."

When he went to Wagner's office, the inspector pulled his comfortable roll chair out from behind his desk and sat himself close to Inspector Nagil. He smiled. "Now this is my unofficial seating arrangement." Wagner watched as Nagil filled his pipe and lit it.

381

There was a knock on the door and Liesl, the waitress came in and brought a pot of coffee. She smiled at Anton. "Hello, Julie." They laughed as Inspector Wagner knew the story about Julie. They filled their cups.

Anton looked at Wagner, "How much do you wish to know?"

"Let me ask you first, I gather it is about a terrorist act you were involved with? Yes? Did it involve you as a police inspector from Munich?"

"No, it was very private."

"Then I wish to know all of it." He used the intercom. "Frau Maria, hold all calls and visitors unless it is the commissioner or an emergency. Also, call Inspector Keller and tell him that Nagil is with me." He smiled at Nagil. "Just in case he looks for you. Now, please."

"All unofficial?" Inspector Wagner nodded.

It was almost noon by the time Inspector Nagil had explained what he called the second incident."

"And nothing was reported in the local papers, no names?"

"Just the little report that the children were found on the street by the IDF."

"IDF means?"

"Israeli Defense Forces; that is what they call their army. Not even the rape of Esther was mentioned."

"Do you have that cyanide pen on you?"

"No. It is locked up in my cabinet."

"Yes, good. I like to see it some day." Inspector Wagner stood up. "What can I say, a job well done, Inspector Nagil. I don't think anyone else here needs to know. As far as we are concerned, no Munich policeman was involved."

When Anton asked "How are things on the home front?" Inspector Wagner assured him that all was quiet, "The Neos are behaving at the moment. Having their tantrums at times and we have had not any problems with people from the Islamic Center, at least not terror-wise. Criminal activities of Muslims or Arabs, Inspector Keller can fill you in."

He smiled. "And congratulations on becoming a father to three children." His eyes looked sincere and his handshake was strong.

Anton returned to his office to open his mail.

All mail that came to his office was opened by the secretary and most was official business, which had been taken cared of. Only mail addressed to him by name was unopened. There was one letter from the Egyptian Embassy in Berlin.

It was from Brigadier Abed al-Hakim Amer.

He gave the names of nine Egyptian Islamic Jihad members, they had been identified from the list he had sent of Egyptians living in Munich. Also the names of two Iranian who were known to have recently come to Munich for the stated purpose of attending the technical university. In a footnote, the brigadier warned that these two Iranians are known scientists, "so identified by our intelligence," had recently graduated from MIT, majoring in nuclear physics, and that American authorities were not aware that they are members of the Iranian Revolutionary Guard. Beware. Nagil included their names in his computer under the heading of identified terrorist suspects and capitalized them:

AHMED REZA JAAFARI, age 40, Iranian n.s. (nuclear scientists)
AYAT WAHAJ, age 43, Iranian, n.s.

He would have to make inquiries, both at the *Technische Universitaet* (Technical University) and with Imam Aref at the mosque. Anton knew from newspaper reports that Iran was working clandestinely on nuclear weapons.

Every evening, he checked his computer and found an e-mail from Hanna telling about her, Amal and the children. In the latest message she wrote,

> The children get along fine with each other. For Esther and David, I have bought little bicycles with training wheels they can use in the nearby park, Danny shuffling along on his little tricycle. David is waiting for you Toni, to come home to teach him to use the bike without training wheels. Esther is mothering Danny, as she was also mothering the monkey and she has taken its sticks off its legs, now the monkey was healed as she was. They love to sit around when I play the piano and sing along with me. In the evening, when I sing Danny Boy, Danny would look proudly at the other two, as it is his song. Now Esther and David want their own songs—do you have any ideas? Also every evening, we sit together and look at pictures we have taken and always want to look at pictures of *aba'*—Daddy Toni, as David calls you and "the Man" as Danny and Esther refer to you. We all love you, your Hanna.

Hanna also wrote that Shimon Herzog came by several times during the week, he had become a real friend to her, Amal, and the children loved him. He was a kind man. Eliahu, the caretaker came by almost every morning to see if he can do anything for them. He had contracted with a builder to add another guest room downstairs. Even Commander Amir came by occasionally and he was the best of friends with David as he wore his uniform. David trusted anybody who wore a uniform.

Anton made an arrangement with the local Lufthansa office who already knew him as a frequent flyer with their airline. While they didn't give him a discount, they assured him that all he needed was to buy economy class and they would upgrade him to first class or business class, whatever was available. All he needed to do was to make his reservation three days before his flight to Israel via Frankfurt. He would always look forward to fly first class, as it was luxurious and relaxing.

He had spoken to personnel and with Inspector Keller's blessing could take, once a month, four days off. His next trip would be the long weekend at the end of November.

TUESDAY, 1 NOVEMBER

After lunch, Anton went to the technical university in the Arcisstrasse. In the admission office, he identified himself as a police inspector and asked to see the director of the university. He was taken to the office of Director Schiller, again showed his credentials and asked the director if two Americans of Iranian descent were studying at the university and gave their names.

"It is really confidential, Herr Inspector."

"So are police inquiries."

"I see." Schiller went to a filing cabinet and brought two files. "Dr. Ahmed Reza Jaafari and Dr. Ayat Wahaj are registered here as researchers. They at once transferred over to Max Planck Institute near the Aumeister, Are you familiar with its location, out in Freimann?"

"I have never been to the institute but I'll find it. If they came here for studies, why the transfer?"

"The object of their research is not available in our university, highly specialized research."

"And what might that be?"

"*Strahlung Forschung der Kernphysik*—radiation research, neutron emission of unstable matter."

"They speak German then? What other languages?"

"They learned German at their American university. In addition, they came here last January and took an intensive course in technical German at the Language Institute. Besides? Persian and English."

"One more thing, Director Schiller, the police department requests that you do not mention to anyone that I came here to inquire about these two men." Anton knew enough about nuclear science that he understood that this was the last step in making a nuclear weapon. A critical mass of Uranium 235 brought together with a source of neutrons in the center, which was usually an element like radium.

Anton finally had his friend Sepp for supper at the Heide inn one evening. Rosemarie didn't wish to come, so they were alone. He told Sepp about the second incident.

All Sepp could do was shake his head. "I don't know Toni, are you very lucky or do you have a guardian angel watching over you? Or you are just a daredevil and get away with it? How many lives have you used up? You know, the saying goes some men have nine lives."

Anton laughed, "That is about cats. I have more lives, the nine I already used up. But really Sepp, I am neither a cat nor a daredevil. I am just well-trained in police work and very careful in what I do."

"What you do is taking risks, like these fanatics following you. How easily they could have shot you, just one bullet and that is it."

"No risk really. I knew what I was doing. Well, at the end when all I had was my toy pistol against Kalashnikovs, it got a little dangerous. But then the cavalry came to rescue us."

"Your guardian angel came to rescue you."

Anton changed the subject.

"How old are you, Sepp? Are you close to retire? You are already driving for me some twenty years, and even then you were not the youngest?"

"Twenty-four years to be exact. I am sixty-three, no retirement for me. Else I would have to sit home and listen to my old lady all day long. By the way, Toni, if you ever need me for police work or a private expedition, don't fail to call on me."

Anton put his hand on Sepp's shoulder. "Thank you, friend."

WEDNESDAY, 2 NOVEMBER

Anton wished to speak to FBI Special Agent Johnson and to catch him the first thing in the morning, he called him at a little past two in the afternoon.

"Agent Johnson."

"Good morning, Mr. Johnson. Inspector Anton Nagil from the Munich police here." They talked briefly about the serial killer Ludolf Hanfnagel, and Johnson thanked him for the evaluation report and then added, "You know, here he would not have gotten away with his insanity plea."

"I realize this. Politics, Mr. Johnson. Germany could not afford to have a serial killer in its midst, but any country can have insane criminals. Look Mr. Johnson, something else. I have a report that two scientists who studied nuclear physics at MIT have turned up in Munich at the Max Planck Institute to research neutron emission. While both are American citizens, they are Iranian born. I have a report that they belong secretly to the Iranian Revolutionary Guard." There was a momentary pause. "This is dangerous, Inspector Nagil. Where did this report emanate from? Can it be trusted?"

"From the Head of Egyptian Military Intelligence. I know Brigadier Amer very well; it came as a private communication to me, a warning."

"I see. And the names of the two scientists?" Anton gave the names. "I get back to you Inspector, probably in a couple days. Where can I reach you? You are six hours ahead of us?"

"Please call me at home. I am usually home by seven in the evening. Or at work, you have my number at headquarters." He gave Johnson his home phone number.

Next, he drove by Pension Freizeit and saw Mrs. Cohn. He told her he needed to see a member of M (Mossad), on an important matter, and as soon as possible.

"Your code name still 'sav'? Mrs. Cohn asked. He told her yes. "And where can you be reached? I imagine you wish for a personal meeting?" He told her during the day at police HQ. "Just have the M person ask for me at the reception booth. If it is an Israeli, don't have him show his passport, just ask for me and the guard will call me. If it is in the evening, have him call me first at home. How do you send the message, Mrs. Cohn?"

"By encoded e-mail. All right?" It was.

It was too late to drive out to Freimann.

THURSDAY, 3 NOVEMBER

In the morning, Inspector Nagil signed out to the Max Planck Institute and drove out there. It was just a few blocks short of Freimann. In the lobby was a receptionist. He showed his police pass and asked to see the director on police matters. She made a call and advised him to go to room 3, "Director Glaser is expecting you." Anton knocked on the door and entered. A tall, elderly man with a goatee stood up.

"Inspector Nagil, what can I do for you? Please have a seat."

"I wish to inquire about two researchers in your institute. Both Americans who came recently. They registered with the technical university and then were assigned to your institute for further research."

"I believe I know whom you are looking for, but please, their names?"

Anton knew their names, but it was more proper for him to read from his notebook.

"A Dr. Ahmed Reza Jaafari and Dr. Ayat Wahaj. Did I pronounce their names correctly?"

"Yes, you do. Dr. Jaafari and Dr. Wahaj. You are right, they came to the Technical University, both graduates of MIT in the United States, actually graduates of the Teheran University. Both took studies at MIT in nuclear engineering. They are doing advanced radiation research in our institute. Anything wrong that the police is interested in these gentlemen?"

"No, nothing wrong. Just routine check as they were both born in Iran."

"Well, this is true, but both moved with their families to the United States a long time ago, and as I was told, both are in opposition to the present regime in Iran."

"May I ask who gave you that information?"

"What? That they were born in Iran?"

"No, that they are in opposition to the present regime in Iran?"

"Do I have to answer all these questions, Inspector? We just don't give out information about our research colleagues to any outsider."

Inspector Nagil smiled. "I am not an outsider but police. I work with the immigration department and there are some irregularities in their applications for studying in Munich. I neither wish to see the gentlemen nor bother you in any depths. All I need to see is their passports if they are available."

"That they are not forgeries?"

"Exactly."

"I can assure you, Inspector, that they are genuine. I was so told by Professor Max Klausner that he checked their passports and background information. All above board so to speak."

"And the information that they dislike the regime in Iran and fled from it also from the professor?"

"Yes."

"Please?"

"Well, I have their passports here. We make it a practice to keep passports of foreign researchers in my office once they have local identification papers. Both have German driver licenses. One moment, please." The director went into a walk-in safe and soon returned with the two passports. He gave them to the inspector.

Anton first looked at the pictures, their faces burned into his memory. Both passports issued two years ago. Profession was listed as nuclear engineers. Home addresses listed in Boston, Massachusetts. He thumbed around in the visa section, found interesting entries. He handed the passports back. "Yes, genuine. One more question director Glaser. You mentioned Professor Klausner before, their sponsor?"

"Yes. He did all the paperwork. As I understand it, both came here last January and spoke with the professor who then invited them to do their research here in our institute. They were interested in radiation research, advanced research which is not available at the university."

"And Professor Klausner is the head of this specialized department?"

"Yes. He has done his research in *Kernphysik und Strahlungforschung*—nuclear science and radiation research for many years. You probably don't understand what this research is all about, Inspector?"

"No idea." Anton smiled. "One more thing, Director, please keep my visit to you and my interest in these gentlemen confidential."

"Yes, I understand. And this ends your interest in these two researchers?"

"Yes. Wrong information from the immigration department I am certain. However, just in case we need to contact these gentlemen and we wish to do so privately, where do they live?"

In Professor Klausner's villa. They rented the upstairs of his villa. The professor lives alone, so he has plenty of room and as I understand, they are rich and pay a princely sum for renting the space."

"This is not really important to us. Goodbye and thank you."

In the foyer he had seen a sign pointing to the cafeteria. It was closed. He went to the coffee room. It was really just a small room with a half dozen tables and vending machines. He took his cup of coffee and sat down. The coffee tasted horrible.

Just then, the receptionist walked in and got a cup of coffee from the machine. She was a blond, middle aged, certainly past her prime but still pretty. She stopped by his table, "Well, did you see the director on police matters, Inspector?"

"Yes. Just some information I needed about Professor Klausner."

She laughed, "Don't tell me he raped a young girl?" Anton's ears pricked up.

"What makes you say that? Surely you are kidding?"

Her laugh was forced, "Yes, I am kidding."

"Please sit down, young lady."

She sat down on his table, sipped. "Terrible tasting coffee but it is hot. It is cold out there in the foyer."

Anton put on his charm; "You had a bad experience with the good professor?"

She glanced down on his hand; no ring. "Everybody knows I was his mistress."

"And?"

"And he chucked me for a younger woman, a mere college girl."

"The Romeo type?"

The woman looked at him with a frown, "You didn't come here to snoop about his love affairs?"

"No. I am interested in the two researchers who live with him."

"Oh, the Iranians."

"They are Americans. What makes you think they are Iranians?"

"Well, they were speaking in this foreign tongue and when I asked what language they were speaking. They said Farsi. Isn't that what they speak in Iran?"

"Yes, I guess so. I am not a language expert. Dr. Jaafari and Dr. Wahaj live with your ex-boyfriend I heard."

"And their two guards."

"What for do they need personal guards?"

"Big shots, I guess. Filthy rich, they bought a new Mercedes since they came here. So, what are you investigating about the two?"

"What do you think I am investigating them for?" I don't even know how to address you?"

"I am Ingrid, and you? I hate to have to call you just inspector?"

"I am Inspector Nagil. Just call me Anton. So, why do you think I am asking about the two good doctors?"

"Well, I know that they have high school girls over to their place."

"They like their ladies young? Your professor, too?"

"I don't wish to talk about Klausner."

"Why? If he jilted you?"

"I have a girl with him and he pays."

"As young as you are and look?"

She laughed, "Now you are flirting with me, Anton. I am 42, and my girl is five. Through him I have a lot of benefits, like this lousy job here. I sit there most of the day and do nothing. How many visitors come? Rarely. But it pays well. A make-believe job Klausner instituted."

"I am also forty-two. Not married as you noticed."

"I am always free. Just let me know and I get a babysitter for my girl. So, tell me, What have the two doctors done that you have police work with them?"

"Just some irregularities with the registration of their car. I work for the traffic police. May I call you Ingrid, you don't mind?"

"No, of course not, Anton. Did you get to see them?"

"No. They are busy. I can just write to them and they can fill out the necessary forms. There is really no need to bother them. But I might bother you, Ingrid?"

"Any time," they laughed. She left and Nagil looked after her. She had turned and saw him looking, smiled and waved to him.

Anton didn't finish his awful coffee and left.

Next he drove out to the Islamic Center. He saw only one man who could be a guard. Things between them and the Neos must have cooled down. He went into the foyer and met the caretaker, told him he wished to see to see either Imam Aref or al-Dulaimi.

He was led into Aref's office who greeted him friendly. "A long time that you visited us, Achmed. What can I do for you, may I order coffee?" Anton nodded.

"I had taken vacation and went to Cairo, to visit an old friend of mine."

"Sidqi Suliman?"

Anton laughed, "You are always well-informed, Imam Aref. No, my friend Adolf Lutz."

"From Lutz Import-Export?"

"Yes. Adolf and I grew up together. His father, Gerhard Lutz and Otto Nagil worked together in camps in Lithuania."

The coffee came and the imam poured him a cup.

"But you did not come here to tell me about your visit to Cairo, Achmed?"

"No. Police work. Recently two Americans came here, both Iranian descent; Muslims of course. We had a complaint from the parents of a high school girl, under age, that she has spent nights at the house of these two men."

The imam smiled. "Except for not coming home, in our country, in Egypt as you know very well, the age limit for girls to have affairs is younger than here."

"But not ilicit love affairs. To marry a young girl, yes."

"You are right, of course, Achmed. And who are the two, do you know their names?"

"Yes. A Dr. Wahaj and Dr. Jaafari."

"Yes, I know them both, Shiites. We are Sunnis and we have our differences. However, here in our mosque we welcome all Muslims. So, how can I help you?"

"I don't know them. I was just asked to investigate them clandestinely. What they look like, their behavior, if they bother your younger girls also."

"They are both handsome men, Americans but Iranian descent. You wish for me to introduce them to you? They come every Friday evening to worship."

"No, not at this point. What I like to do is come here Friday and observe them. You don't mind if I visit your mosque to do that?"

The imam smiled. "Come, you are almost one of us. We have nonbelievers come occasionally and observe our rituals. You are always welcome. But please, if you do not observe our ways of praying, remain in the back."

"I am not against praying to Allah, he is our God also, just a different name."

"Then when you come in remove your shoes please, take a Koran if you wish and observe our rituals."

"I shall do so. When you spoke with them, in what language?"

"I do not know if they speak Arabic, as devout Shiites they should. I don't speak Farsi. We spoke German and their German is better then mine."

"I thank you for your hospitality."

After their usual salutations, Anton left and returned to his office.

First, he looked up the address of Professor Max Klausner in the telephone book. Fuchsstrasse 2a, it must be the corner villa facing the Ungererstrasse. From the vehicle registration department, he got the license number of the two doctors' white Mercedes, it was registered to Ayat Wahaj.

When he came home, his mother told him, "A man had come by an hour before and wished to speak to you. I spoke to him through the intercom. He had said he came for Sav, whatever that meant. He would come back at eight." Anton assured Rosemarie that it was all right. "Mother, can you lay a cold supper for both of us? How was his German?"

"Fluently, with just a slight foreign accent."

"Mother, he is an Israeli and I need to speak to him."

"So you want me to leave when he comes? Yes? And what can I serve? I don't have any kosher food."

"Just serve cold cuts and cheese, he can chose what he wants. And tea, please."

Rosemarie laid the table with different cold cuts and cheese, bread and rolls and had a pot of tea ready by eight. Then, punctually the bell rang. Rosemarie disappeared into the living room and Anton let the man in who identified himself as Aaron Bergman from the Israeli Embassy. While they ate, Anton told him about the two American nuclear scientists, both Iranian descent, gave their names and that he suspected that they had visited Pakistan to see Khan, and then spent three months in Iran. Now they were in Munich at the Max Planck Institute to learn about neutron emission of radium, the end-stage of producing a nuclear bomb. Aaron Bergman said he would return at once to Berlin and cable the Mossad.

FRIDAY, 4 NOVEMBER

At work, shortly after two in the afternoon, Anton received a call from Agent Johnson.

"Just came to work, Inspector Nagil. Is it safe to talk, no tapes or anything?"

"My phone in my office is not bugged, Mr. Johnson."

"Here is what I found out about these two men. First, Dr. Ahmed Reza Jaafari. Born in 1965 in Teheran. Usual schooling then later attended the University in Teheran and majored in nuclear physics. Graduated and came to the United States in 1997, as a refugee. Asked for political asylum as he was a Sunni Muslim and persecuted in Shiite Iran. Took graduate studies at MIT. Graduated as a doctor in nuclear physics in 2002 and applied for further research at the Lawrence Livermore Laboratories in California. He was accepted but then asked to leave when his interest became neutron emission, which has to do with nuclear weapons research; this was in spring of 2004."

"Why was he asked to leave?"

"Someone at the laboratory finally went through his history of previous schooling and his admission to the United States seeking asylum. That he had studied at the University in Teheran. This alone did not arouse suspicion, but that he left Iran alone. Though not married, he left his family behind. Usually, asylum seekers bring their families from these types of countries to escape persecution.

He did not. The mills at Livermore work slowly, they are rather careless, but someone finally became suspicious and he was asked to leave."

"Did they report it to your FBI?"

"Of course not. We sent several agents to the lab to question the faculty and people he associated with, also at MIT. The story on Dr. Ayat Wahaj is the same, only that he is three years older. They came together to the United States in 1997, identical request for asylum, again without family. Also did research at Livermore. Same story, he too asked to be transferred to the radiation laboratory. Was finally checked out and asked to leave in the spring of 2004. Again, no report to our FBI office. And now they are doing research in Munich? What else and new have you found out, Inspector?"

"In September of 2004, they spent a month in Pakistan. In Ocotober of 2004, they turned up in Iran and probably stayed three months there. As refugees from Iran? What is interesting and suspicious is that they entered Iran from Pakistan with their passports stamped with a dated entry to Iran. However, there was no exit stamp. In January, they came to Germany as their passport shows. They registered with the Technical University in Munich. Made full payment for doing radiation research at the Max Planck Institute. They stated in their application that they left Iran with their families to escape persecution, as they are Sunni Moslems. This, of course, is a lie. They also spent three months in Munich studying technical German. Began to do their research here a month and a half ago under the tutelage of a well-known radiation scientist, a Professor Klausner. Rented part of Klausner's villa, in fact live with him. Bought a new Mercedes, spend money freely on high school girls. And last if not least, they are both Shiites and not Sunni Muslims."

Agent Johnson said, "They were both naturalized in 2002, but since they lied on their application, we can deport them. Look, Inspector Nagil, they must be prevented from further research. We can work through the Germany Embassy here. I am certain they understand the significance of the research they do in Munich. Have them returned to the States, we arrest them at the airport, go to court and deport them to Iran."

"And bring their knowledge to Iran? Give me a week or two before you do anything official, Mr. Johnson. We are working on this matter also, and urgently. I get back to you in a week or so. Goodbye."

Next, Anton called Sepp and arranged for him to pick him up at police headquarters at five and take him to the mosque.

November in Munich means early darkness and Muslim services start earlier. At the entrance to the prayer hall, Anton took his shoes off and from a table took a small Koran offered. He went inside the ornate hall and stood to the side observing everyone who came in. Most of the men who came in wore suits like he did, some in sweaters, a few in robes. Hot air ducts warmed the place. That he spotted his two men at once was that their Korans were larger, probably private editions in Farsi and Arabic and he recognized them from their passport pictures. With them were two young men, also in suits. Anton followed them in with others who had come and when they took their place next to each other, he was right behind them. Imam al-Dulaimi was conducting the service. When all knelt down with their heads to the floor, Anton observed that is was possible to use his cyanide pen on one's outstretched hand. It would be a one-shot affair; he would never be able to reload.

He had seen enough. He mumbled in Arabic about not feeling well to his neighbor and left. He had to do one more thing. Out in the well-lit parking lot, he looked for the white Mercedes. For this he had Sepp help him. With maybe three hundred cars, it took about ten minutes before he spotted the car. The license plates matched. While it was unlikely that the next time they would park in the same place it should be somewhere near as people tend to park in a favorite area as a force of habit. Sepp drove him home. When his friend asked what was going on, Anton did not reply at first.

"Police matter or private expedition, Toni?"

"Private, very private. I hate to involve you but I might need your help, Sepp."

"I trust you, Toni. Whatever you need me for, I help you."

"And no questions asked?"

"Unless you wish to tell me, Toni."

"If I have you help me you deserve to know, but not now. I need you next Friday, same time, same place. Pick me up at headquarters. Come by train and leave your taxi at home. Wear something old, something that is in the back of your closet and you are ready to discard. Did you ever get a pistol?"

"No, but a friend of mine has one, legal."

"Borrow it from him. It would be just as a show of force. I don't care if it is loaded or not, yours is not meant to be fired."

"I don't even know how to fire the thing."

"I know, some warrior you are." They laughed.

SUNDAY, 6 NOVEMBER

After a good lunch at the Heide Inn, Anton walked with his mother in the nearby park. Soon the old lady felt tired and wished to be taken home. Anton walked alone, deep in thought about the problem. He knew what the solution was; the two scientists had to be done away with. He was not a killer, though by necessity he had killed many men and one old woman. They all had deserved to die. Assassinations were not to his liking. Yet he knew it had to be done. He was hardly aware of the cold wind that had begun to blow until he began to shiver in his light coat. By the time he returned home, it had begun to snow. Chilled to the bones, he went down into the jacuzzi. He relaxed in the hot swirling water.

Then his mother called down, "Toni, there is a man on the gate. He says his name is Mordechai Nevot."

"Mother, Nevot is a good friend of mine. He must be cold too. Give him one of my trunks and bathrobe and send him down."

Ten minutes later, his friend Nevot from the Mossad came down and eased into the hot water.

"Do you know there is a regular snowstorm outside, Anton? Ah, that feels good. I came dressed in just a suit; I had no idea that it is already winter in Munich."

"It came up suddenly. I was taking a walk and suddenly felt chilled. Then I saw that it was snowing and had turned ice cold. It isn't the cold but the wind."

"And you were thinking about our problem?"

"My problem."

"No, Anton, it is our problem. Now tell me."

Anton told Nevot what he knew and had found out from his own investigations and what the FBI told him.

Nevot said, "I would have thought that after 9/11, they are more careful whom they admit into the country and . . ."

"They came before 9/11."

"I realize that, but to become citizens. Then let them do research at the Livermore Laboratory, a facility where highly classified research is done. Iranians who stated that they are Sunnis, didn't that make them suspicious?"

"Most Americans don't know or don't understand the difference between Sunnis and Shiites. At the Livermore Lab, part of it is just an extension of the University of California where they do not have secret work and research. It was only when they applied for classified research that someone became suspicious, mainly because they were naturalized Iranians, supposedly fled Iran for political reasons and came without their families. How dangerous is their research within the overall work of producing a nuclear weapon, Nevot?"

"It is within the framework of putting it all together. Like when America made the first atom bomb. In Oak Ridge, they produced the purified uranium; in Hanford, the plutonium and in Los Alamos, they put the bomb together, the final assembly. These two scientists would belong to Los Alamos."

"How far along does Israel believe the Iranians are producing a bomb?"

"They have the know-how. They are working on purifying Uranium-235. The best method is with centrifuges. They have installed a number of high-speed double centrifuges and are in the process of enriching the uranium. They need many more and repeat the process countless times. What they are doing now is for propaganda purpose, to be able to say that they are in the enrichment process. It will take many centrifuges and continuous operations of enrichment to get enough for a nuclear device. We estimate they will have enough for one bomb in about four years. Then after, they can produce continuously 235; and make three or four bombs a year. The other method is to make plutonium, but for that they need a reactor. A by-product of the fissionable uranium is plutonium, and here they can use the plentiful 238 or slightly enriched 235. The Russians are building them a reactor, perhaps even two. It is understood by everyone that the Iranians with their plentiful oil reserves need a nuclear power plant like a hole in the head. Everybody knows that they want bombs."

"What is the matter with the Russians? Why are they supporting this evil regime? Don't they realize that once the Iranians have a number of bombs they might give one to the Chechnians who would happily blow up Moscow?"

"It is their president, Putin. He needs hard currency for his corrupt regime. He is a former KGB agent, ruthless and immoral. He would sell his soul to the devil for power and money. Putin wants to recreate the former Soviet Union under the mantle of Russia. That is why he is meddling in the former Republics."

"You mean bring communism back?"

"No, not communism. He knows this system was a colossal failure. However, back under Russian and his dictatorship. He has to fight his own terrorists and yet supports the Axis of Evil, Iran, Syria, and North Korea."

"So, how far away is a plutonium bomb?"

"Two years to build a factory for the reactor, two more years to get enough plutonium. Again, we think in term of four years. Then their Los Alamos where the bomb would be assembled; another year perhaps, or less. But here is where your two scientists come in. They are already researching ways and means to trigger a nuclear device. If we can stop these two scientists from bringing their learned knowledge to Iran, we can gain perhaps a year."

"I am certain the German authorities would cooperate once they become aware of their research and the purpose of it," suggested Anton.

"Yes, but they cannot prove anything illegal. They can deport them to the United States. As you told me the FBI would arrest them, the courts strip them off their citizenship and deport them back to Iran. We don't know how much they have learned so far. The Germans and the Americans might just play into their hands by sending them back. This brings me to the real purpose of my visit here. We have to stop them permanently."

"Kill them?"

"Yes. That is the only way. We cannot kidnap them and bring them to Israel. If anything went wrong and the Germans found out, Israel would be isolated from Europe. The Americans would understand but also lash out at us. Killing them secretly, it could be made to look like a robbery. They live in a villa, you said?"

"The problem is that they are always guarded by two men. Then there is also Professor Klausner in the house. You eliminate five men, including a well-known and famous German scientist and you make a mess. Nobody would believe that it was robbery, but rather the work of the Mossad. You cannot attack them at the research institute."

"That would be even worse, I agree."

"So would be to intercept their car going to and from their home."

Nevot smiled. "Ah, that water feels good to my old bones. Knowing you Anton, what do you have in mind? You have a plan?"

"Yes. Give me a couple weeks. If I fail, you can always bring your team here and do it your way."

"It could still be robbery of sort. The men would wear masks, don't utter a word, only the two scientists need to be done away with, the guards and the professor tied up. The house ransacked, all done silently. Let me hear from you in two weeks."

"Let's go upstairs and eat, Mordechai. You can stay here tonight?"

"No, I like to return to the *Pension*. Tomorrow morning, I fly back to Israel. You can work through Esther. She knows how to get hold of me, and you are still *sav*."

FRIDAY, 11 NOVEMBER

Inspector Nagil told his secretary that he was leaving at four o'clock, "Shopping with my mother," he explained. Down at the booth, Sepp was waiting. He wore an old jacket, a scarf around his neck and grimy trousers.

"You look like a vagabond," Anton laughed. He took his friend down into the police garage where his BMW was. He put on an old and long coat.

While he drove, he explained to his friend, "Look Sepp, there are two scientists who have to be eliminated. Yes, killed. They are both Iranians and study here to work on the atom bomb for Iran. You must have read about Iran and their nuclear work? Good. Killing them would mean at least a year away from building an atom bomb. There is no other way. If we go to the authorities, they just deport them to America as they have become citizens, and America would return them to Iran, which doesn't help."

"Let me ask you Toni, who . . . in whose interest do you do this?"

"Let's just say for the good of the world, not just Germany. Gives more time for diplomatic efforts to stop the Iranians or as a last resort, the Americans will attack them. Now I have a plan but as all plans go, I have to be flexible. I cannot go into details of what will happen. Here is where you come in and how I need you to help me. When we get to the mosque, I park the car near where I expect the two scientists will park their white Mercedes, it will be dark by then. You stay in the car. Sit low so no one can see you, but also look around and watch for the white Mercedes. By five, or shortly after, most should be in the mosque and you won't have to hide anymore. I try to have them leave before services are over;

there is a way to do that. When you see them go to the Mercedes I should be right behind them. There will be four of them, the two scientists and their two bodyguards. Immediately, come to me and we put on our facemasks; they must not see our faces. Together we approach them before they get into the car. I will tell them this is a robbery and I want their money. We both point our pistols at the younger ones who are the guards. I will speak only; you just remain quiet. If need be and they resist, I do the shooting, I have a silencer. The idea is for them to hand over their wallets and weapons, get into the car and drive off. I hope there won't be any shooting and they just leave. Then we return to our car and that is it. Do you have any question?"

"Only one, I thought you will kill them?"

"They will be dead within the hour. How, is not important to you at this point."

"One more question, what if there are people around?" asked Sepp.

"It doesn't matter. So they have a witness or witnesses to the robbery."

"There are no guards at the mosque?"

"Only inside the mosque. Here is the facemask, try it on in the car, there are two large holes for the eyes, it fits over the whole head. By the way, is your pistol loaded?"

"Yes. My friend showed me how to operate it. It is on safety now."

"Keep it on safety. Your pistol will be my backup in case mine won't work, which I doubt." Anton drove along the Ungererstrasse, which lead to the Islamic Center. They drove in silence. Anton parked near where he had seen the Mercedes. It was quarter to five and getting dark, the parking lot well lit.

"Nervous, Sepp?"

"Yes, and a little scared. I never robbed anyone. What if they don't show up?"

"Possible. Then we have to repeat next Friday. The services start around five. By a quarter after, we should be coming out. You join me as soon as you see me. Better you keep your mask off until you get to me; then we both put them on. Try not to get too close to them when you come to me, though I expect them to be busy and not pay any attention to you. See you in about a half an hour, Sepp."

"Be careful, Toni." Anton was already walking toward the mosque.

With others, he entered the mosque, took off his long coat in the foyer and hung it up in the small cloakroom. Here the women separated from the man. He did not see the imams or the caretaker. He stayed off to the side until he saw the scientists and their bodyguards enter. It was already after five, they were late. They had their own Korans again; he took one from the table as he entered the prayer hall and followed close behind them. The services had already begun, Imam al-Dulaimi leading the service. The four took a prayer rug close to the back, Nagil right behind them and in the last row; all were standing again. Anton had his pen ready with the front off. The imam had a good voice as he sang the prayers. Then a sura came where all had to cower down again on their knees, head to the floor. Anton was slightly to the left of Ayat Wahaj. All worshippers had their heads to the floor; he only had a few seconds where he was unobserved. He reached forward and from an inch away from Wahaj's hand he activated the pen, felt it discharge, hid the pen in his hand and lowered his head to the floor.

(Wahaj felt the sting, looked around and only saw everyone cowering low. He then rubbed his hand and felt a small protuberance; the rubbing worked the cyanide into his bloodstream.)

Anton dared not reload his pen, besides he was too far away from Jaafari. When all stood up, he left silently. The last he saw was Wahaj rubbing his hand gain. Anton knew that the cyanide would affect the man within minutes. Within the hour, he would be dead.

He had read up on cyanide poisoning. There would be drowsiness, low blood pressure making the man feel dizzy. This should happen within minutes, followed by coma, rapid severe acidosis, convulsions and—death. Out in the foyer, and unobserved by the guards, Anton put a new pellet into his pen, took his coat,and left the mosque. He walked quickly to his car and was at once joined by Sepp.

"What happened, where are they?"

"Where is the Mercedes?" Sepp pointed to it, not far away. The parking lot was empty of people. "Come with me, they should be here shortly," Anton said. A couple cars away fom the Mercedes they crouched down.

"Now the masks." They put them over their heads and adjusted the eyeholes. Anton took his pistol from his holster and attached the silencer.

"Here they come," whispered Sepp.

"If they give the money or their wallets, you pick it up Sepp, also if they are armed and drop their weapons." Nagil watched the four; the two guards were leading the staggering Wahaj. When they reached their Mercedes, Anton jumped up, a few quick steps to them. "Halt. Geld her, schnell (Stop, give me your money)!" Sepp now beside him; both pointing their pistols at them. "Was wollt ihr (What do you want)?" asked Jaafari.

"Your money and fast!" shouted Anton in German.

"Give, give it to them," uttered Wahaj weakly. He was in distress, breathing fast and shallow.

"A robbery, you are robbing us?" asked Jaafari. Anton jabbed the muzzle of his pistol into Jaafari's mouth, at the same time he shot the pellet at this throat. They all took their wallets out and dropped them, except Wahaj, who had collapsed.

"What's the matter with him?" asked Anton.

"He is sick, we have to take him to a doctor," answered Jaafari.

"You two are guards? Out with your weapons and drop them, quick!" When they hesitated, Jaarfai told them, "Do it." Sepp picked up the wallets and pistols.

"Now go, fast!" Anton hissed. The guard opened the door, then both guards picked up Wahaj and put him on the backseat, then Jaafari followed. he at once collapsed inside. One guard went also into the backseat, the other in front and the Mercedes raced off toward the exit. When it was out of sight Anton and Sepp got into their car and drove off in the other direction toward the Autobahn and then toward the west circling the city, and then south. For a while they drove in silence.

(By then the two guards, Mohammad Ganji and Mahmoud Rashid, had reached their villa. Jaafari was dead. The guards carried in both. Wahaj was just going into convulsions. Professor Klausner watched him for a minute. When Rashid called to him to get a doctor, Klausner told him, "It is too late. He is dying.")

"What do I do with the wallets and the pistols, Toni?"

"You can take their money out, keep it. Everything else I cut up and bury it, the pistols too."

"I don't want their money, Toni."

"You are a good man, Sepp. Nor do I, I burry it too." Again they drove in silence.

"Toni, want to talk about it? Might do you good."

"I have become an assassin and I don't like it, Sepp."

"But if it was necessary. I know it was, else you wouldn't have done it. You did something, if not for Germany, then for the whole world."

"You are right of course, Sepp. I just don't like the method. The work of an assassin, like a KGB agent."

"Are they dead, Toni? How did you do it?"

"Yes, they are dead by now. I shot a cyanide pellet into the hand of Wahaj in the mosque. He took longer to die. Jaarafi I shot the pellet into this throat which causes his death within a minute or so."

"I never saw you do it, how?"

"When I shoved the pistol in his mouth, in the other hand I had a poison pen and shot the pellet into his throat. I don't think anyone noticed it. Let us just forget about this incident, Sepp. It never happened." They continued in silence. Anton drove Sepp to his house in Planegg. They shook hands—no words needed.

(Professor Klausner questioned the two guards about what happened. Their German was poor. Rashid, who spoke the language better, explained how Ayat

Wahaj suddenly got sick in the mosque and they left to come home and then were held up by two robbers who took their wallets and pistols, then let them leave. In the car Jaafari, suddenly went into convulsions and died.

Klausner wished to know what was in their wallets, "Anything incriminating?"

"Just money and my driver's license," answered Rashid.

Ganji remembered that he also had Susie's, the young high school girl's picture, her name and her telephone number in his wallet.

Klausner asked, "I hope not the nude picture of the girl?"

Ganji confessed to it, "That was the one I had."

Klausner groaned, "Then we can't even report it to the police. Let's just hope the robbers don't follow up on the telephone number."

When Ganji asked how come that Jaafari and Wahaj suddenly died, the professor thought that they had been poisoned. "Most likely a strychnine compound mixed into their food." Neither Ganji nor Rashid could think of where this might have happened. Obviously, it had happened. On Wahaj, they found his wallet. He had not given it to the robbers.

The next morning, Klausner called the mosque and was able to speak to Imam al-Dulaimi. He told him that he needed a doctor who was a Muslim, as one of his houseguest who was also a Muslim got sick suddenly; then he added, "A doctor who is discreet, I can trust."

Al-Dulaimi gave him the name and number of Dr. Salah Mahmud. Klausner called the doctor and told him it was an emergency. When Dr. Mahmud came and examined the two dead man, he said that they had been poisoned with cyanide. When Klausner asked when that might have happened Dr. Mahmud said that most likely, it happened within minutes of their death. Klausner then realized that the two robbers had been an assassination team. He also realized that he was in danger and surprised that he was not killed also. He asked Dr. Mahmud how he can ship their bodies back to America. The doctor told him that if he wrote on their death certificate that they had been poisoned, there would be a police investigation.

"And how can we avoid that the police becomes involved?" The doctor told him that it can be avoided if he wrote a fake certificate, that they died suddenly of a heart infarct.

"And how much would that cost me, Dr. Mahmud?"

"One thousand euros for each body."

He had the doctor wait while he consulted with Ganji and Rashid. Explained to them that the shipping back of the bodies would cost a lot of money. While the guards did not have much money, when Klausner searched the belongings of the two scientists, he found more than twenty thousand euros. Klausner took two thousand and gave it to Dr. Mahmud, who then wrote out a death certificate for Jaafari, who died of a heart infarct. He wrote the same certificate for Wahaj.

After the doctor left, they debated to whom to ship the bodies. Klausner wished to have them returned to the United States, as they were American citizens. However, Ganji and Rashid insisted to have them returned to their families in Iran.

The same day, professor Klausner went to the airport to arrange the shipping. They told him he would have to transfer the bodies first to a morgue and from there they could be transported with the proper paperwork to Iran. Klausner arranged that, giving the morgue the death certificates. He also had to get their passports from the Max Planck Institute. On Tuesday with all the documents completed, the bodies were shipped to Iran. Ganji and Rashid returned with the same flight.

Professor Klausner was wise enough to realize that most likely the robbers were an assassination team of the Israeli Mossad. He was surprised that they had let him live. Of course, he could no go to the police because of the picture. It was he who had taken the picture of her and had an affair with the young girl. He could be blackmailed. What could he do? He was desperate and even thought of suicide, but that option was always open to him. For now he would just sit tight. How did Ganji get hold of this picture? He must have searched through his things while he was at the Institute. Klausner at once destroyed his collection of young ladies' photos.)

When Anton was home, his mother asked him why he was so quiet. He told her that he was working on an investigation that pertained to the rape of a high school girl and it was unpleasant business.

Saturday morning, Anton went into the forest. It was a cold and cloudy morning, no one about. The snow had melted, only here and there a patch. He dug a hole and took the three wallets; first examined their contents. There was over three thousand euros. The money he tore into pieces and threw it into the hole, the same with their identifications. The picture of a young girl with the telephone number and her name he kept. In the deep hole he also buried the two pistols.

He would need to have a talk with the professor and warn him to never teach Iranians restricted nuclear science, or for that matter anyone of the Moslem religion. Anton then drove to the Pension Freizeit and saw Frau Cohn, wrote a short note for her to send to Mordechai Nevot: 'Business deal completed, sav.' She noticed his serious and quiet demeanor and when she asked him what was the matter, he only told her that it had been bad business.

Inspector Nagil had to work on Sunday. Wednesday he was off and took the fast train out to the airport. There he spoke to the supervisor of baggage handling, showed him his identification as a police inspector and then asked him if two bodies had been recently shipped from the airport. The supervisor told him that on Tuesday, two bodies had been shipped to Iran, he then produced the manifests. Their names were Ahmed Reza Jaafari and Ayat Wahaj. Both had died Friday night of heart infarct. The certifying physician was Dr. Salah Mahmud. When the supervisor asked if anything was wrong, Inspector Nagil said, "No, just verifying that the bodies were shipped to the right address." Later he called Agent Johnson, who was not in his office. He left a message for the agent to call him.

Early Thursday afternoon, Agent Johnson called. Anton told Mr. Johnson of the sudden demise of Dr. Ahmed Reza Jaafari and Dr. Ayat Wahaj.

"Anything you wish to add to that, Inspector Nagil?"

"No. Both died suddenly of a heart condition. The bodies were shipped to Iran."

"Of course, our investigation will continue here," replied Mr. Johnson.

"I would appreciate if nothing is communicated to German authorities."

"I think I understand. It is just an internal investigation of why these two scientists were granted citizenship without their families being in the United States and why they were ever accepted to the Livermore facility. Also we have to teach our authorities to differentiate between Sunnis and Shiites, the two don't mix."

"Unless they combine for terrorist mischief."

"You are right there, Inspector Nagil. The case is officially closed then on your end? No problems of any sort?"

"There was never a case."

"Good. Congratulations on a job well done, Inspector. You saved the United States a lot of trouble. Are you certain you don't wish to work here? We have certain teams with the CIA where your expertise would be welcomed. No? You have the skills to be a fine agent. Please visit me if you ever come to Washington. I'd like to show you around, be my guest. And goodbye."

For a week, Inspector Nagil was morose, reflective. Even his colleagues mentioned it and asked him if anything was wrong. Inspector Wagner was especially worried and asked if anything happened he should learn about, "Unofficially, of course."

"No, there was no problem."

Hanna noticed it in his e-mails. "What is the matter, Anton Nagil" started one e-mail. Anton, he knew he had to end his lingering doubts about having done the right thing. For that, he had his friend Sepp over.

After a brisk walk in the nearby forest on the cold Saturday afternoon, a little over a week after the happening, Anton invited his friend down into the jacuzzi. Sepp had never been in the jacuzzi and they immersed themselves in the hot, churning water.

"Oh Jesus, that is great! How come you have never invited me down here, Toni?"

"Because you never asked me. Also we have never walked together through the forest on a cold Saturday winter afternoon."

"Some excuse. Well, while we relax, you want to talk about it? It is still on your mind. Look, Toni, I am just a simple man, old enough to be wise, maybe wiser than you are if only by age. Perhaps because I am a simple man and have led a decent life, I can tell right from wrong. So unburden yourself as a friend to a friend."

"Yes, Sepp, it is grinding in my soul. I haven't told you all about myself. A difficult life it is. I have been involved in too many killings. I shot my father when I was thirteen; he brutalized my mother and might have killed her if I hadn't stopped him. Strangely, that never bothered me. I have executed men who deserved it. I have killed men in fighting. You know what I did to Karl Seitz. None of that is on my conscious. But the assassination is." "Well, Toni, to go back to the kidnapping of Rosemarie and what they did to her, and they may have killed her. You did that to Seitz what you had to do to get the information you needed. I might have done it differently. Beat the shit out of him until he told me, probably messed him up more than you did. I understand, you were desperate for a quick answer and you were right. Poor Rosemarie lying in that foul place, cold and without food and water, you were very lenient with her kidnappers. I would have killed all of them if Rosemarie had been my mother. You did not. You are really a very good man. Now, you told me about killing these SS officers who were, as you called them, child-murderers, shooting down tens of thousand Jewish children, right? You executed them for their terrible crimes because there was no justice that punished them. Now think! If you knew what they were up to before and you had the power to kill them, would you have done it?"

"Yes."

"So what is the difference in killing these two scientists who were ready and willing to produce an atomic bomb and murder tens of thousand of children in New York or Tel Aviv? Don't give me that stuff about assassinating them. Assassination is just a form of killing, and it doesn't matter if you use bullets or poison."

"Maybe you are right, Sepp. The manner of killing those who need to be killed is not as important as the reason for it."

"And the reason for preventive killing is as important, if not more so, than for punishing the bastards afterward. This is just my opinion, the thoughts of a simple man."

Anton reached over and shook Sepp's hands, "You are right, Sepp. You might not know it, but your straightforward way of thinking has taken a big burden off my mind. Come on, let's get dressed and I take you over to the Heide Inn and we have a good supper, then we go home and get drunk." That they did. Before that, Sepp called his wife Inge and told her what he was up to. Sepp stayed overnight in the guest room.

Sunday morning, they were sitting down to breakfast when Inge called. Anton laughed, "She doesn't trust you, Sepp. Look, I need you for one more trip this morning." Sepp talked to his wife who seemed satisfied that his story was true. He assured her he would be home by noon.

Anton also showed his friend his collection of knives and daggers which he kept in a box.

"People always wanted to attack me with knives and daggers. Some I kept as souveniers. This one is an SS dagger I took off the war criminal Lutz in Cairo. The next one who threatened me was an Arab in the Old City of Jerusalem. I showed him my pistol and he backed off. I would have loved to take his dagger away; it looked wicked with a curved blade and the handle jewel-encrusted. Then I had an encounter with a robber in Moscow who flashed his knife at me. I threw him and the knife into the river. This simple dagger is from Boris, the Russian in Uzbekistan. He wanted to take my money but decided it wasn't worth to try. This switch-blade I took off Freddy. I told you the story when Gustav Bachleiter and Freddy followed me to Stanberg, to the memorial. This knife is from Ludolf Hanfnagel, the Car Killer. He didn't threaten me with it but a girl he held; then passively handed it to me. They let me have it after he was declared insane. This dagger I took from the old woman Najiba when she threatened to cut the boy's throat." Sepp held it and admired the beautiful workmanship; a curved dagger with a silver handle and jewels on each side. "What did you do Toni, how did you stop her?"

"A quick karate job to her throat, and she dropped it."

Sepp remarked, "It isn't just the knives and daggers, but the stories they tell."

After breakfast, they drove in Sepp's taxi to Fuchsstrasse 2a. Anton had him park right in front of the villa so the taxi could be seen from the house.

"Any danger here, Toni?"

Anton smiled. "No. Just a conversation with a very disturbed professor. Wait in the taxi and read the newspaper."

He went to the door of the villa and rang the bell. There was no answer though he realized that he might be observed through the peephole. After a few more rings and no one came to the door he returned to the taxi. "I guess the professor isn't home or he doesn't wish to let me in."

"I saw the curtain move a little by the window, someone is home," answered Sepp. Anton returned to the door and took a small envelope from his pocket with a copy of a certain photo inside and pushed it under the door. He didn't need to ring again as the door opened and he finally met professor Max Klausner. Max Klausner was a heavybuilt man with a pouch, a small mustache, partially bald, at least bald over his high forehead and he guessed him to be in his early sixties, perhaps good looking to the female gender. Klausner held the envelope in his hand and while he tried to smile, it was more of a nervous and even frightened grin. "You wish to talk to me?"

"Yes, are you alone?"

Again the frightened grin; "Yes, since about a week."

"May I come in, Professor?"

"Is that your taxi? No one else with you?" asked the professor.

"No. I am all alone." Anton turned and gave Sepp the thumbs-up sign. He then followed the professor through the door into the elegant living room.

"You live very nice here, Professor," Anton looked around, "better than a jail cell."

"Yes, thank you. May I ask, is this going to be just a friendly conversation or . . . ?"

"Or what, Professor?"

"Or are you going to kill me?"

"Why should I wish to kill you, Max Klausner?"

"Here, the envelope. You and I know what is in it. I know who you are."

"And who am I, Professor?"

"You are the Israeli Mossad. I . . . I expected you."

"And if I tell you that I am not?"

"Then who are you? We both know where the photo came from, so?"

"We both know that it came from Mohammad Ganji. That doesn't mean that I am with the Mossad."

"The picture is a copy, you have the original. So, what do you want from me, blackmail me?"

"Just a friendly conversation. I smell coffee, I love to be your guest." Anton smiled.

"I just made a pot full. Please sit down and I bring coffee, anything with it? Fresh rolls, a piece of cake?"

"No, coffee is fine." Anton followed the professor into the kitchen.

"You don't trust me?"

Anton smiled. "Should I?"

"You can. You have me in your power with that picture, her name and phone. The girl would talk. If you are not the Mossad, and I doubt very much you are with the police, who are you then?"

"If you wish to use a name, just call me Julius would do fine."

The professor poured the freshly made coffee into a porcelain pot, sat it on a tray, added two delicate cups, his fingers shaking, and carried it to the table in the living room. He tried to pour, his hands shaking. "Here let me," Anton poured two cups.

Anton tasted . . . "Arabian coffee, excellent."

"You are an enigma to me, Herr Julius, if I may say."

"Why do you say so, Professor?"

"You are from Munich, your dialect. You brought me a picture and we both know where it came from."

"I could have found it?"

"Then you would not have connected me to the photo. Besides you mentioned the man who had the picture in his wallet. You at once knew that this is Arabian coffee. You are playing games with me, Herr Julius. So, please again, what do you want from me?"

"You live alone? I mean, since your friends departed?"

"Two of whom you assassinated."

"Tsk, tsk . . . and why would I have done that?"

"We both know why."

"And why did you teach two Iranian scientists what is forbidden to teach them?"

"They were American nuclear scientist, graduates from MIT. Yes, from Iran, but refugees."

"Now you are playing games with me, Professor. We both know that they were Shiites, though they claimed they were Sunnis. They came without their families, as refugees? You saw their passports and you knew they were for three months in Iran, a month before that in Pakistan, probably visiting with Dr. Khan. Please be honest with me and perhaps we can handle this affair discreet."

"What do you wish to know?"

"Three things. How much did they learn about neutron emission of radium? Secondly, who else did you teach this delicate subject? And also, why did you do it?"

The professor hung his head. "If I am honest with you, no harm will befall me? No one else will know?"

"It depends on your answers. By now, you realize that I know more about you and the Iranians than you thought."

"I will be honest, and I trust you, I have no choice. First, let me tell you that I never taught anyone this subject who was not authorized. Dr. Wahaj and Dr. Jaafari learned enough to build a nuclear device. However, as we know, they took their knowledge to the grave. Your third question is more difficult to answer. The why? I am a widower. My wife was very religious. I am a man of certain passions and they pertain to young ladies. I met the two Iranians, as you call them, last January. Then I did not know of their background, I did not see their passports. I only knew that they were graduates from MIT and doctors of nuclear science.

I met them a few times and our conversation delved into the erotic. I realized that they were connoisseurs of young ladies."

"As you are or were professor?"

"Were. Let me assure you it is part of my past. I had a companion, a college girl. Let me just call her Monica. She became infatuated with the Iranians. They were younger, handsome and very rich. At once, they bought a new Mercedes, spent their money freely. I rented them the upstairs and they paid me royally. I shared with them everything."

"Monica also."

"Yes. Monica brought them these young ladies. I said I shared with them everything. We took compromising pictures and they had me in their power, this is how I became involved. Do you know the story or have seen the movie 'The Blue Angel?' No? Well, there was this Professor Unrat, played by Emil Jannings. He fell in love, or should I say in lust, with this dancer who was played by Marlene Dietrich. A last passion in his life and his ruin. I became this Professor Unrat. These Iranians left after three months, they were taking technical German at the Language Institute. They promised to return in September for certain studies on neutron emission at the Max Planck Institute, which I would teach. When they returned beginning of September to begin their studies with me, they again rented my upstairs. They continued their liaison with Monica and the young ladies. It was when I examined their passports that I realized who they were. I did not wish to let them study at our institute. Then they threatened me with exposure. The rest you know."

"Do you wish to resign from the institute?"

"My work is my life. If you wish so, I have to resign. But let me assure you, never again."

"Never again what?"

"Professor Unrat finished his life as a tragic clown. If I have the choice, I like to finish it as the respected Max Klausner."

"Can you, Professor? It is nothing new that respectable men give in to their passions, get blackmailed and wind up as this Professor Unrat."

Klausner looked straight into the eyes of Nagil. "Yes, I can!" He said it sure—and honest?

"I tend to believe you, Professor Klausner."

"May I asked, Herr Julius, are you a professional man? Your speech, your demeanor, you seem educated? Are you also into nuclear science? I wouldn't be surprised. Also you know about cyanide and how to use it. I gather, if you permit me to make this observation, that you are not alone. Whoever sent you, sent me an expert on this subject. Yes?"

"You are very observant but in my case wrong. I work alone. However, I am a chemist and I know about cyanide. I have a rudimentary knowledge of nuclear science. My hobby is however astronomy, or to be exact, astrophysics."

"Oh really? I too am fascinated by astronomy and have written a number of papers."

Anton replied, "I am very unconventional in my ideas of what makes the universe tick, so to speak."

"Interesting. I like to hear your unconventional ideas. I am serious, I really do. Perhaps you can visit me and we can discuss this subject."

"I am a dangerous man, Professor."

Klausner smiled. "Yes, I believe you are. However, not under normal circumstances, I rather see in you a fine man, a gentleman if I may say so. Else"—and his smile vanished and he looked serious—"I would be dead by now."

"You have a fine feeling for people, Professor. I might just take you up on your invitation. Are you certain you are no longer that unfortunate professor from the movie?"

"I am fully cured. As the Jewish people say, NEVER AGAIN."

"Are you Jewish?"

"No. Are you, Herr Julius?"

"No. How about Frl. Ingrid? She has your child."

"Little Erika. Yes, I am her father. You seem to know everything about me."

"So?"

"I would sincerely love to be, or become, Erika's father if . . . Ingrid can forgive me and wants me."

"Work on it. Women can be forgiving with the right man. Now I have to leave. I have a taxi waiting outside."

"Will you visit me again, Herr Julius? I would be honored."

"Call me when Ingrid and Erika are with you. Then I know you are the right professor. Make it after the New Year; that gives you enough time to arrange things. Here is my card." He gave him his card which stated his name and grade, and the address of the *Polizeipraesidium*.

Klausner read and looked up in surprise, "Then you are with the police department, Inspector Nagil?"

"What happened was a private endeavor of mine and did not involve me in an official capacity. However, Professor Klausner, in my safe is a full report of what happened and the original picture. Just an added insurance that nothing happens to me, and that Professor Klausner is no longer in the same situation as Professor Unrat was in. One more thing Professor Klausner, the Iranian authorities might be interested to learn what happened to their two men. They might send emissaries to you. If you feel threatened, call me, my number is on the card. *Auf Wiedersehn*, Professor." And without shaking hands he turned and walked out of the house.

When he entered the taxi, he said to his friend Sepp, "I think we have Professor Klausner cured of all of his bad habits. Let's go and eat somewhere."

CHAPTER XXVI

JERUSALEM

Later Anton sent an e-mail to Hanna:

Dearest Hanna,

Anton Nagil has solved all his problems with the help of the more sensible thinking taxi driver, Sepp. Coming next Sunday morning for my four-day stay. Can't wait to take you into my arms. Hug and kiss our children. I enclose a CD with the Don Cossacks Choir. The first song is EVENING BELLS, which Sasha taught us back in Afghanistan. You can easily learn it and play it on the piano, it will be Esther's song. We teach the children how to imitate the bells. Here is a simple refrain I thought up for you to sing her song. I am not a great poet but it rhymes and goes with the melody and bells:

> *Oh Esther dear . . .*
> *It is your song . . .*
> *The bells sound clear . . .*
> *Now ring along . . .*
> **bing (Esther)** . . . ***bing (David)*** *. . . **bong (Toni)** . . . biiing (Danny)*
> *And Esther tells . . .*
> *I make the chimes . . .*
> *For evening bells . . .*
> *To tell the times . . . etc.*

Oh, how I miss you all. A thousand kisses.

Toni

Monday, when Inspector Nagil came to work, he was his old self again. Anton was a serious person but friendly with most, quick to smile, and much appreciated by both his superiors and staff, and by his friends.

On Saturday, the twenty-sixth, Anton had duty till three in the afternoon. He then rushed home, and Sepp took him to the airport. The plane was full to Frankfurt, and he traveled economy class. But for his midnight Lufthansa flight to Tel Aviv, he had first-class accommodation.

When he was through customs, he found Hanna awaiting him. While Hanna was telling Anton about their life and the children, Anton loved the drive to Jerusalem over mainly empty highways with the sun coming up over the city.

It was only six when they drove through the gate. Amal was waiting for them with a pot of good coffee. Much to tell and Anton was happy about the many male visitors who seemed to make it their business to guard over the family while he was absent.

At seven o'clock, Amal and Hanna went upstairs to awaken the children, wash and dress them. Soon Amal came back to prepare breakfast.

The first one who came into the kitchen was Esther. When she saw Anton, she flew into his arms crying "The Man," and Anton held her tight, her face on his. And at once there were quick steps running down the stairs and David rushed at Anton, "Daddy is here." And when Esther did not want to be put down, Hanna lifted David up and Anton held both children in his arms. The children were already sitting at the table eating when little Danny came and it was his turn to be held and cuddled by Anton. With Danny came a surprise, a little black and white Schnauzer puppy with the cutest face. Amal said wisely, "Every boy should have two things: a dog and a mother willing to let him have a dog. Of course, Maxi belongs to all of them." While they had their breakfast, Hanna could not keep Esther quiet as she needed to tell Anton all about the doings in the kindergarten.

When the children had left for kindergarten and school and Danny was playing with a little battery powdered car Anton had brought for him from Germany, Anton asked Hanna, "Has Esther forgotten about the incident?"

"Yes and no. She is a bubbly child again, but sometimes I catch her alone in her room, crying and talking to her monkey. The monkey becomes her mother. The first time I heard her talk, I listened and after I felt ashamed and never did it again. The talk of a child to her mommy is something very precious and private. It was just child-talk telling her mommy about things that happened, a spat she had with David, that Maxi pooped in the house, that she didn't like her lunch at kindergarten, that the veggies tasted bad and she made me eat it. And then she talked about you, Toni. She said, 'The man came not again today. Mommy, you are not mad at me that I love the man? But I love you and daddy the more. I like Hanna and Amal.' I walked away and cried, Toni. Now when I come in and she talks to the monkey she stops talking and when I take her in my arms and kiss her tears away, she is kind of sad for a while. No, she hasn't forgotten and she misses her mom and dad. But Dr. Herzog believes that she will overcome these moments of remembering and just be a happy child. He also says that kids are so resilient and overcome tragedies in life more easily than adults do."

Anton took Hanna in his arms. "You are the best of mother she can have."

"No, Toni, there is no better mother than your own. All I can do is try." Anton spent the morning with his wife and son, and they went for a stroll in the neighborhood; it was the old story, only Anton could push the stroller. Danny would look back repeatedly to see that he was pushed by the proper person. Together with Hanna and Danny in his car seat, they picked up Esther from kindergarten and when David had came home from school, he did not forget about daddy suppose to teach him riding his tricycle without training wheel. Off to the sportgoods store to buy a safety helmet and then to the nearby Talpiot park, where there were smooth walks. Anton took the training wheels off, David got on his bicycle and with Anton holding the back, running along, still holding while David made a few leisurely circles on to the straight path and Anton let go. David did fine alone until he couldn't take a curve, went into the grass and fell off. A few more times with Anton helping him to get started and David had become a bicyclist. Esther's was still too little to ride without training wheels. She rode hers with training wheels and Danny trying to keep up with his little tricycle pushing frantically with his feet but not making it. By the time they returned home, Amal was back and had supper ready.

Then came the highlight of the evening when they all gathered around the piano and Hanna played Evening Bells. She had taught herself with the children to make the bells. Then after Hanna sang the first stanza she pointed to Esther who made the high sound of a bell—**biing,** then David who sang a little louder—**bing,** pointed at Anton who made it sound very deep—**booong.** "You growl, Toni," Hanna complained, and the children laughed. Last came Danny who squeaked **biiiing,** and they all laughed. After the second stanza she sang, the bells sounded better.

Hanna then said, "This was your song, Esther. Now I sing David's song, it is with the melody of the Lullaby. Don't laugh, Toni, it is the best I could put together.

> *Good evening, good night . . .*
> *For David we sing this so'ong . . .*
> *Our protector, our knight . . .*
> *David, Esther and Danny sing along . . .*
> *Morrow morning, when we wake . . .*
> *We wash and dress up . . .*
> *We have Amal's piece of cake . . .*
> *And warm milk in a cup."*

All clapped joyfully, only Hanna made a sour puss. "Not very good, Toni."

"It is wonderful!" He assured her, but all she could do was grin embarrassed. Then it was time to put the children to bed. First, Danny was hugged and kissed by Amal, Hanna and last by Anton. Then David was likewise put to bed and last Esther, and she clung to Anton until Amal took her arms off him. Later, Eliahu came by and they sat together with a glass of wine.

Monday, after the children had left and Hanna took care of Danny, Anton drove out to Police Headquarters and visited Deputy Avi Barlev. They shook hands, "Welcome, Inspector Nagil, or is it still Toni?'

"Toni, please."

"Before I make us tea, Toni, let me call Nahik Rubin, he wants to hear the story."

"What story, Avi?"

Avi smiled. "Mordechai Nevot said he received a communication from you that the business was taken cared of."

"I thought that was between him and me only?"

"He is the Mossad. But this is something we all needed to learn about and it is only known in the higher echelon of the Mossad, the Shin Bet and between Nahik and me." Avi called and soon Rubin came and greeted Anton comradely.

They sat together with freshly brewed tea and Anton told how he completed the business.

Rubin said, "It might give us and the Americans extra time. On the EU, (European Union) we cannot count on to do anything but talk and negotiate and in the end do nothing. In the UNO, it is China and Russia playing their sinister game."

Avi asked, "And this German, Klausner?"

"No one knows how much he taught the two. He told me in a conversation we had later, that they learned enough to make a bomb explode, but he might have been bragging a little. It doesn't matter now."

"No, it doesn't matter. And that woman, Ingrid with his child?" Avi asked.

"If he is smart, he becomes the girl's father and marries the woman, if she still wants and can forgive him. However, she seems more interested in a fine house and become a housewife, not have to work. I doubt for love."

Rubin said, "Most likely there were plenty of funds the two Iranians had on hand. He had the use of that also."

Avi further said, "You did a great service to all of us. Did you tell your FBI contact?"

"Agent Johnson? Yes. That the two Iranians passed away suddenly. I think he knew very well what I meant but their investigation is continuing. They should have never been permitted to become American citizens. The Livermore

Laboratory should have done a more thorough job investigating them before they admitted them."

Avi said, "Toni, I understand that you looked for a job with both the Mossad and Shin Bet in Israel. They couldn't help you because you are not an Israeli citizen. If you ever want a job with the Israeli police here in Jerusalem, we have a position for you."

Anton had to leave Wednesday afternoon to be back at work Thursday morning. Except for saying goodbye to Hanna, Amal and Danny, he did not to Esther and David as he left before they returned from school. Hanna told him the next day in an e-mail that Esther cried bitterly when he was gone. Hanna told them that soon *Aba* Toni would be back for Hanukkah, which this year came right with Christmas.

On the sixth of December, Commissioner Kolb held a small ceremony in his office, promoting Inspector Nagil to *Polizeioberkommissar*—Head Inspector. For this ceremony, his mother Rosemarie had been invited and the commissioner presented her with a bouquet of roses.

Also, his immediate supervisors, Inspector Keller, Chief of the CID Kirsch and Inspector Wagner attented the ceremony. This promotion upped his salary by six hundred euros. As the commissioner stated and smiled when he said, "I understand your family suddenly increased by three children, congratulations!" Commissioner Kolb lauded his accomplishment with the bomb squad which together with Oettinger and Maurer had become the foremost bomb defusing squad in Germany and was requested by other states. He added, "Prepare yourself to give seminars to other units in Germany in 2006." Kolb also cited him for the invaluable work in dismantling the Russian Mafia in Munich and finding the serial killer Ludolf Hanfnagel.

When Wagner congratulated him, with no one else present, he said "And we could have added a few other accomplishments: the letter bombs disposal, or should I say disposal of the bomber? A certain kidnapping case which never came to the attention of the police and rescue work in the Holy Land."

When Anton answered, "We better not," both laughed.

He then took Rosemarie out for lunch to a fine restaurant. No one was as proud of Head-Inspector Anton Nagil as his beloved mother.

Of course, he e-mailed the news at once to Hanna. In her reply, she told him of telling the children that their papa had become a chief of the Munich Police. When David asked where Munich was, she told him, in a far away country. And when daddy comes home, he has to fly in an airplane. She then wrote that David wishes for Hanukkah a plane like the one his daddy flies in. Esther, who has become fond of animals, wants a little play zoo.

Anton went to the Obletter toy store and bought a replica of an Airbus plane and a zoo for Esther. For Danny an assortment of Matchbox cars and a garage.

It was the week before Christmas, Saturday the 17th, that Inspector Nagil received a phone-call from the duty officer at headquarters, that an urgent message had come in from a Herr Max Klausner, "To please, call him at the institute" and the officer gave the phone number. It was three o'clock in the afternoon when Anton called and was connected to Max Klausner.

"Ah, Inspector Nagil, I am glad you called back so fast. I have good and bad news. First the wonderful news; Ingrid and our daughter Erica live with me and we are getting married."

Anton said, "Congratulations, Professor. You are not disappointing me."

"Yes, I know, you trusted in me. Now the other news which I consider bad news, Ingrid had a call before from a Herr Maliki; he wanted to visit me. She did not tell him that I was at the institute but told him I was in town and would be back at six. He made an appointment for seven. The name, the slight foreign accent Ingrid detected. Our friends perhaps?"

"Most likely."

"What do you advice, Inspector Nagil?"

"I will be at your house before seven."

"Do you think they came to kill me? Take revenge?"

"No. They want to learn what happened. Perhaps repeat the visit of scientists to you. We have to scare them off, permanently."

"No violence then? I thought I send Erica and Ingrid to her mother, just to be safe."

"That is a good idea; do that."

"May I ask how you scare them off?"

Anton laughed, "This call is kind of unexpected. Let me think about it. I see you at 6:30, Professor."

"Max, please."

"All right, Max. I have to be your best friend, someone you trust, confided in. Let me do most of the talking."

"Maybe, just identifying yourself as a police inspector will scare him off?"

"Perhaps. I see you later, Max. Better you leave soon for home."

Anton had thought about the possibility of a visit by the Iranians but didn't think they would dare. They must be desperarate to learn how to make a nuclear device work. He had a stand-by plan but had done nothing about it. He went to a nearby printing shop where he had his police inspector's cards made. He asked for a dozen cards with the name of Julius Hagen, criminal reporter for the *Sueddeutsche Zeitung*. The owner, who knew Inspector Nagil and after being told that the cards were for undercover work, made him genuine press-cards in the name of JULIUS HAGEN, Criminal Reporter for the *Sueddeutsche Zeitung* and included the logo of the paper.

Next, he called his friend Sepp, who was home and asked him to pick him up at 5:30. Anton dressed neatly as a reporter; in his shoulder holster his Beretta and his pen in his breast pocket, in his jacket pocket a small tape recorder. On their way to Klausner's house, Anton explained to his friend what the trip was about.

Anton said, "The idea is to break off any future contact between Iran and Professor Klausner."

"And how will you accomplish that?"

"With threatening to go public if there is any pressure brought on Klausner."

"And what do you want me to do, Toni?"

"Just sit in your taxi in front of the house and let him see you. Listen to the radio."

"Good, the Bayern Club is playing now. No danger to you or Klausner?"

"I don't think so. Change your sign to OCCUPIED when we get there."

The taxi stopped in front of Klausner's house and the professor let Inspector Nagil in. He had already prepared a pot of good coffee. He didn't object that Anton smoked his pipe and nervously lit one of Ingrid's cigarettes, though it was seldom that he smoked.

Anton showed him his press card and explained that most likely it would be later that he would reveal that he is a reporter. "For now I am just your best friend and I know all about the affair as you confided in me. My name is Julius Hagen, so call me Julius and in the familiar per 'du.' We have to play it by ear to see what he wants, how much pressure he puts on you to continue teaching, if that is what he has in mind."

They drank their coffee, Anton smiled. "Just relax, Max. Everything will be all right."

It was shortly before seven that the bell rang. Klausner opened and two men came in. One was elderly, in a suit and sported a trimmed gray beard; the other was a big man in a black training suit. The elegant man frowned when he saw that the professor was not alone and at once said, "I would prefer . . ." but the professor already introduced himself and added, "This is my best friend Julius Hagen."

The man said, "As I tried to say, I would prefer to speak with you alone, Professor Klausner." His German was excellent with just a hint of a Middle Eastern accent.

The professor asked, "May I ask who you are, please?"

"I am Herr Maliki from the Teheran University and I came to speak to you privately."

Anton stood up and smiled pleasantly. "Herr Maliki, I am not only the professor's best friend but also his—well, let's say—his personal guardian." He then turned to the big man. "And who are you?" The giant looked at Maliki.

Maliki said, "This is Raed Zubaida, my driver, he doesn't speak German. Do you speak Arabic?"

"Sorry, I know only German," Anton replied.

"Nor do I speak Arabic," said the professor.

Raed spoke up in Arabic, "Who is this man with the professor?"

Maliki answered, "The professor introduced him as Julius Hagen, he is supposed to be his friend and I guess his bodyguard."

"You want me to get rid of him?" Raed asked.

"No violence. I can't help it if he stays." He turned to professor Klausner, "My driver Raed wanted to know who this man is with you. I explained to him that this man is your friend."

"May I serve coffee? It is good Arabian coffee from—well, I cannot read the inscription on the can but I believe it is from Egypt. I have to get another set for your driver, please sit down," the professor invited them. Anton poured the coffee for all.

Professor Klausner asked, "Herr Maliki, may I ask why you came to see me? It honors me that someone from the prestigious Teheran University visits me."

"It is a delicate subject," he looked at Anton, "this is why I wished we could speak privately. I would appreciate it very much if you send your friend away. Is this his taxi outside?"

The professor answered him, "My friend is fully informed of the delicate subject. You may speak freely."

Maliki shrugged his shoulders. "This was an unfortunate happening to our two scientists. What can you tell me about the matter, Professor?"

Klausner replied, "Very little. The two scientists went to the mosque on Friday evening and when they came back, Ganji and Rashid brought both into the house. Dr. Wahaj was dead and Dr. Jaafari was dying. I called a Muslim physician and he confirmed the death as cardiac arrest. However, I felt that both had been poisoned and told so Ganji and Rashid. The drivers also told me about a robbery at the Islamic Center."

"Yes. Our medical examiners confirmed death by cyanide poisoning. Also that is must have occurred a short time before. It was part of the robbery, an assassination team; most likely by a Mossad team or perhaps by the CIA. We are not certain as one of the team spoke German with a Munich dialect, perhaps a local CIA agent? It doesn't matter at this point. I came here to renew our relationship with you, Professor Klausner. We have a new scientist whom we wish to send to you for the same type of research."

Professor Klausner inquired, "An Iranian scientist? With the last two I had trouble hiding their true identity. Their passports showed that they had visited Pakistan and Iran; as refugees?"

Maliki explained, "I understand; an oversight by our people. No, this scientist is from Lebanon, one of the Palestinian refugees who studied nuclear science in Beirut and is now a Lebanese citizen. A Dr. Omar Ahmed, and Raed Zubaida is his assistant or guardian.," He smiled. "Both would be living with you again."

"I think I am no longer available, too much trouble," Klausner replied.

Maliki further said, "I understand you were well paid and also participated in their extra-curricular activities?"

"I was blackmailed."

"You are still compromised and we would pay well."

Anton spoke up, "How much would you pay, Herr Maliki?"

Maliki turned to Anton, "One million euros."

"How would the money be transferred?" Anton asked.

"I can write a bank draft right now" replied Maliki.

Anton continued to ask, "To be drawn from where?"

"From the Iranian National Bank in Teheran."

"Please complete the transaction," Anton said.

"Made out in your name professor, or perhaps for Herr Hagen?"

Anton answered him, "Please make it out to Professor Klausner."

Maliki took out his checkbook and Anton gave him his pen. He wrote out the draft and then gave it to the professor. Anton took the check, read it and said to Maliki,

"This check for one million euros of the Iranian Government it to be payment for Professor Klausner to teach your scientist how to make an atomic bomb explode?"

Maliki said, "You put it in such extreme language, Herr Hagen."

"How would you describe the agreement?"

"Well, let us say it is payment for teaching our scientist the fissioning of nuclear material," Maliki explained.

Anton drew his pistol, clicked the safety off and held it against Raed. "Please tell your driver to hand over his weapon."

Maliki looked surprised, shocked, "What is this?" I don't understand, Professor. What is going on here?"

Klausner said, "Please do as Herr Hagen told you. Just a precaution, he will explain it all in a moment."

Maliki turned to the driver and spoke Arabic, "Give him your weapon, Raed. I don't know what is going on but for now do as I tell you." Raed took his pistol out and handed it to Anton. To Maliki he said, "I still have my dagger in my sock. You tell me when and I kill Hagen, he looks like a Jew with his black hair. I love to cut his throat."

Maliki said, "Do it as soon as you can."

Anton said, "Max, pat down Maliki and see if he is armed." Max did, Maliki was unarmed.

Anton continued, "Maliki, tell your driver to stand up, face the wall, stretch out his arms and lean with his hands agains the wall. Tell him that I shoot him if he makes the slightest move to resist or not obey me." Maliki told his driver and Raed was leaning against the wall. Anton kept his pistol pointed at Raed and his eyes on him. Raed was a dangerous man and Anton had learned his lesson a long time ago.

"Maliki, give me your driver's license," Anton asked him.

Maliki replied, "I don't see any reason why I should."

Anton glared at him dangerously for a moment, "Please!" Maliki gave it to him.

"It is a diplomatic license for an Iranian. You came from Berlin? What is your position at the Embassy?" inquired Anton.

Maliki answered, "I am the cultural attaché. Yes, at the Iranian Embassy in Berlin."

Anton said, "When we are finished, you may return to Berlin and take your driver with you. Please, sit back down." Maliki now complained bitterly to the professor that he still did not understand what was going on, and as a diplomat, he protested to be treated like a criminal.

He did not turn around and see that Anton stepped behind Raed and gave him a powerful chop against his neck and the driver collapsed into Anton's arms. A sharp pulling and twisting of his head and Raed's neck was broken. The cracking of the neck was audible but Maliki, now in a heated harangue that his diplomatic status was violated did not pay attention.

Anton stood before Maliki and gave him his card. "Not only I am the professor's personal friend and guardian, but I work for this Munich newspaper, you should be familiar with this prominent paper." He reached into his pocket and produced the tape recorder. "Our conversation is on this tape; your attempt to bribe the professor with money from the Iranian Government is recorded. Professor Klausner is no longer available to teach your scientists what is forbidden to teach. I shall write up our conversation and publish it if you persist in contacting the professor or in any way harm him. Do you understand, Mahmoud Maliki? It is all over. Finished!"

Maliki was white in the face, radiating shock and anger, and when he looked over to the lifeless figure of his driver, with his head at a strange angle, also fear. "And the check?"

Anton said, "Evidence, it won't be cashed."

Anton took the card back from the shaking hand of Maliki. "You may leave as soon as we have put Raed into your car. Max, would you please tell the taxi-driver to come in?"

Anton with Sepp carried the body to the Mercedes and laid it on the backseat. Anton pulled the dagger from the sock. "This man wanted to cut my throat with it." He put it in his belt, then took the pistol he had taken from Raed, wiped it clean and put it into Raed's pocket. Then he returned to the house.

Anton said, "You may return to Berlin, Herr Maliki. And remember, no contact, no reprisal, or the whole world will read about what happened here."

Maliki said nothing, got into his car and drove off. After reassuring the professor that Iran could do nothing but forget about the episode and leave him alone, Anton left with Sepp. The only comment his friend Sepp made was, "Another dagger for your collection, Toni."

(What puzzled Mahmoud Maliki later, when the body of Raed Zubaida was examined, was that the pistol was found on him but the dagger was missing. He surmised that this man Hagen understood Arabic. He further thought that this man was the one with the assassins. His inquiry to the Munich Newspaper about their criminal reporter Julius Hagen proved fruitless. No such person existed. Iranian Secret Service then dropped the matter. Iran could not afford any publicity about their nuclear research.)

On Christmas Eve, Anton had volunteered for duty. However, he was home for the Eve when the school children came for the traditional singing of carols, and of course Sepp came with them. Later, Sepp came by with his wife Inge for some spiced wine and cake. For Inge, Anton had a special gift, a silver replica of Jerusalem like he had bought for Rosemarie and Hanna a long, long time ago. Sepp and Inge were pleased with the gift.

Anton had to forego the night flight to Israel, which he was fond of taking, but had managed to get a day flight on Christmas, the twenty-fifth, a Sunday. With all flights booked, he had to pay for first class. He had forgotten the many tourists who wanted to celebrate Christmas in Bethlehem. Sepp drove him to the airport and he was off to Frankfurt in the morning and on the afternoon flight to Tel Aviv.

Anton had told Hanna not to come and pick him up but rather to get the children ready for Hanukkah. She had written how excited they were, having been told the story of the Maccabbes, and why candles would be lit for eight days and they made things in school and kindergarten. Danny was excited by what Esther and David told him.

It took a long time to get through customs. No taxis and the buses and vans were full. He finally called Hanna and asked her if Eliahu could pick him up.

"Guess what, Toni, Commander Amir is here and brought David a present and he would love to get you."

He had to wait another hour and then Amir's jeep came to a screeching stop by the terminal. To the commander, Anton was the hero who rescued the children; to Anton, Amir was the man at the head of the cavalry who saved them. Amir helped him load all his baggage in the back and they were off for Jerusalem. There was heavy traffic along the highway because it was Hanukkah and Christmas on the same day.

Dusk came and Anton called Hanna, "Can you wait with the candle lighting? I know it is sundown but I should be home in a half hour."

"What do you think Toni, that we can't wait? The children wouldn't let me light the candle without you being here. Don't rush; just get home safely. You don't know what Ben brought for David, a BIG surprise."

"Who is Ben?"

"My God, don't you know that Commander Amir's first name is Ben, Benjamin?"

"No, I didn't. I always called him commander or Amir."

"Oh Toni, you have such good friends and don't even know their names. That comes from being away from your family and friends all the time."

"Hanna, you know I can't help it."

"I am so sorry, Toni. You are right, forgive me, please. Rush on home, but you men are careful. Shalom."

Anton turned to the commander, "So it is Ben. I never knew."

"You never asked me, Toni. And by the way, thanks."

"Thanks for what, Ben?"

"Look Toni, I am a good friend with Deputy Barlev."

"Oh that."

"I am just glad to have you as a friend and not an enemy," said Ben.

"Ben, you are a good man. My enemies are always bad, very evil men. So what did you bring for David? Hanna is raving about it."

"My mother is good in tailoring; she made a little uniform for David."

Anton laughed, "David loves men in unifom, now he can wear one. Can you come up for a glass of wine?"

"No, Toni. Hanukkah is a family affair. My mother is waiting for me."

"How come you are not married, Ben?" asked Anton.

"I am engaged. Police work kept me from finding the right woman until now. Rachel is home with my mother."

"If you get married, Ben, I love to be your best man. I am always home the last four days of the month."

"I would be honored. You are almost home." They could see the lights of Jerusalem. When Ben stopped, it was already dark. They unloaded.

"*Yom tov*—A Good Holiday Toni and a Happy Hanukkah."

"*Yom tov* Ben. Give my best to your mother and Rachel." They shook hands and Ben gunned the jeep and drove off. That Hanna heard, and by the time Anton picked up all his bundles, Hanna was at the gate and he dropped everything and embraced his wife.

"The children are waiting, Toni."

"How come they are not down here and all over me?"

"They are waiting for you in the living room. Come, I help you. So many packages, you are spoiling the kids, Toni."

When they came into the living room, the three stood in line and by height. First David, then Esther and last Danny, and Maxi the Schnauzer sat by Danny, his tail swishing the floor, all were beaming up at Anton.

"Now let's say it together, "HAPPY HANUKKAH, PAPA." And then, like let loose from a leash, they ran to papa and each one wanted to be taken in his arms. He finally flopped on the floor and they were all over him. Esther on top of Anton with her little arms around his neck—she could be very possessive, and Maxi trying to get in and lick Anton's face.

Hanna said, "It is time to light the candle." Amal gave each a Yarmulke.

"Amal made them for all of us," said Hanna. Each one was of white silk with the name in blue embroidery; only Anton's larger and had gold embroidery. They stood around the beautiful Menorah made from pink marble—a gift from Dr. Herzog. David said the first short prayer, Hanna the second and Anton read from the prayer book the third. Then David got to light the first candle. They gathered around the piano, Danny wanted to be taken in Anton's arms, and once there, whispered in his ear *ishi* and smiled mischievously. However, Esther began to call him papa. She needed a father.

Hanna played the *moas zur*, the beautiful song sung on Hanukkah which David and Esther had learned in school. Then it was dinnertime, but first the children wanted to know what papa had brought for them. When Hanna told them that it was for later, after eating, they begged to know which wrapped present was theirs. Luckily the one for David and Esther were about the same size. Danny didn't mind that his was a smaller package. But they had to touch their presents, lift it up to see how heavy it was.

Then downstairs into the dining room. Amal knew better than to have cooked an elaborate dinner; she had prepared little breads with mayonnaise for a spread and little smoked and marinated fish pieces the children liked.

At last it was time for the children to open their presents. That they would appreciate what their papa had brought for them. Hanna and Amal did not buy any toys and they had requested from their friends not to bring anything for the children, the exception was the uniform Amir's mother had made for David.

Instead, their friends had brought wine, a basket of fruit, flowers; things for the big people who took care of the little people.

For Hanna, Anton had brought a *Smaragd*—blue diamond necklace, matching earrings and bracelet; for Amal a silver service. Anton received from Hanna a beautiful photo album with all their pictures pasted in and from Amal a blue and white sweater she had knitted.

The wrapping paper was torn off. Danny played at once with his little cars. David found the button that made the large plane blink lights and give off the sound of jet engines. For Esther, Hanna brought in the small play table and on it she set up the zoo. Papa helped her to put the plastic wire cages together for the lions and tigers, the moat around the elephant enclosure, the trees, bushes and flowers to set up. Esther asked many of the names of animals as she had never seen them or been to a zoo. When David had enough flying his plane around, Hanna showed him Commander Amir's present and David wanted at once to put on the uniform.

"Now you are an Israeli warrior, David," Anton told him.

"But I don't have a cap like soldiers do." Anton said he would buy one tomorrow.

"Every soldier needs a cap."

That the children did not want to go to bed was understood. However, by ten, Hanna became firm in demanding that they go to bed. Amal and Hanna saw to it that each one swished a wet washcloth in the face, did a quick job brushing teeth, then once in bed Hanna would sing for each one his or her song with papa present, for Esther without the bells. A hugging and good night kiss . . . Esther holding on longest around papa's neck.

At last, Amal, Hanna and Anton could sit together with a glass of wine, relax and let Toni tell about Rosemarie, Munich, his friends there and his police work or rather he told of his promotion ceremony.

The next day, the first day of Hanukkah, the children were home from school. After breakfast, Esther at once attended to her zoo. Anton went with David into the city to buy a cap for him in a store that sold uniforms for soldiers. Even the smallest size cap was too large for David. Amal could do some sewing that it fit.

That evening, when Anton checked the house and closed the window shutters on the first floor, David accompanied him dressed in his uniform. From that day on, David all dressed up as a soldier, would accompany Amal in the evening when she secured the house. David was very much concerned that they were safe. Between visiting friends, playing with Danny during the day or taking him out in his stroller to the nearby park, then taking Esther and David out to ride their cycles, taking pictures of all for Rosemarie, and being with all his children in the evening, the four days Anton had went by much too fast. Wednesday afternoon he had to leave his family. He took a taxi to the airport and arrived in Munich in the evening.

Thursday morning he was back at work. In the evening, Arthur MacKenzie called and invited Anton for a New Year bash in Edinburgh. It being mandatory that all higher police officers were present for the New Years Party, Anton had to decline but promised to visit the MacKenzies in spring.

With his mother Rosemarie feeling up to it, Anton had made reservation for the two of them.

SYLVESTER

Rosemarie was proud of her son being decked out in his elegant police uniform, showing the two stars. He carried his Russian medal in his pocket until Inspector Keller asked where it was and then pinned it on his jacket.

It was a nice party and he danced many times the waltz and even a polka with his mother. Good food and drink, good company.

Then at midnight, they all stood up with raised glasses, the lights went out and just the strobe lights flashed, "*PROSIT NEUJAHR* (HAPPY NEW YEAR)." Horns and other noisemakers tooted. It was 2006.

BIBLIOGRAPHY

Bergen, Peter L. *Holy War Inc.* Free Press: New York, New York, 2001.

Bodansky, Yossef. *BIN LADEN, The Man Who Declared War on America.* Prima Publishing: Roseville, California, 1999.

Moore, Robin. *The Hunt for bin Laden.* Random House: New York, New York, 2003.

Carew, Tom. *JIHAD! The Secret War in Afghanistan.* Mainstream Publishing Co.: Edinburgh, England, 2000.

Rashid, Ahmed. *TALIBAN* Yale University Press: 2000.

Library of Congress Federal Research Division. "Afghanistan, a country study." Claitor's Publishing Division, 2001.

Federal Research Division. "Kazakstan, Kyrgyzstan, Tajikistan, Turkmenistan, and Uzbekistan: country studies." Edited by Glenn E. Curtis. Headquarters, Department of the Army. DA Pam, March 1996 (550-114).

Yusuf Ali, Abdullah. *The Qur'an.* Tahrike Tarsile Qur'an Inc.: Elmhurst, New York, 1934.

Trifkovic, Serge, ed. "The Koran and Truth about Prophet Mohammed" in *Chronicles Magazine.* Publication on internet, dated 7/23/05.

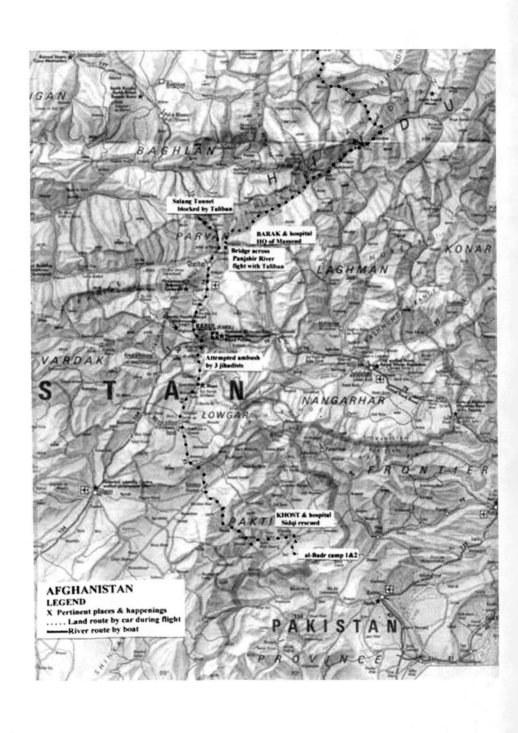

AFGHANISTAN
LEGEND
X Pertinent places & happenings
..... Land route by car during flight
⎯⎯⎯ River route by boat

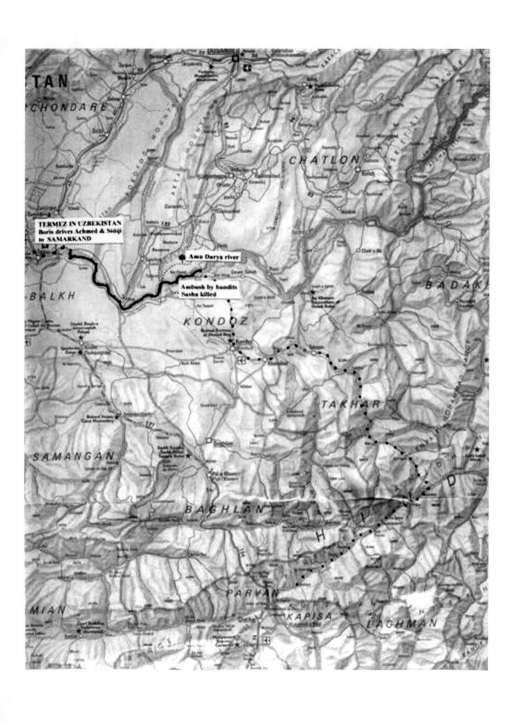

Printed in the United States
124689LV00003B/16/P

9 781436 318709